Houghton Mifflin Mathematics

Authors

Lelon R. Capps

William L. Cole

W.G. Quast

Leland Webb

Mary Ann Haubner

Charles E. Allen

Coordinating Author

Ernest R. Duncan

Houghton Mifflin Company   BOSTON

Atlanta   Dallas   Geneva, Ill.   Lawrenceville, N.J.   Palo Alto   Toronto

Authors

Lelon R. Capps
University of Kansas
Lawrence, Kansas

Mary Ann Haubner
Mount Saint Joseph College
Cincinnati, Ohio

Leland Webb
California State College
Bakersfield, California

W. G. Quast
Slippery Rock University
Slippery Rock, Pennsylvania

William L. Cole
Michigan State University
East Lansing, Michigan

Charles E. Allen
Los Angeles Center for Enriched Studies
Los Angeles Unified School District
Los Angeles, California

Coordinating Author

Ernest R. Duncan
Professor Emeritus
Rutgers University
New Brunswick, New Jersey

Consultants

Elmer A. Koch, Jr.
Principal
Cooper Elementary School
Minneapolis, Minnesota

Sylvia Thomas
Principal
Green Grove Elementary School
Neptune, New Jersey

Farryl Weitzman
Teacher
Hoover Street School
Los Angeles, California

Printed in U.S.A.

ISBN: 0-395-38618-7

CDEFGHIJ–D–943210/8987

CONTENTS

1 NUMERATION AND UNITS OF MEASURE 1

2 ADDITION AND SUBTRACTION OF WHOLE NUMBERS 31

6 MULTIPLICATION AND DIVISION OF DECIMALS 143

7 GEOMETRY, PERIMETER, AREA 179

8 NUMBER THEORY AND DEVELOPING FRACTIONS 211

9 ADDITION AND SUBTRACTION OF FRACTIONS 247

10 MULTIPLICATION AND DIVISION OF FRACTIONS 275

11 RATIO, PROPORTION, PERCENT 303

12 GEOMETRY AND VOLUME 333

13 STATISTICS AND PROBABILITY 367

14 INTEGERS AND GRAPHING 395

A tub holds about 9 hundred pounds of oranges. If a machine called a grovegoat loads 10 tubs of oranges onto the truck, about how many pounds is that?

NUMERATION AND UNITS OF MEASURE

1

PLACE VALUE TO BILLIONS

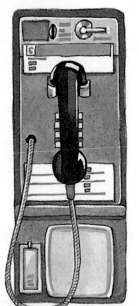

The telephone is used by millions of people throughout the world. Can you estimate the number of telephones in the world? In one particular year there were 472,136,700,020.

Billions			Millions			Thousands			Ones		
hundreds	tens	ones	hundreds	tens	ones	hundreds	tens	ones	hundreds	tens	ones
4	7	2	1	3	6	7	0	0	0	2	0

472 billion   136 million   700 thousand   20

The number above is read *four hundred seventy-two billion, one hundred thirty-six million, seven hundred thousand, twenty.* This is the **word form.** The **standard form** is 472,136,700,020.

The digit 6 is in the millions' place. Its value is 6,000,000. The **expanded form** of 472,136,700,020 is 400,000,000,000 + 70,000,000,000 + 2,000,000,000 + 100,000,000 + 30,000,000 + 6,000,000 + 700,000 + 20.

To help you read large numbers, commas are used between billions, millions, thousands, and ones. Often there are no commas in a calculator display. **Think:** What is the word form for 2563147?

CLASS EXERCISES

What is the word form for the number?

1. 1934

2. 297,654

3. 432,090

4. 27,000,016

5. 40,000,007,000

6. 142,000,000,000

What is the value of the underlined digit?

7. 3<u>5</u>2,482,796

8. 27,2<u>5</u>3,482

9. 9<u>9</u>8,999,999,999

PRACTICE

Write the standard form.

10. 4 thousand 8 **11.** 2 thousand 83 **12.** 32 thousand, 438

13. 6 million, 250 thousand, 4 hundred

14. 68 billion, 206 million, 145 thousand, 16

15. one hundred ninety-five million, two hundred one

16. thirteen billion, twelve million, eleven thousand, ten

Write the expanded form.

17. 4332 **18.** 700,882 **19.** 30,091 **20.** 6891 **21.** 100,298

Write the word form.

22. 7020 **23.** 50,087 **24.** 26,043,000 **25.** 96,058,000,000

26. 30,000 + 7000 + 800 + 70 + 2 **27.** 400,000 + 8000 + 700 + 40

28. 26,000,000 + 300,000 + 90,000 **29.** 7,000,000,000 + 600,000

★ **30.** ten hundreds ★ **31.** one hundred hundreds ★ **32.** one thousand thousands

Use a calculator or count one more. Write the word form.

33. 999 + 1 **34.** 13,999 + 1 **35.** 40,999 + 1

36. 109,099 + 1 **37.** 7,099,999 + 1 **38.** 23,000,789 + 1

CALCULATOR

PROBLEM SOLVING APPLICATIONS
Nonroutine Problems

Match. Write the letter of the correct number.

39. No digits the same; 6 in ten millions' place. **A.** 40,369,375

40. Two digits the same; 0 in millions' place. **B.** 9,057,365

41. Two digits the same; 8 hundred millions. **C.** 560,431,827

42. Two digits the same; no hundred thousands. **D.** 3,817,596,142

★ **43.** Using all four digits 1, 2, 3, and 4, and no other digits, how many different four-digit telephone extension numbers can you write?

COMPARING AND ORDERING WHOLE NUMBERS

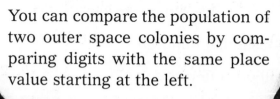

You can compare the population of two outer space colonies by comparing digits with the same place value starting at the left.

Mariner
Pop. 3856

Cladon
Pop. 3757

The thousands are the same.
Look at the hundreds. Compare them.

thousands	hundreds	tens	ones
3	8	5	6
3	7	5	7

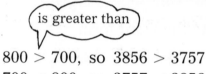

is greater than

$800 > 700$, so $3856 > 3757$
$700 < 800$, so $3757 < 3856$

is less than

 You can compare numbers and put them in order mentally.
To order 359, 353, and 361,

Think: Which has the most hundreds?
Which has the most tens?
Which numbers are left?
Which has more tens?
Which has more ones?

The order from least to greatest is 353, 359, 361.

CLASS EXERCISES

Which number is greater?

1. 30 or 20
33 or 29
33 or 129

2. 79 or 81
179 or 181
279 or 181

3. 57 or 58
257 or 258
10,257 or 10,258

4. 107 or 92
1070 or 920
10,700 or 9200

5. Think: If you compare two whole numbers with different numbers of digits, how can you tell which number is greater?

PRACTICE

Compare. Write < or >.

6. 123 ▨ 127   **7.** 339 ▨ 768   **8.** 654 ▨ 554   **9.** 121 ▨ 122

10. 745 ▨ 738   **11.** 486 ▨ 480   **12.** 4338 ▨ 9098   **13.** 9691 ▨ 10,020

14. 4910 ▨ 4109   **15.** 3741 ▨ 3746   **16.** 20,990 ▨ 20,909

17. 59,009 ▨ 50,990   **18.** 8768 ▨ 10,250   **19.** 64,928 ▨ 16,492

20. 234,567 ▨ 45,678   **21.** 578,376 ▨ 1,578,376   **22.** 3,984,303 ▨ 3,909,443

List the numbers in order from least to greatest mentally.

23. 235; 378; 364   **24.** 3470; 3740; 3047

25. 909; 1001; 910   ★ **26.** 1911; 1899; 1908; 1987; 1897

★ **27.** 10,682; 9862; 10,826; 8962; 10,089

MENTAL MATH

PROBLEM SOLVING APPLICATIONS
Reading Information from a Chart

Solve.

28. Which colony has the most people?

29. Which colony has the fewest people?

30. Which colonies have more than 1,000,000 people?

31. Which colonies have less than half a million people?

★ **32.** The number of people on Gemini is more than on Illiohydron but less than on Urgantis. What is the greatest number of people Gemini could have? the least?

★ **33.** I am thinking of a colony that has an "o" in its name but no "h" and that has more people than Delawane but fewer than Centabiland. Which colony is it?

COLONY	POPULATION
Astrolony	226,671
Centabiland	16,489,000
Delawane	384,639
Illiohydron	6,441,191
Urgantis	8,707,025
Zadon Island	500,213

ROUNDING WHOLE NUMBERS

Sail-a-Boat has 28 sailboats for rent on Conservatory Lake. You can use a rounded number and say *about* 30 sailboats are for rent since 28 is close to 30. Here are other examples.

Round 42 to the nearest ten. Since 42 is nearer to 40 than 50, round down to 40.

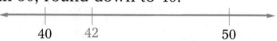

Round 650 to the nearest hundred. When a number is exactly halfway between two numbers, we round up. Round 650 up to 700.

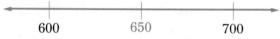

Round 9837 to the nearest thousand. Since 9837 is nearer 10,000 than 9000, round up to 10,000.

CLASS EXERCISES

Round to the nearest ten. Use the number line for help.

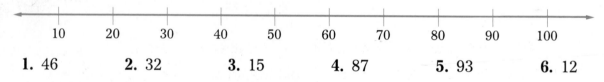

1. 46   **2.** 32   **3.** 15   **4.** 87   **5.** 93   **6.** 12

Round to the nearest hundred. Use the number line.

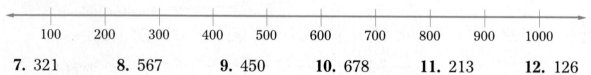

7. 321   **8.** 567   **9.** 450   **10.** 678   **11.** 213   **12.** 126

Round to the nearest thousand. Use the number line.

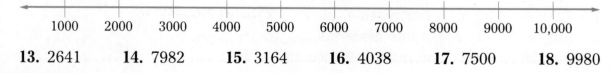

13. 2641   **14.** 7982   **15.** 3164   **16.** 4038   **17.** 7500   **18.** 9980

PRACTICE

Round to the place of the underlined digit.

19. 3̲2   **20.** 1̲58   **21.** 4̲170   **22.** 6̲43   **23.** 7̲9   **24.** 7̲70

25. 2̲813   **26.** 89̲5   **27.** 9̲1   **28.** 20̲1   **29.** 8̲341   **30.** 129̲9

Round to the greatest place value.

31. 31   **32.** 9501   **33.** 555   **34.** 11   **35.** 86   **36.** 138

37. 9399   **38.** 786   **39.** 1304   **40.** 59   **41.** 25   **42.** 439

★ **43. Think:** When rounding to the greatest place value, what is the greatest whole number that can be rounded to 70? What is the least whole number?

PROBLEM SOLVING APPLICATIONS
Using Estimates

When you report information, you often give readers an estimate instead of an exact number. Decide whether each number used in this letter is an estimate or an exact number.

Write *estimate* or *exact* for Exercises 44 through 52.

Dear Mary,

    Here we are in N.Y. City! We drove about 350̲ mi (44.) to visit my 3̲ (45.) cousins. The Lincoln Tunnel is over 8000 ft (46.) long!

    Over 7̲ million (47.) people live here. The buildings are so tall! The World Trade Center is about 1350̲ ft (48.) high and has 110̲ (49.) stories. We also went to see the Statue of Liberty. It was given to the U.S. by France in 1886̲ (50.). It weighs about 450,000̲ lb (51.). We climbed all 168 (52.) steps inside!

                 See you soon,
                 Annie

ROUNDING GREATER NUMBERS

You would use rounded numbers to talk about distances in our solar system because rounded numbers are easier to remember. Look at the table to see how numbers are rounded.

EXACT NUMBER	ROUND TO THE NEAREST	DIGIT TO THE RIGHT	IS IT 5 OR MORE?	ROUND
7842	hundred	4	no	down to 7800
15,633	thousand	6	yes	up to 16,000
125,643	ten thousand	5	yes	up to 130,000

CLASS EXERCISES

Complete the chart.

	EXACT NUMBER	ROUND TO THE NEAREST	DIGIT TO THE RIGHT	IS IT 5 OR MORE?	ROUNDED NUMBER
1.	8342	hundred	4	no	?
2.	19,672	hundred	7	?	?
3.	32,831	thousand	8	?	?
4.	889,201	thousand	2	?	?
5.	163,071	ten thousand	3	?	?
6.	4,748,802	ten thousand	8	?	?

PRACTICE

Round to the place of the underlined digit.

7. 3<u>2</u>06 **8.** <u>8</u>746 **9.** <u>4</u>2,175 **10.** 9<u>4</u>61 **11.** <u>4</u>5,560

12. <u>1</u>7,508 **13.** 49<u>5</u>0 **14.** 6<u>0</u>,774 **15.** 2<u>0</u>9,319 **16.** 50,5<u>5</u>2

17. 42<u>8</u>,400 **18.** 1,5<u>9</u>8,266 **19.** 287,<u>0</u>03 **20.** 24<u>7</u>,813 **21.** 35,2<u>9</u>9,012

Round to the greatest place value.

22. 3385 **23.** 74,806 **24.** 9099 **25.** 950 **26.** 27,368

27. 41,801 **28.** 7500 **29.** 891,197 **30.** 2,500,001 **31.** 78,210,043

32. Think: What is the least number that can be written as 1,000,000,000 when rounded to its greatest place value?

Write the answer.

33. 10×10 **34.** $500 \div 5$ **35.** 5×100

36. $700 \div 100$ **37.** 8×1000 **38.** 4×2000

MIXED REVIEW

PROBLEM SOLVING APPLICATIONS
Using Estimates

Pretend that you will be quizzed on this information. Your teacher will accept estimates of the measures. Rewrite the information rounding each measure to its greatest place value.

39. An astronaut on the moon climbed to an elevation of 25,688 ft.

40. The diameter of the moon is 2159 mi.

41. The distance from Earth to the sun is 92,957,209 mi.

42. The diameter of the sun is 865,400 mi.

43. In about 200 years there will be an eclipse of the sun that will last for 449 seconds.

PROBLEM SOLVING
Strategy: The Four-Step Plan

Leaving Georgia
Drive Safely!

The Mertzes drove from Atlanta to Boston. They drove 753 km from Atlanta to Cincinnati on Monday. On Tuesday, they drove 1939 km more to Boston. On which day did they drive farther? To solve a problem, it may help to follow a series of steps that will lead you to the information you need. Here are four steps to guide you to the correct solution to the problem above.

1. Understand the problem.

2. Make a plan.

3. Use the plan to do the work.

4. Answer and check for reasonableness.

1. What do you know? What do you want to know?	Mon.: 753 km Tues.: 1939 km On which day did the Mertzes drive farther?
2. What do you do to solve the problem?	Compare the distances.
3. Show your work.	1939 has 1 thousand. 753 has 0 thousands. So 1939 km > 753 km.
4. Is the answer reasonable? Does it answer the question?	1939 km is greater, but the question is *On which day?* Tuesday is the answer that is reasonable.

CLASS EXERCISES

For the problem, answer the questions, *What do you know*, *What do you want to know*, and *What do you do to solve the problem*. Then solve the problem.

1. Roberta drove 161 km today. To the nearest hundred, how many kilometers did Roberta drive?

2. Stan spent $185 on the first day of a trip and $165 on the second. On which day did he spend more?

3. On a four-day trip Ann's lunches cost $3.21, $4.33, $3.19, and $3.98. What is the least she paid for a lunch? the most?

PRACTICE

Use what you know and the plan that is given to write a question. Then solve the problem.

You Know	**The Plan**
4. The Chins are 715 km from home.	Round to the nearest hundred.
5. Sam's trip took 95 hours of driving. Tom's trip took 79 hours of driving.	Compare the numbers.
6. We stopped at the zoo. It has 23 deer, 15 monkeys, and 12 zebras.	Order the numbers from least to greatest.
7. The Ricardos traveled 653 km one way and 603 km the other way.	Compare the numbers.
★ 8. The shortest distance Ed drove in a day was 78 km. The longest distance he drove in a day was 700 km more than the shortest distance.	Add the numbers.

CHECKPOINT 1

Write the standard form. *(pages 2–3)*

1. one thousand eleven

2. 9 million, 2 hundred 7

3. 71 billion, 302 million, 70

Complete. Write < or >. *(pages 4–5)*

4. 5069 ▨ 5100

5. 49,009 ▨ 40,990

6. 3,383,326 ▨ 383,326

Round the number to its greatest place value. *(pages 6–9)*

7. 8498   8. 36,123   9. 235,011

10. 269,020,001 11. 1,449,999,823

Solve. *(pages 10–11)*

12. The Ace Company earned $168,724,369 last year and $168,724,693 this year. Did earnings increase or decrease this year?

Extra Practice on page 420

USING A CENTIMETER RULER

The idea of measurement to compare objects has been used by people for thousands of years. To measure objects and draw line segments, you can use a ruler. On the centimeter ruler shown below, each **centimeter (cm)** is marked off into ten smaller units. Each smaller unit is a **millimeter (mm).**

Remember

1 cm = 10 mm

Here's how to draw a segment 7 cm or 70 mm long. Use a sharp pencil close to the ruler.

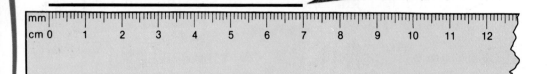

E Estimate the length before using a ruler to measure a segment. Compare your estimate with the measurement. In this way you will improve your sense of how long objects are.

CLASS EXERCISES

Measure the segment to the nearest centimeter. Then measure to the nearest millimeter.

1.

2.

3.

4.

5.

6. **Think:** What is the order of these measurements from least to greatest? 39 cm   78 mm   350 mm   125 cm

PRACTICE

Draw a segment with the given length.

7. 2 cm   **8.** 3 cm   **9.** 18 cm   **10.** 4 cm   **11.** 7 cm

12. 70 mm   **13.** 33 mm   **14.** 85 mm   **15.** 168 mm   **16.** 135 mm

Estimate the length in centimeters.
Then measure to the nearest centimeter.

17.    **18.** 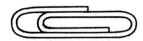   **19.**

Estimate the length in millimeters.
Then measure to the nearest millimeter.

20.    **21.**    **22.**   **E** ESTIMATE

PROBLEM SOLVING APPLICATIONS
Applying Measurements

Write *yes* or *no*.

23. Will the vase stand
on a bottom shelf
if the shelves
are 34 cm apart?

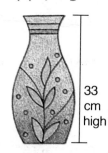

33 cm high

24. Will the toolbox fit under
a bench 36 cm high?

31 cm high

25. Can the dog stretch out in a
dog bed 473 mm long?

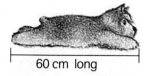

60 cm long

26. Can the goldfish swim
in a bowl 40 cm long?

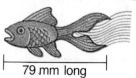

79 mm long

27. Will a wood plank 270 cm
long fit across the stream?

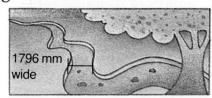

1796 mm wide

★ **28.** The real pencil is 8 times
as long as the drawing.
Will it fit in a box
20 cm long?

METRIC UNITS OF LENGTH

It is easy to get a sense of how long metric units are by working with everyday objects.

 The runner's feet are about one **meter (m)** apart.

The distance between eyelets on his shoe is about one **centimeter (cm)**.

The tip of his shoelace is about one **millimeter (mm)** wide.

The distance he can walk in ten minutes is about one **kilometer (km)**.

Since these units are related by 10's, 100's, and 1000's, it is easy to change from one unit to another.

10 mm = 1 cm   100 cm = 1 m   1000 m = 1 km

CLASS EXERCISES

Complete.

1. 10 mm = ▨ cm
20 mm = ▨ cm
30 mm = ▨ cm

2. 100 cm = ▨ m
300 cm = ▨ m
900 cm = ▨ m

3. 1000 m = ▨ km
2000 m = ▨ km
4000 m = ▨ km

What are two likely metric units for measuring the object?

4. length of a crayon

5. width of a book

6. height of a door

7. height of a mountain

PRACTICE

Choose the better estimate. Write *a* or *b*.

8. thickness of a dime
  a. 1 mm   **b.** 1 cm

9. length of a dining table
  a. 135 cm   **b.** 135 mm

10. length of a river
  a. 1080 m   **b.** 1080 km

11. height of a desk
  a. 73 mm   **b.** 73 cm

12. length of a pencil
    a. 15 cm   **b.** 150 cm

13. height of a flagpole
    a. 10 m   **b.** 200 m

14. height of a room
    a. 240 cm   **b.** 240 km

15. length of a belt
    a. 65 mm   **b.** 65 cm

Match. Estimate and write the letter of the most likely measurement.

ESTIMATE

16. length of a carrot   **A.** about 5 km

17. height of a person   **B.** about 300 m

18. height of a tall building   **C.** about 170 cm

19. length of an unshelled peanut   **D.** about 15 cm

20. thickness of a book cover   **E.** about 4 cm

21. distance you can hike in an hour   **F.** about 2 mm

PROBLEM SOLVING APPLICATIONS
Choosing the Operation

Solve.

22. A pole vaulter uses a pole that is about 5 m long. How many centimeters is the pole? How many millimeters is this?

23. Which event covers the least distance; a 1 km walk, an 800 m dash, or a 1500 m race?

24. An early Olympic shot-put competition was won with a distance of 1350 cm. A later shot-put competition was won with a distance of 26 m. At which competition did the shot-put travel the farthest?

★ **25.** A runner sprints 500 m and jogs 500 m. If the runner follows this pattern of running and jogging 5 times in all, how many kilometers will be covered?

METRIC UNITS
OF CAPACITY AND MASS

In the metric system, **capacity** is measured in **milliliters** (mL) and **liters** (L). Remember:

$$1000 \text{ mL} = 1 \text{ L}$$

 To help estimate capacity, keep in mind that one teaspoon holds about 5 mL and one liter holds about four cups.

Things Usually Measured
in Milliliters

Things Usually Measured
in Liters

Mass is measured in **grams** (g) and **kilograms** (kg). Remember:

$$1000 \text{ g} = 1 \text{ kg}$$

To help you estimate mass, keep in mind that a dollar bill has a mass of about 1 g and this book has a mass of about 1 kg.

Things Usually Measured
in Grams

Things Usually Measured
in Kilograms

CLASS EXERCISES

Choose the better estimate. Write *a* or *b*.

1. amount of gas in a car
   a. 53 mL   **b.** 53 L

2. amount of milk in a glass
   a. 240 mL   **b.** 240 L

3. mass of a raisin
   a. 1 g   **b.** 1 kg

4. mass of a dog
   a. 18 g   **b.** 18 kg

PRACTICE

Match. Estimate to write the letter
of the most likely measurement.

5. amount of water in a fish tank   **A.** about 1 mL

6. amount of water in a fishpond   **B.** about 1 L

7. amount of water in a raindrop   **C.** about 40 L

8. amount of juice in a carton   **D.** about 250 mL

9. amount of soup in a bowl   **E.** about 70,000 L

10. mass of a roast beef   **A.** about 10 g

11. mass of a pencil   **B.** about 250 g

12. mass of a wedge of cheese   **C.** about 20 kg

13. mass of a heavy suitcase   **D.** about 1000 kg

14. mass of a car   **E.** about 3 kg

Write the answer.

**MIXED
REVIEW**

15. 16 + 16   16. 12 + 12 + 12   17. 2 × 12

18. 3 × 9   19. 2 × 1000   20. 3 × 2000

PROBLEM SOLVING APPLICATIONS
Choosing the Operation

Solve.

21. Delia has a 750 mL container and a 2 L container.
    Which of the two containers holds more?

22. Kurt bought a 4 L container of liquid laundry deter-
    gent. How many milliliters is this?

23. The watermelon that Brian bought has a mass of
    4135 g. About how many kilograms is this?

★ 24. How many grams are in six and one-half kilograms?

PROBLEM SOLVING
Strategy: Using Pictures and Maps

1. Understand
2. Plan
3. Work
4. Answer/Check

Temperature in the metric system is measured in **degrees Celsius (°C).**

We call the point at which water freezes 0°C (zero degrees Celsius). We call the point at which water boils 100°C. Between 0° and 100° this thermometer is marked off in intervals of ten degrees, labeled 10, 20, 30, and so on to 100. The smaller markings show intervals of two degrees.

You can get an idea of some other temperatures by looking at the thermometer at the right. Count from 30 to determine that normal body temperature is 37°C. The temperature of a cold winter day shown is written −8°C and is read as *eight degrees below zero Celsius.*

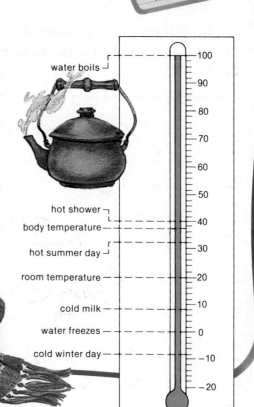

CLASS EXERCISES

What is the temperature shown on the thermometer?

1. hot summer day   **2.** hot shower   **3.** room temperature   **4.** cold milk

Choose the most likely temperature. Write *a, b,* or *c.*

5. raking leaves
   a. 40°C **b.** 13°C **c.** 2°C

6. planting a garden
   a. 25°C **b.** 0°C **c.** 5°C

7. swimming in a pond
   a. 21°C **b.** 12°C **c.** 32°C

8. ice-skating on a pond
   a. 20°C **b.** 35°C **c.** −1°C

9. picking strawberries
   a. 3°C **b.** 24°C **c.** −10°C

10. wearing a winter coat
   a. 75°C **b.** 28°C **c.** −6°C

11. building an igloo
   a. 22°C **b.** −5°C **c.** 35°C

12. washing a car
   a. 25°C **b.** 5°C **c.** 10°C

PRACTICE

The temperature map shows average July temperatures around the world. Places with the same average temperature are joined by a smooth curve called an *isotherm*.

You can tell by looking at the key that most of Australia is warm in July. Temperatures there will vary from about 10°C to 21°C.

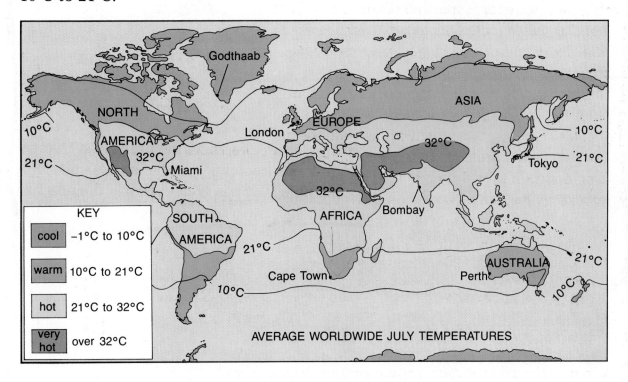

AVERAGE WORLDWIDE JULY TEMPERATURES

KEY
cool   −1°C to 10°C
warm   10°C to 21°C
hot   21°C to 32°C
very hot   over 32°C

Use the temperature map to answer the question.

13. Which city has the coolest temperature in July?

14. Name one continent where you would expect a temperature of 34°C in July.

15. Find three cities where you would expect a temperature of 25°C in July.

16. By about how many degrees does the temperature vary in South America in July?

17. Write expected temperatures for Perth, London, and Tokyo in July.

U.S. CUSTOMARY UNITS OF LENGTH

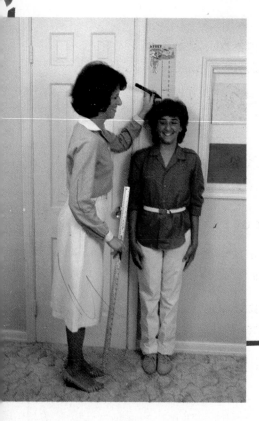

In the United States the most commonly used units of length are the **inch (in.)**, the **foot (ft)**, the **yard (yd)**, and the **mile (mi).**

1 inch (in.)

⊢—————————————⊣

12 in. = 1 ft
3 ft = 1 yd
5280 ft or 1760 yd = 1 mi

Ⓜ To compare distances mentally, first change all measurements to the same unit. For example, 13 in. is greater than 1 ft since 1 ft is 12 in.

CLASS EXERCISES

Choose the best estimate. Write *a*, *b*, or *c*.

1. distance of a marathon
   a. 26 yd   **b.** 26 mi   **c.** 26 ft

2. length of a football field
   a. 100 ft   **b.** 100 yd   **c.** 100 mi

3. length of a book
   a. 4 ft   **b.** 2 yd   **c.** 14 in.

4. length of a couch
   a. 1 yd   **b.** 20 ft   **c.** 120 in.

5. distance around the outside of a house
   a. 120 ft   **b.** 1200 yd   **c.** 12 mi

PRACTICE

Complete.

6. 20 in. = ▦ ft ▦ in.

7. 2 ft 5 in. = ▦ in.

8. 10 ft = ▦ yd ▦ ft

9. 45 in. = ▦ yd ▦ in.

10. 18 ft 19 in. = ▢ yd ▢ ft ▢ in.   **11.** 5 yd 2 ft = ▢ ft

12. 1769 yd = ▢ mi ▢ yd   **13.** 5284 ft = ▢ mi ▢ yd ▢ ft

Choose the best estimate. Write *a*, *b*, or *c*.

14. length of a bicycle
    a. 6 yd **b.** 6 in. **c.** 6 ft

15. length of your arm
    a. 24 in. **b.** 1 yd **c.** 1 ft

16. length of a living room
    a. 6 yd **b.** 6 in. **c.** 6 ft

17. width of a street
    a. 1 mi **b.** 10 yd **c.** 1 ft

Compare the two measurements mentally. Which is greater?

MENTAL MATH

18. 23 in. or 2 ft

19. 4 yd or 14 ft

20. 2 mi or 9876 ft

21. 9 ft or 90 in.

PROBLEM SOLVING APPLICATIONS
Mental Math, Estimation, or Calculator

Tell whether you would choose mental math, estimation, or a calculator to solve. Write M, E, or C. Then solve.

22. Lyle Hill works in a tree nursery. He has planted 100 fir seedlings that each grow about 24 in. a year. In 10 years about how many feet will each seedling have grown?

23. The directions for building a birdhouse call for a piece of wood 38 in. long. Should you buy 3 ft or 4 ft of wood?

★ **24.** Kite string is sold in lengths of 525 ft. About how many spools of kite string must Ronald buy to fly a kite a distance of 1 mi?

★ **25.** David Diaz needs 54 ft of the same carpeting for the living room, 21 ft for the dining room, and 42 ft for the bedroom. Rug King carpet store is having a sale, but all carpet must be bought in rolls of 10 yd. How much carpet must David Diaz buy?

U.S. CUSTOMARY UNITS
OF CAPACITY AND WEIGHT

In the United States, the most commonly used units of capacity are the **cup (c)**, the **pint (pt)**, the **quart (qt)**, and the **gallon (gal).**

Weight is measured in **ounces (oz)**, **pounds (lb)**, and **tons (t).**

$$16 \text{ oz} = 1 \text{ lb}$$
$$2000 \text{ lb} = 1 \text{ t}$$

$$2 \text{ c} = 1 \text{ pt}$$
$$2 \text{ pt or } 4 \text{ c} = 1 \text{ qt}$$
$$4 \text{ qt} = 1 \text{ gal}$$

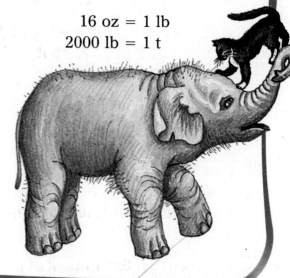

CLASS EXERCISES

Match. Choose the letter of the most likely measurement.

1. weight of a bunch of bananas   **A.** 1 c

2. capacity of a small milk container   **B.** 8 oz

3. weight of a car   **C.** 2 t

4. capacity of an aquarium   **D.** 4 lb

5. capacity of a glass of water   **E.** 20 gal

6. weight of a kitten   **F.** 1 pt

PRACTICE

Complete.

7. 6 pt = ☐ c   8. 2 lb = ☐ oz   9. 8 qt = ☐ c

10. 16 c = ☐ gal   11. 5 t = ☐ lb   12. 160 oz = ☐ lb

13. 2297 lb = ☐ t ☐ lb   14. 19 c = ☐ gal ☐ c   15. 38 qt = ☐ gal ☐ qt

Choose the best estimate. Write *a*, *b*, or *c*.

16. lawn mower gas tank's capacity
    a. 1 pt **b.** 1 qt **c.** 1 gal

17. weight of a watermelon
    a. 16 oz **b.** 16 lb **c.** 16 t

18. weight of a box of cereal
    a. 6 oz **b.** 16 oz **c.** 60 oz

19. capacity of a goldfish pond
    a. 5 qt **b.** 55 c **c.** 555 gal

20. weight of a tenpin bowling ball
    a. 1 t **b.** 8 oz **c.** 15 lb

21. capacity of a bowl of soup
    a. 2 c **b.** 2 pt **c.** 2 qt

PROBLEM SOLVING APPLICATIONS
Choosing the Operation

Solve.

22. One brand of milk only comes in quarts or pints. A recipe calls for 1 c of milk. Should you buy a quart or a pint?

23. Sue Adams owns a dairy. Each of her 100 cows weighs about 500 lb. About how many tons do Sue Adams's cows weigh in all?

★ 24. Lee used half the amount of paint shown to repaint the inside of his house. How much did he use?

hallways	1 gal, 3 qt
dining room	1 gal, 3 qt
living room	3 gal

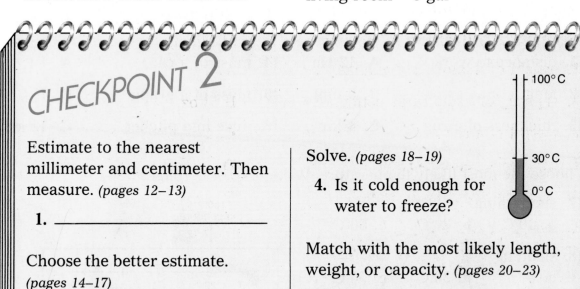

CHECKPOINT 2

Estimate to the nearest millimeter and centimeter. Then measure. *(pages 12–13)*

1. _____

Choose the better estimate. *(pages 14–17)*

2. tea in a cup
   a. 240 mL **b.** 240 L

3. mass of a carrot
   a. 100 kg **b.** 100 g

Solve. *(pages 18–19)*

4. Is it cold enough for water to freeze?

100° C

30° C

0° C

Match with the most likely length, weight, or capacity. *(pages 20–23)*

5. city block **A.** 2000 lb

6. bucket **B.** 2 gal

7. elephant **C.** 200 ft

Extra Practice on page 420

CHAPTER 1 TEST

Write the standard form. *(pages 2–5)*

1. three thousand five hundred

2. 200,000 + 6000 + 500 + 80 + 7

3. eleven million, two hundred one

4. 7 billion, 3 million, 392 thousand

Round to the place of the underlined digit. *(pages 6–9)*

5. <u>7</u>6

6. <u>3</u>081

7. 2<u>0</u>6,415

8. <u>7</u>52,149

Solve. *(pages 10–11)*

9. The farmer had 63 cows, 119 chickens, and 87 pigs. List in order from least to greatest.

10. The Millers traveled 5287 km. To the nearest thousand, how many kilometers is this?

Match. Estimate to write the letter of the most likely measurement. *(pages 12–17)*

11. distance to work

A. 12 cm

12. length of a carrot

B. 5 mm

13. thickness of a rug

C. 4 km

14. mass of a cat

A. 1 L

15. mass of a grape

B. 1 g

16. juice in a pitcher

C. 12 kg

Choose the most likely temperature. Write *a*, *b*, or *c*. *(pages 18–19)*

17. sunbathing
   a. 10°C   **b.** 20°C   **c.** 30°C

18. sledding
   a. 0°C   **b.** 30°C   **c.** 50°C

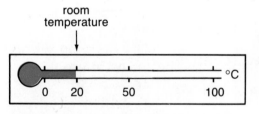

Choose the best estimate. Write *a*, *b*, or *c*. *(pages 20–23)*

19. length of a worm
   a. 3 in.   **b.** 10 yd   **c.** 30 ft

20. weight of a bunch of bananas
   a. 4 oz   **b.** 4 t   **c.** 4 lb

Extra Practice on page 421

MATHEMATICS and LANGUAGE

Many times a word has several meanings. You may not know the meaning of a word unless you hear it used in a sentence.

HOW MANY FEET IN YOUR YARD?

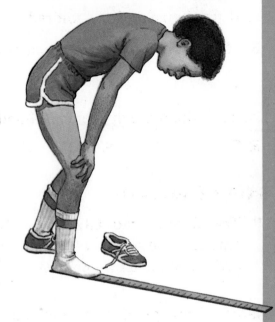

Match the words below with their non-mathematical description. Write the letter of the description.

1. digit
2. foot
3. inch
4. pound
5. yard
6. degrees
7. meter
8. round
9. ruler

A. a piece of ground near a house

B. a finger or a toe

C. a place for keeping stray animals

D. the part of the leg that usually rests on the floor

E. to move or proceed very slowly

F. the division of music into measures

G. a person who governs a country

H. academic titles awarded by a university

I. a rung of a ladder or chair

10. Write a mathematical definition of each of the words in Exercises 1–9.

Enrichment

The Romans used a number system without place value. They just combined basic numerals by addition and subtraction rules to form other numerals. As time passed no numeral was ever used more than three times in a row.

These are the basic Roman numerals.

I	V	X	L	C	D	M
1	5	10	50	100	500	1000

You can follow these rules when using Roman numerals.

• **Add when a numeral is repeated.**

XXX = 10 + 10 + 10 = 30
CCC = 100 + 100 + 100 = 300

• **Add when a numeral for a lesser number follows a numeral for a greater number.**

XV = 10 + 5 = 15   LXXVII = 50 + 20 + 5 + 2 = 77

• **Subtract when a numeral for a lesser number comes before a numeral for a greater number.**

IV = 5 − 1 = 4
XL = 50 − 10 = 40
CM = 1000 − 100 = 900

ROMAN NUMERALS

Complete.

1. DCL = 500 + ▇ + ▇ = ▇

2. CCXXI = ▇ + 20 + ▇ = ▇

3. XIV = 10 + ▇ = ▇

4. MCXL = ▇ + ▇ + ▇ = ▇

Write the standard form.

5. XII   **6.** VI   **7.** IV   **8.** III   **9.** XVI   **10.** XX

11. XXV **12.** XL   **13.** XLV **14.** LXI **15.** XCVII **16.** CMXL

17. DCVII **18.** MDC **19.** CCXX **20.** CDXCI **21.** LXVII **22.** MMDCXXX

Write the Roman numeral.

23. 38   **24.** 75   **25.** 13

26. 168   **27.** 324   **28.** 504

29. 985   **30.** 759   **31.** 2222

32. 1889 **33.** 1987 ★ **34.** 4444

Write the standard form.

35. Sound movies were invented in MCMXXVII.

36. Air conditioning was invented in MCMXL.

37. The toaster was invented in MCMXVIII.

38. The lawn mower was invented in MDCCCLXVIII.

★ **39.** The Roman numeral for 5000 is $\overline{V}$. Copy and complete the table.

ROMAN NUMERAL	$\overline{V}$	$\overline{X}$	$\overline{L}$	$\overline{C}$	$\overline{D}$	$\overline{M}$
Standard Form	?	?	?	?	?	?

CUMULATIVE REVIEW

Choose the correct answer. Write a, b, c, or d.
Compare the numbers.

1. 398 ▨ 389
   a. >
   b. <
   c. =
   d. none of these

2. 5061 ▨ 6501
   a. >
   b. <
   c. =
   d. none of these

3. 2,842,313 ▨ 2,823,243
   a. >
   b. <
   c. =
   d. none of these

What is the standard form?

4. 32 thousand, 576
   a. 320,576
   b. 32,576
   c. 3,200,576
   d. none of these

5. 6 million, 250
   a. 625,250
   b. 6,250,000
   c. 6,000,250
   d. none of these

6. 400,000 + 500 + 70 + 3
   a. 450,073
   b. 405,703
   c. 400,573
   d. none of these

Round to the greatest place value.

7. 384
   a. 380
   b. 300
   c. 400
   d. none of these

8. 8751
   a. 9000
   b. 8000
   c. 8800
   d. none of these

9. 62,597
   a. 63,000
   b. 60,000
   c. 62,000
   d. none of these

Solve.

10. A pencil company had these sales:
   Monday   20,698 pencils
   Tuesday   601,395 pencils
   Wednesday   49,080 pencils
   List the number of pencils sold in
   order from least to greatest.
   a. 20,698   601,395   49,080
   b. 601,395   49,080   20,698
   c. 49,080   20,698   601,395
   d. none of these

11. Mei-Su's home is 1392 km from
   her cousin's home. To the nearest
   thousand, how many kilometers
   apart do Mei-Su and her cousin
   live?
   a. 1000 km
   b. 1400 km
   c. 11,000 km
   d. none of these

Choose the best estimate.

12. the length of
a fingernail
  a. 9 cm
  b. 9 mm
  c. 9 km
  d. 90 mm

13. the length of
a baseball bat
  a. 76 m
  b. 76 km
  c. 76 cm
  d. 76 mm

14. the height of a giant
redwood tree
  a. 100 m
  b. 100 cm
  c. 100 mm
  d. 100 km

15. the mass of
a rose
  a. 180 g
  b. 18 kg
  c. 18 g
  d. 8 kg

16. the amount of
soup in a can
  a. 35 L
  b. 35 mL
  c. 350 L
  d. 315 mL

17. the mass of peanut
butter in a jar
  a. 510 kg
  b. 51 g
  c. 510 g
  d. 51 kg

LANGUAGE and VOCABULARY REVIEW

Find 16 different measurement words in the puzzle.
Write them on a piece of paper.

m	i	l	e	a	r	q	u	s	b	k	r
e	m	l	b	d	m	e	t	e	r	l	e
s	v	w	g	r	a	m	i	o	n	l	t
c	s	t	a	o	p	i	n	t	d	o	e
u	l	p	l	l	g	l	e	d	p	g	m
p	m	i	l	l	i	l	i	t	e	r	o
o	k	p	o	m	n	i	c	m	t	a	l
u	o	u	n	c	e	m	f	t	b	m	i
n	j	l	o	n	a	e	r	o	i	s	k
d	c	e	f	o	o	t	o	n	b	m	t
i	n	c	h	g	m	e	q	u	a	r	t
y	r	s	t	y	a	r	d	l	p	s	r

HISTORY

The abacus was one of the earliest counting devices. Later, Pascal's Arithmetic Machine (1642) could do simple calculations. It could add and subtract.

In 1830, Charles Babbage invented a machine called the Analytical Engine. It could do calculations and store information. Lady Ada Augusta Lovelace developed the first programming language for Babbage's machine.

For the 1890 U.S. Census, Hollerith's Tabulating Machine was used. It was the first machine used to sort and calculate such large amounts of information.

Until 1946 all the machines that were used for calculating had gears inside them. After that electric circuits took the place of gears and the first real computer was invented. Since then computers have developed in stages based on their circuitry.

Copy the time line. Write the letter for the fact where it belongs on the line.

1940   1950   1960   1970   1980   1990

A. ENIAC, the first electronic computer, was introduced in 1946.

B. One year before the seventh decade of the 1900's, transistors took the place of vacuum tubes inside a computer.

C. UNIVAC, the first computer sold to business, was developed 5 years after ENIAC.

D. The first microcomputer, Altair 8800, was available 28 years after ENIAC first appeared.

E. Two years after the beginning of the seventh decade of the 1900's the BASIC language was developed at Dartmouth College.

F. The first computer store opened 25 years before the beginning of the twenty-first century.

On a shelf are 3 stacks containing 50, 20, and 40 hats. Another shelf holds three stacks of 20, 42, and 50 hats. Which shelf has more hats?

2

ADDITION AND SUBTRACTION OF WHOLE NUMBERS

PROPERTIES

You need to know the basic facts to add and subtract.

$$7 + 6 = 13 \qquad 13 - 7 = 6$$

addends　sum　　　　　difference

Commutative Property of Addition

Changing the order of the addends does not change the sum.

$$4 + 3 = 7 \text{ and } 3 + 4 = 7$$
$$\text{so } 4 + 3 = 3 + 4$$

Opposites Property of Addition and Subtraction

Addition and subtraction are opposites. One undoes the other.

$$3 + 5 = 8 \qquad 8 - 5 = 3$$

Associative Property of Addition

Changing the grouping of the addends does not change the sum. The parentheses tell you what to do first.

$$(2 + 4) + 3 = 9 \text{ and}$$
$$2 + (4 + 3) = 9, \text{ so}$$
$$(2 + 4) + 3 = 2 + (4 + 3)$$

Zero Properties

The sum of zero and any number is that number.

$$6 + 0 = 6 \qquad 0 + 6 = 6$$

The difference between any number and zero is that number. The difference between any number and itself is zero.

$$7 - 0 = 7 \qquad 7 - 7 = 0$$

 You can use the properties to help you add and subtract mentally.

To add: $7 + 9 + 5 + 3$
Think: $(7 + 3) + (9 + 5) =$
$$\qquad\quad 10 \quad + \quad 14 \quad = 24$$

CLASS EXERCISES

Add or subtract. Name the property illustrated.

1. $4 + 9$
　　$13 - 9$

2. $4 + 6$
　　$6 + 4$

3. $2 + (7 + 3)$
　　$(2 + 7) + 3$

4. $18 + 0$
　　$18 - 0$

5. Think: Are there commutative and associative properties for subtraction? Give examples to explain.

PRACTICE

Use one of the properties to complete.

6. $6 + 4 = \boxed{} + 6$

7. $9 + 8 = 8 + \boxed{}$

8. $(3 + 7) + 1 = 3 + (\boxed{} + 1)$

9. $(0 + 6) + 0 = \boxed{}$

10. $5 + 2 = \boxed{}$, so $\boxed{} - 2 = 5$

11. $8 - 3 = \boxed{}$, so $5 + \boxed{} = 8$

★ **12.** $0 + 5 = \boxed{}$, so $\boxed{} - \boxed{} = 0$

★ **13.** $\boxed{} + \boxed{} = 0$

Add or subtract mentally.

14. $7 + 6 + 3 + 2$

15. $8 + 3 + 2 + 5$

16. $7 + 5 + 5 + 5$

17. $1 + 9 - 3$

18. $5 - 2 + 5$

19. $3 + 4 + 6 - 3$

MENTAL MATH

PROBLEM SOLVING APPLICATIONS
Using Patterns

Solve.

20. Find the pattern. Complete.
6, 10, 16, 26, $\boxed{}$, $\boxed{}$, $\boxed{}$, $\boxed{}$, $\boxed{}$

21. a. Complete the table. Suppose each addition fact counts as one. Two facts related by the commutative property count only as one. Facts involving 0 do not count.

For example, count two facts for the sum 4:
$1 + 3 = 4, 2 + 2 = 4$.

Sum	2	3	4	5	6	7	8	9	10	11	12
Number of facts	1	1	2	?	?	?	?	?	?	?	?

b. Continue the table through the sum 18.

c. If you know the commutative property and the zero property, how many basic facts are there for the sums 2 through 18?

VARIABLES AND EQUATIONS

Sometimes a letter is used to represent a number. A letter used in this way is called a **variable.**

n	$12 + n$
3	15
5	17
9	21

For example, suppose your age is 12 and you want to find out how old you will be in 3, 5, or 9 years. You can write $12 + n$ and let n stand for 3, 5, or 9.

An **equation** is a mathematical sentence with an equals sign. An equation tells you that two quantities are the same. Here are three examples:

$$3 + 8 = 11 \qquad 4 + n = 9 \qquad t - 4 = 6$$

An equation may include a variable. When you find what number the letter stands for, you **solve** the equation. The answer is the **solution.**

$4 + n = 9$

Think: $4 + 5 = 9$
so $n = 5$

$t - 4 = 6$

Think: $10 - 4 = 6$
so $t = 10$

CLASS EXERCISES

Complete the chart.

1.

n	$n + 4$
0	?
1	?
5	?
8	?

2.

a	$a - 0$
1	?
2	?
3	?
4	?

3.

x	$x - 7$
16	?
14	?
10	?
7	?

Write *true* or *false.*

4. If $n = 5$, then $n + 3 = 8$.

5. If $x = 7$, then $15 - x = 9$.

6. If $b = 0$, then $b + 5 = 5$.

7. If $t = 0$, then $5 - t = 0$.

PRACTICE

Write the sum or difference when $n = 4$.

8. $8 + n$　　　　　**9.** $10 - n$　　　　　**10.** $n + 0$　　　　　**11.** $4 - n$

Solve the equation.

12. $2 + a = 7$　　　**13.** $n - 9 = 9$　　　**14.** $x - 7 = 5$　　　**15.** $7 + a = 11$

16. $4 + y = 9$　　　**17.** $2 + a = 4$　　　**18.** $6 + n = 9$　　　**19.** $x + 3 = 12$

20. $3 + n = 3$　　　**21.** $7 + n = 10$　　　**22.** $a + 6 = 9$　　　**23.** $n + 7 = 7$

★ **24. Think:** In the equation $n - n = \rule{1em}{0.8em}$, what will always be the difference? Why?

_____

Write the answer.

25. $9 + 9$　　　**26.** $15 - 8$　　　**27.** 6×7　　　**28.** $56 \div 7$

29. 7×9　　　**30.** $11 - 7$　　　**31.** $6 + 7$　　　**32.** 8×8

33. $72 \div 9$　　　**34.** $9 + 4$　　　**35.** $24 \div 3$　　　**36.** $8 + 5$

37. $17 - 9$　　　**38.** 8×9　　　**39.** $49 \div 7$　　　**40.** $8 + 9$

MIXED REVIEW

PROBLEM SOLVING APPLICATIONS
Choosing Equations

Match the equation with the property.

41. Changing the order of the addends does not change the sum.

42. The difference between any number and zero is that number.

43. Changing the grouping of the addends does not change the sum.

44. Addition and subtraction are opposites. One undoes the other.

45. The difference between any number and itself is zero.

A. $3 + n = 8$, so $8 - n = 3$

B. $h - h = 0$

C. $13 + s = s + 13$

D. $(6 + 8) + n = 6 + (8 + n)$

E. $b - 0 = b$

ADDITION

When you add 168 and 236, you have to rename 10 ones as 1 ten and 10 tens as 1 hundred.

 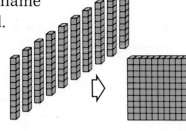

Add the ones. Rename.	Add the tens. Rename.	Add the hundreds.

h	t	o
	1	
1	6	8
+ 2	3	6
		4

h	t	o
1	1	
1	6	8
+ 2	3	6
	0	4

h	t	o
1	1	
1	6	8
+ 2	3	6
4	0	4

Adding dollars and cents is like adding whole numbers. Remember to line up the decimal points.

$$\begin{array}{r} 1\ 1 \\ \$2.49 \\ +\ \ 4.75 \\ \hline \$7.24 \end{array}$$

 Sometimes you can calculate a sum mentally. For example, to add 48 + 35:

Add 2 to 48 to make the next ten. $48 + 2 = 50$
Then add 35. $50 + 35 = 85$
Decrease the sum by 2. $85 - 2 = 83$
   Thus, $48 + 35 = 83$.

CLASS EXERCISES

Add.

1.   23   23   23
   + 46   + 47   + 48

2.   166   167
      + 224   + 224

3.   418   418
      + 382   + 383

4. **Think:** Look at the addition in Exercise 1. How could you have used the first sum to find the second?

PRACTICE

Add.

5. 37
 + 35

6. 57
 + 8

7. 379
 + 355

8. 345
 + 208

9. $8.14
 + 2.79

10. $2.75
 + 8.23

11. 883
 + 15

12. 545
 + 689

13. 791
 + 98

14. 246
 + 373

15. 682
 + 9

16. $9.29
 + 3.81

17. 463 + 35

18. 507 + 372

19. 348 + 27

20. $9.63 + $4.75

21. 659 + 2

22. 462 + 393

23. 247 + 505

24. $6.58 + $7.03

25. 487 + 526 + 65

26. 456 + 4 + 424 + 89

27. 78 + 221 + 45 + 625

Solve the equation.

28. $365 + n = 365$

29. $125 + x = 150$

30. $r + 350 = 550$

31. $116 + 32 = 148$ so, $m - 32 = 116$

★ **32.** $25 + (10 + y) = 85$

Write the sum using mental math.

33. 49 + 3

34. 76 + 89

35. 28 + 57

36. 118 + 74

37. 232 + 9

38. 666 + 5

39. 289 + 6

40. 9992 + 9

MENTAL MATH

PROBLEM SOLVING APPLICATIONS
Mental Math or Paper and Pencil

Tell whether you would choose mental math or paper and pencil to solve. Write *M* or *P*. Then solve.

41. If you buy 2 king-size jigsaw puzzles, how many pieces will you have?

42. How much do a puzzle and a record cost?

43. Dover's sold 78 tapes Thursday, 102 Friday, and 97 Saturday. How many tapes were sold?

44. If you have $25.00, can you buy a pair of skates and a record?

Dover's

ALL records and tapes
NOW just $4.98

Chess Sets $ 5.95
Chemistry Sets   25.89
Skates   19.98
King-Size Jigsaw Puzzles   6.98
• 1000 pieces
Electronic Kits   21.99
• over 1000 experiments

ESTIMATING SUMS

Paul Sanchez owns a sporting goods store. He has 48 tennis rackets on display and another 97 in the storeroom. He wants to estimate how many tennis rackets he has in stock.

To estimate a sum, first round each number to its greatest place value, then add.

$$
\begin{array}{r}
48 \\
+\ 97
\end{array}
\quad \Rightarrow \quad
\begin{array}{r}
50 \\
+\ 100 \\
\hline
150
\end{array}
$$

Paul Sanchez has about 150 rackets in stock.

To estimate sums of money, round to the greatest place value and then add. For example, suppose you plan to purchase a tennis racket for $28.99, a sun visor for $3.29, and a head band on sale for $1.75. About how much would these items cost?

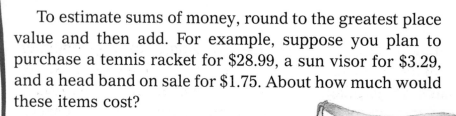

$$
\begin{array}{r}
\$28.99 \\
3.29 \\
+\quad 1.75
\end{array}
\quad \Rightarrow \quad
\begin{array}{r}
\$30 \\
3 \\
+\quad 2 \\
\hline
\$35
\end{array}
$$

You can expect to pay about $35.

CLASS EXERCISES

Complete.

1. To estimate $5.64 + $1.33, add ▢ + ▢.

2. To estimate 1460 + 702, add ▢ + ▢.

3. To estimate 142 + 378 + 691, add ▢ + ▢ + ▢.

4. To estimate $26.84 + $7.49, add ▢ + ▢.

5. **Think:** Name a job and discuss how estimation may be used in it.

PRACTICE

Estimate.

6.	84 + 69	7.	$.65 + .12	8.	860 + 232	9.	$5.55 + 4.50	10.	902 + 77

11.	3752 + 2180	12.	2061 + 1898	13.	$91.03 + 76.15	14.	$33.81 + 4.66	15.	2617 + 5107

16.	128 354 + 328	17.	$422 157 + 124	18.	$5.73 1.47 + 2.83	19.	2481 374 + 85	20.	$11.42 3.78 + .97

PROBLEM SOLVING APPLICATIONS
Using Estimation

Solve.

21. A shoe buyer ordered 378 pairs of tennis shoes, 182 pairs of sneakers, and 593 pairs of jogging shoes. Estimate the total number of pairs of shoes ordered.

22. Joanne wants to buy jogging shoes for $37.86, a cap for $7.40, and a key chain for $1.89. About how much will these purchases cost Joanne?

★ **23.** Paul Sanchez decided to hold a 3-day sale. The first day he took in $1826. The next day sales increased by $694. Sales for the last day totaled $432 more than the day before. Estimate the amount received from the sale. Then, find the exact amount received.

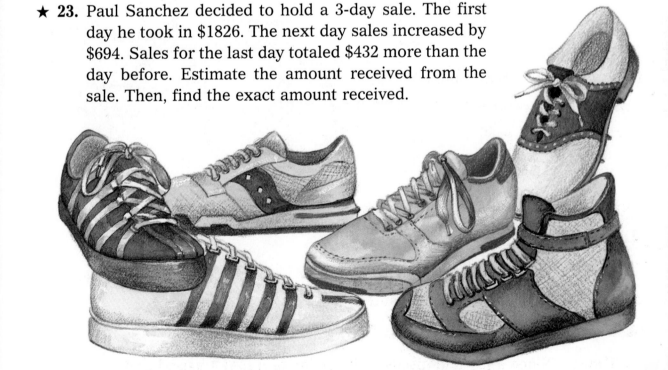

ADDING GREATER NUMBERS

Look at the election results shown on the TV screen. How many votes were cast for Wright and Godin altogether?

You add greater numbers by using the same rules for renaming that you used for adding smaller numbers.

$$\begin{array}{r} \overset{1\quad1}{50{,}848} \\ +\ 53{,}735 \\ \hline 104{,}583 \end{array}$$

They received 104,583 votes altogether.

Think: About how many votes were cast in all?

ELECTION RESULTS

Candidate	Votes
Adam Wright	50,848
Jane Godin	53,735
Ben Taylor	46,521
Nora Zubin	26,079

Even if you use a calculator when adding greater numbers, it's good to estimate to check the reasonableness of your answer.

CLASS EXERCISES

What is the sum?

1.
$$\begin{array}{r} 733 \\ +\ 378 \\ \hline \end{array}\qquad \begin{array}{r} 7335 \\ +\ 3785 \\ \hline \end{array}\qquad \begin{array}{r} 73{,}356 \\ +\ 37{,}856 \\ \hline \end{array}$$

2.
$$\begin{array}{r} 483 \\ +\ 314 \\ \hline \end{array}\qquad \begin{array}{r} 4836 \\ +\ 3142 \\ \hline \end{array}\qquad \begin{array}{r} 48{,}369 \\ +\ 31{,}426 \\ \hline \end{array}$$

3.
$$\begin{array}{r} 438 \\ +\ 146 \\ \hline \end{array}\qquad \begin{array}{r} 4383 \\ +\ 1462 \\ \hline \end{array}\qquad \begin{array}{r} 43{,}838 \\ +\ 14{,}628 \\ \hline \end{array}$$

4.
$$\begin{array}{r} 941 \\ +\ 34 \\ \hline \end{array}\qquad \begin{array}{r} 9412 \\ +\ 340 \\ \hline \end{array}\qquad \begin{array}{r} 94{,}122 \\ +\ 3{,}407 \\ \hline \end{array}$$

PRACTICE

Add.

5.
$$\begin{array}{r} 7264 \\ +\ 8891 \\ \hline \end{array}$$

6.
$$\begin{array}{r} 4728 \\ +\ 1389 \\ \hline \end{array}$$

7.
$$\begin{array}{r} 7536 \\ +\ 274 \\ \hline \end{array}$$

8.
$$\begin{array}{r} 5169 \\ +\ 3926 \\ \hline \end{array}$$

9.
$$\begin{array}{r} 8989 \\ +\ 346 \\ \hline \end{array}$$

10.
$$\begin{array}{r} 3579 \\ +\ 82 \\ \hline \end{array}$$

11.
$$\begin{array}{r} 9028 \\ +\ 69 \\ \hline \end{array}$$

12.
$$\begin{array}{r} 2037 \\ +\ 5888 \\ \hline \end{array}$$

13.
$$\begin{array}{r} 5700 \\ +\ 6800 \\ \hline \end{array}$$

14.
$$\begin{array}{r} \$36.57 \\ +\ 2.36 \\ \hline \end{array}$$

15. 7233 + 644	16. $73.56 + .58	17. 9527 + 8399	18. $5373.47 + 2548.95	19. 38,865 + 7,593

20. 51,609 + 9,723	21. $653.58 + 38.21	22. $4317.71 + 275.85	23. 303,181 + 35,045	24. 663,582 + 227,518

25. 685 4216 387 + 52	26. 75 8168 7 + 892	27. 3004 276 15 + 6172	28. 8869 27 348 + 3	29. 68,819 3,977 850 + 1,136

Add. You may wish to use a calculator.

30. $725 + 30{,}007 + 217{,}583 + 96{,}329$

31. $856{,}021 + 99{,}835 + 67{,}532 + 888{,}003$

32. $92{,}111 + 5768 + 432{,}067 + 95{,}999 + 38{,}271$

33. Would you use a calculator or mental math to add 89,999 and 99,999? Why?

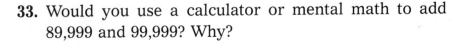

CALCULATOR

PROBLEM SOLVING APPLICATIONS
Choosing the Operation

Solve.

34. After the election Nora Zubin had 7258 bumper stickers left, Jane Godin had 6984, Adam Wright had 7528, and Ben Taylor had 7825 left. Who had the greatest number left? the least?

35. When voters were surveyed about whether or not to build a new school, this was the response: 303 No opinion, 2378 Yes, and 1677 No. How many responded?

36. Beth Roulan spent $37,359 for television advertising and $12,646 for newspaper advertising. How much did she spend in all?

PROBLEM SOLVING
Strategy: Using Estimation

1. Understand
2. Plan
3. Work
4. Answer/Check

One of the most common uses for estimation is when dealing with money. You know the approximate cost of your purchases so that you'll be sure to have enough money. An estimate will also tell you if your bill is reasonable.

Suppose you have $10. Can you buy these items?

Estimate.

$ .90
.70
.50
6.00
———
$8.10

Does the bill seem reasonable?

```
        *SUN MARKET*

     YOU'RE IN THE MARKET
         FOR THE BEST


     Bread          .92
     Milk           .65
     Juice          .54
     Chicken       6.17
     Total         8.28
```

The estimate is well under $10, so $10 is probably enough. The estimate also shows that the bill is reasonable.

CLASS EXERCISES

1. What is the approximate total of this grocery bill?
   Juice $.97 Tissues $.69 Carrots $.45 Bread $.79

2. **Think:** If you round all addends up, will your estimate be less than or greater than the actual sum? Explain.

3. **Think:** When you're estimating how much money you'll need, why might it be best to round all prices up to the *next* dollar instead of to the *nearest* dollar?

PRACTICE

Solve.

4. Sid purchased a pineapple for $2.29, prunes for $1.15, and fish for $4.89. Estimate his grocery bill.

5. Bread costs $1.05 per loaf, broccoli $.79 a head, and milk $.66 a quart. Estimate the total cost of these items.

6. Maria bought items costing $1.97, $2.19, $.63, and $4.05. The clerk charged her $14.51. Was this reasonable? Estimate to decide.

7. Robert bought cheese for $.87 and lettuce for $.69. He gave the clerk a five-dollar bill. He got $2.44 back in change. Was this reasonable? Estimate to find out.

8. Sal bought items costing $3.49, $2.88, $6.79, and $6.48. Was $20.00 enough to pay for the total cost of these items? Estimate to answer *yes* or *no*.

9. Soo-Ling saved these amounts of money in four weeks by using coupons: $3.95, $6.98, $.65, and $10.79. Did she save more or less than $20.00? Estimate to find out.

CHECKPOINT 1

Complete. *(pages 32–35)*

1. $9 + \blacksquare = 9$ 2. $5 - 5 = \blacksquare$

3. $5 + 3 = 8$, so $3 + \blacksquare = 8$

4. $9 - 6 = \blacksquare$, so $3 + \blacksquare = 9$

5. If $x = 9$, then $x + 7 = \blacksquare$.

Estimate. *(pages 38–39)*

6.　468
　+ 731

7.　$17.98
　+　6.20

8. $4.79 + $1.27 + $3.55

Add. *(pages 36–37, 40–41)*

9.　584
　+ 793

10.　$7.57
　+　6.99

11.　1378
　　　82
　+ 653

12.　678,035
　　800,925
　+　37,428

Solve. *(pages 42–43)*

13. For lunch Carmen bought a sandwich for $1.85, an apple for $.24, and a glass of milk for $.75. About how much did Carmen's lunch cost?

Extra Practice on page 422

SUBTRACTION

Hank Aaron hit a record 755 home runs in his major league career. Frank Robinson hit 169 fewer. You can figure out how many home runs Frank Robinson hit by subtracting. In this example you'll need to rename to subtract.

Rename 1 ten as 10 ones. Subtract the ones.

Rename 1 hundred as 10 tens. Subtract the tens.

Subtract the hundreds.

```
      4 15
    7 5 5
  - 1 6 9
  ─────────
          6
```

```
       14
      6 4 15
    7 5 5
  - 1 6 9
  ─────────
        8 6
```

```
       14
      6 4 15
    7 5 5
  - 1 6 9
  ─────────
      5 8 6
```

Frank Robinson hit 586 home runs.

Because of the opposites property, you can add to check your work.

```
  755          586
- 169        + 169
─────        ─────
  586          755 ✓
```

CLASS EXERCISES

Subtract.

1.	62	62	62	2.	243	243	243
	− 32	− 33	− 34		− 143	− 153	− 163

3.	820	820	820	4.	635	635	635
	− 119	− 120	− 121		− 157	− 158	− 159

PRACTICE

Subtract.

5.	45	6.	61	7.	78	8.	83	9.	95
	− 27		− 17		− 9		− 58		− 6

10.	446	11.	582	12.	446	13.	846	14.	324
	− 122		− 37		− 359		− 332		− 55

15.	927	16.	416	17.	734	18.	782	19.	312
	− 553		− 43		− 98		− 643		− 71

20.	$5.30	21.	$9.08	22.	$7.18	23.	$9.13	24.	$6.52
	− 2.18		− 6.34		− .49		− 7.52		− .95

Solve the equation.

25. $675 - 48 = a$ **26.** $895 - 47 = b$ **27.** $913 - c = 913$ **28.** $323 - d = 0$

29. $563 - e = 500$ **30.** $758 - f = 708$ ★**31.** $830 - g = 680$ ★**32.** $h - 21 = 109$

PROBLEM SOLVING APPLICATIONS
Using a Table

The Lakewood Lions have lost their team records. Use the players' numbers and the clues below to help the team figure out its statistics.

33. The Lions' total home runs for the season is the sum of the numbers for the 2nd and 3rd base players.

34. The total hits for the season is the difference between 108 and the left fielder's number.

35. The number of games the team won can be found by subtracting the catcher's number from the shortstop's number.

36. The number of errors the Lions made is the first baseman's number minus the left fielder's number plus the catcher's number.

PLAYER	NUMBER	POSITION
Mazar	56	Pitcher
Sheehan	19	Catcher
Nagy	77	1st base
Burke	8	2nd base
Harrison	13	3rd base
Silva	32	Shortstop
Rost	53	Left Field
Larkin	92	Right Field
Lack	39	Center Field

★ **37.** What are the names of the players whose numbers are greater than 30 more than the least number, and less than 30 less than the greatest number?

ESTIMATING DIFFERENCES

It's easy to make mistakes even when you use a calculator. If you forget to push the clear button between problems, if you enter the wrong number, or if your battery needs replacing, your answer may be wrong. Estimating will help you decide if your answer is reasonable.

Let's look at an example.

Subtract

8736 $\boxed{-}$ 4295 $\boxed{=}$ 13031

To estimate, round to the greatest place value and subtract.

Think: $9000 - 4000 = 5000$

The estimate shows that the difference is not reasonable. Let's subtract again.

8736 $\boxed{-}$ 4295 $\boxed{=}$ 4441

Now you have a reasonable answer.

CLASS EXERCISES

Estimate. Write *a*, *b*, or *c*.

1. 1875 − 934
   a. 3000
   b. 1100
   c. 700

2. 9478 − 3051
   a. 12,000
   b. 6000
   c. 4000

3. 713 − 485
   a. 200
   b. 400
   c. 1200

PRACTICE

Estimate.

4. 75 − 21	**5.** 270 − 19	**6.** 357 − 146	**7.** $3.44 − 1.67	**8.** 4909 − 2311
9. 9396 − 770	**10.** $6.68 − .68	**11.** $11.15 − 9.50	**12.** 6097 − 108	**13.** $31.50 − 19.45
14. 4974 − 3500	**15.** $50.99 − 7.01	**16.** 1904 − 1099	**17.** $26.38 − 15.00	**18.** $23.08 − 10.85

Round to the place of the underlined digit.

19. 238,4̲49   **20.** 1,906̲,701   **21.** 8̲4,792

22. 22,4̲50,000   **23.** 87̲,398,789   **24.** 409̲,500,201,001

MIXED REVIEW

PROBLEM SOLVING APPLICATIONS
Using Estimation

Solve.

25. In one week the outdoor market sold 539 lb of grapefruit, 250 lb of lemons, 119 lb of limes, and 978 lb of oranges. Were more than 2000 lb of citrus fruit sold?

26. Last week 217 cases of eggs were sold at the supermarket. This week 188 cases were sold. About how many cases were sold?

27. In one week 8787 customers shopped at Freeway Market. Of these, 2019 customers went to the market only once a week. About how many customers shopped more than once a week?

★ **28.** Janice bought 2 lb of grapes at $1.09 a pound, 2 lb of tomatoes at $.84 a pound, 3 lb of mushrooms for $3.29, and 4 lb of meat for $18.35. Will two twenty-dollar bills be enough for her purchases?

SUBTRACTING GREATER NUMBERS

Read the signs at the right. How many more people live in Shelton than in Longacre?

You subtract greater numbers by using the same rules of renaming that you learned earlier.

$$
\begin{array}{r}
15\,11\\
4\ \cancel{5}\ \cancel{7}\ 18\\
\cancel{5}\ \cancel{6},\cancel{2}\ \cancel{8}\ 5\\
-\ 1\ 6,7\ 9\ 2\\
\hline
3\ 9,4\ 9\ 3
\end{array}
$$

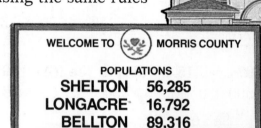

WELCOME TO MORRIS COUNTY

POPULATIONS
SHELTON 56,285
LONGACRE 16,792
BELLTON 89,316

There are 39,493 more people in Shelton.

 Check the reasonableness of your answer by estimating the difference: $60,000 - 20,000 = 40,000$. Both numbers were rounded up, so the exact answer is less than 40,000, and 39,493 is reasonable.

CLASS EXERCISES

What is the difference?

1.	615	6153	61,537	2.	217	2176	21,763
	− 259	− 2593	− 25,937		− 129	− 1296	− 12,963

3.	953	9531	95,318	4.	753	7536	75,369
	− 675	− 6751	− 67,518		− 219	− 2196	− 21,969

PRACTICE

Subtract.

5.	5736	6.	7381	7.	5902	8.	3761	9.	7685
	− 2928		− 5508		− 1881		− 293		− 98

10.	8727	11.	6956	12.	7706	13.	7238	14.	2843
	− 2835		− 6837		− 297		− 4176		− 117

15.	7592 − 398	16.	5868 − 99	17.	6384 − 4096	18.	$89.52 − 63.88	19.	$67.21 − 8.65
20.	64,532 − 43,452	21.	69,679 − 10,651	22.	93,623 − 25,436	23.	43,796 − 26,989	24.	$981.52 − 722.25
25.	39,098 − 11,719	26.	83,596 − 5,897	27.	56,721 − 5,999	28.	563,797 − 89,468	29.	687,492 − 88,840

Estimate. Will the answer be (A) less than 1000, (B) between 1000 and 10,000, or (C) between 10,000 and 30,000? Write A, B, or C.

ESTIMATE

30. 9683 − 8245

31. 125,876 − 99,158

32. 538 + 124 + 286

33. 17,286 − 7948

PROBLEM SOLVING APPLICATIONS
Mental Math, Estimation, or Calculator

Tell whether you would use mental math, estimation, or a calculator. Write M, E, or C. Then solve.

34. Last year the Shelton Library bought books totaling $75,065. This year they purchased books totaling $35,065. How much less was spent this year?

35. Longacre has 250 stop signs, 175 yield signs, 50 one-way signs, and 125 no-turn-on-red signs. How many traffic signs are there in Longacre?

36. The population of Bellton is 89,316 and the population of Longacre is 16,792. About how many more people live in Bellton?

★ 37. The budget for the Bellton summer recreational program was set at $135,000. In June $68,000 was spent. The amount spent in July was $29,000 less than was spent in June. In August $19,500 was spent. How much was in the budget in September?

ZEROS IN SUBTRACTION

You can think of numbers in different ways. For example, you can think of 9000 as 899 tens 10 ones, or 8 thousands 9 hundreds 9 tens 10 ones.

You can use this idea when subtracting from numbers with several zeros.

First rename.

$$\begin{array}{r} {\scriptstyle 8\ 9\ 9\ 10} \\ 9\,0\,0\,0 \\ -\ 6\,8\,6\,9 \\ \hline \end{array}$$

Then subtract.

$$\begin{array}{r} {\scriptstyle 8\ 9\ 9\ 10} \\ 9\,0\,0\,0 \\ -\ 6\,8\,6\,9 \\ \hline 2\,1\,3\,1 \end{array}$$

Here are some other examples.

$$\begin{array}{r} {\scriptstyle 4\ 9\ 9\ 12} \\ 5\,0\,0\,2 \\ -\ \ \ 1\,3\,5 \\ \hline 4\,8\,6\,7 \end{array}$$

$$\begin{array}{r} {\scriptstyle 5\ 9\ 11} \\ 6\,0\,1\,9 \\ -\ \ \ 3\,3\,7 \\ \hline 5\,6\,8\,2 \end{array}$$

Ⓜ There are times when you may be able to use mental math to subtract from numbers with zeros. You can add on to name the difference.

To find $500 - 197$, **think:** $197 + 3 = 200$,
$200 + 300 = 500$,
so $500 - 197 = 303$.

CLASS EXERCISES

Complete.

1. $80 = 7$ tens ▨ ones

2. $60 = $ ▨ tens 10 ones

3. $100 = $ ▨ tens 10 ones

4. $500 = 49$ tens ▨ ones

5. $700 = $ ▨ tens 10 ones

6. $900 = $ ▨ hundreds 9 tens ▨ ones

7. $2000 = 199$ tens ▨ ones

8. $6000 = $ ▨ tens 10 ones

PRACTICE

Subtract.

9.	70 − 11	**10.**	90 − 55	**11.**	36 − 9	**12.**	340 − 93	**13.**	820 − 12		
14.	700 − 243	**15.**	$6.08 − .35	**16.**	$5.00 − 3.82	**17.**	801 − 256	**18.**	$9.00 − .87		
19.	6040 − 2382	**20.**	$90.00 − 7.91	**21.**	8003 − 1106	**22.**	6106 − 209	**23.**	$40.06 − 7.21		

24. $70.00 − 69.09 **25.** 800 − 597 **26.** 200 − 98 **27.** 701 − 333

28. $6.00 − $4.63 **29.** 923 − 251 **30.** 300 − 291 **31.** 500 − 33

Subtract using mental math.

32. 1000 − 499 **33.** 7000 − 1750 **34.** 4000 − 2225

35. $1.00 − $.46 **36.** $2.00 − $1.79 **37.** $5.00 − $4.15

MENTAL MATH

PROBLEM SOLVING APPLICATIONS
Nonroutine Problems

Solve.

38. Lenny and Lulu each have 12 coins that total 49¢. Lulu has one more kind of coin than Lenny. What coins does each have?

39. How many ways can you buy 3 connected stamps? 4 connected stamps?

40. Tillie has an old-fashioned toaster. It toasts 2 slices of bread at once, but only one side of the bread at a time. Each slice must be toasted for one minute and then turned over. How can Tillie toast 3 slices in 3 minutes?

41. Divide the clock into 6 parts so that the sum of the numbers in each part is the same.

★ **42.** Replace each ▇ with a digit from 0 to 9 so that the addition is correct. Use each digit exactly once.

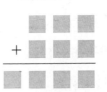

1. understand
2. Plan
3. work
4. answer/ check

PROBLEM SOLVING
Strategy: Using Information
From a Chart

The chart at the right shows the starting and finishing times for some of the trips taken by the Bicycle Touring Club. How long did Trip #1 take from start to finish?

The amount of time that passes between the start and end of an event is the **elapsed time.**

**BICYCLE TOURING CLUB
TRIP TIMES**

TRIP #	STARTING TIME	FINISHING TIME
1	7:30 A.M.	11:15 A.M.
2	8:20 A.M.	3:45 P.M.
3	10:00 A.M.	2:15 P.M.
4	10:20 A.M.	11:15 A.M.

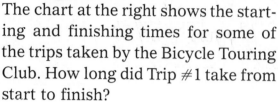

```
          10    75
  11:15    11 h 15 min
-  7:30   -  7 h 30 min
           3 h 45 min
```

Rename 11 h 15 min as 10 h 75 min. Subtract the starting time from the finishing time to find the elapsed time.

How long did Trip #2 take to complete? Since the time period includes noon, you must add 12 before subtracting.

```
                add 12
  3 h 45 min              15 h 45 min
- 8 h 20 min      ⇨      -  8 h 20 min
                           7 h 25 min
```

Trip #2 took 7 h 25 min.

You can also find the answer mentally.

Think: 8:20 to 12:20 is 4 h.
12:20 to 3:20 is 3 h.
3:20 to 3:45 is 25 min.
It is 7 h 25 min from 8:20 to 3:45.

CLASS EXERCISES

1. How many hours before noon did Trip #3 begin?

2. How long after noon did Trip #3 finish?

3. How long did Trip #3 take?

4. How long did Trip #4 take?

PRACTICE

MUSIC LESSON SCHEDULE

STUDENT	MON.	TUES.	WED.	THURS.	FRI.
Zack		5:00–5:45	4:15–5:10		2:30–3:20
Liz	5:00–5:45			4:15–5:10	3:30–4:10

Use the chart to solve.

5. On which days of the week does Zack take music lessons? On which days does Liz take lessons?

6. How much time is there between the time Zack starts his Friday lesson and Liz ends her Friday lesson?

7. Liz practices for an additional 40 minutes immediately after her Thursday lesson. At what time does she finish practicing on Thursdays?

8. Zack's Social Studies class begins 2 hours and 15 minutes before his Friday lesson ends. At what time does Zack's Social Studies class begin?

★ 9. Assuming her schedule is the same each week, how much time in all does Liz spend in 2 weeks taking music lessons?

★10. Who spends more total time each week taking music lessons, Zack or Liz?

CHECKPOINT 2

Estimate. (pages 46–47)

1. 4786
   − 2314

2. $27.04
   − 12.98

Subtract. (pages 44–45, 48–51)

3. $7.15
   − 3.97

4. 136,023
   − 129,415

Solve. (pages 52–53)

RUNNER	START	FINISH
Linda	10:30 A.M.	1:15 P.M.
Laurie	10:40 A.M.	1:07 P.M.

5. How long did the race take Linda? Laurie?

6. Who had the better time? by how much?

Extra Practice on page 422

CHAPTER 2 TEST

Solve the equation. *(pages 32–35)*

1. $3 + y = 9$

2. $x - 3 = 4$

3. $6 + a = 10$

4. $n - 0 = 5$

Estimate the sum. *(pages 38–39)*

5.
```
   93
+  58
```

6.
```
  $6.70
+  2.21
```

7.
```
  34,526
+  8,306
```

8.
```
  $48.92
    4.81
+    .78
```

Write the answer. *(pages 36–37, 40–41)*

9.
```
    67
   313
    52
+  524
```

10.
```
  $98.89
+   2.62
```

11.
```
  722,056
   48,661
+     124
```

12.
```
  27,109
   4,882
     111
+  6,336
```

Solve. *(pages 42–43)*

13. Tanya purchased items costing $.89, $1.27, $2.81, and $.63. Estimate the total cost of her purchases.

Estimate the difference. *(pages 46–47)*

14.
```
   64
-  18
```

15.
```
  $7.60
-  2.88
```

16.
```
  7807
-  411
```

17.
```
  $89.93
-  35.54
```

Write the answer. *(pages 44–45, 48–51)*

18.
```
   931
-  450
```

19.
```
   6002
-  3717
```

20.
```
  392,148
-   4,655
```

21.
```
  $90.01
-  35.67
```

Use the chart to solve. *(pages 52–53)*

22. How long did Mac's deliveries take on Wednesday?

23. On which day did Mac's deliveries take the least time?

MAC'S DELIVERY TIMES

DAY	START	FINISH
Tues.	8:15 A.M.	11:20 A.M.
Wed.	9:45 A.M.	1:15 P.M.

Extra Practice on page 423

MATHEMATICS and PHYSICAL EDUCATION

Telling time plays an important part in many planned events. Below is the sixth-grade schedule of events for the annual Claremont Avenue School Sports Day.

IS IT TIME FOR SPORTS?

Use the schedule to answer these questions.

1. What is the total amount of the time scheduled for the running events and relay races?

2. Pete's favorite event is soccer. From the end of the softball game, how long must Pete wait to play soccer?

3. Which sporting event is scheduled for the least amount of time? the greatest?

4. Sue Spitzer will referee the softball throw and volleyball game. How much time off does she have between these two events?

5. How much time is scheduled for the actual sporting events for the day?

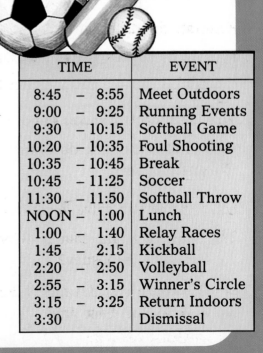

TIME		EVENT
8:45 – 8:55		Meet Outdoors
9:00 – 9:25		Running Events
9:30 – 10:15		Softball Game
10:20 – 10:35		Foul Shooting
10:35 – 10:45		Break
10:45 – 11:25		Soccer
11:30 – 11:50		Softball Throw
NOON – 1:00		Lunch
1:00 – 1:40		Relay Races
1:45 – 2:15		Kickball
2:20 – 2:50		Volleyball
2:55 – 3:15		Winner's Circle
3:15 – 3:25		Return Indoors
3:30		Dismissal

Enrichment

The world is divided into 24 time zones that are one hour apart in time. The map shows time zones around the world. As you move east, add one hour for each time zone you pass through. As you move west, subtract one hour for each time zone.

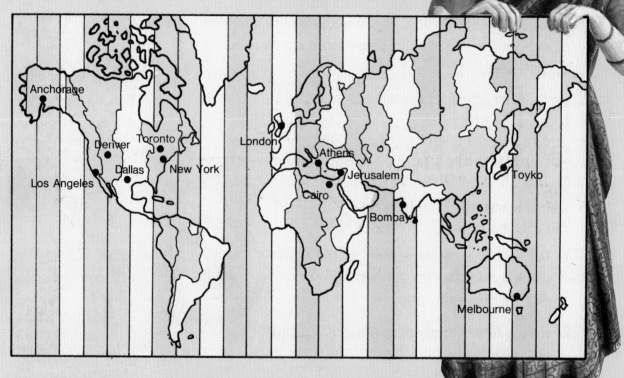

Use the map to answer the questions.

1. What is the time difference between New York and Denver?

2. What is the time difference between Tokyo and Cairo?

3. If it's 2:30 in Dallas, what time is it in Jerusalem?

4. If it's 6:30 in Bombay, what time is it in Melbourne?

TIME ZONES

	ATHENS	ANCHORAGE	LOS ANGELES	LONDON	TOKYO	TORONTO	NEW YORK
ATHENS	0	− 12	− 10	− 2	+ 7	− 7	− 7
ANCHORAGE	+ 12	0	?	+ 10	+ 19	?	+ 5
LOS ANGELES	+ 10	− 2	0	?	+ 17	?	+ 3
LONDON	+ 2	?	− 8	0	?	?	− 5
TOKYO	− 7	?	?	− 9	0	− 14	?
TORONTO	+ 7	− 5	− 3	+ 5	?	0	?
NEW YORK	+ 7	?	?	?	+ 14	?	0

The table above shows time differences between some cities. Here's how to find the time in London when it's 2:00 in Toronto. Find the row containing Toronto and follow it over to the column containing London. Add 5 hours to the Toronto time. Since 2 + 5 = 7, it's 7:00 in London when it's 2:00 in Toronto.

5. Copy and complete the table above. Use the map on page 56 for help.

Use the table from Exercise 5 to answer the question.

6. A flight to New York left Los Angeles at 1:00 A.M. The flying time was 6 hours and 25 minutes. At what time did the plane arrive in New York?

7. A flight to Los Angeles left London at 8:00 A.M. The flying time was 11 hours. At what time did the plane arrive in Los Angeles?

8. A flight from Toronto arrived in Athens at 10:40 A.M. The flying time was 9 hours. At what time did the plane leave Toronto?

9. A flight left Anchorage at 6:00 A.M. and arrived in New York at 7:32 P.M. What was the flying time?

57

Choose the correct answer. Write *a, b, c,* or *d.*
What is the standard form?

1. 22 thousand 76

    a. 2276
    b. 22,760
    c. 22,076
    d. none of these

2. 5 million, 340 thousand, 2 hundred

    a. 500,340,200
    b. 5,340,200
    c. 50,340,200,000
    d. none of these

3. 7000 + 400 + 80 + 3

    a. 700,408,003
    b. 70,483
    c. 7483
    d. none of these

Round to the place of the underlined digit.

4. 3<u>8</u>1

    a. 38
    b. 380
    c. 390
    d. none of these

5. 2<u>7</u>,544

    a. 27,000
    b. 280,000
    c. 28,000
    d. none of these

6. <u>9</u>26,018

    a. 930,000
    b. 800,000
    c. 900,000
    d. none of these

Which is the best estimate?

7. the length of a desk top

    a. 5 in.
    b. 5 mi
    c. 5 yd
    d. 5 ft

8. the capacity of a small container of cream

    a. 1 qt
    b. 1 pt
    c. 1 gal
    d. 10 gal

9. the weight of a sixth grader

    a. 100 lb
    b. 100 oz
    c. 100 t
    d. 10 lb

10. the width of a bookcase

    a. 300 ft
    b. 30 in.
    c. 300 yd
    d. 30 mi

Which is the best estimate?

11.
$$\begin{array}{r} \$4.38 \\ + 3.75 \\ \hline \end{array}$$

    a. $8.00
    b. $6.00
    c. $1.00
    d. $9.00

12.
$$\begin{array}{r} 2661 \\ + 290 \\ \hline \end{array}$$

    a. 330
    b. 3300
    c. 33,000
    d. 330,000

13.
$$\begin{array}{r} 169 \\ 644 \\ + 218 \\ \hline \end{array}$$

    a. 1000
    b. 1100
    c. 1200
    d. 1300

Solve.

14. Shoe laces cost $1.42, white shoe polish costs $3.59, and water-proofing cream costs $2.65. Estimate the total cost of these items.
    a. $6.00
    b. $8.00
    c. $10.00
    d. $12.00

15. Joe purchased items costing $1.81, $.79, $3.16, and $2.88. Estimate the total cost of his purchases.
    a. $9.00
    b. $9.50
    c. $10.00
    d. $10.50

Which is the best estimate?

16. $8.41 − $6.73
    a. $1.00
    b. $14.00
    c. $3.00
    d. $15.00

17. 6042 − 521
    a. 5000
    b. 5500
    c. 6000
    d. 6500

18. 3525 − 2191
    a. 5000
    b. 4000
    c. 3000
    d. 2000

LANGUAGE and VOCABULARY REVIEW

Choose the word that completes the sentence.

equation   difference   variable   solve   estimate   sum

1. To find an answer to a problem is to __?__ the problem.

2. An __?__ is a mathematical sentence with an equals sign.

3. To __?__ a sum, first round each number to its greatest place value, then add.

4. When a letter is used to represent a number, that letter is called a __?__.

5. The answer in subtraction is called a __?__.

6. The answer in addition is called a __?__.

ARTIFICIAL INTELLIGENCE

People solve problems by using thinking strategies. They can plan. They can use what they already know. They can change their minds when something is not working correctly.

When a computer solves a problem, it can do only the steps people give it.

Scientists are looking for ways to program a computer to solve a problem the way people do. This kind of computer problem solving is called **artificial intelligence.**

Here are two areas that scientists are researching.

Robotics

A robot can do the same task over and over. It can pack the same objects over and over. But a robot cannot decide when two objects, in a box full of objects, do not match. Scientists are finding ways to make a robot decide when shapes are different.

Language Translation

People can translate a sentence from one language to another. People *think* about the words they use. For example, people know that "fly," "bear," "cook," and "walk" are used as nouns and verbs. A computer does not think about words. So it often uses them incorrectly. For example:

Correct Sentence: The stone walk in the garden is beautiful.

Computer Sentence: Beautiful stones walk in the garden.

Solve.

1. What is artificial intelligence?

2. How do people solve problems?

3. Can a robot decide that a blue box does not belong with yellow boxes?

4. Why does a computer make mistakes when it translates sentences?

Compare the number of barrels stored in rows 10 long, 3 deep, and 3 high with the number of barrels stored in rows 10 long, 1 deep, and 9 high.

3

MULTIPLICATION OF WHOLE NUMBERS

PROPERTIES
OF MULTIPLICATION

You need to know the basic facts in order to multiply any two numbers.

$$8 \times 9 = 72$$
factors product

These properties of multiplication can help you.

Commutative Property
Changing the order of factors does not change the product.

$8 \times 3 = 24$ and $3 \times 8 = 24$
so $8 \times 3 = 3 \times 8$

Associative Property
Changing the grouping of factors does not change the product.

$(2 \times 3) \times 4 = 24$ and
$2 \times (3 \times 4) = 24$
so $(2 \times 3) \times 4 = 2 \times (3 \times 4)$

Zero Property
The product of zero and any number is zero.

$4 \times 0 = 0$ $0 \times 4 = 0$

Property of One
The product of one and any number is that number.

$7 \times 1 = 7$ $1 \times 7 = 7$

Distributive Property
When two or more numbers are being multiplied by the same factor, you can add and then multiply or multiply and then add.

$3 \times (2 + 3) = 3 \times 5 = 15$ and $(3 \times 2) + (3 \times 3) = 6 + 9 = 15$
so $3 \times (2 + 3) = (3 \times 2) + (3 \times 3)$

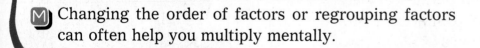 Changing the order of factors or regrouping factors can often help you multiply mentally.

CLASS EXERCISES

What are the products? Name the properties illustrated.

1. 4×5
5×4

2. 8×0
0×8

3. $4 \times (3 \times 2)$
$(4 \times 3) \times 2$

4. $2 \times (3 + 1)$
$(2 \times 3) + (2 \times 1)$

PRACTICE

Use one of the properties to complete.

5. $4 \times 6 = 6 \times \blacksquare$

6. $(7 \times 4) \times 2 = 7 \times (\blacksquare \times 2)$

7. $4 \times 1 = \blacksquare$

8. $\blacksquare \times 7 = 7 \times 5$

9. $(\blacksquare \times 3) \times 4 = 3 \times (3 \times 4)$

10. $0 \times 3 = \blacksquare$

11. $1 \times 8 = 8 \times \blacksquare$

12. $2 \times (3 \times \blacksquare) = (2 \times 3) \times 6$

13. $1 \times 1 = \blacksquare$

14. $(6 \times 2) \times \blacksquare = 6 \times (2 \times 9)$

15. $6 \times (2 + 4) = (\blacksquare \times 2) + (\blacksquare \times 4)$

16. $2 \times (\blacksquare + \blacksquare) = (2 \times 6) + (2 \times 8)$

17. $\blacksquare \times (\blacksquare + \blacksquare) = (9 \times 3) + (9 \times 7)$

Use mental math to name the product.

18. $3 \times 7 \times 2$

19. $3 \times 9 \times 3$

20. $4 \times 8 \times 2$

MENTAL MATH

21. $2 \times 9 \times 5$

22. $2 \times 5 \times 2 \times 5$

23. $9 \times 1 \times 3 \times 0$

24. Think: If you can't remember the product of 9 and 5, how can you use one of the properties to help you?

PROBLEM SOLVING APPLICATIONS
Choosing the Operation

Solve.

25. Doreen Lewis wrote 9 computer programs last week. This week she wrote 8 more programs. How many programs did she write in all?

26. The Eastern Company has 6 branch offices. There are 2 computer terminals at each office. How many computer terminals does the company have?

27. Sidney Greene operates a word processor. The printer can produce about 5 copies of a letter in a minute. About how many copies of the letter can the printer produce in 9 minutes?

★ **28.** Lorne Mazza can type 8 two-page letters in an hour. How many pages can he type in 4 hours?

MULTIPLYING
BY ONE-DIGIT NUMBERS

Lakeville School has 3 bands with 28 students in each band. How many students in all are there in the bands?

To combine 3 groups of equal size, you multiply. The distributive property can help you understand this process. It also helps you multiply mentally.

$$3 \times 28 = 3 \times (8 + 20)$$
$$= (3 \times 8) + (3 \times 20)$$
$$= 24 + 60$$
$$= 84$$

You show the multiplication like this:

Multiply the ones.   Multiply the tens.
Rename 24 ones as   Add the 2 tens from
2 tens 4 ones.   the first product.

$$\begin{array}{r} 2 \\ 28 \\ \times 3 \\ \hline 4 \end{array}$$
Think: $(3 \times 2) + 2$
$$\begin{array}{r} 2 \\ 28 \\ \times 3 \\ \hline 84 \end{array}$$

There are 84 students in all in the bands.

If you use a calculator to multiply, check the reasonableness of the result by a quick mental estimate.

Calculate: 3 ⊠ 6795 ▭ 20385

Check: $3 \times 7000 = 21,000$

CLASS EXERCISES

What is the product?

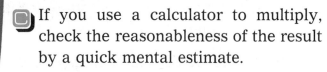

1. $\begin{array}{r} 4 \\ \times 3 \end{array}$ and $\begin{array}{r} 10 \\ \times 3 \end{array}$ ⇨ $\begin{array}{r} 14 \\ \times 3 \end{array}$

2. $\begin{array}{r} 3 \\ \times 6 \end{array}$ and $\begin{array}{r} 20 \\ \times 6 \end{array}$ ⇨ $\begin{array}{r} 23 \\ \times 6 \end{array}$

PRACTICE

Multiply.

3. 45
×8

4. 63
×9

5. 89
×8

6. 24
×9

7. 96
×6

8. 78
×3

9. 916
×4

10. 901
×9

11. 752
×5

12. 163
×2

13. 583
×8

14. 3153
×7

15. 8719
×7

16. 2457
×8

17. 1042
×5

Multiply. Check the reasonableness of your answer.

18. 9876
×9

19. 12,086
×5

20. 31,086
×4

21. 55,319
×3

CALCULATOR

22. 2634
×8

23. 5072
×7

24. 14,302
×5

25. 86,319
×9

26. Think: Would you choose mental math or a calculator to multiply 4 × 92? Explain.

PROBLEM SOLVING APPLICATIONS
Choosing the Operation

Solve.

27. In a workshop, Dale learned that it takes about 32 L of sap to make 1 L of maple syrup. How many liters of sap are needed to make 8 L of syrup?

28. At the Outdoor Center there are 13 workshops on Friday and 8 more on Saturday than on Friday. How many are on Saturday?

29. The Outdoor Center had 5797 students visit last year. The Lakeville School sent 9 groups of 175 students each to the Center. How many student visitors were not from the Lakeville School?

★ 30. The Outdoor Center is sending 15 free tickets worth $2 each to each of 9 schools, and 20 tickets worth $3 apiece to the local senior citizens center. What is the total value of the tickets?

MULTIPLYING BY TENS, HUNDREDS, THOUSANDS

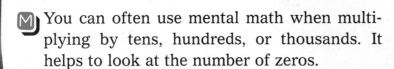

SPACE TAXI SERVICE

413,000 Passenger Miles a Year.

M You can often use mental math when multiplying by tens, hundreds, or thousands. It helps to look at the number of zeros.

413	413	413
×10	×100	×1000
4130	41,300	413,000

When you multiply dollars and cents, remember to write the dollar sign and decimal in your answer.

$4.23	$4.23	$4.23
×2	×20	×200
$8.46	$84.60	$846.00

CLASS EXERCISES

What is the product? Look for a pattern.

1. 25	25	25	2. 733	733	733
×10	×100	×1000	×40	×400	×4000

3. $2.31	$2.31	$2.31	4. 500	500	500
×20	×200	×2000	×10	×100	×1000

5. **Think:** Look at Exercise 4. What pattern do you notice?

PRACTICE

Multiply.

6. 57	7. 87	8. 482	9. 679	10. 346
×10	×200	×40	×700	×1000

11. 37	**12.** 458	**13.** 1825	**14.** 3795	**15.** 18
×20	×300	×100	×10	×500

16. 318	**17.** 1000	**18.** $8.71	**19.** $.27	**20.** $6.48
×2000	×100	×900	×400	×3000

21. 100 × 875 **22.** 20 × 436 **23.** 10 × 844 **24.** 60 × 400

25. 700 × 39,674 **26.** 50 × 783 **27.** 100 × 1358 **28.** 1000 × 2000

Use mental math to name the product. Use the properties to help you make tens and hundreds.

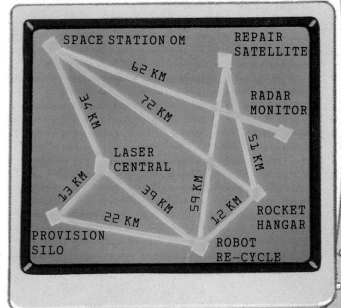

MENTAL MATH

29. 2 × 9 × 5 × 8 **30.** 25 × 3 × 4 × 2 **31.** 6 × 5 × 2 × 5

32. 4 × 5 × 2 × 1 **33.** 10 × 421 × 10 **34.** 5 × 45 × 2

PROBLEM SOLVING APPLICATIONS
Using Information from a Picture

The computer display shows the routes traveled by Space Taxi Service. Use the display to complete the computer printout of the fare schedule.

SPACE STATION OM
REPAIR SATELLITE
62 KM
34 KM
72 KM
RADAR MONITOR
51 KM
LASER CENTRAL
13 KM
39 KM
59 KM
12 KM
ROCKET HANGAR
22 KM
PROVISION SILO
ROBOT RE-CYCLE

FARE SCHEDULE
ROCKET RIDE TAXI

	FROM	TO	COST AT $.80 PER KM
35.	OM	HANGAR	▨
36.	SILO	CENTRAL	▨
37.	RE-CYCLE	SILO	▨
38.	SATELLITE	HANGAR	▨
39.	OM	MONITOR	▨
40.	CENTRAL	OM	▨
41.	HANGAR	RE-CYCLE	▨
ROUND TRIP			
★ **42.**	SATELLITE	RE-CYCLE	▨

ESTIMATING PRODUCTS

Suppose you need to know about how many play booklets to have on hand for a theater performance. If the theater has 188 rows of 31 seats, about how many booklets should you have on hand?

Since an exact answer isn't needed, you can round each factor to its greatest place value and multiply in your head to get a mental estimate. You should have about 6000 booklets.

$$
\begin{array}{ccc}
188 & \longrightarrow & 200 \\
\times 31 & \longrightarrow & \times 30 \\
\hline
& & 6000
\end{array}
$$

You can also estimate a product by stating a range within which the product lies. Round down and multiply to determine a lower limit for this range. Round up to determine an upper limit. For example, 8 × $6.49 is between 8 × $6 and 8 × $7, or between $48 and $56.

CLASS EXERCISES

Round to the nearest ten.

1. 45   **2.** 67   **3.** 14   **4.** 94   **5.** 99

Round to the nearest ten cents.

6. $.17   **7.** $.82   **8.** $.75   **9.** $.39   **10.** $.76

Round to the nearest hundred.

11. 835   **12.** 780   **13.** 964   **14.** 129   **15.** 450

Round to the nearest dollar.

16. $3.45   **17.** $4.72   **18.** $8.89   **19.** $3.50   **20.** $9.13

PRACTICE

Estimate the product.

21. 18	22. 38	23. 45	24. 225	25. 45
×4	×7	×67	×8	×21

26. $5.18	27. $8.47	28. $2.85	29. 334	30. 602
×69	×12	×76	×97	×45

31. 715	32. 464	33. 853	34. $1.32	35. $9.47
×377	×283	×192	×963	×231

Estimate a range for the product.

36. 7 × $1.68   **37.** 24 × $3.39   **38.** 450 × 150   **39.** 799 × 213

Estimate the answer.

40. $47.02	41. 35,438	42. $473.19
+ 23.89	+ 8,236	− 149.68

43. 678,932	44. 703,002	45. $50,596.27
+ 486,755	− 51,309	− 13,904.89

MIXED REVIEW

PROBLEM SOLVING APPLICATIONS
Choosing the Operation

Solve. Estimate the answers.

46. Lena bought 19 packs of writing tablets at $15.10 per pack. About how much did she spend for the tablets in all?

47. A spiral-bound notebook contains 185 pages. About how many pages are in 21 notebooks?

48. Paul Chin sold 25 red pens last week. He also sold 67 blue ones. About how many more blue pens did he sell?

49. Rose Jackson needs 2875 index cards to complete her work. About how many 28-card packs does she need to buy?

PROBLEM SOLVING
Strategy: Drawing a Picture

Sometimes it's hard to know how to solve a problem just by reading it. Drawing a picture can often make solving a problem easier. For example:

Kara is setting up tables for a party. Four people can sit at each square table. How many people can sit at 8 square tables placed end-to-end in two groups of 4?

To solve this problem, draw a picture like the one below. By using the picture, it's easy to determine that 20 people can sit at the tables.

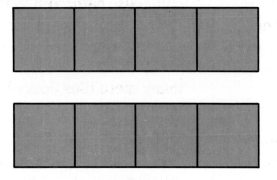

CLASS EXERCISES

Use the picture to help solve the problem.

1. Kara's club has a tent to use for a clubhouse. If each of the four sides of the tent needs 3 stakes, how many stakes are needed for the whole tent?

2. The members are choosing a club sweatshirt. Their color choices are red, blue, and green. Their emblem choices are dolphin, leopard, and panda. How many different ways can they design the club sweatshirt?

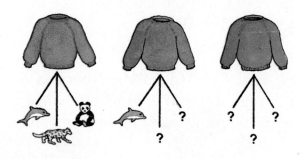

PRACTICE

Solve. Draw a picture that will help.

3. Every time a club member enters the tent, everyone present must shake hands with everyone else. The person entering pays a nickel for each handshake. If you enter the tent and there are already 3 people there, how much must you pay?

4. Each club member does one indoor job and one outdoor job each week. The indoor jobs are vacuuming, dusting, and laundry. The outdoor jobs are mowing and raking. How many weeks can a member go without doing the same two jobs together again?

5. Club members want to saw a log into 10 pieces to make stools for their clubhouse. If it takes 5 minutes to saw through the log, how long will it take to cut the log into 10 pieces?

6. Nan is putting new tiles in the clubhouse bathroom. She needs 7 rows with 4 tiles in each row. If she has completed all of 2 rows and half of the other rows, how many more tiles does she need?

7. Ramon has a 14-link chain to make a plant hanger. He wants to cut it so that one piece has 4 more links than the other. How many links will be on each piece?

★ 8. Sara and Dave shovel a walk 30 m long. They start at opposite ends and work toward each other. Sarah clears 3 m per minute and Dave clears 2 m per minute. How long will it take them to finish the walk?

CHECKPOINT 1

Complete. *(pages 62–67)*

1. $7 \times (3 + 5) =$
   $(\blacksquare \times 3) + (\blacksquare \times 5)$

2. $(3 \times 9) + (3 \times 8) =$
   $3 \times (\blacksquare + \blacksquare)$

3. $496 \times 10 = \blacksquare$

4. $3578 \times 9 = \blacksquare$

Estimate. *(pages 68–69)*

5. 732×1000 6. $\$7.68 \times 578$

Solve. Draw a picture to help.
(pages 70–71)

7. Four people can sit at one square table. How many can sit at 8 square tables placed end-to-end?

Extra Practice on page 424

MULTIPLYING
BY TWO-DIGIT NUMBERS

ARTS and CRAFTS SHOW!
EACH OF OUR SCHOOL'S 32 CLASSES
HAS MADE 24 PROJECTS
NOVEMBER 13,14 10 A.M. – 5 P.M.

To determine how many projects in all, multiply 24 by 32.

Multiply by 2 ones.	Multiply by 3 tens.	Add.
24 ×32 48	24 ×32 48 720	24 ×32 48 720 768

There were 768 projects.

You can estimate the product first and compare the estimate with the exact product to see if your answer is reasonable or not.

Think: Why would you expect the exact answer to be greater than 600 projects?

CLASS EXERCISES

Multiply.

1. 42   42   42   2. 31   31   31
   ×2   ×10   ×12   ×4   ×20   ×24

3. 357   357   357   4. $20.55 $20.55 $20.55
   ×5   ×40   ×45   ×3   ×40   ×43

PRACTICE

Multiply.

5. 52 ×27	**6.** 37 ×81	**7.** 86 ×95	**8.** 91 ×49	**9.** 274 ×68	**10.** 165 ×36
11. 488 ×29	**12.** 9706 ×28	**13.** 1253 ×26	**14.** 585 ×38	**15.** 686 ×92	**16.** 8039 ×17
17. $.46 ×52	**18.** $2.99 ×29	**19.** $68.68 ×79	**20.** $1.07 ×82	**21.** $.35 ×47	**22.** $57.75 ×70

23. 39 × 15   **24.** 65 × 537   **25.** 87 × 4387   **26.** 76 × 7117

27. 11 × 782   **28.** 26 × 2435   **29.** 88 × 945   **30.** 65 × 5355

Is the product greater than 40,000? Estimate to answer.

31. 49 × 726   **32.** 99 × 654   **33.** 85 × 502

34. 36 × 921   **35.** 8 × 4655   **36.** 999 × 40

ESTIMATE

PROBLEM SOLVING APPLICATIONS
Choosing the Operation

Solve.

37. The committee sold 428 tickets at $.75 each. Did they reach their sales goal of $350?

38. The decorating committee had a $35.00 budget. They spent $29.65. How much did they have left?

39. Carlos gave out guide maps. He had 15 boxes with 25 maps in each box. If all the maps were given out, how many did Carlos give out?

★ **40.** On the first day 178 adults and 93 children attended the fair. On the second day 119 adults and 223 children attended. In all, did more children or more adults attend the fair?

MULTIPLYING
BY GREATER NUMBERS

To multiply 617 by 254, think of 254 as 2 hundreds 5 tens 4 ones.

Multiply by 4 ones.	Multiply by 5 tens.	Multiply by 2 hundreds. Add.
617	617	617
×254	×254	×254
2468	2468	2468
	30850	30850
		123400
		156,718

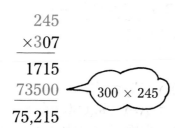

Be careful when there are zeros in a factor.

```
    245
   ×307
   1715
  73500      300 × 245
  75,215
```

Here's how to use a calculator to check each step.

7 ✕ 245 ▭ 1715
300 ✕ 245 ▭ 73500
1715 ✚ 73500 ▭ 75215

CLASS EXERCISES

Multiply.

1.
321	321	321	321
×4	×20	×500	×524

2.
728	728	728	728
×3	×70	×600	×673

PRACTICE

Multiply.

3. 251
×349

4. 617
×181

5. 284
×686

6. 317
×408

7. 1345
×222

8. 302
×687

9. 445
×955

10. 845
×421

11. 4121 ×385	12. 6024 ×619	13. 7853 ×278	14. 6543 ×929	15. 4806 ×613
16. 52,521 ×708	17. 92,809 ×434	18. 4599 ×3613	19. 6007 ×1392	20. 4127 ×5323

21. 615 × 580   22. 92,809 × 434   23. 345 × 6781   24. 713 × 2954

25. 769 × 47,862   26. 252 × 35,914   27. 1299 × 9485   28. 3808 × 1348

You may use a calculator to find an error in each multiplication.

CALCULATOR

29. 427 ×19 3643 4270 7913	30. 261 ×107 1887 26100 27,987	31. 364 ×101 364 3640 4004

PROBLEM SOLVING APPLICATIONS
Choosing the Operation

Solve.

32. One airplane was used on a 4960 mi trip 152 times during the course of a year. How many miles did the plane fly in all?

33. The Flyer Club is for people who fly over 100,000 mi. Paul flew sixteen 2000 mi trips, twelve 4800 mi trips, and six 3000 mi trips. Is he eligible for the club?

34. The airport souvenir shop stocks T-shirts in sizes S, M, L, and XL. There are two designs in each of three colors in stock for all sizes. How many possible choices of T-shirts does a customer have?

★ 35. The security checkpoint can check up to 250 people per hour. What is the greatest number of people that can be checked in 5 days? (Count 1 day as 24 h.)

POWERS AND EXPONENTS

Instead of writing $2 \times 2 \times 2 \times 2$, you may write 2^4. A product that uses the same factor more than once is called a **power** of the factor. 2^4 is called *the fourth power of 2* or *2 to the fourth power.* The raised 4 is called an **exponent.** It means that 2 is to be used as a factor 4 times.

$2^4 = 16$

The number 2^2 is usually read *two squared* and 2^3 is read *two cubed.*

Any number raised to the first power is that number.

$2^1 = 2$

You can use exponents to show powers of ten.

$10^1 = 10$ $10^2 = 100$ $10^3 = 1000$

Think: What do you notice about the exponent and the number of zeros in the standard form of powers of ten?

CLASS EXERCISES

Complete.

1. $3^2 = \square \times \square$

2. $4^2 = \square \times \square$

3. $5^2 = \square \times \square$

4. $2^3 = \square \times \square \times \square$

5. $3^3 = \square \times \square \times \square$

6. $4^3 = \square \times \square \times \square$

7. $5 \times 5 \times 5 = 5^{\square}$

8. $6 \times 6 = 6^{\square}$

9. $2 \times 2 \times 2 \times 2 \times 2 = 2^{\square}$

10. $7 \times 7 \times 7 = \square^3$

11. $4 \times 4 \times 4 = \square^3$

12. $10 \times 10 = \square^2$

PRACTICE

Write using exponents.

13. 9×9

14. $6 \times 6 \times 6$

15. $2 \times 2 \times 2 \times 2$

16. $7 \times 7 \times 7$

17. $8 \times 8 \times 8$

18. $10 \times 10 \times 10$

Write the product.

19. 3^2 **20.** 5^1 **21.** 8^3 **22.** 4^2 **23.** 6^2 **24.** 2^3

25. 4^3 **26.** 6^1 **27.** 7^2 **28.** 3^3 **29.** 2^1 **30.** 7^3

31. 10^2 **32.** 9^2 **33.** 17^2 **34.** 14^2 **35.** 19^2 **36.** 15^2

Solve the equation.

37. $4 \times 10^1 = n$ **38.** $2 \times 10^2 = n$ **39.** $6 \times 10^3 = n$

40. $5 \times 10^4 = n$ **41.** $10^1 \times 10^2 = n$ **42.** $10^3 \times 10^1 = n$

★ **43.** $n \times 10^1 = 50$ ★ **44.** $n \times 10^2 = 1500$ ★ **45.** $10{,}000 = 10^n$

Write the standard form.

46. $5000 + 300 + 40 + 6$ **47.** $10{,}000 + 700 + 90 + 9$

48. $400{,}000 + 800 + 10 + 7$ **49.** $80{,}000{,}000 + 3000 + 200$

50. $70{,}000{,}000{,}000 + 9{,}000{,}000{,}000 + 60{,}000{,}000 +$
$300{,}000 + 80{,}000 + 5000 + 300 + 40 + 9$

MIXED REVIEW

PROBLEM SOLVING APPLICATIONS
Mental Math, Estimation, or Calculator

Tell whether you would choose mental math, estimation, or a calculator. Write *M*, *E*, or *C*. Then solve.

51. In one day a 7-person logging crew chopped down 279 trees. Paul Bunyan chopped down 5 times as many as the 7-person crew. About how many trees did Paul chop down?

52. The camp cook fried 500 eggs for breakfast. Paul Bunyan ate 386 of them. How many fried eggs were left for the other loggers?

★ **53.** The square of my secret number is the same as two times the number. Name two numbers that may be my secret number.

PROBLEM SOLVING
Strategy: Trial and Error

Sometimes the best way to solve a problem is to try several answers. Each try will give you some information to help you reach the correct answer.

Look at this problem:

Lynn has $4.60 in quarters and dimes. She has 4 more dimes than quarters. How many quarters does she have?

First Try   8 quarters   12 dimes
                 $2.00 + $1.20
                     $3.20

> $3.20 < $4.60
> Try again.

Second Try   10 quarters   14 dimes
                  $2.50 + $1.40
                      $3.90

> $3.90 < $4.60
> The total is still not enough.
> Try other numbers.

Third Try   12 quarters   16 dimes
                 $3.00 + $1.60
                     $4.60

> $3.00 + $1.60 = $4.60

Lynn has 12 quarters.

CLASS EXERCISES

Solve. Use the hint for your first try.

1. The sum of 3 consecutive numbers is 219. What are the 3 numbers?

   Hint: $3 \times 70 = 210$

2. Craig bought 72 cm of wood trim to frame a rectangular painting. The frame has to be 4 cm longer than it is wide. How wide is the painting?

   Hint: The frame has 4 sides.

PRACTICE

Solve. Use trial and error.

3. What is the greatest number you can multiply by 78 to get a product between 2000 and 2500?

4. The product of 3 consecutive numbers is 6840. What are the numbers?

5. Karen is 7 years older than Lee. In 5 years she will be twice as old as Lee. How old are Karen and Lee now?

6. Pedro collected $6.50 in tips. He had twice as many dimes as nickels. He had 8 more quarters than dimes. How many of each coin did he have?

7. In a class election, Jeff received twice as many votes as Steven. Steven received twice as many votes as Adam. There were 35 votes altogether. How many votes did Adam receive?

★ **8.** At a school party there were 8 times as many teachers as bus drivers. There was 1 more teacher aide than there were bus drivers. There was 1 principal. There were 32 adults at the party. How many teachers were there?

CHECKPOINT 2

Multiply. *(pages 72–75)*

1. 75 × 684

2. 69 × $14.37

3. $138.97
  ×289

4. 4076
  ×9805

Complete. *(pages 76–77)*

5. $4^2 = $ ▨ × ▨

6. $7 \times 7 \times 7 = $ ▨▨

7. $6^3 = $ ▨

8. $6 \times 10^2 = $ ▨

Solve by trial and error.
(pages 78–79)

9. Lindsay, Elliot, and Ethan played Rocket Derby. Ethan scored 27 more points than Elliot. Lindsay scored 17 fewer points than Ethan. The sum of all the players was 115. What was each player's score?

Extra Practice on page 424

CHAPTER 3 TEST

Write the answer. *(pages 62–67)*

1. 61
$\times 5$

2. 38
$\times 7$

3. 704
$\times 9$

4. 2356
$\times 4$

Estimate. *(pages 68–69)*

5. 26
$\times 13$

6. 54
$\times 78$

7. 120
$\times 37$

8. $7.98
$\times 109$

Draw a picture to help you solve the problem. Then solve.
(pages 70–71)

9. Nick is pasting stamps in an album. There are 9 rows, with places for 6 stamps in each row. If Nick has filled 2 rows and half of the other rows, how many more stamps can he paste on the page?

10. Joyce has oatmeal bread and wheat bread for making sandwiches. For fillings she has cheese, chicken, and tuna fish. If she uses only one filling and one kind of bread for each sandwich, how many possible kinds of sandwiches can Joyce make?

Write the answer. *(pages 72–75)*

11. 92
$\times 36$

12. 536
$\times 70$

13. 5488
$\times 502$

14. 9001
$\times 2481$

Write the product. *(pages 76–77)*

15. 5^2

16. 13^1

17. 8^3

18. 7^2

Use trial and error to solve. *(pages 78–79)*

19. The product of three consecutive numbers is 9240. What are the numbers?

20. Juan has $2.50. He has twice as many dimes as nickels. He has 4 more quarters than dimes. How many of each coin does he have?

Extra Practice on page 425

MATHEMATICS and SOCIAL STUDIES

High energy costs have led people to use less expensive fuels and to use fuel more efficiently.

The energy in fuels used for heating and transportation is measured in British thermal units, or Btu's. The chart shows some fuels and the Btu's they contain. The larger the number of Btu's, the more heat the fuel produces when it's burned.

WHERE DO YOU GET YOUR BTU'S?

1 lb of coal	12,500 Btu's
1 lb of wood	7,500 Btu's
1 gal of gasoline	132,275 Btu's
1 gal of propane	91,740 Btu's
1 gal of heating oil	140,000 Btu's

1. A family uses propane to heat water. They replaced the nozzle on their shower with one that uses less water. They find they are using 12 fewer gallons of propane a month.

   a. How many Btu's will they save a year?

   b. Propane costs $1.20 a gallon. How much money will they save a year?

2. A car uses 5400 Btu's to carry a passenger a mile. A bicycle only needs 310 Btu's to carry a passenger as far. How many Btu's are saved if a person bicycles 5 mi rather than driving the same distance?

3. A gallon of diesel fuel has the same amount of Btu's as heating oil. How many more Btu's are in 10 gal of diesel fuel than 10 gal of gasoline?

Enrichment

We call ten the base of our numeration system because we group in powers of ten. We use the ten digits 0 through 9 to write numbers. Computers do not use a base ten number system as we do. Base two numbers make it possible for computers to complete complicated computations in a very short time. In the base two numeration system we group in powers of two and use only two digits, 0 and 1, to write numbers. The symbol 1101_{two} is read "one one zero one, base two."

Let's look at place value charts for base ten and base two.

In base ten, the values of the places are 1, 10, 100, 1000, and so on. You multiply the value of one place by 10 to find the value of the next higher place.

Base Ten

10^3	10^2	10^1	
1000	100	10	1
			6

$$6_{ten} = 6 \times 1$$

In base two, the values of the places are 1, 2, 4, 8, and so on. You multiply the value of one place by 2 to find the value of the next higher place. To write a base two number as a base ten number, first write it in expanded form as shown.

Base Two

2^3	2^2	2^1	
8	4	2	1
	1	1	0

$$110_{two} = (1 \times 4) + (1 \times 2) + (0 \times 1)$$
$$= 4 + 2 + 0$$
$$= 6_{ten}$$

Complete to name the powers of two. (It's easier if you begin on the right.)

1.

2^8	2^7	2^6	2^5	2^4	2^3	2^2	2^1
?	?	?	?	?	?	?	?

BASE TWO
NUMBERS

Complete the chart to write the base two number as a base ten number.

	BASE TWO	EIGHTS	FOURS	TWOS	ONES	BASE TEN
	1_{two}				1	1
	10_{two}			1	0	2
	11_{two}			1	1	3
2.	100_{two}		?	?	?	?
3.	101_{two}		?	?	?	?
4.	110_{two}		?	?	?	?
5.	111_{two}		?	?	?	?
6.	1000_{two}	?	?	?	?	?
7.	1001_{two}	?	?	?	?	?
8.	1010_{two}	?	?	?	?	?
9.	1011_{two}	?	?	?	?	?
10.	1100_{two}	?	?	?	?	?
11.	1101_{two}	?	?	?	?	?
12.	1110_{two}	?	?	?	?	?
13.	1111_{two}	?	?	?	?	?

Write the base ten number for the base two number.

14. The average sixth grader is 10010110_{two} cm tall.

15. The school year is usually 10110100_{two} days long.

16. The movie was 101001_{two} minutes long.

17. Jerry spent 101101_{two} minutes on his homework.

CUMULATIVE REVIEW

Choose the best answer. Write a, b, c, or d.

Choose the value of the underlined digit.

1. 164,099
   a. 6,000
   b. 600,000
   c. 60,000
   d. none of these

2. 39,465,886
   a. 900,000
   b. 90,000
   c. 9,000,000
   d. none of these

3. 222,222,222,222
   a. 200,000,000,000
   b. 20,000,000,000
   c. 200,000,000
   d. none of these

Order the numbers from greatest to least.

4. 157; 160; 158
   a. 160; 158; 157
   b. 160; 157; 158
   c. 157; 158; 160
   d. none of these

5. 2570; 2750; 2057
   a. 2750; 2057; 2570
   b. 2057; 2570; 2750
   c. 2750; 2570; 2057
   d. none of these

6. 997; 1109; 1110
   a. 1110; 1109; 997
   b. 1109; 1110; 997
   c. 997; 1109; 1110
   d. none of these

Find the answer.

7.   486
      + 474

   a. 950
   b. 970
   c. 960
   d. none of these

8.   576
          25
       + 303

   a. 804
   b. 894
   c. 994
   d. none of these

9. $3344.83
       +   892.51

   a. $4327.34
   b. $4136.34
   c. $4237.34
   d. none of these

Find the answer.

10.   432
        −   51

   a. 381
   b. 483
   c. 481
   d. none of these

11. $80.03
        −   4.64

   a. $76.39
   b. $75.49
   c. $76.49
   d. none of these

12.   95,588
        −   7,044

   a. 92,544
   b. 87,544
   c. 88,544
   d. none of these

Use the chart to solve the problems.

TUMBLING SCHEDULE

CLASS	MON.	TUES.	WED.	THURS.	FRI.
fifth grade	10:00–10:45	1:00–1:45			2:30–3:15
sixth grade	11:00–11:45		2:30–3:15		1:00–1:30

13. On what days of the week does the fifth grade have tumbling?

   a. Mon., Wed., Fri.
   b. Mon., Tues., Fri.
   c. Mon., Wed., Thurs.
   d. none of these

14. The sixth grade has music class 1 hour and 15 minutes after tumbling class ends on Monday. What time does music class begin?

   a. 12:00
   b. 1:00
   c. 10:30
   d. none of these

LANGUAGE and VOCABULARY REVIEW

Match each term with its description.

1. Zero Property

2. Commutative Property

3. Distributive Property

4. Property of One

5. Associative Property

A. The product of one and any number is that number.

B. Changing the grouping of the factors does not change the product.

C. The product of zero and any number is zero.

D. Changing the order of the factors does not change the product.

E. When two or more numbers are being multiplied by the same factor, they may be added and then multiplied or multiplied and then added.

SOFTWARE AND HARDWARE

Software is a set of instructions, called a *program,* that tells the computer what to do.

Hardware is the equipment that makes up a computer. Hardware includes the keyboard, monitor, printer, and disk drive.

When input is given to the computer, the software and hardware work together to change or interpret it.

Data are stored in **memory** until they are ready to be used.

Data are changed or *processed* in the **Central Processing Unit (CPU).** The CPU is made up of Memory, the **Control Unit,** and the **Arithmetic-Logic Unit (ALU).**

The Control Unit directs the way software is used. It sends data into memory and numerical input from memory to the ALU. The Control Unit also sends the results of a process to an output device. The ALU does computations and comparisons.

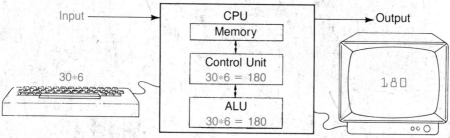

Input → CPU → Output

Memory

Control Unit
30*6 = 180

ALU
30*6 = 180

30*6

180

Solve.

1. What do you call instructions that make the computer work?

2. What is the name for the equipment in a computer system?

3. Which part of the CPU multiplies?

4. Which part processes data?

5. Which part sends data to the ALU?

6. Which part can compare 12 and 17 to find which is greater?

4

If 10 people entered the exhibit of King Tut's treasures every minute, how long would it take a line of 600 people to enter?

DIVISION OF WHOLE NUMBERS

EQUATIONS: MULTIPLICATION AND DIVISION

Dividing by a number is the opposite of multiplying by that number. This is the **Opposites Property** of multiplication and division. Remember that zero divided by any number is zero, but zero cannot be used as a divisor.

We can think of multiplication as repeated addition and division as repeated subtraction.

These ideas can help you recall the division facts. They also can help you solve multiplication and division equations.

$3 \times 4 = 12$, so $12 \div 4 = 3$.

$$0 \div 12 = 0$$

$$
\begin{array}{r}
4 \\
4 \\
+\ 4 \\
\hline
12
\end{array}
\qquad
\begin{array}{r}
12 \\
-\ 4 \\
\hline
8 \\
-\ 4 \\
\hline
4 \\
-\ 4 \\
\hline
0
\end{array}
$$

M You can solve some equations mentally by thinking of the basic facts.

$3 \times n = 12$ — **Think:** $3 \times 4 = 12$, so $n = 4$.

$n \div 4 = 6$ — **Think:** $24 \div 4 = 6$, so $n = 24$.

CLASS EXERCISES

Complete.

1. $4 \times 8 =$ ⬜, so $32 \div 8 =$ ⬜.

2. $6 \times 9 =$ ⬜, so $54 \div 9 =$ ⬜.

3. $6 \times 7 =$ ⬜, so $42 \div 7 =$ ⬜.

4. $8 \times 7 =$ ⬜, so $56 \div 7 =$ ⬜.

5. $7 \times 7 =$ ⬜, so $49 \div 7 =$ ⬜.

6. $9 \times 5 =$ ⬜, so $45 \div 5 =$ ⬜.

7. Six can be subtracted from 30 five times, so $30 \div 6 =$ ⬜.

8. Three can be subtracted from 21 ⬜ times, so $21 \div 3 =$ ⬜.

9. **Think:** Name all the related multiplication and division facts for 6, 5, and 30.

PRACTICE

Solve.

10. $28 \div 4 = n$ **11.** $a \div 6 = 6$ **12.** $36 \div 9 = y$ **13.** $n \div 3 = 8$

14. $72 \div 9 = a$ **15.** $n \div 9 = 5$ **16.** $y \div 7 = 7$ **17.** $a \div 8 = 2$

18. $9 \times n = 81$ **19.** $5 \times a = 25$ **20.** $3 \times y = 12$ **21.** $n \times 7 = 56$

22. $18 \div 6 = a$ **23.** $n \div 7 = 6$ **24.** $y \div 4 = 4$ **25.** $64 \div 8 = a$

26. $9 \times y = 18$ **27.** $n \times 4 = 36$ **28.** $5 \times a = 45$ **29.** $8 \times y = 72$

30. $63 \div 7 = n$ **31.** $y \times 8 = 40$ **32.** $a \div 6 = 5$ **33.** $n \div 9 = 9$

Use mental math to complete. Let $m = 8$ and $h = 9$. Write $<$, $>$, or $=$.

34. $14 + m \quad 22$ **35.** $23 - h \quad 22$ **36.** $3 \times m \quad 18$

37. $63 \div h \quad 14$ **38.** $32 \div m \quad 23$ **39.** $7 \times m \quad 71$

40. $54 - h \quad 34$ **41.** $h \times 5 \quad 45$ **42.** $m - 8 \quad 4$

MENTAL MATH

PROBLEM SOLVING APPLICATIONS
Equations

Write the solution to the equation
to complete the sentence.

43. Lakeville School's annual sports
day was held $\underline{n \div 2 = 7}$ days ago.

44. There were $\underline{n - 6 = 8}$ first-place
winners in various events.

45. Rachel won the $\underline{10 \times 10 = n}$
meter dash.

46. James won the rope-climbing
contest by $\underline{10 - n = 7}$ seconds.

47. There were $\underline{n + 0 = 4}$ members
on the relay team.

★ **48.** In all, there were $\underline{n + n = 24}$ ob-
stacles in the obstacle course.

ONE-DIGIT DIVISORS

Here's how you can divide 227 by 7.

Think of $7\overline{)22}$. — 3 R1

divisor → $7\overline{)227}$ ← dividend

$\dfrac{3}{7\overline{)227}}$
$\underline{-21}$
1 — Subtract 3 × 7.

Is 1 less than 7? Yes.

To check the division, multiply the quotient 32 by the divisor 7. Then add the remainder 3. The sum should equal the dividend.

Think of $7\overline{)17}$.

quotient → 32 R3 ← remainder
$7\overline{)227}$
$\underline{-21}\downarrow$
17
$\underline{-14}$
3 — Subtract 2 × 7.

Check.
```
  32
 ×7
 224
+  3
 227✓
```

 You also could use short division to determine $7\overline{)227}$. Just divide, multiply, and subtract mentally.

$\dfrac{3}{7\overline{)22_17}}$ $\dfrac{3\ 2\ \text{R3}}{7\overline{)22_17}}$

CLASS EXERCISES

Divide.

1. $6\overline{)32}$ $6\overline{)325}$ $6\overline{)3259}$ **2.** $5\overline{)194}$ $5\overline{)1946}$ $5\overline{)19{,}462}$

3. $8\overline{)488}$ $8\overline{)4889}$ $8\overline{)48{,}891}$ **4.** $4\overline{)179}$ $4\overline{)1796}$ $4\overline{)17{,}966}$

5. $9\overline{)706}$ $9\overline{)7063}$ $9\overline{)70{,}632}$ **6.** $7\overline{)582}$ $7\overline{)5824}$ $7\overline{)58{,}249}$

PRACTICE

Divide and check.

7. $8\overline{)89}$ **8.** $7\overline{)84}$ **9.** $2\overline{)59}$ **10.** $9\overline{)100}$ **11.** $5\overline{)133}$

12. $4\overline{)6639}$ **13.** $8\overline{)2034}$ **14.** $6\overline{)9254}$ **15.** $9\overline{)1935}$ **16.** $4\overline{)3168}$

Divide.

17. $3\overline{)23,605}$ **18.** $5\overline{)24,061}$ **19.** $7\overline{)898}$ **20.** $2\overline{)16,675}$ **21.** $3\overline{)2149}$

22. $4\overline{)1769}$ **23.** $6\overline{)37,555}$ **24.** $8\overline{)48,997}$ **25.** $5\overline{)42,687}$ **26.** $9\overline{)1573}$

27. $8\overline{)51,534}$ **28.** $7\overline{)62,946}$ **29.** $5\overline{)26,841}$ **30.** $9\overline{)77,833}$ **31.** $6\overline{)43,217}$

32. $375 \div 5$ **33.** $188 \div 2$ **34.** $328 \div 8$ **35.** $1134 \div 3$ **36.** $7936 \div 8$

Use short division to divide mentally.

37. $3\overline{)775}$ **38.** $4\overline{)679}$ **39.** $7\overline{)848}$

40. $2\overline{)1486}$ **41.** $5\overline{)9368}$ **42.** $6\overline{)3854}$

43. $4\overline{)2751}$ **44.** $9\overline{)87,915}$ **45.** $8\overline{)65,010}$

MENTAL MATH

PROBLEM SOLVING APPLICATIONS
Choosing the Operation

Use the photo to solve.

46. David Lee made paper chains as decorations for his class party. Each loop in the chain was 4 cm long. One of the longest chains he made was 1316 cm long. How many loops were in the chain?

47. Sarah used 95 four-centimeter long loops to make a chain. What was the total length of the chain?

48. How many 5 cm loops would be needed to make a chain 2365 cm long?

★ **49.** David used blue, green, and yellow loops to make the chains. The blue and yellow loops were 4 cm long. The green loops were 5 cm long. How long was the chain that David made with 85 blue, 65 yellow, and 113 green loops?

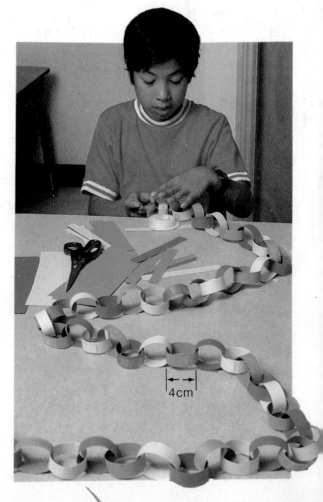

4cm

ZEROS IN THE QUOTIENT

There were 4535 tickets sold for the ice show. There were
5 performances of the show. The same number of tickets
were sold for each performance. How many tickets were
sold for each performance?

Divide 4535 by 5 in three stages.

Think of $5 \overline{)45}$.
The quotient is 9.

Think of $5 \overline{)3}$.
The quotient is 0.

Think of $5 \overline{)35}$.
The quotient is 7.

$$\begin{array}{r} 9 \\ 5 \overline{)4535} \\ -45 \\ \end{array}$$

$$\begin{array}{r} 90 \\ 5 \overline{)4535} \\ -45 \downarrow \\ \hline 3 \\ -0 \\ \hline 3 \\ \end{array}$$

$$\begin{array}{r} 907 \\ 5 \overline{)4535} \\ -45 \\ \hline 3 \\ -0 \downarrow \\ \hline 35 \\ -35 \\ \hline 0 \\ \end{array}$$

907 tickets were sold for each show.

 You can use estimation to check the reasonableness of
your answer. First round the quotient to its greatest
place value and multiply by the divisor.

$$5 \times 907 \triangleright 5 \times 900 = 4500$$

Then compare your estimate and the dividend 4538. If they
are close, your answer is reasonable. **Think:** Is 907 a
reasonable answer?

CLASS EXERCISES

Divide.

1. $8 \overline{)48}$ $8 \overline{)486}$ $8 \overline{)4867}$ **2.** $3 \overline{)21}$ $3 \overline{)212}$ $3 \overline{)2124}$

3. $5 \overline{)450}$ $5 \overline{)4506}$ $5 \overline{)45,063}$ **4.** $6 \overline{)420}$ $6 \overline{)4201}$ $6 \overline{)42,019}$

5. $7 \overline{)154}$ $7 \overline{)1542}$ $7 \overline{)15,428}$ **6.** $4 \overline{)612}$ $4 \overline{)6123}$ $4 \overline{)61,235}$

PRACTICE

ESTIMATE

Divide. Estimate to check as shown on page 92.

7. $4\overline{)815}$ **8.** $5\overline{)154}$ **9.** $9\overline{)8172}$ **10.** $8\overline{)97,631}$

11. $6\overline{)44,457}$ **12.** $5\overline{)3000}$ **13.** $7\overline{)4948}$ **14.** $9\overline{)62,373}$

Divide.

15. $8\overline{)23,210}$ **16.** $4\overline{)16,123}$ **17.** $6\overline{)42,457}$ **18.** $7\overline{)24,503}$

19. $7\overline{)63,546}$ **20.** $8\overline{)16,647}$ **21.** $4\overline{)16,322}$ **22.** $3\overline{)21,025}$

23. $6\overline{)63,020}$ **24.** $2\overline{)13,000}$ **25.** $5\overline{)35,352}$ **26.** $9\overline{)78,030}$

27. $5\overline{)78,025}$ **28.** $2\overline{)21,068}$ **29.** $3\overline{)10,530}$ **30.** $6\overline{)48,186}$

31. $63,873 \div 9$ **32.** $37,632 \div 4$ **33.** $14,515 \div 5$ **34.** $20,510 \div 7$

35. $21,510 \div 9$ **36.** $12,234 \div 6$ **37.** $11,545 \div 5$ **38.** $16,744 \div 8$

Complete. Name the divisor.

★ **39.** $\blacksquare\overline{)7412}$ (823 R5) ★ **40.** $\blacksquare\overline{)62,504}$ (8 929 R1) ★ **41.** $\blacksquare\overline{)4372}$ (874 R2)

Estimate the answer.

MIXED REVIEW

42. $42,768 + 38,001$ **43.** $678,832 + 549,999$

44. 368×7202 **45.** $\$190.00 + \$25.50$

46. $\$7100.00 - \$429.29$ **47.** $5 \times \$96.87$

PROBLEM SOLVING APPLICATIONS
Trial and Error

Complete. Use the same number on each side of the equation to make the equation true. (*Hint:* Each answer is a one-digit number.)

48. $2 \times \blacksquare = 12 - \blacksquare$ **49.** $5 \times \blacksquare = 28 + \blacksquare$ **50.** $9 \div \blacksquare = 6 - \blacksquare$

51. $36 + \blacksquare = 405 \div \blacksquare$ **52.** $6 \times \blacksquare = 294 \div \blacksquare$ ★ **53.** $2106 \div \blacksquare = 357 - \blacksquare$

PROBLEM SOLVING
Strategy: Writing Equations

When you solve word problems, it's helpful to be able to write number phrases and equations for word phrases and sentences.

Write the word phrase as a number phrase.

Example.

word phrase ⟹ number phrase
   a minus 12 $a - 12$

The Lopez family bought tickets for the beach at $4.00 each. What is the total cost?

Let *c* be the total cost of the tickets.
Let *n* be the number of tickets bought.

You can write an equation that shows the total cost. The total cost is the number of tickets times $4.00.

$$c = n \times 4$$

CLASS EXERCISES

Write the word phrase as a number phrase.

1. 4 times *n*

2. 8 less than *x*

3. 14 more than *a*

4. the sum of 16 and *y*

5. 26 minus *a*

6. 12 plus *y*

7. *r* divided by 3

8. the number of hours in *n* days

9. the number of pennies in *t* dollars

10. the product of 15 and *n*

11. the difference 47 minus *x*

12. the number of days in *h* weeks

Write an equation for the word sentence. Then solve.

13. The product of 6 and *w* is 24.

14. The sum of *n* and 25 is 50.

15. The quotient when 72 is divided by 9 is *y*.

16. The difference when 4 is subtracted from *b* is 29.

PRACTICE

Write a number phrase to complete the sentence.

17. Vi spent $16 more than Pam. Let p = the amount Pam spent. The amount Vi spent = ▦.

18. Norman's books cost $7 each. Let b = the number of books. Then ▦ = the cost of the books.

19. Liz's mass is 8 kg less than Donna's. Let m = Donna's mass. Then ▦ = Liz's mass.

20. The price of gas is increased by $.12. Let p = the original price of gas. Then ▦ = the new price.

21. Bo, Mia, and Phil shared the cost of their dinner equally. Let c = the cost of the dinner. The amount paid by each = ▦.

22. Dave rented a typewriter for 75 hours. Let h = the cost per hour to rent the typewriter. Then ▦ = the total cost of the rental.

Write the letter for the equation that matches. Then solve.

23. What is the cost of 25 rides at 75¢ a ride?

24. Curt scored 25 points. He needs 75 points to win. How many more points does he need?

A. $75 \div 25 = b$
B. $75 \times 25 = a$
C. $75 + 25 = y$
D. $75 - 25 = n$

25. The 25-member Glee Club won 75 free tickets to the park. If the tickets are shared equally, how many will each member get?

CHECKPOINT 1

Solve. *(pages 88–89)*

1. $9 \times c = 45$ **2.** $49 \div x = 7$

3. $g \div 6 = 4$ **4.** $h \times 9 = 81$

Write the answer. *(pages 90–93)*

5. $4\overline{)3165}$ **6.** $6\overline{)29,364}$

7. $7\overline{)30,405}$ **8.** $9\overline{)49,555}$

Write an equation for the word sentence. Then solve. *(pages 94–95)*

9. Evelyn packed 2412 seashells, 9 to a box. How many boxes did Evelyn pack?

Extra Practice on page 426

DIVIDING BY TENS

The Sky High Kite Company packs their dragon kites in boxes of 30. How many boxes of 30 kites can be packed with 8364 dragon kites? How many are left over?

Divide 8364 by 30.

For 30)83, think of 3)8.   For 30)236, think of 3)23.   For 30)264, think of 3)26.

$$
\begin{array}{r} 2 \\ 30)\overline{8364} \\ -\ 60 \\ \hline 23 \end{array}
\qquad
\begin{array}{r} 27 \\ 30)\overline{8364} \\ -\ 60\!\!\downarrow \\ \hline 236 \\ -\ 210 \\ \hline 26 \end{array}
\qquad
\begin{array}{r} 278 \text{ R}24 \\ 30)\overline{8364} \\ -\ 60 \\ \hline 236 \\ -\ 210 \\ \hline 264 \\ -\ 240 \\ \hline 24 \end{array}
$$

There can be 278 boxes of dragon kites with 24 kites left over.

 If you had used a calculator to do this division, the display would have shown 278.8. Here is how to determine the remainder.

Notice that the quotient is to the left of the decimal point.
Multiply the quotient by the divisor.
Subtract the product from the dividend to determine the remainder.

278
278 ⊠ 30 ▣ 8340
8364 ⊟ 8340 ▣ 24

CLASS EXERCISES

What is the quotient?

1. 30)90

30)120

30)270

2. 40)160

40)280

40)360

3. 70)140

70)420

70)560

4. 50)150

50)300

50)500

5. 30)60

30)600

6. 60)180

60)1800

7. 90)3600

90)3690

8. 20)2000

20)2400

PRACTICE

Divide and check.

9. $20\overline{)502}$ 10. $30\overline{)1038}$ 11. $50\overline{)1352}$ 12. $40\overline{)1204}$

13. $80\overline{)8055}$ 14. $70\overline{)2730}$ 15. $60\overline{)4212}$ 16. $90\overline{)7483}$

Divide.

17. $50\overline{)918}$ 18. $20\overline{)719}$ 19. $30\overline{)1266}$ 20. $70\overline{)731}$

21. $60\overline{)4702}$ 22. $90\overline{)3562}$ 23. $80\overline{)4286}$ 24. $40\overline{)825}$

25. $30\overline{)1970}$ 26. $20\overline{)608}$ 27. $20\overline{)672}$ 28. $70\overline{)6674}$

29. $1980 \div 60$ 30. $3400 \div 40$ 31. $6660 \div 90$ 32. $4560 \div 60$

33. $5840 \div 80$ 34. $6930 \div 70$ 35. $700 \div 50$ 36. $420 \div 30$

Determine the remainder.

37. $4383 \div 40 = 109$ R   38. $4115 \div 60 = 68$ R

39. $5789 \div 50 = 115$ R   40. $6969 \div 70 = 99$ R

CALCULATOR

PROBLEM SOLVING APPLICATIONS
Choosing the Operation

Solve.

41. Sky High shipped 960 kites. The kites were packed 20 to a box. How many boxes of kites were shipped?

42. A super dragon kite is 25 ft long. A regular dragon kite is 13 ft long. How much longer is the super dragon kite?

43. In one day Sky High sold 35 red kites, 14 blue kites, 18 green kites, and 23 multicolored kites. How many kites were sold in all?

★ 44. A roll of kite string is 2200 ft long. Karl uses one half of the string to fly his kite. Then he uses one half of the remaining string on the roll to make the kite go higher. How much string does Karl use in all?

TWO-DIGIT DIVISORS
ONE-DIGIT QUOTIENTS

To divide 98 by 37, mentally round 37 up to 40.
To estimate the quotient, think of $4\overline{)9}$.

$$\begin{array}{r} 40 \end{array} \qquad \begin{array}{r} 2 \text{ R24} \\ 37\overline{)98} \\ -74 \\ \hline 24 \end{array}$$

Sometimes your first estimate isn't great enough.
Look at 326 divided by 45.

Round 45 up to 50. Think of $5\overline{)32}$.

Try 6 as the quotient.   Try 7 as the quotient.

$$50 \quad \begin{array}{r} 6 \\ 45\overline{)326} \\ -270 \\ \hline 56 \end{array} \quad \begin{array}{l} \text{Since 56 is greater than} \\ \text{45, try a greater quotient.} \end{array}$$

$$\begin{array}{r} 7 \text{ R11} \\ 45\overline{)326} \\ -315 \\ \hline 11 \end{array}$$

Sometimes your first estimate is too great.
Look at 121 divided by 44.

Mentally round 44 down to 40. Think of $4\overline{)12}$.

Try 3 as the quotient.   Try 2 as the quotient.

$$40 \quad \begin{array}{r} 3 \\ 44\overline{)121} \\ -132 \end{array} \quad \begin{array}{l} \text{Since 132 is greater than} \\ \text{121, try a smaller quotient.} \end{array}$$

$$\begin{array}{r} 2 \text{ R33} \\ 44\overline{)121} \\ -88 \\ \hline 33 \end{array}$$

CLASS EXERCISES

Divide.

1. $20\overline{)81}$ $19\overline{)81}$ **2.** $30\overline{)65}$ $27\overline{)65}$ **3.** $40\overline{)243}$ $36\overline{)243}$

4. $60\overline{)186}$ $64\overline{)186}$ **5.** $50\overline{)316}$ $54\overline{)316}$ **6.** $70\overline{)436}$ $66\overline{)436}$

PRACTICE

Divide and check.

7. $28\overline{)60}$ **8.** $34\overline{)65}$ **9.** $39\overline{)170}$ **10.** $25\overline{)163}$ **11.** $44\overline{)153}$

12. $53\overline{)193}$ **13.** $88\overline{)753}$ **14.** $74\overline{)400}$ **15.** $34\overline{)259}$ **16.** $72\overline{)588}$

17. $65\overline{)264}$ **18.** $52\overline{)463}$ **19.** $53\overline{)174}$ **20.** $44\overline{)364}$ **21.** $78\overline{)393}$

22. $85\overline{)782}$ **23.** $25\overline{)118}$ **24.** $18\overline{)110}$ **25.** $50\overline{)462}$ **26.** $62\overline{)289}$

27. $225 \div 45$ **28.** $164 \div 41$ **29.** $217 \div 31$ **30.** $280 \div 35$ **31.** $520 \div 8$

Write the answer.

32. $706 - 308$ **33.** 6×97 **34.** 9×85

35. 8×407 **36.** $428 + 637$ **37.** 8×547

38. 7×86 **39.** 9×967 **40.** $832 - 765$

41. $600 - 147$ **42.** $273 + 727$ **43.** 486×7

44. 608×8 **45.** $369 - 296$ **46.** $989 + 898$

MIXED REVIEW

PROBLEM SOLVING APPLICATIONS
Choosing the Operation

Solve.

47. Jeff can print 60 T-shirts from one stencil. How many T-shirts can he print from 15 stencils?

48. Shirley needs 38 leather loops to make one belt. How many belts can she make from 160 loops? How many loops will be left over?

49. Chris has 357 beads. He wants to make 37 necklaces. How many beads will each necklace have if each has the same number?

★ **50.** Melba sold 38 clay pots at a crafts show. She collected $119.70 which included $5.70 for taxes. Each pot was the same price. How much did she charge for each pot including tax?

TWO-DIGIT DIVISORS
TWO-DIGIT QUOTIENTS

Greenways' Plant Shop has a special display that has 18 shelves. There are 215 African violet plants on display. Each shelf contains the same number of plants. The extra plants are placed on the floor. How many plants are on each shelf? How many plants are on the floor?

To determine the answer, divide.

Round 18 to 20. Think of $2\overline{)2}$.   Think of $2\overline{)3}$.   Write the remainder.

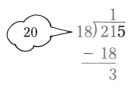

$$\begin{array}{r} 1 \\ 18\overline{)215} \\ -18 \\ \hline 3 \end{array}$$

$$\begin{array}{r} 11 \\ 18\overline{)215} \\ -18\downarrow \\ \hline 35 \\ -18 \\ \hline 17 \end{array}$$

$$\begin{array}{r} 11 \text{ R17} \\ 18\overline{)215} \\ -18 \\ \hline 35 \\ -18 \\ \hline 17 \end{array}$$

There are 11 plants on each shelf and 17 plants on the floor.

When you divide money by a whole number, put the decimal point in the quotient over the decimal point in the dividend. Then divide as with whole numbers.

$$\begin{array}{r} \$\ .21 \\ 12\overline{)\$2.52} \\ -2\ 4 \\ \hline 12 \\ -12 \\ \hline 0 \end{array}$$

CLASS EXERCISES

Divide.

1. $40\overline{)875}$ **2.** $30\overline{)1285}$ **3.** $60\overline{)689}$ **4.** $80\overline{)895}$

$37\overline{)875}$ $26\overline{)1285}$ $55\overline{)689}$ $78\overline{)895}$

PRACTICE

Divide and check.

5. $33\overline{)757}$ **6.** $18\overline{)537}$ **7.** $93\overline{)6542}$ **8.** $44\overline{)1425}$ **9.** $51\overline{)789}$

10. $64\overline{)4973}$ **11.** $38\overline{)714}$ **12.** $77\overline{)873}$ **13.** $29\overline{)2143}$ **14.** $17\overline{)984}$

15. $50\overline{)2475}$ **16.** $76\overline{)6238}$ **17.** $56\overline{)1512}$ **18.** $39\overline{)1238}$ **19.** $85\overline{)7025}$

20. $14\overline{)290}$ **21.** $82\overline{)1000}$ **22.** $87\overline{)7118}$ **23.** $35\overline{)1273}$ **24.** $21\overline{)461}$

25. $\$13.20 \div 40$ **26.** $\$26.60 \div 28$ **27.** $\$47.12 \div 76$ **28.** $\$59.50 \div 85$

29. $\$8.16 \div 17$ **30.** $\$27.65 \div 79$ **31.** $\$14.08 \div 32$ **32.** $\$9.02 \div 41$

PROBLEM SOLVING APPLICATIONS
Using Information from a Chart

Use the production report to solve.

33. Cartons hold 36 pairs of tennis shoes. How many cartons are needed?

34. The Footprint received a shipment of tennis shoes. The bill was $1296. How many pairs of tennis shoes were received?

35. Heel and Toe employs 56 people to make sandals. They work at about the same rate. About how many pairs of sandals did each employee make the week of March 18?

HEEL AND TOE SHOE COMPANY			
Production Report			
Week of *March 18* Dept. 23			
Style Number	Type	Number of Pairs	Price Per Pair
68	tennis shoes	1512	$18.00
59A	sandals	2016	$15.00
90C	rainboots	3564	$20.00
90B	workboots	2664	$25.00

★ **36.** Heel and Toe received the following special order to be filled in 11 days: #68—740 pairs, #59A—850 pairs, #90C—230 pairs, and #90B—380 pairs. Each pair takes the same amount of time to make. How many pairs must be made in a day to fill the order on time?

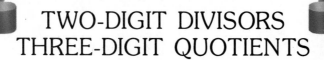

TWO-DIGIT DIVISORS
THREE-DIGIT QUOTIENTS

The Forest Service planted 15,648 trees to replace part of a forest that had been destroyed. They planted 84 trees in each row. How many complete rows of trees did they plant?

Divide to determine the answer.

```
        1              18               186 R24
84) 15,648     84) 15,648        84) 15,648
  - 8 4          - 8 4↓            - 8 4
    7 2            7 24              7 24
                - 6 72            - 6 72
                    52              528
                                  - 504
                                     24
```

They planted 186 complete rows.

CLASS EXERCISES

Divide.

1. 38) 842   38) 8429   2. 27) 1122   27) 11,223

3. 81) 983   81) 9835   4. 81) 3413   81) 34,135

5. 46) 5128   46) 51,287   6. 63) 2440   63) 23,960

PRACTICE

Divide and check.

7. 48) 6576   8. 47) 12,367   9. 66) 7173   10. 24) 15,997

11. 92) 48,321   12. 35) 23,520   13. 69) 37,536   14. 73) 20,052

15. 27) 5808   16. 29) 3430   17. 78) 60,996   18. 37) 25,019

Divide.

19. $70\overline{)28{,}241}$ **20.** $31\overline{)9427}$ **21.** $25\overline{)10{,}070}$ **22.** $72\overline{)54{,}884}$

23. $84\overline{)19{,}020}$ **24.** $85\overline{)15{,}995}$ **25.** $19\overline{)10{,}971}$ **26.** $64\overline{)23{,}040}$

27. $17{,}577 \div 81$ **28.** $28{,}576 \div 32$ **29.** $13{,}464 \div 66$ **30.** $12{,}384 \div 24$

31. $\$75.87 \div 27$ **32.** $\$25{,}152 \div 48$ **33.** $\$151.68 \div 16$ **34.** $\$284.76 \div 84$

Tell whether you would use mental math or a calculator. Write *M* or *C*. Then divide.

35. $27\overline{)2700}$ **36.** $7\overline{)651}$ **37.** $22\overline{)880}$ **38.** $95\overline{)6725}$

39. $35\overline{)70{,}070}$ **40.** $42\overline{)32{,}256}$ **41.** $9\overline{)63{,}927}$ **42.** $23\overline{)15{,}962}$

PROBLEM SOLVING APPLICATIONS
Choosing the Operation

Solve.

43. One wagon can move 85 evergreens. How many wagons are needed to move 15,648 evergreens?

44. The Paper Perfect Company planted 239 trees in each of 187 acres. Altogether, how many trees did they plant?

45. One bag of fertilizer is needed for every 64 trees planted. How many trees can be fertilized with 205 bags?

46. If a logging crew chopped down 31,365 ft of logs and the average tree was 85 ft tall, how many trees did the crew chop down?

★ **47.** A forest worker can plant 96 trees in one day. How many workers are needed to plant 15,648 trees in two days?

THREE-DIGIT DIVISORS

The Smiths are packing for a picnic. This sandwich has about 1592 milligrams (mg) of sodium. Sodium is in table salt. Most people need no more than 250 mg of sodium a day. Divide to compare the sodium in this sandwich with the amount Joanne Smith needs in a day.

Round 250 to 300. Think of $3\overline{)15}$.
Try 5 as the quotient.

$$\begin{array}{r} 5 \\ 250\overline{)1592} \\ -\ 1250 \\ \hline 342 \end{array}$$

300

Since 342 is greater than 250, try 6 as the quotient.

$$\begin{array}{r} 6 \text{ R}92 \\ 250\overline{)1592} \\ -\ 1500 \\ \hline 92 \end{array}$$

The sandwich has about 6 times as much sodium as Joanne needs in a day.

Think: What steps can you take to determine the quotient and the remainder if you divide 1592 by 250 on a calculator?

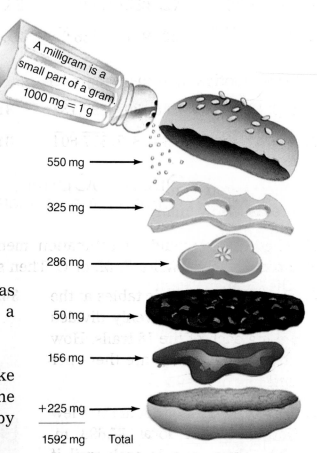

A milligram is a small part of a gram.
1000 mg = 1 g

550 mg ⟶

325 mg ⟶

286 mg ⟶

50 mg ⟶

156 mg ⟶

+225 mg ⟶

1592 mg   Total

CLASS EXERCISES
Divide.

1. $200\overline{)768}$ **2.** $500\overline{)9311}$ **3.** $700\overline{)56,608}$ **4.** $400\overline{)28,773}$

$179\overline{)768}$ $492\overline{)9311}$ $665\overline{)56,608}$ $382\overline{)28,773}$

PRACTICE

Divide and check.

5. $375\overline{)1578}$ **6.** $202\overline{)3667}$ **7.** $495\overline{)7546}$ **8.** $917\overline{)75,679}$

9. $422\overline{)26,984}$ **10.** $901\overline{)78,954}$ **11.** $322\overline{)46,721}$ **12.** $608\overline{)85,030}$

13. $346\overline{)91,861}$ **14.** $159\overline{)54,616}$ **15.** $708\overline{)43,708}$ **16.** $645\overline{)37,691}$

17. $491\overline{)28,776}$ **18.** $248\overline{)84,307}$ **19.** $831\overline{)70,661}$ **20.** $965\overline{)77,650}$

21. $191\overline{)83,700}$ **22.** $682\overline{)71,061}$ **23.** $316\overline{)28,124}$ **24.** $787\overline{)50,368}$

25. $769\overline{)\$669.03}$ **26.** $987\overline{)\$8586.90}$ **27.** $209\overline{)\$1985.50}$ **28.** $742\overline{)\$6581.54}$

Write the quotient and the remainder.

29. $492\overline{)180,090}$ **30.** $708\overline{)899,132}$ **31.** $202\overline{)188,008}$

32. $609\overline{)357,609}$ **33.** $817\overline{)357,604}$ **34.** $909\overline{)497,723}$

CALCULATOR

PROBLEM SOLVING APPLICATIONS
Estimation, Mental Math, or Calculator

Tell whether you would use estimation, mental math, or a calculator to solve. Write *E*, *M*, or *C*. Then solve.

35. There are 450 picnic tables at the Center. They are evenly divided among each of the 18 trails. How many picnic tables are there per trail?

36. During a one-year period 365,000 people visited the Nature Center. On the average, how many people visited each day?

37. The 18 trails at Mountain View Nature Center total 17,698 m. About how long is each trail if they are approximately the same length?

★ **38.** In one year the Center sold 111,960 T-shirts, 67,320 binoculars, and 284,760 sun visors. On an average, how many of each item were sold each day? (The Center is open 360 days a year.)

PROBLEM SOLVING
Strategy: Choosing the Operation

1. Understand
2. Plan
3. Work
4. Answer/Check

Choosing the correct operation is often the most difficult part of problem solving. Study the examples to see why the operation was chosen.

How many campers signed up for an activity?

> **Add** since you want to determine a total.
> $17 + 9 + 23 + 12 = 61$

How many more chose volleyball than hiking?

> **Subtract** since you want to determine how much greater one group is than another.
> $17 - 9 = 8$

Each hiker picked 15 wild flowers. How many is that in all?

> **Multiply** since you want to combine groups of equal size. $15 \times 9 = 135$

There are 3082 beads for crafts. How many beads can each camper have?

> **Divide** since you want to know how many in each group. $3082 \div 23 = 134$

CLASS EXERCISES

Write *add, subtract, multiply,* or *divide* to tell which operation you'd use to solve the problem.

1. A canoe can carry ▓ campers. How many canoes are needed to carry ▓ campers?

2. Max bought ▓ postcards that cost ▓ each. How much did he spend?

3. Teddy says his cat Hippo has a mass of ▓ kg. Arnold says his cat Lillian has a mass of ▓ kg. How much heavier is Arnold's cat?

4. Susan got ▓ mosquito bites in the morning and ▓ bites in the afternoon. How many bites did she get in all?

PRACTICE

Match each problem with the correct example. Solve the problem.

A. $15 \div 3$ **B.** $15 + 3$ **C.** 15×3 **D.** $15 - 3$

5.

> Dear Sam,   CG
>   Today I found 15 spiders.
> I'll give three of them to
> you when I get home.
>   Your friend,
>   Al

How many spiders will Al keep?

6.

> Dear Emily,   CG
>   We went hiking today and
> 3 kids got poison ivy. The
> other 15 of us just got blisters.
>   See you soon,
>   Laurie

How many campers went hiking?

7.

> Dear Willy,   CG
>   Today was my turn to cook.
> I made Campfire Nuggets
> for 15 people. Everyone ate 3.
>   Yours truly,
>   Ned

How many Nuggets were eaten?

8.

> Dear Carol,   CG
>   I've collected 15 different
> beetles. I'll split them
> with you and Ellie when
> I get home.
>   Your sister,
>   Mimi

How many beetles will each get?

Solve. Be sure to check your answer.

9. In her first week at camp, Melina spent $1.89 on insect spray, $.98 on bandages, and $1.57 on snacks. If she has $10.56 left, how much did she have to start with?

10. In a camp softball game, the Donkeys beat the Mules by 9 runs. If the Donkeys' final score was 37, what was the Mules' final score?

11. "I played Magic Maze with the camp computer 41 times today," said Lorna, "and I won 15 times." How many times did the computer win?

12. James took 7 rolls of film to camp. Each roll had 24 pictures. If he used 5 complete rolls, how many pictures did he take?

★ **13.** The camp cook makes granola. His recipe makes enough for 15 servings. How many times should he increase the recipe to make 140 servings?

ESTIMATING QUOTIENTS

Sandra Ling works for the Board of Health. She often travels while doing her job. Last week she drove 548 mi in 7 days. About how many miles did she drive each day?

You can answer the question by estimating the quotient. If you round to the greatest place value, estimating the quotient mentally may be difficult.

$$\frac{?}{7)\overline{500}}$$

In cases like this, it's easier to estimate the quotient by using **compatible numbers,** that is, numbers that you can divide easily. Choose a number close to 548 that is easily divided by 7.

$$\frac{80}{7)\overline{560}}$$

She drove about 80 mi each day.

CLASS EXERCISES

Complete.

1. $4)\overline{331}$ ⇨ $4)\overline{320}$

2. $46)\overline{487}$ ⇨ $50)\overline{500}$

3. $12)\overline{375}$ ⇨ $12)\overline{360}$

4. $26)\overline{928}$ ⇨ $30)\overline{900}$

5. $44)\overline{1571}$ ⇨ $40)\overline{1600}$

6. $65)\overline{2218}$ ⇨ $70)\overline{2100}$

PRACTICE

Estimate the quotient.

7. $7)\overline{283}$

8. $6)\overline{314}$

9. $7)\overline{6217}$

10. $4)\overline{2657}$

11. $85)\overline{7242}$

12. $29)\overline{1153}$

13. $51)\overline{4832}$

14. $68)\overline{5640}$

15. $21\overline{)4423}$ **16.** $93\overline{)44,687}$ **17.** $64\overline{)31,477}$ **18.** $42\overline{)2541}$

19. $76\overline{)4842}$ **20.** $93\overline{)27,113}$ **21.** $35\overline{)27,431}$ **22.** $83\overline{)3642}$

23. $189\overline{)9932}$ **24.** $621\overline{)538,009}$ **25.** $773\overline{)478,554}$ **26.** $582\overline{)239,112}$

PROBLEM SOLVING APPLICATIONS
Using Estimation

BOOKKEEPER
Full charge, $19,865 plus benefits. Send resume to:
   Box L
   Phoenix, AZ 85008

PROGRAMMER Excellent opportunity with a small computer firm. Experience necessary, $22,480. Send resume to: Box R, Boulder, CO 80301

Estimate to solve. Use the newspaper clipping.

27. John earns $300 per week in his present job. Would he earn more if he took the bookkeeper job?

28. If Sally takes the programmer job, will she earn more than or less than $2000 per month?

29. Sally earns $315 per week. If she took the programmer job, would she earn more or less than $315 each week?

★ **30.** Paul has been offered a trainee job that pays $2140 a month plus an annual bonus of $2000. He presently earns $22,250 per year. Which job would pay more?

CHECKPOINT 2

Write the answer. *(pages 96–105)*

  1. $49\overline{)368}$ **2.** $86\overline{)7086}$

  3. $514\overline{)47,007}$ **4.** $246\overline{)49,073}$

Estimate. *(pages 108–109)*

  5. $87\overline{)62,899}$ **6.** $212\overline{)587,302}$

Solve. *(pages 106–107)*

  7. Nicole planted 1343 flower seeds in 17 rows. How many were planted per row?

  8. Marco sold 179 fans a day. How many did he sell in a week?

Extra Practice on page 426

Solve. *(pages 88–89)*

1. $18 \div 3 = n$ **2.** $y \div 7 = 7$ **3.** $5 \times a = 20$ **4.** $n \times 4 = 32$

Write the answer. *(pages 90–93)*

5. $6\overline{)74}$ **6.** $7\overline{)446}$ **7.** $5\overline{)4000}$ **8.** $8\overline{)40,328}$

Match each problem with an equation. Then solve. *(pages 94–95)*

9. A paintbrush costs $.80. What is the cost of 20 brushes?

10. Jeff earned $80 painting fences. With this money he bought 20 cassettes. If the cassettes were all the same price, what was the price of one?

11. Jeff painted 80 fence posts on Saturday and 20 fence posts on Monday. How many fence posts did he paint in all?

A. $80 \div 20 = a$
B. $80 - 20 = b$
C. $80 \times 20 = n$
D. $80 + 20 = y$

Write the answer. *(pages 96–105)*

12. $30\overline{)2031}$ **13.** $67\overline{)478}$ **14.** $76\overline{)841}$ **15.** $66\overline{)7835}$ **16.** $502\overline{)24,912}$

Solve. *(pages 106–107)*

17. Nan and Phil played checkers 33 times. Nan won 14 times. How many times did Phil win?

18. Hannah solved 5 crossword puzzles. She spent 18 min on each puzzle. How long did she spend on all the puzzles?

Estimate the quotient. *(pages 108–109)*

19. $158 \div 8$ **20.** $4114 \div 37$ **21.** $19,637 \div 53$ **22.** $8888 \div 274$

Extra Practice on page 427

MATHEMATICS and HEALTH

A healthful diet includes a number of different foods to give your body the nutrients it needs. Two important nutrients are calcium and vitamin C. A twelve-year-old's diet should provide 80 mg of vitamin C and 1200 mg of calcium a day.

DOES YOUR DIET BALANCE?

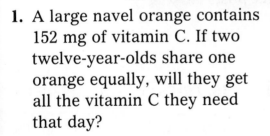

1. A large navel orange contains 152 mg of vitamin C. If two twelve-year-olds share one orange equally, will they get all the vitamin C they need that day?

2. A loaf of raisin bread contains 324 mg of calcium. If the loaf is sliced into 18 equal pieces, how much calcium will each slice provide?

3. A cup of skim milk contains 296 mg of calcium. A large egg contains 28 mg of calcium. Will 4 cups of skim milk and an egg provide a twelve-year-old with the daily amount of calcium?

4. A nine-year-old needs 800 mg of calcium a day. Will three cups of skim milk a day provide enough? To solve, find the information you need elsewhere on this page.

★5. Calcium and vitamin C are just two of the minerals and vitamins in a healthful diet. Name another mineral and another vitamin that contribute to your health.

111

Enrichment

The mathematicians of ancient Greece called the numbers 1, 3, 6, 10, 15, and so on *triangular numbers*. From one dot, a triangular pattern of 3 dots, 6 dots, 10 dots and so on can be built up.

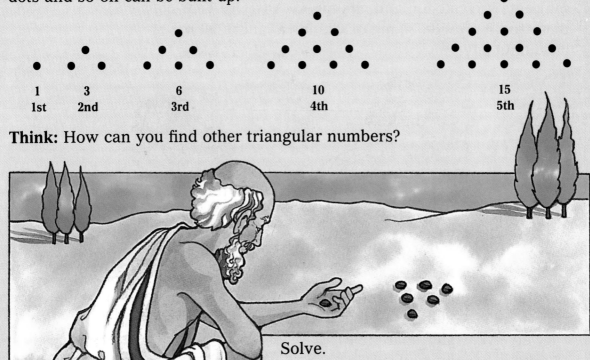

1	3	6	10	15
1st	2nd	3rd	4th	5th

Think: How can you find other triangular numbers?

Solve.

1. What is the 6th triangular number?

2. What is the 10th triangular number?

3. Nine people meet for lunch. They all shake hands. How many handshakes would there be in all? (Hint: Draw a picture letting a point represent a person.) Is your answer a triangular number?

4. If the number of people that met had been 12, how many handshakes would have taken place?

TRIANGULAR NUMBERS

5. What is the sum of the numbers from 1 to 10? Is this a triangular number?

6. What is the 15th triangular number? Is it the same as the sum of the numbers from 1 to 15?

The Greeks also studied *square* numbers.

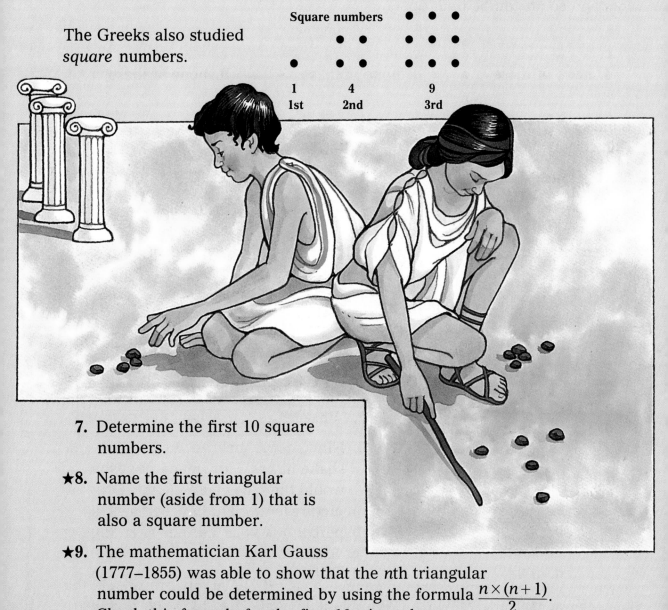

Square numbers

1   4   9
1st   2nd   3rd

7. Determine the first 10 square numbers.

★**8.** Name the first triangular number (aside from 1) that is also a square number.

★**9.** The mathematician Karl Gauss (1777–1855) was able to show that the *n*th triangular number could be determined by using the formula $\frac{n \times (n+1)}{2}$. Check this formula for the first 10 triangular numbers by substituting each of the first 10 counting numbers for *n*.

Choose the correct answer. Write *a*, *b*, *c*, or *d*.

Compare the numbers.

1. 3810 ▨ 3108

   a. >
   b. <
   c. =
   d. none of these

2. 50,099 ▨ 50,900

   a. >
   b. <
   c. =
   d. none of these

3. 4,686,101 ▨ 4,153,300

   a. >
   b. <
   c. =
   d. none of these

Round to the greatest place value.

4. 431

   a. 430
   b. 500
   c. 400
   d. none of these

5. 7608

   a. 7000
   b. 7600
   c. 8000
   d. none of these

6. 92,635

   a. 90,000
   b. 92,000
   c. 100,000
   d. none of these

Choose the most likely temperature.

7. water-skiing

   a. 1°C
   b. 11°C
   c. 31°C
   d. none of these

8. snow-skiing

   a. 100°C
   b. −2°C
   c. 32°C
   d. none of these

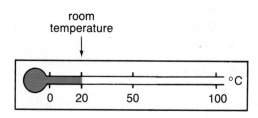

room temperature

Which is the best estimate?

9.   22
  + 37

   a. 40
   b. 60
   c. 80
   d. 100

10. $.76
  + .13

   a. $.60
   b. $.70
   c. $.90
   d. $1.00

11. $48.91
  + 32.70

   a. $100
   b. $90
   c. $80
   d. $60

12.   354
  + 249

   a. 600
   b. 900
   c. 400
   d. 800

13.   790
  + 426

   a. 1400
   b. 1200
   c. 1000
   d. 2800

14. $314.06
  + 870.98

   a. $2400
   b. $1800
   c. $1600
   d. $1200

Find the answer.

15.
```
   4873
+ 3685
```
    a. 8548
    b. 8558
    c. 8458
    d. none of these

16.
```
  $4562.53
+   139.84
```
    a. $4701.37
    b. $4702.47
    c. $4702.37
    d. none of these

17.
```
   4166
    765
+    73
```
    a. 4004
    b. 5004
    c. 5094
    d. none of these

Which is the best estimate?

18. 387 − 33
    a. 430
    b. 330
    c. 340
    d. 370

19. $31.25 − $8.50
    a. $21.00
    b. $28.00
    c. $38.00
    d. $40.00

20. $40.89 − $11.10
    a. $50.00
    b. $40.00
    c. $30.00
    d. $20.00

Find the answer.

21.
```
   6686
−   509
```
    a. 6187
    b. 6087
    c. 6077
    d. none of these

22.
```
  $426.25
− 134.42
```
    a. $391.83
    b. $291.83
    c. $292.83
    d. none of these

23.
```
  171,512
− 115,325
```
    a. 56,287
    b. 57,197
    c. 56,187
    d. none of these

LANGUAGE and VOCABULARY REVIEW

Use the examples to match.

```
    6 R3
9)57
− 54
   3
```

```
  26
+ 33
  59
```

1. 57   **A.** quotient
2. 33   **B.** dividend
3. 6   **C.** addend
4. 59   **D.** remainder
5. 9   **E.** sum
6. 3   **F.** divisor

MEMORY

Computers store information in memory. **Primary memory** is located inside the computer. There are two kinds.

Read Only Memory, or **ROM,** is built into a computer. ROM includes permanent instructions such as telling the computer how to add and how to send output to a monitor or a printer.

Random Access Memory, or **RAM,** is temporary memory. RAM stores programs and data while the computer is on. Data stored in RAM is usually erased when the computer is turned off.

Secondary memory is located outside the computer. Tapes and disks are used to store data and programs outside the computer.

Memory is measured by the number of characters it can store. Two common measures of memory are K and M.

K = 1024 characters, so
16K = 16 × 1024
= 16,384
M = 1,048,576 characters, so
10M = 10 × 1,048,576
= 10,485,760

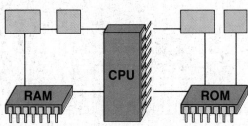

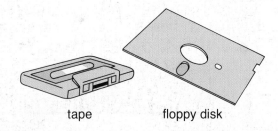

tape   floppy disk

Write *true* or *false*.

1. Directions for finding 676 + 287 are stored in ROM.

2. A computer with 32K memory can store 35,840 characters.

3. Information in RAM can be changed.

4. One K of memory equals 2^{10} characters.

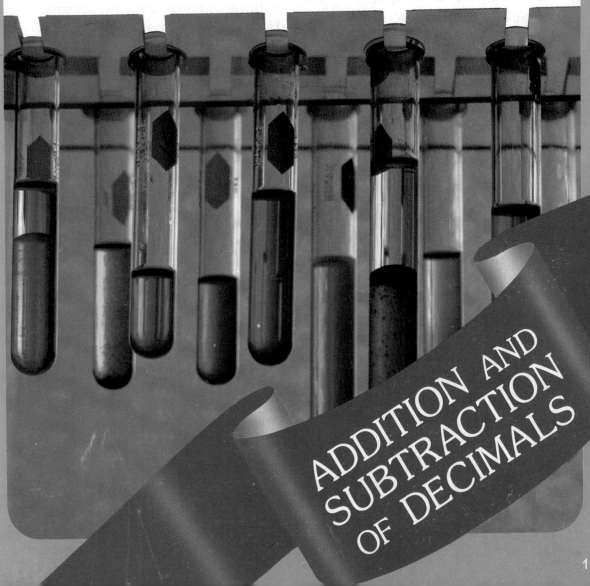

A cosmetic may contain only a few parts of one ingredient in 1000 parts of a mixture of ingredients. How many parts in 1000 are equal to 1 part in 100?

5

ADDITION AND SUBTRACTION OF DECIMALS

PLACE VALUE TO HUNDREDTHS

When a whole is divided into ten equal parts or a hundred equal parts, you can write **decimals** to describe the parts.

1 whole	10 equal parts	100 equal parts

  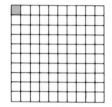

one whole ◊ 1.00   one tenth ◊ 0.1   one hundredth ◊ 0.01

Seven hundredths is written 0.07. If you press ⊡ 0 7 on a calculator, the screen will show 0.07 .

The place value chart below shows how decimals fit into our place value system. A **decimal point** is used to separate the whole numbers (ones, tens, and hundreds) from the decimals (tenths and hundredths).

hundreds	tens	ones	tenths	hundredths
		5	. 2	
		0	. 8	9
1	2	3	. 0	2

Look at the numbers shown in the chart.

5.2	Read:	*5 and 2 tenths*
0.89	Read:	*89 hundredths*
123.02	Read:	*123 and 2 hundredths*

CLASS EXERCISES

Complete.

1. 0.7 = ▓ tenths

0.07 = ▓ hundredths

2. 0.9 = ▓ tenths

0.09 = ▓ hundredths

3. 0.4 = ▓ tenths

0.04 = ▓ hundredths

4. 6.08 = ▓ and ▓ hundredths

5. 17.28 = ▓ and ▓ hundredths

PRACTICE

Write the decimal.

6. 8 and 2 tenths   7. 6 tenths   8. 4 and 1 tenth

9. 3 hundredths   10. 27 hundredths   11. 4 tenths

12. 5 and 49 hundredths   13. 329 and 7 tenths   14. 73 and 27 hundredths

15. 95 and 3 hundredths   16. 4 and 2 hundredths   17. 703 and 47 hundredths

18. 241 and 3 tenths   19. 3 and 70 hundredths   20. 71 and 20 hundredths

21. 2 and 8 hundredths   22. 6 hundredths   23. 892 and 7 hundredths

24. 177 and 2 tenths   25. 11 hundredths   26. 568 and 5 hundredths

Write the decimal that a calculator will show if you push these keys.

27. 1 · 0 6   28. · 1 9   29. · 2 8

30. 0 1 ·   31. 9 0 0 ·   32. · 1 2

CALCULATOR

PROBLEM SOLVING APPLICATIONS
Organizing Information

There are 10 vehicles parked in the rest area. Complete the table to show the number of vehicles named and then the decimal part for the vehicles named. For example: vehicles from Rhode Island, number 1, decimal 0.1.

	TYPE OF VEHICLE	NUMBER	DECIMAL
33.	car	?	?
34.	truck	?	?
35.	motorcycle	?	?
36.	California vehicles	?	?
37.	not from Florida	?	?
38.	cars from Kansas	?	?

PLACE VALUE TO HUNDRED-THOUSANDTHS

tens	ones		tenths	hundredths	thousandths	ten-thousandths	hundred-thousandths
	0	.	2	1	9		
	6	.	0	0	0	3	
1	1	.	3	7	6	5	4

Basketball free-throw results are given to the nearest thousandth.

Use the place value chart to the left to help you read the numbers in the chart.

Read: *219 thousandths*

Read: *6 and 3 ten-thousandths*

Read: *11 and 37,654 hundred-thousandths*

In 0.219, the 9 is in the thousandths' place. Its value is 9 thousandths.

In 6.0003, the 3 is in the ten-thousandths' place. Its value is 3 ten-thousandths.

In 11.37654, the 4 is in the hundred-thousandths' place. Its value is 4 hundred-thousandths.

You can read decimals in another way. The decimal 11.37654 can be read *eleven point three seven six five four.*

You can also write decimals in expanded form. This shows the place value of each digit in the number 0.8958.

$$0.8958 = 0.8 + 0.09 + 0.005 + 0.0008$$

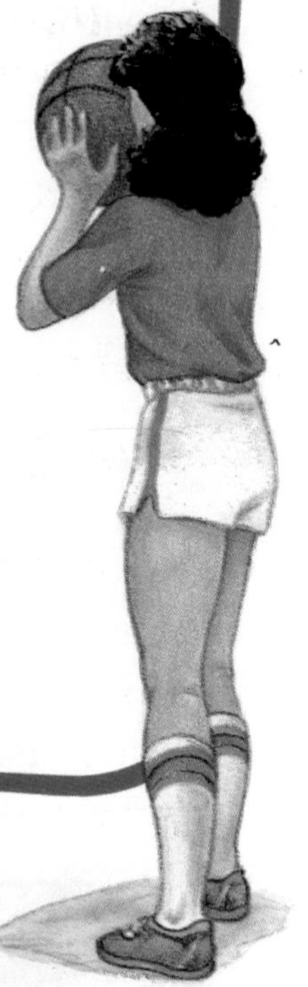

CLASS EXERCISES

Complete.

1. 0.3 = ▨ tenths
   0.37 = ▨ hundredths
   0.374 = ▨ thousandths

2. 0.9 = ▨ tenths
   0.91 = ▨ hundredths
   0.917 = ▨ thousandths

3. 0.25 = ▨ hundredths
   0.256 = ▨ thousandths
   0.2568 = ▨ ten-thousandths

4. 0.403 = ▨ thousandths
   0.4031 = ▨ ten-thousandths
   0.40316 = ▨ hundred-thousandths

PRACTICE

Write the value of the underlined digit.

5. 75.<u>8</u>   **6.** 78.3<u>2</u>   **7.** 4.56<u>8</u>2   **8.** 52.648<u>1</u>   **9.** 21.6038<u>7</u>

Write the decimal.

10. 6 and 123 thousandths   **11.** 2 and 41 hundredths

12. 3 and 4128 ten-thousandths   **13.** 427 thousandths

14. 64 hundredths   **15.** 5 and 5243 ten-thousandths

16. 47 and 241 thousandths   **17.** 52 and 20 hundredths

18. 59 and 104 ten-thousandths   **19.** 471 and 47 ten-thousandths

20. 621 hundred-thousandths   **21.** 89 and 28 thousandths

22. 16 and 16 hundredths   **23.** 5 and 5 hundred-thousandths

In the number 658.01492, what digit is in the place shown?

24. tens' place?   **25.** hundreds' place?   **26.** ten-thousandths' place?

27. tenths' place?   **28.** thousandths' place?   **29.** hundred-thousandths' place?

Write in expanded form.

30. 0.42   **31.** 0.659   **32.** 0.028   **33.** 0.1257

34. 1.5   **35.** 2.76   **36.** 12.0209   **37.** 1.70206

PROBLEM SOLVING APPLICATIONS
Open-Ended Problems

Use all the cards to solve.

38. Write two decimals with a 7 in the thousandths' place and a 2 in the ten-thousandths' place.

39. Write all the decimals you can make with a 7 in the tens' place and a 2 in the tenths' place.

40. Write all the decimals you can make with a 3 in the tenths' place and an 8 in the ones' place.

COMPARING AND ORDERING DECIMALS

You can write a zero after the last digit in a decimal without changing its value. The shaded squares to the right show that

$$0.4 = 0.40.$$

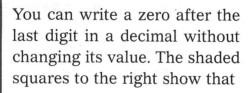
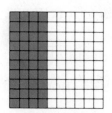

4 tenths = 40 hundredths
0.4 = 0.40

To compare 0.3 and 0.28, you can rewrite 0.3 as 0.30.

You can see from the shaded squares that

$0.30 > 0.28$ and $0.28 < 0.30$.

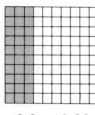
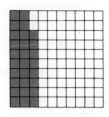

0.3 = 0.30   0.28

$0.3 > 0.28$

You can also write zeros to help you write a group of decimals in order from least to greatest.

1.9, 1.5, 1.65   The order from least to greatest is:
 ↓   ↓   ↓
1.90 1.50 1.65   1.5, 1.65, 1.9

 You should be able to compare decimals mentally by comparing the values of the digits in each place, beginning at the left.

CLASS EXERCISES

Write *true* or *false*.

1. $4.3 = 4.30$ **2.** $0.80 = 0.8$ **3.** $0.51 = 0.510$

4. $6.08 = 6.80$ **5.** $0.9 = 0.09$ **6.** $3.80 = 3.800$

7. $48.3 = 48.30$ **8.** $17.7 = 170.7$ **9.** $3.7 > 3.6$

10. $0.03 < 0.01$ **11.** $0.15 > 0.2$ **12.** $1.68 < 1.680$

PRACTICE

Write <, >, or = to compare the numbers.

13. 0.3 ▨ 0.4   **14.** 0.73 ▨ 0.71   **15.** 0.513 ▨ 0.519

16. 0.8 ▨ 0.80   **17.** 0.9 ▨ 0.76   **18.** 8.45 ▨ 0.967

19. 1.009 ▨ 0.8314   **20.** 123.5 ▨ 12.35   **21.** 5.35 ▨ 5.5

22. 17.35 ▨ 18.35   **23.** 0.1456 ▨ 0.15   **24.** 1.04 ▨ 1.0400

25. 1.23 ▨ 1.023   **26.** 17.38 ▨ 17.3791   **27.** 0.4 ▨ 0.384

28. 4.005 ▨ 4.01   **29.** 6.0189 ▨ 6.02   **30.** 10.090 ▨ 10.009

Order from least to greatest.

31. 2.4, 1.9, 2.6   **32.** 0.35, 0.62, 0.47   **33.** 2.2, 2.22, 2.202

34. 4.5, 3.95, 4.2, 4.19   **35.** 0.03, 0.029, 0.031   **36.** 1.10, 1.01, 1.011, 1.101

37. 6.75, 5.67, 7.65, 6.57, 7.56, 5.76

Estimate the answer.

38. 1986 + 7099   **39.** 1265 − 350

40. 640 + 222 + 798   **41.** 37,260 − 15,404

42. 78,012 + 46,500   **43.** 225,321 − 126,300

MIXED
REVIEW

PROBLEM SOLVING APPLICATIONS
Using Information from a Chart

Arrange the finishers in order from first to last place.

44. EVENT: LONG JUMP

STUDENT	DISTANCE IN METERS
David	3.78
Costa	4.02
George	3.90
James	4.10

45. EVENT: 80 METER HURDLES

STUDENT	TIME IN SECONDS
Sasha	26.806
Marie	28.371
Joanne	25.916
Leslie	26.842

ROUNDING DECIMALS

On one space voyage, astronauts traveled 102.25 million miles. You can say that they traveled *about* 102 million miles. You can round the decimal when you don't need a number as exact as 102.25 million.

You round decimals by using the same rules you use for rounding whole numbers.

EXACT NUMBER	ROUND TO THE NEAREST	DIGIT TO THE RIGHT	IS IT 5 OR MORE?	ROUND
36.73	whole number	7	Yes	up to 37
15.21	tenth	1	No	down to 15.2
4.903	hundredth	3	No	down to 4.90
73.8425	thousandth	5	Yes	up to 73.843

Rounded to the greatest place value, 0.635 is 0.6.

CLASS EXERCISES

Complete the chart.

	EXACT NUMBER	ROUND TO THE NEAREST	DIGIT TO THE RIGHT	IS IT 5 OR MORE?	ROUNDED
1.	3.7	whole number	7	Yes	?
2.	48.26	tenth	6	?	?
3.	0.342	hundredth	2	?	?
4.	0.6878	thousandth	8	?	?
5.	126.08	tenth	8	?	?
6.	37.003	hundredth	3	?	?
7.	19.61	whole number	6	?	?
8.	682.1105	thousandth	5	?	?

PRACTICE

Complete. Round the number to each place shown.

	NUMBER	THOUSANDTH	HUNDREDTH	TENTH	WHOLE NUMBER	TEN
9.	23.4792	?	?	?	?	?
10.	86.5555	?	?	?	?	?
11.	169.2468	?	?	?	?	?
12.	597.8352	?	?	?	?	?

Round to the greatest place value.

13. 1.2   **14.** 2.6   **15.** 229.5   **16.** 0.86   **17.** 10.291

18. 14.87   **19.** 0.14   **20.** 156.62   **21.** 24.072   **22.** 0.1882

★ **23.** Name five numbers that will round to 0.25.

★ **24.** Name five numbers that will round to 0.763.

PROBLEM SOLVING APPLICATIONS
Nonroutine

25. Round the decimal for each letter to the nearest hundredth. Use the code to complete the title of the picture.

A–0.045
B–0.1990
E–0.073
F–0.4346
G–0.181
H–0.435
I–0.3831

L–0.082
M–0.3901
N–0.273
O–0.286
R–0.043
S–0.085
U–0.1932

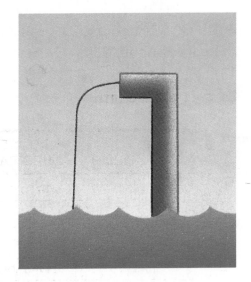

0.09 0.05 0.38 0.08 0.29 0.04 0.43 0.38 0.09 0.44 0.38 0.27 0.18

0.43 0.04 0.29 0.39 0.05 0.09 0.19 0.20 0.39 0.05 0.04 0.38 0.27 0.07

ESTIMATING DECIMAL SUMS AND DIFFERENCES

In the Bayville Annual Model Airplane Trials, Sheila's plane traveled a distance of 151.3 m and then 132.8 m. About how far did it travel altogether?

For a quick mental estimate of the total distance, round each addend to its greatest place value. Then add the rounded numbers.

$$
\begin{array}{rcr}
151.3 \text{ m} & \Diamond & 200 \text{ m} \\
+ \ 132.8 \text{ m} & \Diamond & + \ 100 \text{ m} \\
\hline
& & 300 \text{ m}
\end{array}
$$

The plane traveled about 300 m altogether.

If you need a closer estimate, here is another method. Use the **front-end** digits to form your addends and then adjust as shown below. Use this method for subtraction, too.

Estimate 151.3 + 132.8.

Think: 100 + 100 = 200

51.3 + 32.8 is about 80.
The sum is about 280.

Estimate $81.40 − $24.65.

Think: $80 − $20 = $60

Subtract more from the estimate since $4.65 > $1.40. The difference is about $56.

CLASS EXERCISES

Are the numbers rounded correctly? Write *yes* or *no*. If not, give the correct rounded numbers. (Round to the nearest whole number.)

1.
$$
\begin{array}{rcr}
6.5 & \Diamond & 7 \\
+ \ 3.1 & \Diamond & + \ 3 \\
\hline
& & 10
\end{array}
$$

2.
$$
\begin{array}{rcr}
9.46 & \Diamond & 10 \\
+ \ 6.8 & \Diamond & + \ 7 \\
\hline
& & 17
\end{array}
$$

3.
$$
\begin{array}{rcr}
17.6 & \Diamond & 17 \\
- \ 4.31 & \Diamond & - \ 5 \\
\hline
& & 12
\end{array}
$$

4.
$$
\begin{array}{rcr}
0.99 & \Diamond & 1 \\
+ \ 1.156 & \Diamond & + \ 2 \\
\hline
& & 3
\end{array}
$$

5.
$$
\begin{array}{rcr}
76.11 & \Diamond & 76 \\
- \ 18.99 & \Diamond & - \ 19 \\
\hline
& & 57
\end{array}
$$

6.
$$
\begin{array}{rcr}
437.2 & \Diamond & 438 \\
- \ 288.9 & \Diamond & - \ 289 \\
\hline
& & 149
\end{array}
$$

PRACTICE

Round to the greatest place value. Then estimate the answer.

7. 5.36
  + 2.75

8. 8.98
  − 4.79

9. 10.29
  + 3.471

10. 11.87
  − 5.62

11. 20.01
  + 11.22

12. 6.83
  + 12.376

13. 6.35
  + 10.901

14. 85.176
  + 5.617

15. 13.9
  − 6.91

16. 12.75
  − 2.498

Estimate using front-end estimation.

17. 15.75
  + 42.8

18. 815.75
  + 360.2

19. 457.8
  − 349.7

20. 6637.88
  + 2781.43

21. 4578.25
  − 3215.9

PROBLEM SOLVING APPLICATIONS
Estimating the Answer

Solve.

22. In 3 trials one plane traveled 231.6 m, 179.9 m, and 268.7 m. About how far did it travel in all?

23. Brian's plane costs $46.75 and Patti's plane costs $34.25. About how much do both planes cost?

24. The trial planes traveled 2947.80 m. The planes in the finals traveled 4306.75 m. About how much less did the trial planes travel?

★ 25. If a plane travels about 180 mi on each trial flight, about how many trials will it take to go a distance of 3000 mi?

CHECKPOINT 1

Write the decimal. (pages 118–121)

1. 4 tenths   2. 17 hundredths

Order from least to greatest. (pages 122–123)

3. 4.107, 4.9, 4.0176, 4.0109

Round each to the nearest tenth, hundredth, and thousandth. (pages 124–125)

4. 4.0267   5. 268.70049

Estimate the answer. (pages 126–127)

6. 468.9 + 143.1 7. 37.64 − 24.9

Extra Practice on page 428

PROBLEM SOLVING
Strategy: Too Much or Too Little
Information

1. Understand
2. Plan
3. Work
4. Answer/ Check

Sometimes a problem contains more information than you need to know in order to solve it. For example:

The annual budget for the town of Lowton is 14.35 million dollars. $1.2 million is spent on the town's recreation program. Another $7.25 million is spent for education. About how much more is spent for education than for recreation?

In order to solve the problem, you need to know how much is spent for recreation and for education. You do *not* need to know the annual budget. This problem contains **too much** information.

Estimate to determine the answer.

$$\begin{array}{r} \$7.25 \text{ million} \longrightarrow \$7 \text{ million} \\ - \ 1.2 \ \ \text{million} \longrightarrow - \ 1 \text{ million} \\ \hline \$6 \text{ million} \end{array}$$

About $6 million more is spent for education.

Here is another problem.

How much more did Lowton spend on recreation last year? You cannot solve this problem because you have **too little** information.

CLASS EXERCISES

Tell whether the problem contains too much or too little information. State the extra information.

1. Police officers in Lowton were paid $482.50 per week to start. Recently, that amount was raised. How much do the officers earn now as a starting salary?

2. The main road in Lowton is 14.75 km long and is being repaved. It has cost $2.5 million to repave 11.5 km so far. How much of the road is left to repave?

PRACTICE

If the problem contains too little information, tell what you need to know. If the problem contains too much information, write the extra information and estimate to answer.

ESTIMATE

3. The town of Lowton has a population of 75.2 thousand. Highland, which is 12.8 km south of Lowton, has a population of 39.2 thousand. About how much greater is the population of Lowton?

4. Each spring Lowton sponsors a marathon. There are 213 runners entered in this year's race. About how many more runners entered this year than last?

Use the information in the picture. If the problem contains too little information, tell what you need to know. If the problem contains too much information, write the extra information and solve the problem.

HIGHLAND PUBLIC LIBRARY
USED BOOK SALE

Kind	Price
General Hardcovers	$3.75 each
Paperbacks	$1.25 each
Reference Books	$6.50 each

Buy 3 of a kind → Get 1 FREE of same kind

5. Chul bought 2 hardcover books. How much did he save by buying the hardcover books used, instead of new?

6. Norma Gibbs purchased a set of encyclopedias, 5 hardcover books, and 2 paperbacks. In what amount should she write out her check?

7. Kim had $20.00 to spend on books. She bought 1 reference book, which cost $18.75 when new. She also bought 2 paperbacks. Does Kim have any money left? Estimate to answer.

★ 8. Laura Ruscetta went to the sale with $100. She bought a 10-book set of encyclopedias, 3 hardcover books, and 9 paperbacks. How many books did she take home from the sale?

ADDITION OF DECIMALS

Earl ran 10.75 km this morning. Yesterday he ran 12.5 km. How many kilometers did he run in all?

To determine how far Earl ran, add. You add decimals just as you add whole numbers. Be sure to line up the decimal point in the answer with the decimal point in the addends.

$$
\begin{array}{r}
10.75 \text{ km} \\
+ 12.50 \text{ km} \\
\hline
23.25 \text{ km}
\end{array}
$$

You may wish to write a zero so that both addends have the same number of decimal places.

Earl ran 23.25 km in all.

 You can estimate to determine if your answer is reasonable. Since 10.75 + 12.5 is about 10 + 10, your answer of 23.25 seems reasonable.

Here are some other addition examples.

$$
\begin{array}{r}
82.43 \\
+ 65.96 \\
\hline
148.39
\end{array}
\qquad
\begin{array}{r}
14.02 \\
9.3 \\
+ 75.15 \\
\hline
98.47
\end{array}
$$

CLASS EXERCISES

Are the decimal points lined up correctly? Write *yes* or *no*.

1. $\begin{array}{r} 0.3 \\ + 0.5 \\ \hline \end{array}$
2. $\begin{array}{r} 0.8 \\ + \ \ 0.8 \\ \hline \end{array}$
3. $\begin{array}{r} 0.9 \\ + \ \ \ 0.41 \\ \hline \end{array}$
4. $\begin{array}{r} 27.3 \\ + 48.5 \\ \hline \end{array}$
5. $\begin{array}{r} 7.46 \\ + 2.9 \\ \hline \end{array}$

6. $\begin{array}{r} 11.3 \\ + \ \ 2.61 \\ \hline \end{array}$
7. $\begin{array}{r} 7.8 \\ + 1.45 \\ \hline \end{array}$
8. $\begin{array}{r} 17.9 \\ + 6.7 \\ \hline \end{array}$
9. $\begin{array}{r} 4.68 \\ + \ \ 7.7 \\ \hline \end{array}$
10. $\begin{array}{r} 324.5 \\ + 468.9 \\ \hline \end{array}$

PRACTICE

Add.

11. $\begin{array}{r} 3.8 \\ + 4.7 \\ \hline \end{array}$
12. $\begin{array}{r} 4.12 \\ + 6.38 \\ \hline \end{array}$
13. $\begin{array}{r} 5.29 \\ + 6.4 \\ \hline \end{array}$
14. $\begin{array}{r} 4.129 \\ + 47.384 \\ \hline \end{array}$
15. $\begin{array}{r} 4.1497 \\ + 2.3786 \\ \hline \end{array}$

16.	8.057	17.	12.3	18.	7.098	19.	33.981	20.	13.6546
	+ 59.128		+ 324.7		+ 6.98		+ 4.83		+ 2.39

21.	4.8	22.	8.23	23.	7.8	24.	3.4914	25.	28.97
	2.7		3.4		3.621		7.0057		3.2
	+ 4.9		+ 7.01		+ 6.91		2.421		4.39
							+ 3.2846		+ 11.68

26. 4.0 + 0.623 **27.** 4.8 + 3.6 + 2.41 **28.** 8.37 + 9.84 + 17.994

Estimate the sum. Tell if the given answer is reasonable. Write *yes* or *no*.

ESTIMATE

29.	82.19	30.	43.16	31.	221.95	32.	891.7
	+ 45.02		+ 9.9		+ 505.1		+ 188.4
	127.21		53.06		327.05		1080.1

PROBLEM SOLVING APPLICATIONS
Too Much Information

Solve.

33. Carla hiked 14.4 km on Monday and 14.25 km on Thursday. How far did she hike on the two days?

34. David hiked 7.5 km in 1.2 h. He hiked 3.7 km more in 0.6 h. How far did he hike?

35. The Skyward Hiking Club members hiked for a total of 56.74 h this week. The Bird's Eye Club hiked for a total of 42.06 h this week. Which club hiked more?

★ **36.** The trail to the top of Mt. Moore is 10.8 km long. After 2 h, Phillip had hiked 7.2 km. About how much longer will it take him to reach the top?

SUBTRACTION OF DECIMALS

The distance between Duran and Fords is 175.7 km. The distance between Fords and Amboy is 207.25 km. How much farther is it from Fords to Amboy than from Duran to Fords?

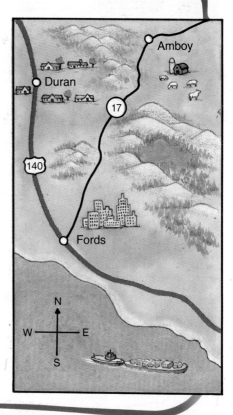

Subtract to determine the answer. Remember to line up the decimal points.

```
  207 | 25
− 175 | 70
───────────
   31 | 55
```

You may wish to write a zero so that both numbers have the same number of decimal places.

It is 31.55 km farther.

Here are some other examples.

```
  48 | 26        3 | 70        7 | 00
−  5 | 90      − 0 | 29      − 5 | 67
───────────    ───────────    ───────────
  42 | 36        3 | 41        1 | 33
```

CLASS EXERCISES

Are the decimal points lined up correctly? Write *yes* or *no*.

1.	2.	3.	4.	5.
0.8 − 0.5	17.8 − 1.5	46.3 − 27.8	92.81 − 24.8	4.81 − 2.1

PRACTICE

Subtract.

6.	7.	8.	9.	10.
2.3 − 1.6	17.8 − 9.7	23.2 − 4.6	16.8 − 7.9	67.3 − 43.6

11.	12.	13.	14.	15.
3.82 − 1.2	7.38 − 2.9	13.3 − 0.6	9.81 − 3.9	41.07 − 2.68

16.	17.	18.	19.	20.
4.38 − 0.09	4.27 − 1.836	2.483 − 1.97	16.08 − 3.751	179.4 − 59.6

21. 3.926 − 1.845   **22.** 9.831 − 6.060   **23.** 9.005 − 2.346   **24.** 163 − 76.35

25. 75 − 1.09   **26.** 7.5 − 1.239   **27.** 83 − 7.2   **28.** 37.9 − 28.8

29. 9.483 − 2.68   **30.** 48.41 − 22.4   **31.** 266 − 13.75   **32.** 0.308 − 0.02

Write the answer.

33. $47.89
    ×64

34. 62)‾50476‾

35. 5076
    ×724

MIXED REVIEW

36. 30,701 ÷ 27   **37.** 781 × $60.27   **38.** 76,105 ÷ 398

PROBLEM SOLVING APPLICATIONS
Consumer Applications

Which product costs less if the coupon is used?
Tell how much less.

39. Happy Pup Dog Food $1.59
Doggie Burgers Dog Food $1.69

40. Best Broccoli and Cheese $3.75
Best Green Beans $3.20

41. Mountain Swiss $2.98
Tasty Cheddar $2.69

42. Freshtime Apple Juice $1.39
Chuckles Apple Juice $1.59

43. Whoosh Detergent $3.15
Losuds Detergent $2.89

★ **44.** Best Bet Clam Chowder $.89
Sea Star Clam Chowder $.75

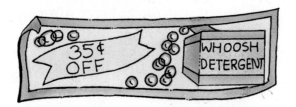

PROBLEM SOLVING
Strategy: Organizing Information in a Table

1. Understand
2. Plan
3. Work
4. Answer/Check

It is often necessary to arrange information in an organized way. If you have a checking account, keeping a checkbook record is a way of organizing information. It's important to record the checks you write and the deposits you make.

DATE	CHECK NUMBER	CHECKS OR DEPOSITS	AMOUNT OF CHECK	✓	AMOUNT OF DEPOSIT	BALANCE
		BALANCE BROUGHT FORWARD →				289 13
12/1	325	Village Market	18 45			270 68
12/7	326	Edwards Electric	62 89			207 79
12/10		Deposit			165 85	373 64
12/13	327	Dr. Tracy (dentist)	32 00			341 64
12/22		Deposit			75 00	416 64
12/27	328	Brighton Lumber	84 12			?
12/27	329	Alpha Airlines	119 65			?
1/5		Deposit			165 85	?

Subtract when you write a check.

$289.13	◊ balance
− 18.45	◊ check number 325
$270.68	◊ new balance

Add when you make a deposit.

$341.64	◊ balance
+ 75.00	◊ deposit of 12/22
$416.64	◊ new balance

CLASS EXERCISES

Use the checkbook record above.

1. What was the amount of the check to Edwards Electric?

2. What was the amount of the deposit made on December 10th?

3. What was the balance before check number 327 was written?

4. What was the balance after check number 326 was written?

5. To whom was check number 325 made out?

6. What was the amount of the check written to Dr. Tracy?

PRACTICE

Use the checkbook record below. Write the balance after
the check or deposit.

	DATE	CHECK NUMBER	CHECKS OR DEPOSITS	AMOUNT OF CHECK	✓	AMOUNT OF DEPOSIT	BALANCE
			BALANCE BROUGHT FORWARD →				839 02
7.	6/17	541	Last National Bank	315 27			?
8.	6/20	542	Heat Wave Insulation	75 89			?
9.	6/23	543	Sea Breeze Health Club	125 00			?
10.	6/25		Deposit			289 75	?
11.	6/27	544	A-1 Garage	49 75			?
12.	6/30		Deposit			150 00	?

Solve.

13. Use the information to the right to make a checkbook record like the one above. The beginning balance is $375.17. What was the balance at the end of the month?

Checks: 3/2 $28.45, 3/5 $50.00, 3/7 $125.88, 3/8 $89.99, 3/16 $175.80, 3/18 $17.65, 3/20 $9.99, 3/24 $235.00.
Deposits: 3/7 $250.00, 3/10 $64.50, 3/15 $250.00, 3/21 $250.00.

CHECKPOINT 2

Write *too much* or *too little* information. Solve for too much. (*pages 128–129*)

1. At a sale Kate bought a cassette for $6.99 and a book for $3.50. The book originally cost $5.95. How much did Kate spend at the sale?

Write the answer. (*pages 130–133*)

2. 5.0167 + 385.01

3. 457.1 − 97.98

4. 1.00792 − 0.7656

Complete. (*pages 134–135*)

AMOUNT OF CHECK	✓	AMOUNT OF DEPOSIT	BALANCE
BALANCE BROUGHT FORWARD →			361 87
5. 47 80			?
6.		118 00	?
7. 298 50			?

Extra Practice on page 428

Write the decimal. *(pages 118–121)*

1. 3 and 21 hundredths

2. 5 and 577 thousandths

3. 614 ten-thousandths

4. 5 hundred-thousandths

Order the numbers from least to greatest. *(pages 122–123)*

5. 4.5, 3.5, 4.3

6. 0.73, 0.69, 0.81

7. 2.20, 2.02, 2.022, 2.202

Estimate the sum or difference. *(pages 124–127)*

8. $\begin{aligned} 7.41 \\ + 3.64 \end{aligned}$

9. $\begin{aligned} 9.81 \\ - 4.71 \end{aligned}$

10. $\begin{aligned} 63.15 \\ + 6.807 \end{aligned}$

11. $\begin{aligned} 18.46 \\ - 7.644 \end{aligned}$

Solve. If there is not enough information, write *too little.*
(pages 128–129)

12. Al wants to plant 12 rows of corn. Seed costs $1.25 a package. How much does Al need for the seed?

13. Alex drove 22.4 km to the seed store and then 14.35 km to the hardware store. He spent $35.83. Then he drove 29.45 km home. About how far did Alex drive?

Write the answer. *(pages 130–133)*

14. $\begin{aligned} 6.13 \\ + 7.37 \end{aligned}$

15. $\begin{aligned} 44.524 \\ + 3.81 \end{aligned}$

16. $\begin{aligned} 19.9 \\ - 5.7 \end{aligned}$

17. $\begin{aligned} 388.3 \\ - 58.5 \end{aligned}$

Organize the information to solve the problem.
(pages 134–135)

18. Tim has a balance of $372.46. He writes checks for $35.21 and for $18.90. He has a service charge of $2.00. What is his balance now?

19. Liz has a balance of $415.52. She deposits $64.00. She writes checks for $36.15, $122.00, and $51.88. What is her balance now?

Extra Practice on page 429

MATHEMATICS and SCIENCE

A barometer measures air pressure. Weather forecasters use changes in air pressure to predict changes in the weather. Barometer readings are often expressed in hundredths of inches.

ARE YOU UNDER PRESSURE?

1. A barometer in Topeka, Kansas, rose 0.23 in. from 29.92 in. A barometer in St. Louis, Missouri, fell 0.17 in. from 30.22 in. Which city's reading is shown on the barometer at the right?

2. A barometer reading above 30.30 in. usually means fair weather. A reading of 29.80 in. or below usually means a storm. What is your forecast if a barometer is 29.75 in. and falling?

3. A rapid rise on a barometer is 0.05 in. or more in 3 h or less. A barometer rose from 29.98 in. to 30.02 in. between 8:30 A.M. and 11:30 A.M.. Was this a rapid rise?

4. On Monday a barometer reading was 30.12 in. It fell 0.16 in. on Tuesday and the weather became rainy. It rose 0.21 in. on Wednesday as the weather cleared. What was Wednesday's barometer reading?

★5. Both *mercury* and *aneroid* barometers are used to measure air pressure. Find out how they work.

Enrichment

Each card has a number, either 3, 6, or 7, on the back. Can you use the clues below to find out which number is on which card?

Clue A. The number on ● is less than the number on ▲.

Clue B. The number on ★ is an odd number.

Clue C. The number on ● is not an even number.

To solve the problem, make a chart showing all the possibilities. Make an X in each box as the possibilities are eliminated.

	★	▲	○
3		X	
6	X		X
7			X

From Clue A you know that 7 is not on ● and 3 is not on ▲.

From Clue B you know that 6 is not on ★.

From Clue C you know that 6 is not on ●.

Since ● has all possibilities crossed out except one, 3 is on ●. You can see that 6 is on ▲ so 7 must be on ★.

Make a chart to solve the problem.

1. Each card has the number 4, 8, or 12 on the back. Use the clues to decide which number is on which card.

   a. The number on ■ is greater than the number on ⬡.
   b. The number on ☾ evenly divides the number on ⬡.

2. Each card has the number 12, 15, 18, or 20 on the back. Use the clues to decide which number is on which card.

   a. The number on 🌶 is less than the number on 🥕.
   b. The number on 🍋 is greater than the number on 🍎.
   c. The numbers on 🥕 and 🍎 can be evenly divided by 5.

LOGIC

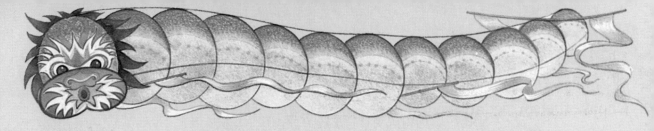

Solve.

3. Sue Brown, Mary Green, and Jane Blue are flying brown, green, and blue kites. What color kite is each girl flying? You have these clues.

   a. No girl's kite color is the same as her name color.

   b. Sue Brown is not flying a green kite.

5. The president, vice-president, and treasurer of a company are Bob White, Sue Adams, and Rita Ramos. Which job does each person hold? You have these clues.

   a. The president has the highest salary.

   b. Bob White earns less than Sue Adams.

   c. The treasurer is the brother-in-law of Rita Ramos.

   d. The president has no brothers or sisters.

4. Sonya, Richard, Caitlin, and Dylan are artists. Each is a writer, dancer, painter, or singer. Which person is which? You have these clues.

   a. Sonya and Caitlin have seen the singer perform.

   b. Both Richard and the writer have portraits done by the painter.

   c. The writer has written biographies of both Dylan and Sonya.

   d. Sonya has never met Caitlin.

6. Greg, Joanne, Sheryl, and Jamie work in the same office building. Each is an engineer, architect, accountant, or private detective. Which person has which job? You have these clues.

   a. Sheryl is younger than Jamie but older than the accountant.

   b. The engineer earns more than either Greg or Jamie.

   c. The detective is the oldest and Joanne is the youngest.

   d. The accountant makes the most money and Greg makes more than the detective.

CUMULATIVE REVIEW

Choose the correct answer. Write *a, b, c,* or *d.*

Find the answer.

1. $48.90
   +   7.65

a. $41.25
b. $45.55
c. $46.55
d. none of these

2. 7118
   + 937

a. 8055
b. 8155
c. 8145
d. none of these

3. $2314.51
   +   447.82

a. $2751.33
b. $2762.33
c. $2761.33
d. none of these

4. 33
   ×5

a. 155
b. 255
c. 165
d. none of these

5. 802
   ×7

a. 564
b. 5614
c. 5604
d. none of these

6. 1464
   ×8

a. 8612
b. 11,612
c. 8282
d. none of these

Which is the best estimate?

7. $6.65
   + 3.40

a. $3
b. $4
c. $8
d. $10

8. $5.73
   ×41

a. $240.00
b. $300.00
c. $24.00
d. $30.00

9. 606
   ×177

a. 60,000
b. 140,000
c. 120,000
d. 12,000

Draw a picture to help you solve the problem.

10. You have a 16 in. piece of wood. You want to cut it so that one piece is 5 in. longer than the other. How long will each piece be?

a. 10 in. and 6 in.
b. 11 in. and 5 in.
c. 16 in. and 21 in.
d. none of these

11. The decorator is buying curtains. The color choices are blue, gold, or white. The fabric choices are rayon, cotton, or nylon. How many different choices are there?

a. 9
b. 8
c. 6
d. none of these

Find the answer.

12. 61
　　$\times 35$

a. 1135
b. 2035
c. 2135
d. none of these

13. 4747
　　$\times 28$

a. 132,816
b. 131,816
c. 131,916
d. none of these

14. 9033
　　$\times 464$

a. 4,191,212
b. 4,201,312
c. 4,191,312
d. none of these

15. 4^2

a. 6
b. 16
c. 8
d. none of these

16. 6^3

a. 18
b. 216
c. 36
d. none of these

17. 8^1

a. 8
b. 16
c. 0
d. none of these

18. $7\overline{)44}$

a. 6 R2
b. 7 R2
c. 6
d. none of these

19. $6\overline{)200}$

a. 33 R3
b. 30 R2
c. 33 R2
d. none of these

20. $8\overline{)3299}$

a. 49 R3
b. 412 R3
c. 312 R3
d. none of these

LANGUAGE and VOCABULARY REVIEW

Choose the correct word to complete each sentence.

1. When you combine addends, the answer is the (sum, difference).

2. In writing amounts of money, you place a (dollar sign, decimal point) between the dollars and cents.

3. When you write 2,500,000 for two million, five hundred thousand, you are writing the number in (expanded form, standard form).

4. When something is divided into 1000 equal parts, each part is a (hundredth, thousandth).

BINARY CODE

All of the information that is given to the computer is changed to binary code.

Binary code uses base two numeration to represent letters, numbers, and symbols. You use the digits zero and one to write numbers in base two. In binary code each digit is called a **bit**.

$$0 \nwarrow \quad \nearrow 1$$

bit

In some computers, the binary code is written by putting together eight bits. The eight bits are called a **byte.**

$$\underbrace{0\ 1\ 0\ 0\ 0\ 1\ 0\ 0}_{\text{byte}}$$

This is the binary code for D.

Each character on the keyboard has been assigned a decimal number by the manufacturer. The decimal number is changed to binary code in the computer.

In base two the value of each place is a power of two.

The table below shows the binary code for several characters.

CHARACTER	DECIMAL NUMBER	2^7	2^6	2^5	2^4	2^3	2^2	2^1	
		128	64	32	16	8	4	2	1
A	65	0	1	0	0	0	0	0	1
P	80	0	1	0	1	0	0	0	0
3	51	0	0	1	1	0	0	1	1
+	43	0	0	1	0	1	0	1	1

Find the decimal number for each character.

1. >; 00111110

2. H; 01001000

3. 7; 00110111

4. F; 01000110

5. d; 01100100

6. <; 00111100

7. W; 01110111

8. Q; 01010001

9. 1; 01001001

6

A freighter has been loaded with 1250 stacks of lumber, each of which weighs about 0.8 tons. Does the cargo of lumber weigh about 1000 tons?

MULTIPLICATION AND DIVISION OF DECIMALS

ESTIMATING DECIMAL PRODUCTS

Kevin bought 6 decals that cost $.89 each from states he visited. Did he spend more than $5.00?

Kevin estimates that he spent more than $5.00. He used these rules to estimate:

- Round a number that has more than one digit.
- Round the number to its greatest place value.

Since Kevin rounded *up*, his estimate is more than he spent.

Look at these examples.

$$\begin{array}{r} 1.8 \\ \times 6.3 \\ \hline \end{array} \Rightarrow \begin{array}{r} 2 \\ \times 6 \\ \hline 12 \end{array} \qquad \begin{array}{r} 48.72 \\ \times 2.78 \\ \hline \end{array} \Rightarrow \begin{array}{r} 50 \\ \times 3 \\ \hline 150 \end{array}$$

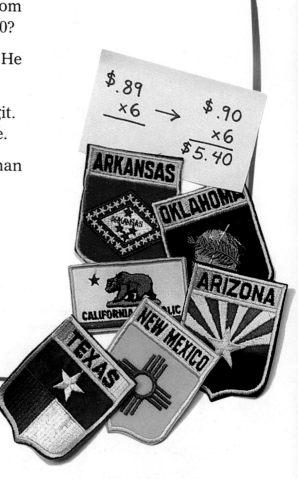

$$\begin{array}{r} \$.89 \\ \times 6 \\ \hline \end{array} \rightarrow \begin{array}{r} \$.90 \\ \times 6 \\ \hline \$5.40 \end{array}$$

CLASS EXERCISES

Estimate the product.

1.
$$\begin{array}{r} 12 \\ \times 1.8 \\ \hline \end{array} \Rightarrow \begin{array}{r} 10 \\ \times 2 \\ \hline \blacksquare \end{array}$$

2.
$$\begin{array}{r} 3.76 \\ \times 24 \\ \hline \end{array} \Rightarrow \begin{array}{r} \blacksquare \\ \times 20 \\ \hline \blacksquare \end{array}$$

3.
$$\begin{array}{r} 8.45 \\ \times 9 \\ \hline \end{array} \Rightarrow \begin{array}{r} \blacksquare \\ \times 9 \\ \hline \blacksquare \end{array}$$

4.
$$\begin{array}{r} 3.9 \\ \times 2.1 \\ \hline \end{array} \Rightarrow \begin{array}{r} \blacksquare \\ \times \blacksquare \\ \hline \blacksquare \end{array}$$

5.
$$\begin{array}{r} 7.65 \\ \times 3.3 \\ \hline \end{array} \Rightarrow \begin{array}{r} \blacksquare \\ \times \blacksquare \\ \hline \blacksquare \end{array}$$

6.
$$\begin{array}{r} 23.79 \\ \times 42.25 \\ \hline \end{array} \Rightarrow \begin{array}{r} \blacksquare \\ \times \blacksquare \\ \hline \blacksquare \end{array}$$

7. **Think:** If you round both factors down, will the estimated product be greater than or less than the actual product? Explain.

PRACTICE

Estimate the product.

8. 3.4 ×4.3	**9.** 2.68 ×3.9	**10.** 20.40 ×6.6	**11.** 1.08 ×3.78	**12.** 18.12 ×5.9
13. 217 ×3.8	**14.** 86.5 ×4.85	**15.** 93.486 ×1.59	**16.** 436.7 ×29.3	**17.** 53.78 ×53.78
18. 6.8 ×9.4	**19.** 10.7 ×3.2	**20.** 18.3 ×4.1	**21.** 5.4 ×9.8	**22.** 19.09 ×6.4
23. 74.98 ×9.5	**24.** 950.1 ×19.2	**25.** 3.768 ×18.64	**26.** 1.547 ×27.8	**27.** 876.14 ×49.01

PROBLEM SOLVING APPLICATIONS
Using Estimation

The *exchange rate* determines how much of the local money a traveler visiting another country would get for $1 of U.S. currency. For example, if you were in Sweden recently, you could exchange $1 for 8.805 Swedish kronor.

Use the table to estimate the amount of local currency you would get for the dollar amount given.

28. Francs for $200?

29. Shekels for $20?

30. Rupees for $600?

31. Pesos for $80?

32. Riyals for $1000?

33. Francs for $2000?

RECENT EXCHANGE RATES

COUNTRY	MONEY USED	DOLLAR VALUE IN LOCAL CURRENCY
Colombia	Peso	96.15
France	Franc	9.465
Israel	Shekel	596.1
Saudi Arabia	Riyal	3.56
Pakistan	Rupee	14.78

MULTIPLYING DECIMALS BY WHOLE NUMBERS

When you multiply a decimal by a whole number, the product will have the same number of decimal places as the decimal. Look at the examples below to see why this happens. Remember, you can think of multiplication as repeated addition.

$$\begin{array}{r} 3.8 \\ 3.8 \\ 3.8 \\ + 3.8 \\ \hline 15.2 \end{array}$$

$$\begin{array}{r} 3.8 \\ \times 4 \\ \hline 15.2 \end{array}$$ ◁ 1 decimal place

◁ 1 decimal place

$$\begin{array}{r} 47.439 \\ 47.439 \\ + 47.439 \\ \hline 142.317 \end{array}$$

$$\begin{array}{r} 47.439 \\ \times 3 \\ \hline 142.317 \end{array}$$ ◁ 3 decimal places

◁ 3 decimal places

E When several addends cluster around the same number, you can estimate the sum by multiplying. For example, these addends are all close to $1.50:

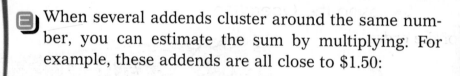

$1.47 + $1.53 + $1.57 + $1.42 ⇨

$$\begin{array}{r} \$1.50 \\ \times 4 \\ \hline \end{array}$$

Estimated sum ⇨ $6.00

CLASS EXERCISES

Multiply.

1.
$$\begin{array}{r} 24 \\ \times 6 \\ \hline \end{array}$$
$$\begin{array}{r} 2.4 \\ \times 6 \\ \hline \end{array}$$
$$\begin{array}{r} 0.24 \\ \times 6 \\ \hline \end{array}$$

2.
$$\begin{array}{r} 32 \\ \times 7 \\ \hline \end{array}$$
$$\begin{array}{r} 3.2 \\ \times 7 \\ \hline \end{array}$$
$$\begin{array}{r} 0.32 \\ \times 7 \\ \hline \end{array}$$

3.
$$\begin{array}{r} 543.1 \\ \times 2 \\ \hline \end{array}$$
$$\begin{array}{r} 54.31 \\ \times 2 \\ \hline \end{array}$$
$$\begin{array}{r} 5.431 \\ \times 2 \\ \hline \end{array}$$

4.
$$\begin{array}{r} 45 \\ \times 36 \\ \hline \end{array}$$
$$\begin{array}{r} 4.5 \\ \times 36 \\ \hline \end{array}$$
$$\begin{array}{r} 0.45 \\ \times 36 \\ \hline \end{array}$$

PRACTICE

Multiply.

5. 8.7
×4

6. 17.8
×9

7. 37.6
×8

8. $27.84
×3

9. 72.69
×5

10. 7.9
×41

11. 41.6
×73

12. $.87
×62

13. 55.45
×25

14. 278.1
×37

15. 78.3
×823

16. 68.4
×946

17. $39.44
×125

18. 6.472
×232

19. 8.119
×349

20. 24.71
×5334

21. 4.123
×6247

22. 19.8
×5641

23. 5.981
×9056

24. 7.247
×6617

Multiply to estimate the sum.

25. $.53 + $.48 + $.51

26. 23.5 + 24.4 + 24 + 23.8

27. 1.19 + 1.24 + 1.16 + 1.22

28. $7.01 + $6.89 + $7.23

ESTIMATE

PROBLEM SOLVING APPLICATIONS
Choosing the Operation

Determine the cost of the order.

29. 6 Colossal Clubs

30. 1 Burly Beef sandwich and 1 Super Soup

31. 5 orders of the Cheese Choice

32. 7 Titan Tunas

33. 1 Chunky Chicken sandwich, 1 Super Soup, 1 Spinach Salad, 1 milk

★ **34.** The Magicians' Club is meeting at Food Glorious Food. Each of the 12 members orders Chunky Chicken, Spinach Salad, and milk. Is $100.00 enough to pay the bill?

MENU

SANDWICHES
Titan Tuna $3.65
Colossal Club $4.35
Burly Beef $3.95
Chunky Chicken $5.60
Huge Ham and Cheese $4.60

SIDE ORDERS
Super Soup $1.25
Spinach Salad $2.75
Veggies and Dip $3.85
Cheese Choice $2.75

DRINKS
Milk . . . . $.85
Juice . . . . $.95

MULTIPLYING DECIMALS

The model shows what happens when you multiply decimals.

5 tenths
0.5

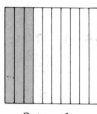

3 tenths
0.3

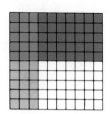

The green part
is 15 hundredths.
0.3 of 0.5 is 0.15

You can see that when you multiply tenths by tenths the product is hundredths.

$$0.3 \times 0.5 = 0.15$$

When you multiply hundredths by tenths the product is thousandths.

$$1.2 \times 0.16 = 0.192$$

The number of decimal places in a product is the sum of the number of decimal places in the factors.

Look at these examples.

```
  4.116  ——  3 decimal places
    ×3   ——  + 0 decimal places
 12.348  ——  3 decimal places
```

```
  417.6  ——  1 decimal place
 ×0.48   ——  + 2 decimal places
200.448  ——  3 decimal places
```

 You can use a calculator to multiply decimals. Be sure to enter the decimal point by pressing $\boxed{\cdot}$. Check the position of the decimal point in the answer.

CLASS EXERCISES

Which is the product? Write a or b.

1. 0.4×6.1
  a. 2.44
  b. 24.4

2. 1.7×0.33
  a. 56.1
  b. 0.561

3. 10.2×1.11
  a. 11.322
  b. 113.22

4. 1.5×5.5
  a. 8.25
  b. 0.825

PRACTICE

Multiply.

5. 0.8×0.9

6. 5.1×0.3

7. 7.2×0.24

8. 0.8×0.35

9. 0.2×15.3

10. 0.05×4.6

11. 213.1×0.01

12. 1.2×0.11

13.
$$\begin{array}{r} 1.2 \\ \times 2.3 \\ \hline \end{array}$$

14.
$$\begin{array}{r} 3.2 \\ \times 0.8 \\ \hline \end{array}$$

15.
$$\begin{array}{r} 0.207 \\ \times 1.2 \\ \hline \end{array}$$

16.
$$\begin{array}{r} 36.5 \\ \times 0.3 \\ \hline \end{array}$$

17.
$$\begin{array}{r} 10.4 \\ \times 2.5 \\ \hline \end{array}$$

18.
$$\begin{array}{r} 28.1 \\ \times 6.9 \\ \hline \end{array}$$

19.
$$\begin{array}{r} 2.071 \\ \times 21.3 \\ \hline \end{array}$$

20.
$$\begin{array}{r} 61.2 \\ \times 0.8 \\ \hline \end{array}$$

21.
$$\begin{array}{r} 25.4 \\ \times 35.6 \\ \hline \end{array}$$

22.
$$\begin{array}{r} 32.84 \\ \times 0.15 \\ \hline \end{array}$$

23.
$$\begin{array}{r} 14.317 \\ \times 2.1 \\ \hline \end{array}$$

24.
$$\begin{array}{r} 15.6 \\ \times 267.9 \\ \hline \end{array}$$

25.
$$\begin{array}{r} 1.148 \\ \times 10.16 \\ \hline \end{array}$$

26.
$$\begin{array}{r} 0.4 \\ \times 167.5 \\ \hline \end{array}$$

27.
$$\begin{array}{r} 2.53 \\ \times 175.9 \\ \hline \end{array}$$

Multiply. A calculator will be helpful.

28. $22.8 \times 39.1 \times 6.7$

29. $4.708 \times 3.65 \times 5.4$

30. $8.66 \times 9.44 \times 2.65$

31. $151 \times 16.79 \times 5.342$

CALCULATOR

PROBLEM SOLVING APPLICATIONS
Choosing a Strategy

Solve.

32. Sound is used to measure ocean depth. In one second a sound will travel 1.5 km through water. If it takes 2.6 s for a sound to reach the bottom of the ocean, how deep is the water?

33. With scuba gear, a beginning diver can dive to a depth of about 30.5 m. A professional diver can reach a depth 48.8 m deeper. To what depth can a professional diver go?

34. Underwater, a fish appears to be 1.25 times larger than it actually is. To a diver underwater, how many meters long would a 33.8 cm fish appear to be?

★ **35.** Ramona used sound to measure how far she was from the ocean's bottom. Her first sounding took 3.8 s to reach the bottom. Her next sounding took 2.1 s. How much closer to the bottom was Ramona when she took the second sounding? (Missing information can be found in Exercise 32.)

ZEROS IN
THE PRODUCT

Polly needs to buy 0.04 m of gold braid to finish trimming a hat. How much will it cost her if the braid sells for $1.08 per meter?

Multiply to find out.

$$\begin{array}{r} \$1.08 \\ \times 0.04 \\ \hline \$.0432 \end{array}$$

Stores usually round up to the next cent. The braid will cost $.05. Notice that you need to write an extra zero in the product to make the correct number of decimal places.

Look at these examples.

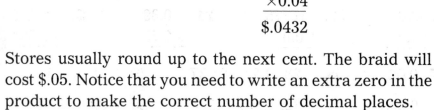

| $\begin{array}{r} 4.08 \\ \times 0.002 \\ \hline 0.00816 \end{array}$ | ← 2 decimal places
← + 3 decimal places
← 5 decimal places | $\begin{array}{r} 0.06 \\ \times 0.03 \\ \hline 0.0018 \end{array}$ | ← 2 decimal places
← + 2 decimal places
← 4 decimal places |

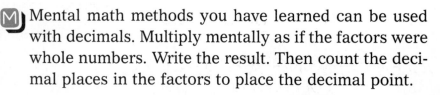

Ⓜ Mental math methods you have learned can be used with decimals. Multiply mentally as if the factors were whole numbers. Write the result. Then count the decimal places in the factors to place the decimal point.

Multiply: 0.04×0.37
  Think: $4 \times 37 = 4 \times (30 + 7) = 120 + 28 = 148$
  Write: 0.0148

CLASS EXERCISES

Write the product with the decimal point in the correct place.

| **1.** $\begin{array}{r} 0.19 \\ \times 0.06 \\ \hline 114 \end{array}$ | **2.** $\begin{array}{r} 0.25 \\ \times 0.07 \\ \hline 175 \end{array}$ | **3.** $\begin{array}{r} 0.149 \\ \times 0.4 \\ \hline 596 \end{array}$ | **4.** $\begin{array}{r} 0.38 \\ \times 0.003 \\ \hline 114 \end{array}$ | **5.** $\begin{array}{r} 2.48 \\ \times 0.06 \\ \hline 1488 \end{array}$ |
| **6.** $\begin{array}{r} 0.49 \\ \times 0.13 \\ \hline 637 \end{array}$ | **7.** $\begin{array}{r} 0.29 \\ \times 0.68 \\ \hline 1972 \end{array}$ | **8.** $\begin{array}{r} 5.1 \\ \times 0.24 \\ \hline 1224 \end{array}$ | **9.** $\begin{array}{r} 0.31 \\ \times 0.2 \\ \hline 62 \end{array}$ | **10.** $\begin{array}{r} 2.5 \\ \times 0.03 \\ \hline 75 \end{array}$ |

PRACTICE

Multiply.

11. 1.45 ×0.05	**12.** 4.79 ×0.2	**13.** 0.388 ×0.09	**14.** 7.42 ×0.3	**15.** 0.98 ×0.08
16. 1.89 ×0.03	**17.** 0.21 ×0.08	**18.** 0.39 ×0.102	**19.** 0.09 ×0.06	**20.** 0.07 ×0.005
21. 2.06 ×0.34	**22.** 0.056 ×0.25	**23.** 0.175 ×0.084	**24.** 0.39 ×0.73	**25.** 0.478 ×0.684

26. 1.6 × 0.63   **27.** 0.025 × 0.98   **28.** 1.2 × 0.027   **29.** 0.38 × 0.12

30. 0.73 × 0.06   **31.** 0.018 × 0.05   **32.** 2.9 × 0.004   **33.** 0.09 × 0.34

34. 0.16 × 2.961   **35.** 6.38 × 8.82   **36.** 0.065 × 0.747   **37.** 0.316 × 0.0068

Use mental math to multiply.

38. 0.3 × 0.04   **39.** 0.4 × 0.22   **40.** 0.3 × 0.19

41. 0.02 × 0.56   **42.** 0.08 × 8.08   **43.** 1.2 × 0.012

MENTAL MATH

PROBLEM SOLVING APPLICATIONS
Mental Math or Pencil and Paper

Tell whether you would use mental math or pencil and paper. Write *M* or *P*. Then solve.

44. Randy uses 0.3 m of ribbon on each band hat he trims. He has 7 hats finished. How much ribbon has he used?

45. Shakeena used 3.74 m of blue yarn and 2.09 m of red yarn to trim vests. How much more blue yarn did she use?

46. Erin needs 0.08 m of ribbon to trim a shirt. If ribbon costs $.50 a meter, how much will the ribbon cost?

47. Kate has 6.45 m of silver braid with which to trim 3 jackets. Can she put 2.05 m of braid on each jacket?

PROBLEM SOLVING
Strategy: Reasonable Answers

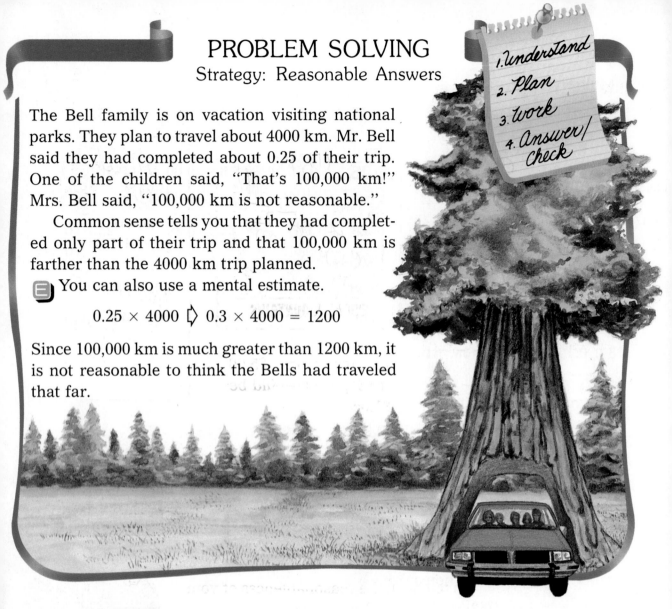

1. Understand
2. Plan
3. Work
4. Answer/Check

The Bell family is on vacation visiting national parks. They plan to travel about 4000 km. Mr. Bell said they had completed about 0.25 of their trip. One of the children said, "That's 100,000 km!" Mrs. Bell said, "100,000 km is not reasonable."

Common sense tells you that they had completed only part of their trip and that 100,000 km is farther than the 4000 km trip planned.

You can also use a mental estimate.

$$0.25 \times 4000 \Rightarrow 0.3 \times 4000 = 1200$$

Since 100,000 km is much greater than 1200 km, it is not reasonable to think the Bells had traveled that far.

CLASS EXERCISES

Which answer is most reasonable? Write a, b, or c.

1. The road up Pike's Peak is about 35 km long. The Bells drove up about 0.5 of the way. How many kilometers up did they drive?
   a. 1.75 km **b.** 17.5 km **c.** 175 km

2. Gas costs $.36 per liter. The Bells bought 50 L. How much did they pay?
   a. $.18 **b.** $180.00 **c.** $18.00

3. The Petrified Forest covers 93,490 acres, while the Redwood National Park covers 110,130 acres. How much larger is the Redwood National Park?
   a. 16,640 acres **b.** 82,477 acres **c.** 203,620 acres

PRACTICE

Is the answer reasonable? Write *yes* or *no*.

4.

The Park Motel

The Tinker Family
5 Members

Motel Room	$55.00
Dinner	36.79
Breakfast	17.27
Telephone	4.75
Tax	3.30
Total	$ 117.11

5.

$2.95

ROCKY MOUNTAINS

Change from $5.00 for 1 poster would be $1.05.

6.

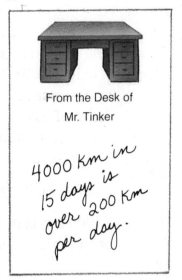

From the Desk of
Mr. Tinker

4000 km in 15 days is over 200 km per day.

Write < , > , or = to complete.

7. 2^3 ▢ 3^2 **8.** 2^4 ▢ 4^2 **9.** 5^3 ▢ 3^5

10. 7^3 ▢ 18^2 **11.** $3^2 + 4^2$ ▢ 5^2 **12.** 100^2 ▢ 10^5

MIXED REVIEW

Solve. Use estimation to check the reasonableness of your answer.

13. Mr. Bell used 6 pieces of rope each 2.6 m long to tie luggage on top of the car. How many meters of rope did he use in all?

14. The Bells visited Sequoia National Park in California. They saw Mt. Whitney, which is 14,494 ft high. The highest point in North America is Mt. McKinley in Alaska, which is 20,320 ft high. How much shorter is Mt. Whitney than Mt. McKinley?

15. The Bells' vacation lasted 15 days. They budgeted $60 per night for a motel room and $75 per day for food. How much did they budget for these items altogether?

DIVIDING DECIMALS
BY WHOLE NUMBERS

Look at the example below to see how to divide a decimal
by a whole number.

First divide as you
would whole
numbers.

$$\begin{array}{r} 1\,9 \\ 8\overline{)\,15.2} \\ -\ 8 \\ \hline 7\,2 \\ -\,7\,2 \\ \hline 0 \end{array}$$

Then write the decimal
point in the
quotient above the
decimal point in
the dividend.

$$\begin{array}{r} 1\,|\,9 \\ 8\overline{)\,15\,|\,2} \\ -\ 8 \\ \hline 7\ 2 \\ -\,7\ 2 \\ \hline 0 \end{array}$$

Watch out for problems like these.

Sometimes you'll
need to write
zeros in the
quotient.

$$\begin{array}{r} 0.029 \\ 13\overline{)\,0.377} \\ -\ 26 \\ \hline 117 \\ -\,117 \\ \hline 0 \end{array}$$

Sometimes you'll
need to write
zeros in the
dividend.

$$\begin{array}{r} 5.45 \\ 6\overline{)\,32.70} \\ -\ 30 \\ \hline 2\ 7 \\ -\,2\ 4 \\ \hline 30 \\ -\,30 \\ \hline 0 \end{array}$$

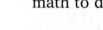 You can use short division to find $5\overline{)\,68.5}$. Use mental
math to divide, multiply, and subtract in your head.

Here's how.
$$5\overline{)\,6_18.5} \quad\quad 5\overline{)\,6_18._35} \quad\quad 5\overline{)\,6_18._35}$$
(quotients: 1, $1\,3$, $1\,3.7$)

TRIM
NEEDED
68.5 cm

CLASS EXERCISES

What is the quotient?

1. $5\overline{)\,365}$ $5\overline{)\,36.5}$ **2.** $4\overline{)\,506}$ $4\overline{)\,50.6}$

3. $12\overline{)\,516}$ $12\overline{)\,51.6}$ **4.** $35\overline{)\,7070}$ $35\overline{)\,70.70}$

5. $78\overline{)\,117}$ $78\overline{)\,1.17}$ **6.** $54\overline{)\,6858}$ $54\overline{)\,6.858}$

PRACTICE

Divide.

7. $3\overline{)38.4}$	**8.** $6\overline{)11.7}$	**9.** $4\overline{)5.2}$	**10.** $8\overline{)249.6}$
11. $9\overline{)97.2}$	**12.** $4\overline{)34.16}$	**13.** $7\overline{)448.7}$	**14.** $3\overline{)128.04}$
15. $8\overline{)0.72}$	**16.** $7\overline{)101.64}$	**17.** $6\overline{)0.084}$	**18.** $5\overline{)15.52}$
19. $7\overline{)1.141}$	**20.** $8\overline{)2.462}$	**21.** $9\overline{)0.72}$	**22.** $6\overline{)3.453}$
23. $38\overline{)5.51}$	**24.** $15\overline{)16.2}$	**25.** $29\overline{)83.52}$	**26.** $41\overline{)2.1156}$
27. $59\overline{)1.1977}$	**28.** $24\overline{)152.4}$	**29.** $18\overline{)2.43}$	**30.** $32\overline{)280.32}$

Divide using short division. Be sure to write the decimal point in the quotient.

MENTAL MATH

31. $7\overline{)37.1}$ **32.** $8\overline{)65.04}$ **33.** $4\overline{)3.396}$ **34.** $6\overline{)46.014}$

PROBLEM SOLVING APPLICATIONS
Choosing the Operation

Solve.

35. Batik Designs Unlimited received a shipment of 6.5 kg of wax. The shipment was equally divided into 5 boxes. How many kilograms of wax were in each box?

36. Suppose your bill for 12 m of fabric is $35.76. What would be the cost of one meter of that fabric?

37. If you have 27 m of a fabric and you sell 11.6 m in the morning and 2.3 m in the afternoon, how much fabric is left at the end of the day?

★ **38.** You have 10 m of cloth. An elephant pillow pattern requires 1.3 m of cloth. A bear pattern requires 0.9 m. If you make 5 elephants, how many bears can you make with the remaining cloth?

MULTIPLYING OR DIVIDING BY POWERS OF 10

 Multiplication and division with powers of 10 can be done mentally.

Multiplying or dividing a decimal by 10 moves the decimal point one place.

$$74.5 \times 10 = 745.$$
$$74.5 \div 10 = 7.45$$

Multiplying or dividing a decimal by 100 moves the decimal point two places.

$$6.831 \times 100 = 683.1$$
$$6.831 \div 100 = 0.06831$$

Multiplying or dividing a decimal by 1000 moves the decimal point three places.

$$4.25 \times 1000 = 4250.$$
$$4.25 \div 1000 = 0.00425$$

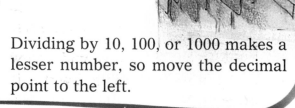

Multiplying by 10, 100, or 1000 makes a greater number, so move the decimal point to the right.

Dividing by 10, 100, or 1000 makes a lesser number, so move the decimal point to the left.

CLASS EXERCISES

Write the product with the decimal point in the correct place.

1. $10 \times 3.15 = 315$
$100 \times 3.15 = 315$
$1000 \times 3.15 = 315$

2. $10 \times 0.78 = 78$
$100 \times 0.78 = 78$
$1000 \times 0.78 = 78$

3. $10 \times 22.9 = 229$
$100 \times 22.9 = 229$
$1000 \times 22.9 = 229$

Write the quotient with the decimal point in the correct place.

4. $64.3 \div 10 = 643$
$64.3 \div 100 = 643$
$64.3 \div 1000 = 643$

5. $8.61 \div 10 = 861$
$8.61 \div 100 = 861$
$8.61 \div 1000 = 861$

6. $0.21 \div 10 = 21$
$0.21 \div 100 = 21$
$0.21 \div 1000 = 21$

PRACTICE

Multiply or divide.

7. 100×82.11 **8.** $0.473 \div 1000$ **9.** 1000×210.5 **10.** $0.762 \div 100$

11. $93.84 \div 10$ **12.** 1000×7.48 **13.** $12.3 \div 100$ **14.** 10×10.78

15. 1000×24.7 **16.** $36.43 \div 100$ **17.** 10×83.01 **18.** $2.755 \div 1000$

19. $0.371 \div 10$ **20.** 100×0.146 **21.** $0.8615 \div 1000$ **22.** 100×0.315

To complete, multiply or divide by the power of ten shown.

23.

×	0.315	6.217	8.75	17.6
10	3.15	?	?	?
100	?	?	?	?

24.

÷	16.5	4.08	9.65	27.31
100	?	?	?	?
1000	?	?	?	?

PROBLEM SOLVING APPLICATIONS
Choosing a Strategy

Solve.

25. Movie tickets are 4.5 cm long. How long is a roll of 2000 tickets?

26. Tickets are 0.5 mm thick. How thick is a stack of 1000 tickets?

★ **27.** Movie seats are 40 cm wide. How many seats can fit in a row that is 10 m wide?

★ **28.** A side row is 7 m wide. What is the greatest number of seats 40 cm wide that can fit in the row?

CHECKPOINT 1

Estimate. *(pages 144–145)*

1. 5.2×6.8 **2.** 6.85×71.6

Write the answer. *(pages 146–151)*

3. 7×3.2 **4.** 0.2×0.14

Is the answer reasonable? *(pages 152–153)*

5. One dozen eggs cost $1.19, so 6 dozen cost $7.14.

Write the answer. *(pages 154–157)*

6. $14.65 \div 5$ **7.** 100×18.63

8. $0.625 \div 10$ **9.** 100×0.483

Extra Practice on page 430

DIVIDING BY TENTHS

These examples show that multiplying the dividend and the divisor by the same number doesn't change the quotient.

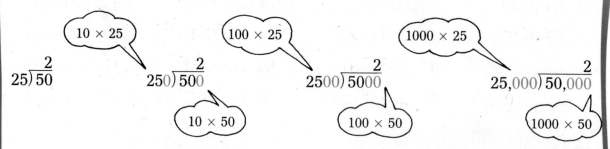

$$\overset{2}{25\overline{)50}}$$ (10 × 25)

$$\overset{2}{250\overline{)500}}$$ (100 × 25) (10 × 50)

$$\overset{2}{2500\overline{)5000}}$$ (1000 × 25) (100 × 50)

$$\overset{2}{25{,}000\overline{)50{,}000}}$$ (1000 × 50)

Here's how to divide 25.75 by 0.5.

First multiply the ~~dividend~~ *divisor* and the ~~divisor~~ *dividend* by the power of 10 that will make the divisor a whole number. Then divide.

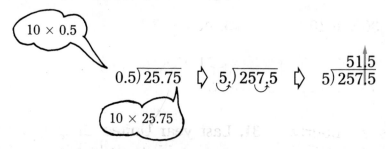

(10 × 0.5)

$$0.5\overline{)25.75} \quad \Rightarrow \quad 5.\overline{)257.5} \quad \Rightarrow \quad \overset{51|5}{5\overline{)257|5}}$$

(10 × 25.75)

You can think of division with decimals as repeated subtraction. Some calculators have a *constant* feature that lets you subtract the same number several times by repeatedly pressing the ⊟ key. To determine $1.5 \div 0.5$, subtract 0.5 as shown until you reach 0.

1.5 ⊟ 0.5 ⊟ ⊟ ⊟ 0

The number of times you pressed ⊟ is the quotient, 3.

2500 ft

CLASS EXERCISES

Complete.

1. $0.7\overline{)4.2} \ \lozenge \ 7.\overline{)42.}$ **2.** $0.9\overline{)6.48} \ \lozenge \ 9.\overline{)64.8}$ **3.** $1.6\overline{)3.36} \ \lozenge \ 16.\overline{)33.6}$

PRACTICE

Divide.

4. $0.6\overline{)7.8}$ 5. $0.4\overline{)4.8}$ 6. $0.3\overline{)1.56}$ 7. $0.5\overline{)0.395}$

8. $0.8\overline{)2.512}$ 9. $0.6\overline{)13.92}$ 10. $0.9\overline{)0.774}$ 11. $0.7\overline{)2.464}$

12. $1.3\overline{)27.82}$ 13. $2.7\overline{)8.424}$ 14. $4.2\overline{)35.49}$ 15. $1.8\overline{)0.234}$

16. $2.4\overline{)2.244}$ 17. $3.3\overline{)0.891}$ 18. $1.6\overline{)9.088}$ 19. $4.5\overline{)30.78}$

20. $23.9\overline{)320.26}$ 21. $22.1\overline{)18.785}$ 22. $55.8\overline{)887.22}$ 23. $23.6\overline{)42.48}$

Determine the quotient using repeated subtraction. Try the constant feature on your calculator if you have one.

CALCULATOR

24. $2.5 \div 0.5$ 25. $8.8 \div 2.2$ 26. $24.8 \div 6.2$

27. $15.5 \div 3.1$ 28. $30.3 \div 10.1$ 29. $49.7 \div 7.1$

PROBLEM SOLVING APPLICATIONS
Choosing the Operation

Solve.

30. Janice Wildes earns an hourly wage of $19.50 as an electrician. She is paid 1.5 times the hourly wage for overtime. What would she be paid for 40 hours at the regular rate and 8 hours overtime?

31. Last year United Gadgets Company sold its gadgets for $34.96 each. Because of inflation, it raised the price this year to $37.20 per gadget. How much was the price increased?

32. Joe Pannone is an accountant. He is looking for file number 88.532. He opens a file drawer labeled 87.500–88.250. Will he find the file in this drawer?

★ 33. On a business trip to Port Warren, Ann York determined that she had spent $166.86 on gas. If Ann paid 30.9¢ per liter, how many liters did she buy?

DIVIDING BY HUNDREDTHS AND THOUSANDTHS

Marty and Mindy's Fish Mart packaged 2.88 kg of fish in portions of 0.24 kg each. You can divide 2.88 by 0.24 to find out how many portions there are.

First multiply the dividend and divisor by 100. This will make the divisor a whole number.

$$100 \times 0.24$$

$$0.24\overline{)2.88} \quad \Rightarrow \quad 24.\overline{)2\,88.}$$

Next divide as with whole numbers.

$$100 \times 2.88$$

$$\begin{array}{r} 12 \\ 24\overline{)288} \end{array}$$

There are 12 portions of fish.

To divide by thousandths, first multiply the dividend and divisor by 1000. You may need to write a zero in the dividend. Then divide.

$$0.842\overline{)993.56} \quad \Rightarrow \quad \begin{array}{r} 1180 \\ 842.\overline{)993\,560.} \end{array}$$

Here's another example. Write the decimal point in the quotient.

$$1.27\overline{)3.937} \quad \Rightarrow \quad \begin{array}{r} 3.1 \\ 1\,27.\overline{)3\,93.7} \end{array}$$

CLASS EXERCISES

What are the quotients?

1. $8\overline{)192}$ $0.08\overline{)1.92}$ 2. $742\overline{)24,486}$ $0.742\overline{)244.86}$

3. $13\overline{)364}$ $0.13\overline{)3.64}$ 4. $53\overline{)3392}$ $0.053\overline{)3.392}$

5. $142\overline{)3976}$ $1.42\overline{)3.976}$ 6. $6.2\overline{)318.06}$ $0.062\overline{)0.31806}$

PRACTICE

Divide.

7. $0.03\overline{)0.837}$ **8.** $0.005\overline{)1.425}$ **9.** $0.009\overline{)7.56}$ **10.** $0.03\overline{)7.194}$

11. $0.04\overline{)0.956}$ **12.** $0.007\overline{)1.512}$ **13.** $0.59\overline{)9.44}$ **14.** $0.11\overline{)2.783}$

15. $0.08\overline{)3.936}$ **16.** $0.005\overline{)13.15}$ **17.** $2.34\overline{)13.572}$ **18.** $0.315\overline{)7.56}$

19. $0.047\overline{)94}$ **20.** $0.028\overline{)6.916}$ **21.** $5.04\overline{)957.6}$ **22.** $0.816\overline{)3.9984}$

23. $0.17\overline{)68}$ **24.** $0.12\overline{)5.532}$ **25.** $7.01\overline{)24.535}$ **26.** $8.83\overline{)35.32}$

27. $0.602\overline{)28.294}$ **28.** $0.023\overline{)22.08}$ **29.** $0.035\overline{)12.88}$ **30.** $0.985\overline{)0.788}$

PROBLEM SOLVING APPLICATIONS
Using Decimals

Exercises 31–40 are records of sales at John's Bait and
Tackle shop. Determine how many items were purchased
per sale.

Fishing lures cost $1.39 each.

31. $4.17   **32.** $8.34   **33.** $15.29   **34.** $23.63   **35.** $41.70

Deluxe fishing hooks cost $.75 each.

36. $3.75   **37.** $7.50   **38.** $11.25   **39.** $21.00   **40.** $27.00

41. Maureen sold 122.5 kg of scrod. If each piece of scrod
weighed about 1.75 kg, how many pieces of scrod did
Maureen sell?

★ **42.** Work backwards to determine the starting number.

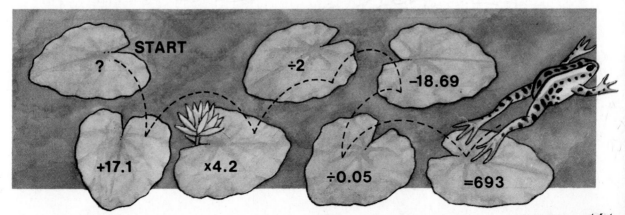

ROUNDING THE QUOTIENT

To the nearest gram, how large is one serving?

To find out, divide 448 g by 15. Divide to the tenths' place since you want to round to the nearest whole number.

$$
\begin{array}{r}
29.8 \\
15\overline{)448.0} \\
-30 \\
\hline
148 \\
-135 \\
\hline
130 \\
-120 \\
\hline
10 \\
\end{array}
$$

BROWN RICE

NUTRITIONAL INFORMATION

PACKAGE
 WEIGHT 448g

SERVINGS PER
 PACKAGE 15

VITAMIN CONTENT

PROTEIN.........4*
THIAMINE 6
NIACIN. 6
IRON 2

* % of U.S.
 RECOMMENDED DAILY
 ALLOWANCES
 (U.S. RDA)

To the nearest gram, each serving is 30 g.

When you divide with decimals, the division may go on and on. In this case, you need to round the quotient to have a usable answer.

Always divide to one place further than the place to which you're rounding. When rounding to the nearest tenth, divide to the hundredths' place. When rounding to the nearest hundredth, divide to the thousandths' place.

CLASS EXERCISES

Divide to the hundredths' place. Round the quotient to the nearest tenth.

1. $6\overline{)2.23}$ **2.** $8\overline{)7.15}$ **3.** $0.3\overline{)0.52}$ **4.** $1.2\overline{)3.46}$

Divide to the thousandths' place. Round the quotient to the nearest hundredth.

5. $16\overline{)37.8}$ **6.** $82\overline{)0.991}$ **7.** $3.7\overline{)6.812}$ **8.** $15.2\overline{)9.681}$

PRACTICE

Divide. Round the quotient to the nearest tenth.

9. $7\overline{)125}$ **10.** $9\overline{)22.4}$ **11.** $4\overline{)31.7}$ **12.** $3\overline{)74}$

13. $0.6\overline{)3.85}$ **14.** $0.04\overline{)1.431}$ **15.** $0.7\overline{)92.5}$ **16.** $0.9\overline{)16.18}$

17. $1.32\overline{)0.756}$ **18.** $0.231\overline{)0.7441}$ **19.** $8.71\overline{)2.235}$ **20.** $6.07\overline{)13}$

Divide. Round the quotient to the nearest hundredth.

21. $8\overline{)45.3}$ **22.** $4\overline{)11.5}$ **23.** $6\overline{)52.19}$ **24.** $7\overline{)61.03}$

25. $0.3\overline{)22.9}$ **26.** $0.08\overline{)0.795}$ **27.** $0.6\overline{)45.2}$ **28.** $0.7\overline{)3.893}$

29. $4.44\overline{)73.6}$ **30.** $0.361\overline{)4.793}$ **31.** $1.75\overline{)31.47}$ **32.** $2.09\overline{)58.8}$

PROBLEM SOLVING APPLICATIONS
Nonroutine Problems

Solve.

33. Yan-Tien had four servings of cereal. The full box held three times as many servings as Yan-Tien ate. If each serving was 37.4 g, how many grams of cereal were in the box before Yan-Tien opened it?

34. An apple tree has 2 main trunks. Each main trunk has 4 limbs and each limb has 4 branches. If each branch has 4 twigs and at the end of each twig is an apple, how many apples are on the tree?

★ **35.** Claude found two dollars and added it to the money he already had. He then had five times as much money as he would have had if he'd lost two dollars. Claude started with less than $10.00. How much did he have after his lucky find?

CHANGING METRIC UNITS
OF LENGTH

The file cabinets are 70 cm tall. Will they fit under a shelf that is 1.2 m tall?

When you compare measurements, you should be certain they are written in the same units.

You can write 1.2 m as 120 cm.
1 m = 100 cm
1.2 m × 100 = 120 cm

Since 70 cm is less than 120 cm, the cabinets will fit under the shelf.

 You can change from meters to any other unit in the metric system by multiplying or dividing mentally by 10, 100, or 1000.

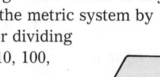

> **When changing from a lesser unit to a greater unit, divide.**
>
> **When changing from a greater unit to a lesser unit, multiply.**

1 meter ÷ 1000 = 1 millimeter	0.001 m = 1 mm
1 meter ÷ 100 = 1 centimeter	0.01 m = 1 cm
1 meter ÷ 10 = 1 decimeter	0.1 m = 1 dm
1 meter	1 m
1 meter × 10 = 1 dekameter	1 dam = 10 m
1 meter × 100 = 1 hectometer	1 hm = 100 m
1 meter × 1000 = 1 kilometer	1 km = 1000 m

In everyday life, hectometers, dekameters, and decimeters are seldom used.

CLASS EXERCISES

Multiply by 100 to write the measure in centimeters.

1. 7.2 m
2. 3.67 m
3. 75.7 m
4. 0.9 m
5. 0.315 m

Divide by 100 to write the measure in meters.

6. 1200 cm
7. 936 cm
8. 64 cm
9. 8 cm
10. 0.9 cm

PRACTICE

Write the measure in meters.

11. 4.8 km   **12.** 9.08 km   **13.** 0.7 km   **14.** 11.006 km   **15.** 0.025 km

Write the measure in centimeters.

16. 63.4 mm   **17.** 7.21 mm   **18.** 0.51 mm   **19.** 56 mm   **20.** 0.01 mm

Complete.

21. 48.9 m =   cm   **22.** 0.80 km =   m   **23.** 598 cm =   m

24. 9.51 km =   m   **25.** 751 m =   km   **26.** 0.25 cm =   mm

27. 27 mm =   cm   **28.** 0.08 m =   mm   **29.** 0.6 m =   cm

30. 117.2 m =   km   **31.** 168 cm =   m   **32.** 90.7 cm =   m

33. 0.85 km =   m   **34.** 82.6 cm =   mm   ★ **35.** 79 mm =   km

PROBLEM SOLVING APPLICATIONS
Pencil, Calculator, or Mental Math

Tell whether you would choose mental math, pencil and paper, or a calculator. Write *P*, *C*, or *M*. Then solve.

36. Can an extension cord that is 58 m long be used to connect a typewriter to an outlet that is 485 cm away?

37. Will a wastebasket that is 36.5 cm tall fit under a desk that is 0.66 m high?

★ **38.** Will a photograph that is 88 mm wide and 128 mm long fit in a frame that is 9.1 cm wide and 11 cm long?

★ **39.** A workshop had strips of lumber of the following lengths: 2.3 m, 233 cm, 2.39 m, 231 cm, 2315 mm, 2.29 m. Arrange these strips in order from least to greatest.

CHANGING METRIC UNITS
OF CAPACITY AND MASS

The pattern used to change metric units of length is also used to change metric units of capacity and mass.

CAPACITY

kiloliter	hectoliter	dekaliter	liter	deciliter	centiliter	milliliter
1000 L	100 L	10 L	1 L	0.1 L	0.01 L	0.001 L
1 kL	1 hL	1 daL		1 dL	1 cL	1 mL

Usually only the liter and milliliter are used in everyday life.

MASS

kilogram	hectogram	dekagram	gram	decigram	centigram	milligram
1000 g	100 g	10 g	1 g	0.1 g	0.01 g	0.001 g
1 kg	1 hg	1 dag		1 dg	1 cg	1 mg

Usually only the kilogram, gram, and milligram are used in everyday life. Truckers, machinery makers, and others may use the metric ton (t).

$$1 \text{ t} = 1000 \text{ kg}$$

 Change metric units of capacity and mass by multiplying or dividing mentally by 10, 100, or 1000.

2.7 kg is 2700 g (multiply by 1000).

275 mL is 0.275 L (divide by 1000).

CLASS EXERCISES

Multiply by 1000 to write the measure in a smaller unit.

1. 6 L   **2.** 0.5 kg   **3.** 8.3 L   **4.** 1.75 kg   **5.** 0.095 kg

Divide by 1000 to write the measure in a larger unit.

6. 1584 g   **7.** 274 mL   **8.** 960 mg   **9.** 80 g   **10.** 7.2 mL

PRACTICE

Complete.

11. 8.3 L = ▨ mL   **12.** 2000 g = ▨ kg   **13.** 0.7 kg = ▨ g

14. 584 mL = ▨ L   **15.** 1.51 kg = ▨ g   **16.** 875 g = ▨ kg

17. 780 g = ▨ kg   **18.** 0.75 L = ▨ mL   **19.** 625 mg = ▨ g

20. 25 mL = ▨ L   **21.** 64 g = ▨ kg   **22.** 4.5 mL = ▨ L

23. 1.875 L = ▨ mL   **24.** 27 t = ▨ kg   ★ **25.** 5842 g = ▨ t

Measure to the nearest centimeter and millimeter.

26. ——————————   **27.** ————————

28. ——————————   **29.** ——————————

MIXED REVIEW

PROBLEM SOLVING APPLICATIONS
Choosing the Operation

Solve.

30. For the party, Tina made 0.95 kg of popcorn, Romona made 790 g and Fred made 0.8 kg. Who made the most popcorn? Who made the least?

31. For the party Todd brought 0.79 kg of peanuts, Anita brought 790 g of cashews, and Lauren brought 0.790 kg of walnuts. Compare the amounts they brought.

32. At the party they had a Guess the Mass contest. "How many of you would make a metric ton?" If Kurt had a mass of 64 kg, how many of him would it take to make a metric ton?

33. SuLin brought 6.5 kg of raisins and 2.45 kg of peanuts to mix together. The guests ate 7.89 kg of the mix. About how much did SuLin have left?

PROBLEM SOLVING
Strategy: Multi-Step Problems

1. Understand
2. Plan
3. Work
4. Answer / Check

Order Form
GOLD MEDAL SPORTS

Ship to: *Hampton Athletic Club*

Item	How many	What is it?	Price	Cost
22B	15	soccer uniform	$12.50	$187.50
25R	5	soccer ball	$26.99	$134.95
		Total Cost		$322.45
		Postage and Handling		$10.00
		Total Order		$332.45

The Hampton Athletic Club is buying new soccer equipment. They are ordering everything from the Gold Medal Sports' catalog.

To find the total cost of the order, you need to solve four small problems.

◇ $15 \times \$12.50 = \$187.50$

◇ $5 \times \$26.99 = \$134.95$

◇ $\$187.50 + \$134.95 = \$322.45$

◇ $\$322.45 + \$10.00 = \$332.45$

CLASS EXERCISES

Complete the order form.

1.

Order Form
GOLD MEDAL SPORTS

Ship to: *Bayville Senior Citizen Center*

Item	How many	What is it?	Price	Cost
173	5	billiard cue	$21.99	?
267	4	inflatable raft	$57.85	?
		Total Cost		?
		Postage and Handling		$12.50
		Total Order		?

2.

Order Form
GOLD MEDAL SPORTS

Ship to: *Port Warren Cycle Club*

Item	How many	What is it?	Price	Cost
122x	25	bikes	$179.99	?
317x	25	helmets	$14.50	?
482c	1	whistle	$3.98	?
		Total Cost		?
		Postage and Handling		$37.50
		Total Order		?

PRACTICE

Solve.

3. Greg wants to buy the following items:

- speedometer for $9.99
- tire pump for $18.99
- mirror for $3.99

How much change should he receive if he pays with 2 twenty dollar bills?

5. John bought a basketball for $21.99. He returned it and bought a football for $13.99 and a jersey for $10.99. How much more does he owe the store?

4. Joanne is using Gold Medal's Layaway Plan. She is buying the following:

- a table tennis table for $48.97
- a set of paddles for $15.88
- table tennis balls for $1.98

Joanne made a deposit of $12.50. How much more does she owe?

6. Maureen wants to buy a bike that costs $88.99. She has saved $35.00. How long will it take to save the rest of the money if she saves $5.00 each week?

Read the letter to answer the questions.

7. What should the amount of the corrected bill be?

8. How much was the boat club overcharged?

9. How much was the boat club overcharged for each life jacket?

Solve.

★ **10.** Gold Medal Sports gives G&M stamps on all purchases. Customers receive 1 stamp for every 25¢ spent up to $50.00. Amounts over $50.00 receive 1 stamp for every 10¢ spent. How many stamps would you receive if you bought hiking boots for $39.95 and a first-aid kit for $12.75?

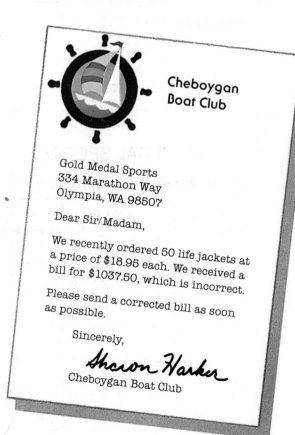

Cheboygan Boat Club

Gold Medal Sports
334 Marathon Way
Olympia, WA 98507

Dear Sir/Madam,

We recently ordered 50 life jackets at a price of $18.95 each. We received a bill for $1037.50, which is incorrect. Please send a corrected bill as soon as possible.

Sincerely,

Sharon Harker

Cheboygan Boat Club

ESTIMATING
DECIMAL QUOTIENTS

When you divide decimals, you can estimate the quotient to check the placement of the decimal point in the quotient.

To estimate a decimal quotient, you may round the dividend and divisor to the greatest place value and divide.

$$6.36\overline{)32.8} \quad \triangleright \quad \overset{5 \text{ Estimate}}{6\overline{)30}}$$

Sometimes the rounded numbers are not easy to divide mentally. Then you may look for compatible numbers, that is, numbers close to the dividend and divisor that are easy to divide.

$$7.36\overline{)43.8} \quad \triangleright \quad \overset{?}{7\overline{)40}} \quad \text{Use } \overset{6 \text{ Estimate}}{7\overline{)42}}$$

Think: The distance a plane traveled and the amount of fuel it used were recorded in decimals. How can you estimate the number of kilometers the plane traveled on 1 L of fuel?

CLASS EXERCISES

Estimate the quotient.

1. $3.2\overline{)12.7} \quad \triangleright \quad 3\overline{)12}$

2. $5.9\overline{)311.3} \quad \triangleright \quad 6\overline{)300}$

3. $28.9\overline{)598.4} \quad \triangleright \quad 30\overline{)600}$

4. $8.14\overline{)5298.5} \quad \triangleright \quad 10\overline{)5000}$

5. $4.89\overline{)91.8} \quad \triangleright \quad 5\overline{)90}$

6. $2.84\overline{)15.732} \quad \triangleright \quad 3\overline{)15}$

PRACTICE

Estimate the quotient.

7. $4.7\overline{)29.47}$ **8.** $7.9\overline{)64.43}$ **9.** $2.1\overline{)718.8}$ **10.** $9.1\overline{)425.7}$

11. $2.93\overline{)89.431}$ **12.** $6.74\overline{)215.7}$ **13.** $4.21\overline{)19.472}$ **14.** $5.28\overline{)29.531}$

15. $78.4\overline{)235.81}$ **16.** $37.6\overline{)578.9}$ **17.** $83.2\overline{)732.55}$ **18.** $2.89\overline{)56.89}$

19. $55.7 \overline{)\, 289.76}$ **20.** $12.7 \overline{)\, 43.81}$ **21.** $37.9 \overline{)\, 7.338}$ **22.** $9.46 \overline{)\, 270.80}$

23. $1.3 \overline{)\, 33.8}$ **24.** $54.7 \overline{)\, 246.15}$ **25.** $2.8 \overline{)\, 6.498}$ **26.** $2.89 \overline{)\, 381.48}$

27. $41.3 \overline{)\, 3386.6}$ **28.** $4.87 \overline{)\, 14.0743}$ **29.** $2.5 \overline{)\, 5075}$ **30.** $69.7 \overline{)\, 144.25}$

PROBLEM SOLVING APPLICATIONS
Using Estimation

Estimate.

31. An airplane flew 1449 km in 2.8 h. About how far did the airplane fly in one hour?

32. An airplane flew 3.5 h at an average speed of 582 km per hour. About how far did it fly?

★ **33.** An airplane uses 1.9 L of gasoline per minute. About how many hours can the airplane fly on 705 L of gasoline?

★ **34.** The Apollo 10 command module reached a speed of 39,896.16 km/h. About how many kilometers per minute is this?

★ **35.** Write and solve a problem that requires the solver to estimate when one decimal is divided by another.

CHECKPOINT 2

Write the answer. If necessary, round to the nearest tenth. *(pages 158–163)*

1. $61.2 \overline{)\, 201.96}$ **2.** $0.123 \overline{)\, 0.4674}$

3. $0.5 \overline{)\, 68.37}$ **4.** $3.91 \overline{)\, 48.6}$

Complete. *(pages 164–167)*

5. 6.7 L = ▮ mL

6. 2.48 m = ▮ cm

7. 0.48 kg = ▮ g
8. 6.02 mg = ▮ g

Solve. *(pages 168–169)*

9. It takes Ben 30 min to make one whistle. If he works 4 h with a 30 min break, how many whistles can he make?

Estimate the quotient. *(pages 170–171)*

10. $2.5 \overline{)\, 58.2}$ **11.** $71.6 \overline{)\, 628.9}$

Extra Practice on page 430

CHAPTER 6 TEST

Estimate the product. *(pages 144–145)*

1. 2.4
×3.3

2. 1.75
×8.1

3. 6.06
×4.88

4. 781.15
×2.145

Write the answer. *(pages 146–151)*

5. 59.4
×297

6. 0.61
×3.4

7. 15.3
×7.8

8. 0.007
×0.081

Divide. Then round the quotient to the nearest tenth. *(pages 154–163)*

9. $37\overline{)227.92}$

10. $100\overline{)47.36}$

11. $5.4\overline{)42.444}$

12. $1.96\overline{)9.7804}$

Complete. *(pages 164–167)*

13. 0.731 km = ▨ m

14. 245 cm = ▨ mm

15. 17 mL = ▨ L

Solve. Estimate to check the reasonableness of your answer. *(pages 152–153)*

16. A ferry boat made 8 round trips. The lake is 4.7 km wide. How far did the ferry travel?

17. A ferry boat ride costs $3.85. How much will it cost for 23 children to have rides?

Solve. *(pages 168–169)*

18. Kirk bought a T-shirt for $6.95, shorts for $8.95, and a pair of sneakers for $17.95. How much change did he receive from two twenty dollar bills?

19. Meredith bought a blouse for $12.99 and a skirt for $19.99. She returned the skirt and bought a blazer for $26.00 and a sweater for $15.65. How much more does she owe the store?

Estimate the quotient. *(pages 170–171)*

20. $67.3\overline{)275.83}$

21. $51.4\overline{)453.88}$

22. $6.9\overline{)35.89}$

23. $77.7\overline{)2400.99}$

Extra Practice on page 431

MATHEMATICS and ART

A life-size picture or sculpture is the same size as what it represents. Artists may represent a subject as life-size, larger, or smaller.

IS THAT THE SIZE OF IT?

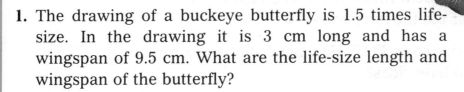

1. The drawing of a buckeye butterfly is 1.5 times life-size. In the drawing it is 3 cm long and has a wingspan of 9.5 cm. What are the life-size length and wingspan of the butterfly?

2. Make a copy 1.5 times the size of the picture of the buckeye butterfly.

3. A ladybug is 0.75 cm long. Measure the drawing. How many times longer than life-size is the drawing?

4. The Statue of Liberty is 46 m tall from her sandals to the top of her torch. Measure yourself in the same pose. Pretend that you are holding a torch that is 30 cm long. About how many times taller is the Statue of Liberty than you?

Enrichment

You can write standard numbers in expanded notation. Here's an example.

$4{,}372{,}895 = (4 \times 1{,}000{,}000) + (3 \times 100{,}000) + (7 \times 10{,}000) +$
$(2 \times 1000) + (8 \times 100) + (9 \times 10) + (5 \times 1)$

This form takes a lot of space, and a lot of time writing zeros! Expanded notation can be shortened by using powers of ten.

$1{,}000{,}000 = 10^6$, so $4{,}000{,}000$ can be written as 4×10^6
$4{,}372{,}895 = (4 \times 10^6) + (3 \times 10^5) + (7 \times 10^4) + (2 \times 10^3) +$
$(8 \times 10^2) + (9 \times 10^1) + (5 \times 1)$

Write these numbers in expanded notation using powers of ten. Use the chart to help.

10^9	1,000,000,000
10^8	100,000,000
10^7	10,000,000
10^6	1,000,000
10^5	100,000
10^4	10,000
10^3	1000
10^2	100
10^1	10

1. 243
2. 3879
3. 4821
4. 63,985
5. 486,093
6. 9,429,876
7. 8,302,481
8. 68,937,498
9. 102,365,299
10. 268,539,740
11. 7,368,366,928
12. 5,854,901,407

The nearest Pluto ever comes to Earth is about 4,260,800,000 km. Scientists must often make calculations with large numbers. To make their work easier, they use **scientific notation**.

A number in scientific notation is shown as the product of a number between 1 and 10 and a power of 10. Here's how to write 4,260,800,000 in scientific notation.

SCIENTIFIC NOTATION

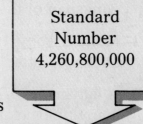

Standard Number
4,260,800,000

Scientific Notation
4.2608×10^9

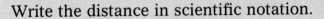

Write the distance in scientific notation.

13. The moon is about 382,000 km away from Earth.

14. The diameter of the sun is about 1,384,000 km.

15. When Saturn is closest to Earth, it is about 1,228,952,000 km away.

16. At its farthest point, Saturn is about 1,630,000,000 km away from Earth.

Write the number in standard form.

17. Venus is about 1.069×10^8 km away from the sun.

18. The star Sirius is about 8.352×10^{13} km away.

19. The diameter of Jupiter is about 1.385×10^5 km.

20. Neptune is about 4.48×10^9 km from the sun.

21. Uranus is about 2.848×10^9 km from the sun.

22. The star Canopus is about 9.6×10^{14} km away from the sun.

23. The orbit of Earth has a diameter of about 2.9728×10^8 km.

This tells the exponent for 10.

Some calculators will automatically change to scientific notation a result that has more than 8 digits. For example, $9728 \times 14,385 = 139,937,280$ might be shown as 1.3994 E8.

Write the number in scientific notation and in standard form.

24. 1.386 E8   **25.** 6.25 E10   **26.** 7.948 E12

CUMULATIVE REVIEW

Choose the correct answer. Write *a*, *b*, *c*, or *d*.
Estimate the difference.

1. 564
  − 188
  a. 550
  b. 500
  c. 450
  d. 400

2. 9093
  − 207
  a. 9200
  b. 8000
  c. 8800
  d. 7000

3. $37.12
  − 6.40
  a. $20.00
  b. $25.00
  c. $34.00
  d. $43.00

Find the answer.

4. $8.24
  − 3.53
  a. $4.61
  b. $4.71
  c. $5.71
  d. none of these

5. 91,474
  − 6,677
  a. 84,897
  b. 84,797
  c. 85,707
  d. none of these

6. 5002
  − 2205
  a. 2797
  b. 2707
  c. 3797
  d. none of these

Find the answer.

7. 54
  ×8
  a. 402
  b. 412
  c. 432
  d. none of these

8. 807
  ×9
  a. 783
  b. 8163
  c. 7263
  d. none of these

9. 7625
  ×6
  a. 42,620
  b. 42,650
  c. 45,650
  d. none of these

Find the answer.

10. 5)685
  a. 137
  b. 135
  c. 139
  d. none of these

11. 7)5318
  a. 759 R8
  b. 759 R5
  c. 759
  d. none of these

12. 4)97,034
  a. 24,258 R4
  b. 24,258 R2
  c. 24,268 R2
  d. none of these

Find the answer.

13. $60\overline{)5978}$
   a. 99 R32
   b. 99 R30
   c. 99 R38
   d. none of these

14. $24\overline{)1873}$
   a. 77 R23
   b. 78 R3
   c. 78 R1
   d. none of these

15. $452\overline{)65,461}$
   a. 143 R473
   b. 144 R383
   c. 144 R373
   d. none of these

Solve.

16. Nicholas has 8 more tadpoles than Marian. If Marian has 24 tadpoles, how many tadpoles does Nicholas have?
   a. 16 tadpoles
   b. 32 tadpoles
   c. 3 tadpoles
   d. none of these

17. The science class has 21 tanks in which to put 147 tadpoles. If the students divide the tadpoles equally, how many will be in each tank?
   a. 168 tadpoles
   b. 126 tadpoles
   c. 7 tadpoles
   d. none of these

Which is the best estimate?

18. $48\overline{)5189}$
   a. 10
   b. 100
   c. 1000
   d. 2000

19. $61\overline{)54,307}$
   a. 900
   b. 80
   c. 70
   d. 600

20. $779\overline{)638,941}$
   a. 80,000
   b. 8000
   c. 800
   d. 80

LANGUAGE and VOCABULARY REVIEW

Write *true* or *false*. If you write *false*, correct the sentence by replacing the underlined word or words.

1. The distance from Chicago to Milwaukee would be measured in <u>centimeters</u>.

2. An <u>equation</u> is a mathematical sentence with an equals sign.

3. To round 58.9 to the nearest whole number, you would <u>round down</u>.

4. Units of <u>capacity</u> are measured in liters and milliliters.

FLOWCHART

Flowcharts are often used by computer programmers to show the step-by-step order of doing a process.

Each shape in the flowchart helps to show the correct instruction for each step of the solution.

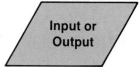

Input or Output

Process

Decision

The flowchart below shows the plan for finding a palindrome for a number. A **palindrome** is a phrase or a number that reads the same forwards and backwards.

"Madam I'm Adam" and **3113** are palindromes.

The flowchart shows a loop. In a loop, certain steps are repeated over and over again.

Which steps are looped in this flowchart?

Use the flowchart. Find a palindrome from the number.

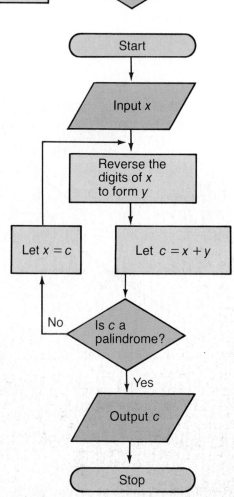

Start

Input x

Reverse the digits of x to form y

Let $x = c$

Let $c = x + y$

No

Is c a palindrome?

Yes

Output c

Stop

1. $x = 27$
2. $x = 431$
3. $x = 7681$
4. $x = 90$
5. $x = 625$
6. $x = 68$
7. $x = 3592$
8. $x = 46{,}071$

7

This dish collects the heat of the sun. Which of its lines do you think are straight? curved? Why do you think this collector is dish-shaped?

GEOMETRY, PERIMETER, AREA

179

POINTS, LINES, PLANES

A **point** shows an exact location. A **line** is a set of points. It extends in both directions without end.

Points A and B
Line AB, written $\overleftrightarrow{AB}$

A **line segment** is part of a line. It has two endpoints.

Line segment AB, written $\overline{AB}$

A **ray** is part of a line. It has one endpoint and goes on and on in one direction. You name the endpoint first.

Ray PQ, written $\overrightarrow{PQ}$

Lines that cross each other are called **intersecting lines.** Intersecting lines that form square corners, or right angles, are **perpendicular.** Lines that will never intersect are called **parallel lines.**

intersecting

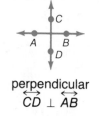

perpendicular
$\overleftrightarrow{CD} \perp \overleftrightarrow{AB}$

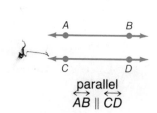

parallel
$\overleftrightarrow{AB} \parallel \overleftrightarrow{CD}$

A **plane** is a set of points on a flat surface that extends without end in all directions.

 Think: Is a wall part of a plane? Can you picture it continuing in all directions?

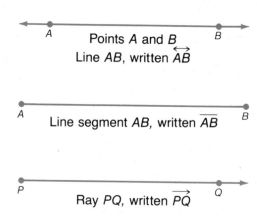

Plane M

CLASS EXERCISES

Name the figure using the letters shown.

1.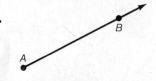

2.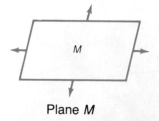

3.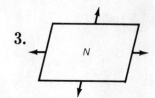

Write the letter for the figure that matches.

4. parallel lines   A.   B.   C.

5. perpendicular lines

6. intersecting lines

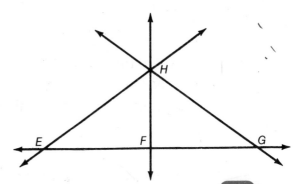

PRACTICE

Use the figure at the right.

7. Name four lines.

8. Name six segments.

9. Name ten rays.

Name the geometric figure you picture.

10. Picture the part of a line that lies between two points.

MENTAL MATH

11. Picture a point and part of a line extending from that point in one direction without end.

12. Picture two rays extending in opposite directions from the same endpoint.

PROBLEM SOLVING APPLICATIONS
Interpreting a Diagram

Write *parallel*, *perpendicular*, or *intersecting* to describe the way the pair of lines looks to you.

13. $\overleftrightarrow{AB}$ and $\overleftrightarrow{CD}$

14. $\overleftrightarrow{EF}$ and $\overleftrightarrow{AI}$

15. $\overleftrightarrow{IJ}$ and $\overleftrightarrow{BJ}$

16. $\overleftrightarrow{EF}$ and $\overleftrightarrow{GH}$

17. $\overleftrightarrow{DC}$ and $\overleftrightarrow{BJ}$

18. $\overleftrightarrow{GH}$ and $\overleftrightarrow{AI}$

19. $\overleftrightarrow{AI}$ and $\overleftrightarrow{IJ}$

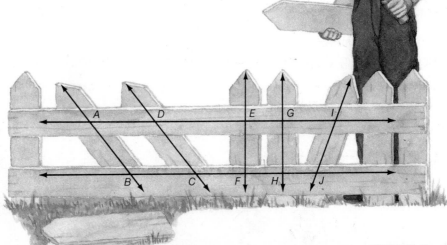

ACUTE, RIGHT, AND OBTUSE ANGLES

Two rays with a common endpoint form an **angle.** The common endpoint is the **vertex** of the angle.

You can use a protractor to measure the number of units, or **degrees,** in an angle.

- First place the center of the protractor on the vertex, B, and the base of the protractor on $\overrightarrow{BA}$.

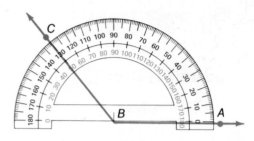

- Then read the measure of the angle where $\overrightarrow{BC}$ passes through the scale.
- The measure of $\angle ABC$ is 130 degrees (130°).
Write $m\angle ABC = 130°$.

Angle B, Angle ABC, or Angle CBA
$\angle B$, $\angle ABC$, or $\angle CBA$

Think: How can you use a protractor to draw an angle of a given size?

$\angle ABC$ measures 90°.
$\angle ABC$ is a **right angle.**
$\overrightarrow{BA}$ is perpendicular to $\overrightarrow{BC}$.

$\angle DEF$ measures less than 90°. $\angle DEF$ is an **acute angle.**

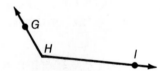

$\angle GHI$ measures more than 90° but less than 180°. $\angle GHI$ is an **obtuse angle.**

The symbol $\sqsupset$ shows a right angle in a diagram.

CLASS EXERCISES

Is the angle *acute, obtuse,* or *right?* Write *A, O,* or *R.*

1.

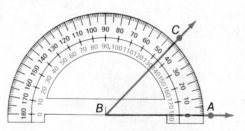

2.

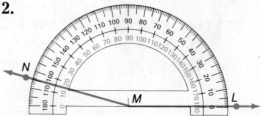

PRACTICE

Use a protractor to determine the measure of the angle.
Write *acute*, *obtuse*, or *right*.

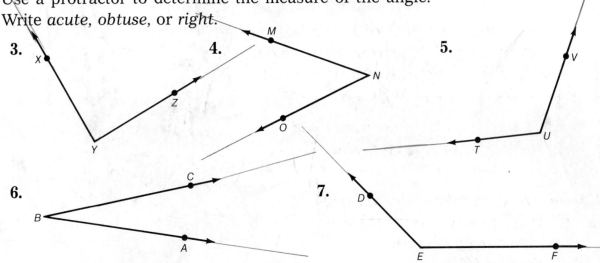

3.   **4.**   **5.**

6.   **7.**

Draw an angle of the given measure.

8. 25°   **9.** 98°   **10.** 46°   **11.** 120°   **12.** 90°   **13.** 75°

PROBLEM SOLVING APPLICATIONS
Drawing Diagrams

Draw the diagram and measure to answer.

14. Draw a line *AB*. Draw a point *C* between points *A* and *B*. Use a protractor to draw a ray *CD* perpendicular to line *AB*. What is the sum of the measures of ∠*DCA* and ∠*DCB*?

15. Draw a line *EF*. Draw a point *G* between points *E* and *F*. Draw a ray *GH*, above line *EF*. Measure ∠*HGE* and ∠*HGF*. What is the sum of the measures of these two angles?

★ **16.** Draw a line *JK*. Draw a point *L* between *J* and *K*. Draw two rays above line *JK* from *L*. Label the left one $\overrightarrow{LM}$ and the right one $\overrightarrow{LN}$. Measure ∠*JLM*, ∠*MLN*, and ∠*NLK*. What is the sum of the measures of these three angles?

POLYGONS

A simple closed figure formed by joining three or more segments is called a **polygon.** The segments that form the polygon are called **sides.** The points where the sides intersect are called **vertexes.**

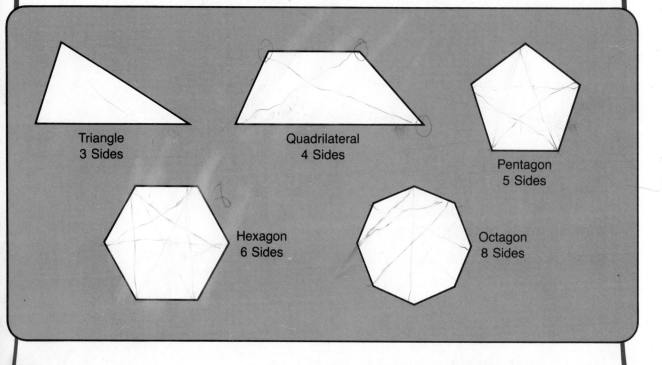

Triangle
3 Sides

Quadrilateral
4 Sides

Pentagon
5 Sides

Hexagon
6 Sides

Octagon
8 Sides

If all the sides of a polygon are the same length, and all the angles have the same measure, the polygon is called a **regular polygon.**

CLASS EXERCISES

Name the polygon.

1.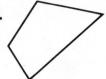

2.

3.

4.

5. **Think:** What do you notice about the number of sides and the number of vertexes for each polygon?

PRACTICE

Use the figure at the right.

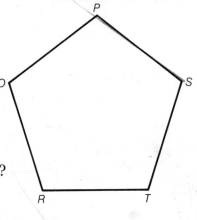

6. Name the sides of the pentagon.

7. Name the angles of the pentagon.

8. Use a centimeter ruler to measure each side. What is the length of each side?

9. Are all the angles of the pentagon the same size?

10. Is this a regular pentagon? Why?

11. What is the sum of the measures of all the angles of this pentagon? Can this sum be evenly divided by 180?

Write the answer.

12. $15.2 + 6.85$ 13. $285 + 75$ 14. $11.5 - 2.9$

15. $85.4 + 2.7$ 16. $13 - 7.8$ 17. $14.7 - 9.9$

MIXED REVIEW

PROBLEM SOLVING APPLICATIONS
Using Patterns

A line segment that joins two vertexes of a polygon but is not a side is called a **diagonal.** Complete the table below.

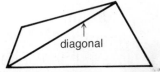

diagonal

	POLYGON	NUMBER OF VERTEXES	NUMBER OF SIDES	NUMBER OF DIAGONALS	SIDES PLUS DIAGONALS
18.	Triangle	?	?	?	?
19.	Quadrilateral	?	?	?	?
20.	Pentagon	?	?	?	?
21.	Hexagon	?	?	?	?
22.	Heptagon	7	?	?	?

★ 23. If you have completed Exercises 18–22, find a pattern in the last column. Predict what the entry would be in this column for an octagon.

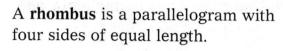

QUADRILATERALS

Some quadrilaterals have special properties.

A **parallelogram** is a quadrilateral with opposite sides parallel.

A **rhombus** is a parallelogram with four sides of equal length.

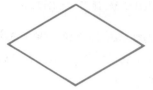

A **rectangle** is a parallelogram with four right angles.

A **square** is a rectangle with four sides of equal length.

A **trapezoid** is a quadrilateral with exactly one pair of opposite sides parallel.

 The sum of the measures of the angles of any quadrilateral is 360°. **Think:** If three angles of a quadrilateral are 45°, 170°, and 87°, how can you use a calculator to find the measure of the fourth angle?

CLASS EXERCISES

Choose the correct name for the figure. Write *a* or *b*.

1.
a. square
b. rhombus

2.
a. rhombus
b. rectangle

3.
a. trapezoid
b. square

4.
a. parallelogram
b. polygon

5.
a. square
b. polygon

6.
a. trapezoid
b. rhombus

PRACTICE

Write *true* or *false*. Drawing a picture may help you decide.

7. The sides of a rectangle are perpendicular to each other.

8. A square is a rectangle.

9. A square is a rhombus.

10. A trapezoid is a parallelogram.

11. If a parallelogram has all angles the same size, it must be a rectangle.

12. A rhombus that isn't a square is a regular quadrilateral.

13. The opposite sides of a parallelogram are equal in length.

★14. A parallelogram cannot have only two right angles.

What is the measure of the fourth angle of the quadrilateral? You may wish to use a calculator by entering 360 and subtracting each angle measure in turn.

CALCULATOR

15. 60°, 60°, 120°   **16.** 75°, 100°, 70°   **17.** 50°, 125°, 140°

18. 82°, 82°, 98°   **19.** 25°, 65°, 130°   **20.** 38.5°, 108°, 37.5°

PROBLEM SOLVING APPLICATIONS
Drawing a Diagram

Draw a diagram to solve.

21. Draw a trapezoid that has two right angles.

22. Draw a rhombus that has sides 6 cm long. Measure the angles. Draw a different rhombus with sides 6 cm long but with different angle measures.

23. Draw a quadrilateral that isn't a parallelogram or trapezoid that has an angle of 90°.

★ 24. Draw a parallelogram with one angle of 45° and another angle of 135°. Measure the other angles. What do you discover?

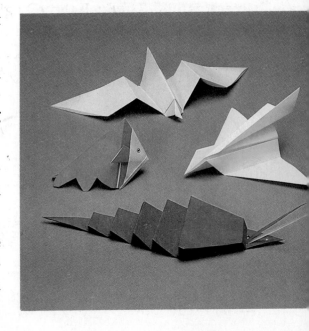

TRIANGLES

Here are some triangles with special properties.

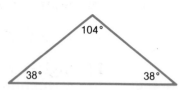

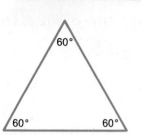

A **right triangle** has one right angle.

An **isosceles triangle** has two sides of equal length and two angles of equal measure.

An **equilateral triangle** has three sides of equal length and three angles of equal measure.

The sum of the angles of any triangle is 180°. You can use this fact to determine the $m\angle C$ in the triangle below.

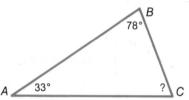

$$m\angle A + m\angle B = 33° + 78° = 111°$$
$$m\angle C = 180° - 111°$$
$$m\angle C = 69°$$

 You can also use mental math to determine a missing angle measure. Start with 180° and subtract the two angle measures you know. The number that is left is the measure of the third angle.

CLASS EXERCISES

Is the triangle *right, equilateral,* or *isosceles*? Write R, E, or I.

1.

2.
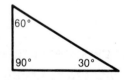

3.
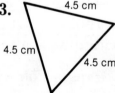

Complete.

4.
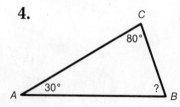

$$m\angle A + m\angle C = 30° + 80° = \blacksquare°$$
$$m\angle B = 180° - \blacksquare° = \blacksquare°$$

PRACTICE

Is the triangle *right*, *equilateral*, or *isosceles*? Write R, E, or I.

5. sides: 3 cm, 7 cm, and 7 cm

6. sides: 4.5 m, 4.5 m, and 4.5 m

7. angles: 35°, 55°, and 90°

8. angles: 37°, 90°, and 53°

9. angles: 60°, 60°, and 60°

10. angles: 55°, 55°, and 70°

11. sides: 6.2 cm, 4 cm, and 6.2 cm

★ **12.** angles: 45°, 90°, and 45°

What is the measure of the third angle of the triangle?
Do as many as you can mentally.

13. 20°, 30°

14. 45°, 10°

15. 10°, 90°

MENTAL MATH

16. 70°, 70°

17. 60°, 60°

18. 65°, 10°

What is the measure of the angle?
Use the drawing at the right.

19. ∠ABC

20. ∠CBD

★ **21.** ∠BAC

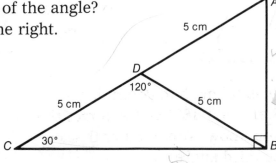

PROBLEM SOLVING APPLICATIONS
Classifying Angles

Use the information in the box to solve the problem. Use a
protractor.

| **Acute triangle** | → All three angles measure less than 90°. |
| **Obtuse triangle** | → One angle measures greater than 90°. |

22. Draw an obtuse triangle with one angle of 100°.

23. Draw a right isosceles triangle.

24. Draw an obtuse isosceles triangle.

★ **25.** Draw an acute triangle with angles of 40°, 75°, and 65°.

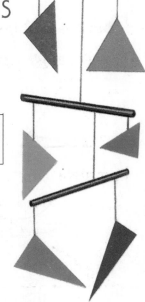

PROBLEM SOLVING
Strategy: Classifying

Venn diagrams can help you understand the use of the words *all*, *some*, and *no* in some word problems.

Are all even numbers whole numbers? Are no even numbers whole numbers? Are some even numbers whole numbers?

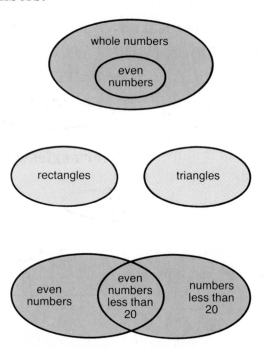

All even numbers are whole numbers but not all whole numbers are even numbers. The Venn diagram at the right shows this.

Are all, some, or no rectangles also triangles?

No rectangles are also triangles. The Venn diagram at the right shows this.

Are all, some, or no even numbers also less than 20?

Some, but not all, even numbers are less than 20. The Venn diagram at the right shows this.

CLASS EXERCISES

Write *all*, *some*, or *no* to complete the sentence.

1.

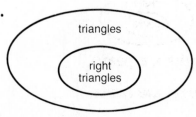

2.

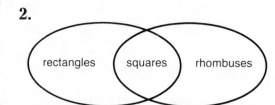

a. ___?___ triangles are right triangles.

b. ___?___ right triangles are triangles.

a. ___?___ squares are rectangles.

b. ___?___ squares are rhombuses.

PRACTICE

Use the Venn diagram below. Write *true* or *false*.

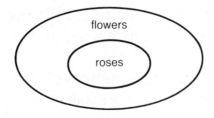

3. All flowers are roses.

4. Some roses are flowers.

5. Some flowers are roses.

6. No roses are flowers.

Copy and complete the Venn diagram to make a true statement.

7. No squares are circles.

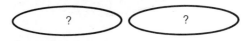

8. All triangles are polygons.

9. Some, but not all, rectangles are squares.

10. Some wild animals are cats.

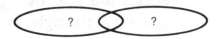

CHECKPOINT 1

Name the figure. *(pages 180–183)*

1.

2.

3.

4.

Name the polygon. *(pages 184–189)*

5. 6.

Use the Venn diagram. Write *true* or *false*. *(pages 190–191)*

7. All fruits are pears.

8. All pears are fruits.

9. Some fruits are pears.

Extra Practice on page 432

PERIMETER

Perimeter (P) is the distance around a figure. You can determine the perimeter of this rectangular cabinet door by adding the two lengths (l) and the two widths (w).

$$65 + 65 + 42 + 42 = 214$$

The perimeter is 214 cm.

In a rectangle the two lengths are the same and the two widths are the same. You can use a **formula** to find the perimeter of any rectangle.

$$P = (2 \times l) + (2 \times w)$$
$$= (2 \times 65) + (2 \times 42)$$
$$= 130 + 84$$
$$= 214$$

Think: Could you also use the formula $P = 2 \times (l + w)$? Why?

The perimeter is 214 cm.

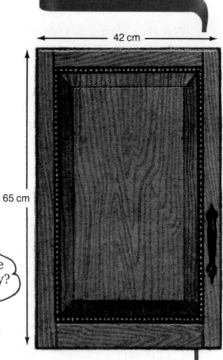

Some calculators have memory keys. Use M+ to add data to the calculator's memory and MR to recall what is in memory. To find the perimeter of the rectangle above, clear the memory and enter:

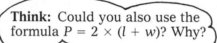

The calculator will display the perimeter 214.

CLASS EXERCISES

Complete.

1.

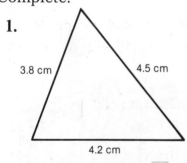

3.8 cm 4.5 cm 4.2 cm

$P = 3.8 + 4.5 + \blacksquare$

The perimeter is ▊ cm.

2.

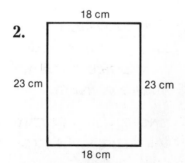

18 cm 23 cm 23 cm 18 cm

$P = 2 \times (l + w)$

$P = 2 \times (\blacksquare + \blacksquare)$

The perimeter is ▊ cm.

PRACTICE

What is the perimeter?

3.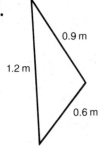
0.9 m
1.2 m
0.6 m

4.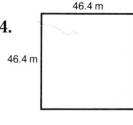
46.4 m
46.4 m

5.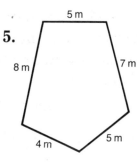
5 m
8 m
7 m
4 m
5 m

6.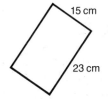
15 cm
23 cm

7.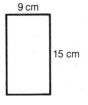
9 cm
15 cm

Determine the perimeter of the polygon. The memory key of your calculator may be helpful.

CALCULATOR

8. Rectangle: $l = 1.7$ cm
$w = 1.9$ cm

9. Rectangle: $l = 65$ cm
$w = 54$ cm

10. Rectangle: $l = 11.5$ m
$w = 8.5$ m

11. Rectangle: $l = 156$ m
$w = 128$ m

★ **12.** Parallelogram: 2 sides each 176.9 cm, 2 sides each 84.9 cm

PROBLEM SOLVING APPLICATIONS
Multi-Step Problems

Solve.

13. A roll of weather stripping is 24 m long. How many rolls are needed to go around 14 square windows that are 0.9 m on each side?

14. How much weather stripping is needed to go around all three windows?

★ **15.** Sue Hong needs to put trim around the outside edge of 4 identical rectangular doors. The perimeter of each door is 9 m. If the height of each door is 3 m, what is the width?

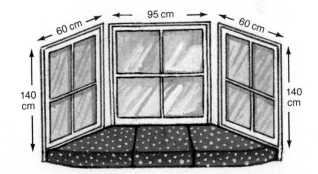
60 cm
95 cm
60 cm
140 cm
140 cm

CIRCLES AND CIRCUMFERENCE

You can use a compass to draw this **circle.** Place the point of the compass at a point that will become the **center** of the circle. Stretch the opening of the compass to 3 cm. Move the pencil around to draw the circle.

The **radius (r)** is the length of a line segment that joins the center and a point on the circle. The **diameter (d)** is the length of a line segment that goes through the center and that joins two points on the circle. The diameter is two times the radius.

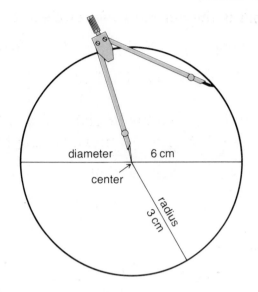

The distance around a circle is called the **circumference (C).** The quotient $C \div d$ is the same number for any circle. You use the symbol π, the Greek letter Pi, to stand for the number which is approximately 3.14. The symbol $\approx$ means *is approximately equal to.*

$C \div d = \pi$ For the circle above $C \approx 3.14 \times 6$

$C = \pi \times d$ $C \approx 18.84$

$C \approx 3.14 \times d$ The circumference is about 18.84 cm.

E For a quick mental estimate of the circumference, multiply the diameter of the circle by 3.

CLASS EXERCISES

What is the circumference?

1. (20 mm)
$C = \pi \times d$
$\approx 3.14 \times$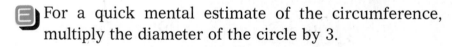
$\approx$ ▨

2. (70 cm)
$C = \pi \times d$
$\approx 3.14 \times$ ▨
$\approx$ ▨

3. (7.5 cm)
$C = \pi \times d$
$\approx 3.14 \times$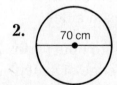
$\approx$ ▨

4. (31.4 cm)
$C = \pi \times d$
$\approx 3.14 \times$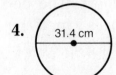
$\approx$ ▨

PRACTICE

What is the diameter of a circle with the given radius?

5. 30 cm	**6.** 16 m	**7.** 35 m	**8.** 167 cm	**9.** 22.9 cm
10. 83.6 m	**11.** 45.91 cm	**12.** 33.9 cm	**13.** 145.87 m	**14.** 32.6 mm

What is the circumference of a circle with the given diameter? Round the answer to the nearest hundredth.

15. 5 cm	**16.** 100 m	**17.** 45 m	**18.** 150 cm	**19.** 0.36 cm
20. 83.6 m	**21.** 736 m	**22.** 0.456 m	**23.** 73.34 km	**24.** 16.81 cm

Write *true* or *false*.

25. π is exactly equal to 3.14.

26. All circles have the same circumference.

27. If two circles have the same radius, they also have the same diameter.

28. All points on a circle are the same distance from the center.

Multiply the diameter by 3 to estimate the circumference.

29. $d = 17$ m	**30.** $d = 3.7$ cm	**31.** $r = 4.5$ m	**32.** $r = 7.2$ m
33. $r = 13$ mm	**34.** $d = 14$ m	**35.** $d = 117$ m	**36.** $r = 2.45$ m

ESTIMATE

PROBLEM SOLVING APPLICATIONS
Using Circumference

Solve.

37. A Ferris wheel's diameter is 15 m. How far will you travel in one turn?

38. The diameter of Tim's bicycle wheel is 68 cm. How many centimeters will the wheel travel in 8 complete turns?

★ **39.** Estimate the distance around the pool at the park shown to the right.

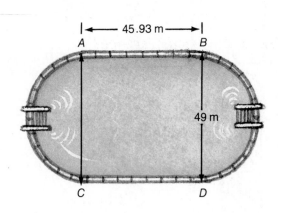

AREA OF RECTANGLES

The **area (A)** of a figure is the amount of surface inside it.

You can count the square units to determine the area of the rectangle.

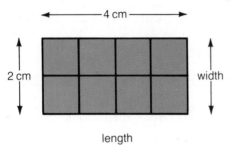

You can also determine the area of a rectangle by multiplying the length *(l)* times the width *(w)*. Use the formula $A = l \times w$.

$A = l \times w$
$= 4 \times 2$
$= 8$

The area is 8 cm².

8 square centimeters

You can count the square units to determine the area of the square.

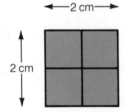

You can also multiply the length of a side *(s)* times the length of a side *(s)* to determine the area of a square.

$A = s^2 \qquad s \times s = s^2$
$= 2 \times 2$
$= 4$

The area is 4 cm².

CLASS EXERCISES

Complete.

1.

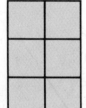

$A = l \times w$
$= \blacksquare \times \blacksquare$
$= \blacksquare$
The area is ▦ cm².

2.

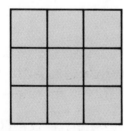

$A = s^2$
$= \blacksquare^2$
$= \blacksquare$
The area is ▦ cm².

3.

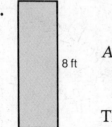

2.5 ft

8 ft

$A = l \times w$
$= \blacksquare \times \blacksquare$
$= \blacksquare$
The area is ▦ ft².

4.

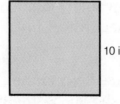

10 in.

10 in.

$A = s^2$
$= \blacksquare^2$
$= \blacksquare$
The area is ▦ in².

PRACTICE

What is the area of the rectangle with the given length and width?

5. $l = 170$ m
$w = 50$ m

6. $l = 350$ m
$w = 170$ m

7. $l = 17$ km
$w = 17$ km

8. $l = 3.4$ m
$w = 1.2$ m

9. $l = 8.1$ cm
$w = 4.0$ cm

10. $l = 0.9$ cm
$w = 0.9$ cm

11. $l = 2.3$ cm
$w = 4.6$ cm

12. $l = 5.5$ cm
$w = 3.0$ cm

What is the area of a square with the given side?

13. $s = 12$ mm

14. $s = 18$ m

15. $s = 2.7$ ft

16. $s = 8.1$ m

★ **17. Think:** If a square has an area of 196 ft², what is the length of each side?

Write the answer.

18. 144
       $\times 0.9$

19. 7.5
       $\times 7.5$

20. 18
       $-\ 1.7$

21. 17.15
       $-\ 3.5$

MIXED REVIEW

22. $11 - 8.75$

23. $4.2 + 13.8$

24. 75.2
       $-\ 6.7$

25. 86.1
       $+\ 0.7$

PROBLEM SOLVING APPLICATIONS
Using Formulas

Solve.

26. A garden shaped like a rectangle is 32 m long and 28 m wide. How much fence is needed to enclose the garden?

27. There are two bare spots in the Gridley's back yard. Each is rectangular in shape and measures 20 m by 30 m. Is a bag of grass seed that covers 500 m² enough to cover both spots?

★ **28.** The Mascari's front porch measures 9 m by 6 m and their back porch measures 7 m by 5 m. Both floors are rectangular. One can of paint will cover 45 m². How much paint do they need to paint both floors?

Any side of a triangle can serve as the base. The height is the length of a perpendicular line segment from the base to the opposite vertex.

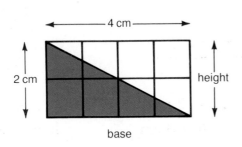

4 cm

2 cm

height

base

The area of each right triangle shown at the left is half the area of the rectangle. You can find the area by multiplying the length of the base (*b*) by the height (*h*) and dividing by 2.

$$A = (b \times h) \div 2$$
$$= (4 \times 2) \div 2$$
$$= 8 \div 2$$
$$= 4$$

4 square centimeters

The area is 4 cm².

The area of the rectangle at the right is $b \times h$, or 80 cm². Try the formula $A = (b \times h) \div 2$ to determine the area of the triangle at the right.

$$A = (b \times h) \div 2$$
$$= (10 \times 8) \div 2$$
$$= 80 \div 2$$
$$= 40$$

The formula $A = (b \times h) \div 2$ can be used for any triangle.

The area is 40 cm².

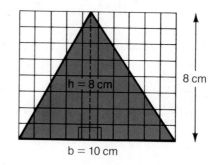

h = 8 cm

8 cm

b = 10 cm

 To estimate the shaded area, count the completely shaded squares and mentally piece together partially shaded squares. The number of square units shaded is about 6.

CLASS EXERCISES

Complete.

1.

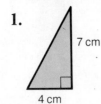

7 cm

4 cm

$$A = (b \times h) \div 2$$
$$= (\boxed{} \times \boxed{}) \div 2$$
$$= \boxed{} \div 2 = \boxed{}$$

The area is $\boxed{}$ cm².

2.

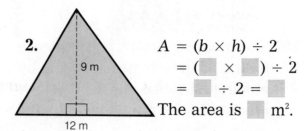

9 m

12 m

$$A = (b \times h) \div 2$$
$$= (\boxed{} \times \boxed{}) \div 2$$
$$= \boxed{} \div 2 = \boxed{}$$

The area is $\boxed{}$ m².

PRACTICE

What is the area of the triangle with the given base and height?

3.

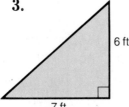

6 ft

7 ft

4.

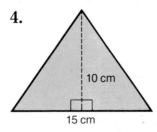

10 cm

15 cm

5.

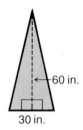

←60 in.

30 in.

6. $b = 14$ cm
$h = 12$ cm

7. $b = 11.8$ mm
$h = 14$ mm

8. $b = 30$ cm
$h = 6$ cm

9. $b = 100$ km
$h = 49$ km

10. $b = 22$ cm
$h = 21$ cm

11. $b = 50$ mm
$h = 30$ mm

12. $b = 7.2$ m
$h = 4.6$ m

13. $b = 200$ km
$h = 200$ km

Estimate the area of each figure in square units.

ESTIMATE

14.

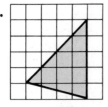

15.

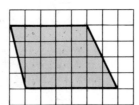

16.

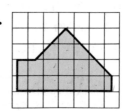

PROBLEM SOLVING APPLICATIONS
Using Area and Perimeter

What are the area and the perimeter?

17.

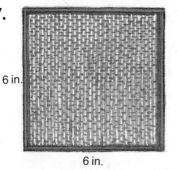

6 in.

6 in.

18.

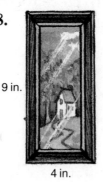

9 in.

4 in.

19.

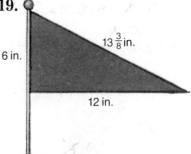

$13\frac{3}{8}$ in.

6 in.

12 in.

20. What do you discover about the areas and the perimeters in Exercises 17, 18, and 19?

AREA OF A CIRCLE

You can estimate the area of the circle by counting the number of square centimeters that are shaded.

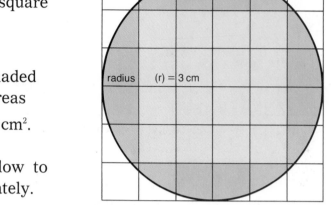

radius   (r) = 3 cm

16 ☐ completely shaded
 8 ◼ almost completely shaded
+ 4 ▨ from other shaded areas
───
28   The area is about 28 cm².

You can use the formula below to calculate the area more accurately.

$$A = \pi \times r^2$$

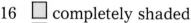 For the circle in the picture you use the formula like this.

$A = \pi \times r^2$
$A \approx 3.14 \times 3^2$
$ \approx 3.14 \times 9$
$ \approx 28.26 \text{ cm}^2$

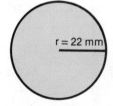 Some calculators have a pi key, $\boxed{\pi}$, with the value 3.1415927. If you use it to find the area of this circle, your answer will differ a little from the one here.

CLASS EXERCISES

Complete to show the area of the circle. Round to the nearest hundredth.

1.
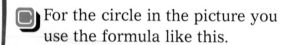
r = 15 cm

$A = \pi \times r^2$
$ \approx 3.14 \times \boxed{}^2$
$ \approx 3.14 \times \boxed{}$
$ \approx \boxed{}$
The area is ▨ cm².

2.
r = 22 mm

$A = \pi \times r^2$
$ \approx 3.14 \times \boxed{}^2$
$ \approx 3.14 \times \boxed{}$
$ \approx \boxed{}$
The area is ▨ mm².

3.
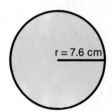
r = 7.6 cm

$A = \pi \times r^2$
$ \approx 3.14 \times \boxed{}^2$
$ \approx 3.14 \times \boxed{}$
$ \approx \boxed{}$
The area is ▨ cm².

4.
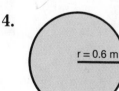
r = 0.6 m

$A = \pi \times r^2$
$ \approx 3.14 \times \boxed{}^2$
$ \approx 3.14 \times \boxed{}$
$ \approx \boxed{}$
The area is ▨ m².

PRACTICE

What is the area of a circle with the given radius?
Use $\pi \approx 3.14$. Round to the nearest hundredth.

5. 2 cm   **6.** 4 mm   **7.** 5 m   **8.** 8 cm   **9.** 9 cm

10. 10 mm   **11.** 30 cm   **12.** 13 m   **13.** 25 m   **14.** 36 km

15. 1.5 m   **16.** 2.2 cm   **17.** 5.5 mm   **18.** 8.1 m   **19.** 9.7 m

Draw a picture to help you answer the question.
Write *yes* or *no*.

20. If two circles have the same radius, will they have the same area?

21. If two circles have the same area, will they have the same radius?

Determine the area. Try using a calculator with a π key if you can. Round answers to the nearest hundredth.

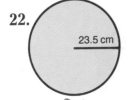

22.
23.5 cm

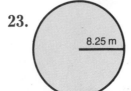

23.
8.25 m

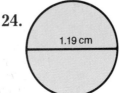

24.
1.19 cm

CALCULATOR

PROBLEM SOLVING APPLICATIONS
Using a Picture

Solve. Use the picture.

25. Anna is trying to decide on a square garden or a circular garden. Which garden would need the most fencing to go around it? Which garden would have the greater area?

16 m

16 m

r = 10 m

★ **26.** How much outdoor carpeting is needed to cover the sidewalk between the pool and the fence? Use $\pi \approx 3.14$.

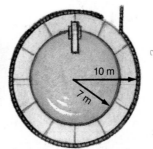

10 m

7 m

PROBLEM SOLVING
Strategy: Using Formulas

1. Understand
2. Plan
3. Work
4. Answer/ Check

Tom needs to put molding around the outside of the picture. He uses the formula for the perimeter of a rectangle.

$$P = 2 \times (l + w)$$
$$= 2 \times (54 + 36)$$
$$= 2 \times 90$$
$$= 180$$

← 54 cm →

36 cm

The perimeter is 180 cm. He will need at least 180 cm of molding.

CLASS EXERCISES

Choose the correct formula.

1.

30 cm
GO BEARS
60 cm

How much felt is needed to make the banner?
a. $A = (b \times h) \div 2$
b. $P = 2 \times (l + w)$
c. $C = \pi \times d$

2.

6 ft

How much fringe is needed to go around the tablecloth?
a. $A = (b \times h) \div 2$
b. $P = 2 \times (l + w)$
c. $C = \pi \times d$

PRACTICE

Solve. Use the correct formula.

3.

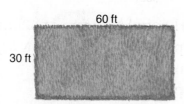

60 ft

30 ft

How many square feet of lawn are there?

4.

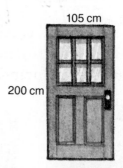

105 cm

200 cm

How much molding will be needed to go around the door frame?

Use a formula to solve. You may wish to draw a picture to help you plan. (Use $\pi \approx 3.14$.)

5. Mindy's yard is in the shape of a rectangle 25 m by 30 m. Andy's yard is twice as long and twice as wide. Does Andy have twice as much yard to mow as Mindy does?

6. Mary King has six triangular herb gardens 2.4 m on each side. If she put edging around each of the triangles, how much edging would she have to buy?

7. A round picnic table has a diameter of 4.2 m. What is the area of a tablecloth that covers just the top of the table? (Round the answer to the nearest hundredth.)

★ 8. Ted King has 36 m of wire fencing. What are the dimensions of the largest rectangular area that he can enclose with the fencing?

Give the area of the shaded region. (Use $\pi \approx 3.14$.)

9.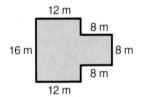

10.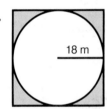

CHECKPOINT 2

Determine the perimeter.
(pages 192–193)

1.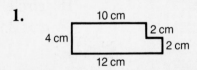

Determine the circumference.
(pages 194–195)

2.

3.

Determine the area.
(pages 196–201)

4. Triangle: $b = 7$ cm, $h = 5$ cm

5. Circle: $r = 4$ m (Use $\pi \approx 3.14$.)

Use a formula to solve.
(pages 202–203)

6. Karl bought a 15 m by 20 m carpet for his room. How many square meters of carpeting did he buy?

Extra Practice on page 432

CHAPTER 7 TEST

Name the figure. *(pages 180–183)*

1.

2.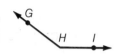

3.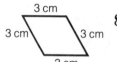

4.

Name the polygon. *(pages 184–189)*

5.

6.
150.9 m
98.2 m   98.2 m

7.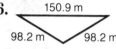
3 cm
3 cm   3 cm
3 cm

8.

Use the Venn diagram. Write *true* or *false*. *(pages 190–191)*

9. All vegetables are tomatoes.

10. No tomatoes are vegetables.

11. Some vegetables are tomatoes.

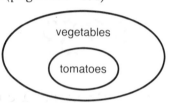

Find the perimeter or circumference. *(pages 192–195)*

12.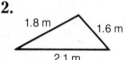
1.8 m   1.6 m
2.1 m

13.
75.5 cm
Regular Hexagon

14.
d = 9.4 cm

15.
r = 8.5 mm

Find the area. When necessary, round to the nearest hundredth. *(pages 196–201)*

16. rectangle
l = 6.4 cm
w = 5.8 cm

17. right triangle
b = 40 mm
h = 35 mm

18. circle
r = 3.9 m

Use the correct formula to solve. *(pages 202–203)*

19. The director of a museum wants to wallpaper a windowless gallery wall that measures 37 m by 12 m. How much wallpaper will the director need?

20. The director wants to rope off a square area around a piece of sculpture. One side of the area is 14 m. Will 60 m of rope be enough?

Extra Practice on page 433

MATHEMATICS and SHOP

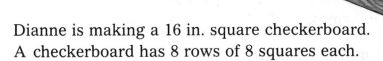

Planning a shop project may call for knowledge of geometry, area, and perimeter.

CAN YOU CUT CORNERS?

Dianne is making a 16 in. square checkerboard. A checkerboard has 8 rows of 8 squares each.

1. What are the dimensions of each square?

2. Dianne plans to make the dark squares out of mahogany. The shop's lumber supply contains a piece which measures 10 in. by 12 in. Will this be enough for Dianne's checkerboard?

Jesse will be cutting a circular table top from a single 4 ft square piece of plywood. He plans to cut the largest possible circle from the piece.

3. He'll use a jigsaw to cut the circle in one single cut. How long will the cut be?

4. A half-pint can of varnish covers about 30 square ft. How many complete coats of varnish can Jesse apply to his table top from a single can?

★5. How much of the 4 ft square sheet of plywood will be scrap?

Enrichment

Networks are made up of paths and vertexes. A vertex is odd if the number of paths that meet there is odd. A vertex is even if the number of paths that meet there is even.

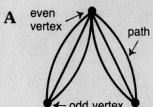

A

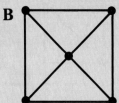

B

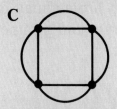

C

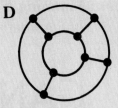

D

A network is *traversable* if you can draw it without lifting your pencil or retracing any path. You can look for a rule

If a network is traversable, it cannot have more than 2 odd vertexes.

NETWORK	NUMBER OF ODD VERTEXES	NUMBER OF EVEN VERTEXES	TRAVERSABLE?
A	2	1	yes
B	4	1	no
C	0	4	yes
D	8	0	no

R

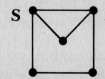

S

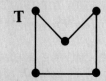

T

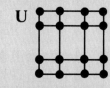

U

Complete the table for the networks to the right.

	NETWORK	NUMBER OF ODD VERTEXES	NUMBER OF EVEN VERTEXES	TRAVERSABLE?
1.	R	?	?	?
2.	S	?	?	?
3.	T	?	?	?
4.	U	?	?	?

NETWORKS

The spaces in a network are called regions. Including the region outside the paths, this network has 3 regions.

Copy and complete the table for the networks to the right.

M **N** **O**  **P**

	NETWORK	VERTEXES	REGIONS	PATHS
5.	M	?	?	?
6.	N	?	?	?
7.	O	?	?	?
8.	P	?	?	?

9. Add the number of vertexes and the number of regions for each network above. Compare this number with the number of paths. Complete the equation.

$$\text{Vertexes} + \text{Regions} - \text{Paths} = \blacksquare$$

Use the equation from Exercise 9. Solve.

10. A network has 5 vertexes and 4 regions. How many paths does it have?

11. A network has 8 paths and 4 vertexes. How many regions does it have?

12. A network has 3 paths and 2 vertexes. How many regions does it have?

13. A network has 12 paths and 6 regions. How many vertexes does it have?

Copy each network. Try to color the network using 4 or fewer colors. No two touching regions can be the same color.

14.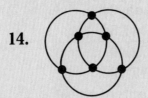

15.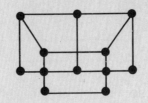

CUMULATIVE REVIEW

Choose the correct answer. Write *a, b, c,* or *d.*

Find the value of the underlined digit.

1. 9<u>6</u>,781
   a. 60,000
   b. 6,000
   c. 600
   d. none of these

2. <u>4</u>52,452,452
   a. 400
   b. 4,000,000
   c. 400,000,000
   d. none of these

3. 6,1<u>7</u>4,333,899
   a. 70 billion
   b. 7 ten-billions
   c. 7 ten-millions
   d. none of these

Order the decimals from least to greatest.

4. 3.72, 2.73, 3.27
   a. 2.73, 3.27, 3.72
   b. 3.72, 3.27, 2.73
   c. 2.73, 3.72, 3.27
   d. none of these

5. 4.6, 4.64, 4.604
   a. 4.6, 4.64, 4.604
   b. 4.64, 4.604, 4.6
   c. 4.6, 4.604, 4.64
   d. none of these

6. 8.80, 8.088, 8.08, 8.808
   a. 8.08, 8.088, 8.80, 8.808
   b. 8.088, 8.08, 8.808, 8.80
   c. 8.808, 8.80, 8.088, 8.08
   d. none of these

Which is the best estimate?

7. 6.47   **a.** 3
    + 3.86   **b.** 4
         c. 8
         d. 10

8. 22.95   **a.** 30
    − 6.105   **b.** 17
          c. 28
          d. 26

9. 48.33   **a.** 56
    − 7.573   **b.** 33
          c. 42
          d. 58

Solve.

10. Firefighters in Flameville were paid $512.75 a week. Recently the amount was raised by $25. The firefighters work a $37\frac{1}{2}$ hour week. What is a firefighter's new weekly salary?

   a. $512.75
   b. $537.75
   c. $737.75
   d. none of these

11. Fines for overdue library books totaled $314.19 in April. Book fines of $82.60 were collected on Monday and $64.90 were collected on Tuesday. How much more was collected on Monday than on Tuesday?

   a. $147.50
   b. $72.40
   c. $17.70
   d. none of these

Find the answer.

12.　14.5
　　　+ 17.3

a. 31.8
b. 21.8
c. 31.2
d. none of these

13.　52.06
　　　− 3.79

a. 49.37
b. 49.27
c. 48.37
d. none of these

14.　30.84
　　　7.009
　　+ 6.233

a. 42.082
b. 43.182
c. 44.082
d. none of these

Solve.

15. Suella has a balance of $178.24 in her checking account. She writes checks for $36.55, $29.08, and $14.93 and deposits $65. What is Suella's new balance?

a. $162.68
b. $160.58
c. $161.68
d. none of these

16. The bank charges $.10 for each check written. There is an $8.25 charge to order 200 new checks. There is also a monthly service charge of $3.50 on all checking accounts. What are Ted Allen's charges if he writes 9 checks and orders 200 new checks in March?

a. $9.15
b. $11.75
c. $12.65
d. none of these

LANGUAGE and VOCABULARY REVIEW

Write the letter of the matching description next to each term.

1. meter

A. the amount of surface inside a figure

2. perimeter

B. the distance around a circle

3. circumference

C. a number that is added

4. area

D. the distance around a polygon

5. addend

E. a metric unit used for measuring length

6. point

F. shows an exact location in space

COMPUTER LOGIC

Programmers use logic statements when they write a plan for a program. Sentences with *IF* and *THEN* are called **conditional statements.** For a computer, the part that begins with IF is the *condition.* The part that begins with THEN is the *action.* For example:

> If the length of each side of a polygon is given, then add the lengths of the sides to determine the perimeter.

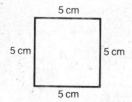

Sometimes the condition has two parts joined by *AND.* When both parts in the condition are *true,* the computer takes the action. When one part of the condition is *false,* the computer does not take the action. For example:

> If the lengths of the sides of a shape are given and they are the same, then multiply the length by the number of sides to determine the perimeter.

> The conditional statement is true. The computer multiplies 5 by 4 to determine the perimeter.

Given the conditional statement, write *true* or *false* for each example. Then write what the computer will do.

If a triangle has 3 equal sides and 3 equal angles, then write "This triangle is equilateral."

If the measure of the angle is less than 90°, then write "Acute Angle."

1.

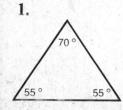

2.

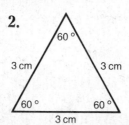

3.   **4.**

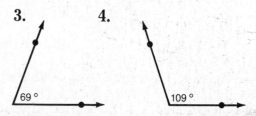

Can a log 28 in. in diameter be sliced into four-inch thick pieces with nothing left over?

NUMBER THEORY
AND DEVELOPING
FRACTIONS

DIVISIBILITY RULES

One number is **divisible** by another if it can be divided with no remainder. Here is a divisibility rule for the number 3 to help you know if a number is divisible by 3 without actually dividing.

A number is divisible by 3 if the sum of its digits is divisible by 3.

Is 29,307 divisible by 3?
Add the digits. 2 + 9 + 3 + 0 + 7 = 21
Is 21 divisible by 3? Yes.
So, 29,307 is divisible by 3.

Here are some other divisibility rules to remember.

DIVISIBILITY RULE	EXAMPLE
A number is **divisible by 2** if the digit in the ones' place is 0, 2, 4, 6, or 8.	37,858 is divisible by 2.
A number is **divisible by 5** if the digit in the ones' place is 0 or 5.	30,015 is divisible by 5.
A number is **divisible by 9** if the sum of its digits is divisible by 9.	73,827 is divisible by 9. (7 + 3 + 8 + 2 + 7 = 27)
A number is **divisible by 10** if the digit in the ones' place is 0.	68,170 is divisible by 10.

 You should be able to use these rules to test numbers mentally for divisibility.

CLASS EXERCISES

What is the sum of the digits?

1. 345　　　**2.** 1000　　　**3.** 27,474　　　**4.** 87,966　　　**5.** 81,810

6. Which of the numbers in Exercises 1–5 are divisible by 2? by 3? by 5?

PRACTICE

Is the first number divisible by the second?
Write *yes* or *no*.

7. 27; 2   **8.** 105; 5   **9.** 206; 10   **10.** 60; 3   **11.** 4761; 9

12. 703,490; 10   **13.** 6790; 2   **14.** 158,602; 3   **15.** 791; 5   **16.** 40,106; 3

17. 87,290; 5   **18.** 44,887; 9   **19.** 97,538; 2   **20.** 598,779; 9   **21.** 123,456; 10

Test to see if the number is divisible by 2, by 3, and by 9.
Write *2, 3, 9,* or *none.*

22. 123   **23.** 666   **24.** 472   **25.** 1872   **26.** 2781

27. 6715   **28.** 6789   **29.** 5697   **30.** 11,112   **31.** 97,884

32. 87,307   **33.** 578,352   **34.** 148,102   **35.** 606,303   **36.** 432,012

37. Think: Is a number that is divisible by 9 also divisible by 3?

38. Think: Is a number that is divisible by 2 and by 3 also
divisible by 6? Write a divisibility rule for 6.

PROBLEM SOLVING APPLICATIONS
Choosing the Operation

Solve.

39. Flo's has 144 bunches of flowers
for the tables. How many more
tables can be decorated if 2
bunches are used per table instead of 3 bunches per table?

40. Flo's has 27 packages of frozen
green beans. Each package contains 8 servings. How many servings of green beans does Flo's
Kitchen have?

41. Flo's served a total of 1724 lunches in 3 days. Could the same number of lunches have been served
on each day?

42. Flo's Kitchen makes lunches for
meetings. The restaurant allows 2
servings of apple juice per person. Can it use 754 servings without any leftovers?

MULTIPLES AND
LEAST COMMON MULTIPLES

When you multiply a whole number by 0, 1, 2, 3, 4, . . ., each product is a **multiple** of the number. The three dots mean that the list goes on and on. Look at these examples.

The multiples of 4: 0, 4, 8, 12, 16, 20, 24, . . .
The multiples of 6: 0, 6, 12, 18, 24, 30, 36, . . .

Since 12 and 24 are multiples of both 4 and 6, they are called **common multiples** of 4 and 6. When talking about common multiples, you do not include 0. There are many other common multiples of 4 and 6. **Think:** What is the next common multiple of 4 and 6 after 24?

The **least common multiple (LCM)** of 4 and 6 is 12, since 12 is the least of the common multiples.

On some calculators you can determine multiples of a number. Follow these steps.

Press a number; then press ⊞ ⊟. You will see the number multiplied by 2.

Press ⊟ again. You will see the number multiplied by 3.

Each time you press ⊟ you will see the next multiple.

CLASS EXERCISES

Complete.

1. The multiples of 2 are 0, 2, 4, ▨, ▨, ▨, 12, . . .

2. The multiples of 3 are 0, 3, 6, ▨, ▨, ▨, 18, . . .

3. The common multiples of 2 and 3 are ▨, ▨, ▨, ▨, . . .

4. The LCM of 2 and 3 is ▨.

PRACTICE

What are the first six multiples of the number?

5. 8   **6.** 5   **7.** 15   **8.** 25   **9.** 150   **10.** 9

What are the first two common multiples of the numbers?

11. 4 and 8   **12.** 5 and 15   **13.** 6 and 9   **14.** 6 and 8   **15.** 25 and 150

Determine the LCM of the numbers.

16. 3 and 4   **17.** 4 and 6   **18.** 2 and 6   **19.** 6 and 10

20. 8 and 12   **21.** 8 and 5   **22.** 12 and 15   **23.** 10 and 20

24. 20 and 25   **25.** 16 and 24   **26.** 18 and 20   ★ **27.** 15, 18, and 20

Determine the answer. A calculator will be helpful.

28. The first 20 multiples of 6   **29.** The first 15 multiples of 13

30. The eighth multiple of 80   **31.** The eleventh multiple of 19

32. The 15th multiple of 78   ★ **33.** The first 3-digit multiple of 7

CALCULATOR

PROBLEM SOLVING APPLICATIONS
Paper and Pencil or Calculator

Tell whether you would choose paper and pencil or a calculator to solve the problem. Write *P* or *C*. Then solve.

34. Mia wants to buy 20 stamps that cost 47¢ each. How much change should she get from $10.00?

35. Peter bought some 12-cent stamps and some 15-cent stamps. He spent the same amount on each kind. What is the least he could have spent on each?

36. Jay will receive *Stamp Fan News* every 6 weeks and *Stamp World* every 8 weeks. If the first issues of both magazines arrive today, when will Jay again receive both magazines in the same week?

★ **37.** The Collector's Showcase has four displays, one each for 20¢, 30¢, 40¢, and 50¢ stamps. If the value of each display is the same, what is the least possible value each display could have?

FACTORS AND GREATEST COMMON FACTORS

Numbers which divide a number with no remainder are called **factors** of the number.

Factors of 8: 1, 2, 4, 8   Factors of 10: 1, 2, 5, 10

$$8 \div 1 = 8$$
$$8 \div 2 = 4$$
$$8 \div 4 = 2$$
$$8 \div 8 = 1$$

$$10 \div 1 = 10$$
$$10 \div 2 = 5$$
$$10 \div 5 = 2$$
$$10 \div 10 = 1$$

Look at the factors above. Since 1 and 2 are factors of both 8 and 10, they are called **common factors** of 8 and 10. The **greatest common factor (GCF)** of 8 and 10 is 2.

 You can use mental math to determine the factors of a number. Since every number has at least two factors, the number itself and 1, you always know at least two of the factors.

To determine the factors of 8, **think:** 1 and 8 are factors. What other numbers from 1 through 8 divide 8 evenly? The factors of 8 are 1, 2, 4, and 8.

$$8 \div 2 = 4$$
$$8 \div 4 = 2$$

CLASS EXERCISES

Complete the chart.

	NUMBERS	FACTORS	COMMON FACTORS	GCF
1.	18	1, 2, 3, ▨, ▨, ▨	1, ▨, ▨	▨
	27	1, 3, ▨, ▨		
2.	45	1, 3, 5, ▨, ▨, ▨	1, ▨	▨
	21	1, ▨, ▨, ▨		
3.	15	1, 3, ▨, ▨	1, ▨	▨
	20	1, 2, 4, ▨, ▨, ▨		
4.	6	1, 2, ▨, ▨	1, 2, ▨, ▨	▨
	12	1, 2, 3, ▨, ▨, ▨		

PRACTICE

Write the factors.

5. 50   **6.** 11   **7.** 26   **8.** 23   **9.** 36   **10.** 24

Write the common factors of the numbers. Then write the GCF.

11. 16 and 20   **12.** 36 and 60   **13.** 24 and 48   **14.** 20 and 100

15. 27 and 63   **16.** 85 and 51   **17.** 9 and 7   **18.** 17 and 51

19. 16 and 24   **20.** 40 and 130   **21.** 75 and 30   **22.** 41 and 17

23. 18 and 36   **24.** 26 and 39   ★ **25.** 8, 12, and 18   ★ **26.** 14, 42, and 51

27. Think: The numbers 4 and 9 each have exactly three factors. What are the next two numbers that have exactly three factors?

Use mental math to list the factors of the number.

28. 10   **29.** 15   **30.** 22   **31.** 79   ★ **32.** 200

MENTAL MATH

PROBLEM SOLVING APPLICATIONS
Choosing a Strategy

Solve.

33. Andrea has 16 buttons on a shirt. There are two colors of buttons, red and blue with more red than blue. The GCF of the two groups is 4. How many buttons are blue?

34. Katura has 26 teaspoons and 13 soupspoons. How many place settings can she complete if she puts 2 teaspoons with each soupspoon?

35. Michael has 90 quarters and 36 nickels. He puts them in piles of only quarters and only nickels with the same number in each pile. What is the greatest number each pile can have?

★ **36.** Use the numbers 12 and 18. Compare their product to the product of their LCM and GCF. What do you discover?

PRIME AND COMPOSITE NUMBERS

A number which is a multiple of 2 is an **even number.** Some even numbers are 0, 2, 4, 6, 8, 10, . . .

A number which is not a multiple of 2 is an **odd number.** Some odd numbers are 1, 3, 5, 7, 9, 11, . . .

A number which has only two factors, 1 and itself, is a **prime number.** The numbers 2, 3, 5, 7, 11, 13, 17, . . . are prime numbers.

A number which has more than two factors is called a **composite number.** The numbers 4, 6, 8, 9, 10, 12, 14, 15, . . . are composite numbers. Notice that 0 and 1 are neither prime nor composite.

Any composite number can be written as the product of prime numbers. This written form is called the **prime factorization** of a number.

To determine the prime factorization of a number such as 60, you can make a factor tree. First, write the number as the product of any two factors.

Then, if those factors are not prime numbers, write each of them as the product of any two factors.

Keep going until you have only prime numbers. All of these prime numbers are factors. The prime factorization of 60 is 2 × 2 × 3 × 5.

Factor Tree

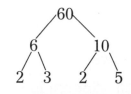

60 MARBLES

CLASS EXERCISES

Is the number even or odd? Write *E* or *O*.

1. 6   **2.** 23   **3.** 87   **4.** 64   **5.** 92   **6.** 145   **7.** 548

Is the number prime or composite? Write *P* or *C*.

8. 20   **9.** 57   **10.** 23   **11.** 31   **12.** 101   **13.** 99   **14.** 531

15. Think: What is the only even prime number?

PRACTICE

16. Follow the steps. Then list all the prime numbers less than 100. (*Hint:* There are 25.)

1	2	3	4	5	6	7	8	9	10
11	12	13	14	15	16	17	18	19	20
21	22	23	24	25	26	27	28	29	30
31	32	33	34	35	36	37	38	39	40
41	42	43	44	45	46	47	48	49	50
51	52	53	54	55	56	57	58	59	60
61	62	63	64	65	66	67	68	69	70
71	72	73	74	75	76	77	78	79	80
81	82	83	84	85	86	87	88	89	90
91	92	93	94	95	96	97	98	99	100

- Copy the table at the right.
- Cross off 1.
- Cross off all multiples of 2 except 2.
- Cross off all multiples of 3 except 3.
- Find the next number that is not yet crossed off. Cross off all multiples of it except for it.
- Repeat the last step until there are no more numbers to cross off.

Make a factor tree to find the prime factorization.

17. 18   **18.** 27   **19.** 35   **20.** 64   **21.** 115   **22.** 210

PROBLEM SOLVING APPLICATIONS
Nonroutine Problems

Christian Goldbach (1690–1764) made two famous statements about some numbers. They are called Goldbach's Conjectures because no one has ever been able to prove them to be true or false.

You can write every even number greater than two as the sum of two prime numbers. For example,

$$18 = 5 + 13.$$

You can write every odd number greater than five as the sum of three prime numbers. For example,

$$27 = 23 + 2 + 2.$$

Test Goldbach's Conjectures with the number. (Remember 1 is not prime.)

23. 24   **24.** 36   **25.** 48   **26.** 17   **27.** 33   ★ **28.** 859

MEANING OF FRACTIONS

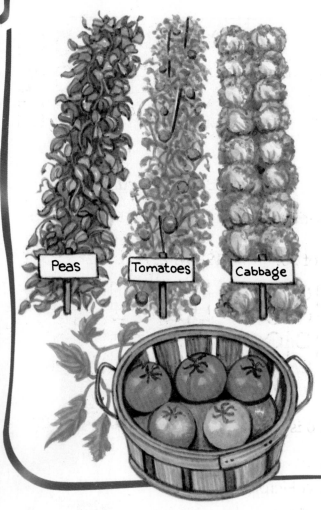

Peas   Tomatoes   Cabbage

The garden is divided into 3 equal parts. Peas are planted in 1 of the parts. You write the **fraction** $\frac{1}{3}$ (read as *one third*) to compare the part of the garden planted in peas to the whole garden.

In a fraction, the top number is the **numerator** and the bottom number is the **denominator.**

$$\frac{\text{numerator}}{\text{denominator}} \rightarrow \frac{1}{3} \leftarrow \frac{\text{part planted in peas}}{\text{total number of parts}}$$

You can write many fractions to describe the tomatoes in the basket.

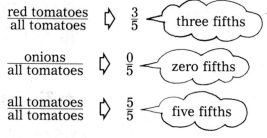

$$\frac{\text{red tomatoes}}{\text{all tomatoes}} \quad \Rightarrow \quad \frac{3}{5} \quad \text{three fifths}$$

$$\frac{\text{onions}}{\text{all tomatoes}} \quad \Rightarrow \quad \frac{0}{5} \quad \text{zero fifths}$$

$$\frac{\text{all tomatoes}}{\text{all tomatoes}} \quad \Rightarrow \quad \frac{5}{5} \quad \text{five fifths}$$

CLASS EXERCISES

Complete the fraction for the shaded part.

1. $\frac{}{9}$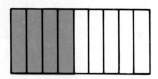

2. $\frac{3}{}$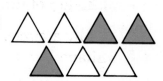

3. $\frac{}{6}$

Copy and shade to show the fraction.

4. $\frac{3}{4}$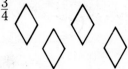

5. $\frac{2}{8}$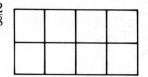

6. $\frac{6}{6}$

PRACTICE

Write the fraction for the shaded part.

7.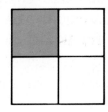

8.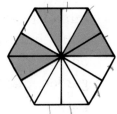

9.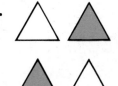

10.

Write the fraction.

11. two sevenths

12. nine tenths

13. four fourths

14. eight twelfths

15. six twenty-fifths

16. forty-three hundredths

17. What is $\frac{1}{3}$ of 9?

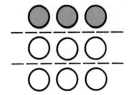

18. What is $\frac{1}{5}$ of 20?

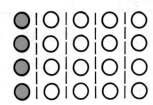

19. What is $\frac{1}{6}$ of 12?

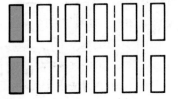

Complete.

20. $\frac{3}{4}$ of 16 is ▢.

★ **21.** $\frac{2}{3}$ of 6 is ▢.

★ **22.** $\frac{4}{10}$ of 30 is ▢.

PROBLEM SOLVING APPLICATIONS
Drawing a Picture

Follow the steps to draw and shade the figure.
Then write a fraction to show how much is *not* shaded.

23. Draw a rectangle.
Shade $\frac{3}{4}$ of it.

24. Draw a square.
Shade $\frac{7}{8}$ of it.

25. Draw a circle.
Shade $\frac{1}{2}$ of it.

26. Draw a square.
Shade $\frac{5}{6}$ of it.

27. Draw a circle.
Shade $\frac{7}{8}$ of it.

★ **28.** Draw a rectangle.
Shade $\frac{4}{4}$ of it.

EQUIVALENT FRACTIONS

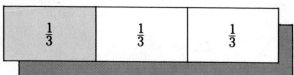

$\frac{1}{3}$ of the unit is shaded

A rectangular unit is shown divided into 3 equal parts, 6 equal parts, 5 equal parts, and 10 equal parts.

You can see that $\frac{1}{3}$ and $\frac{2}{6}$ of the same unit are the same size. Therefore $\frac{1}{3}$ and $\frac{2}{6}$ are **equivalent fractions.**

$$\frac{1}{3} = \frac{2}{6}$$

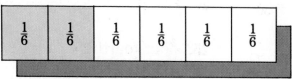

$\frac{2}{6}$ of the unit is shaded

The **terms** of a fraction are the numerator and the denominator. You can multiply the terms of a fraction by the same number, other than zero, to write an equivalent fraction.

$$\frac{2}{5} = \frac{2 \times 2}{5 \times 2} = \frac{4}{10}$$

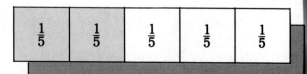

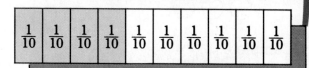

 You can use mental math to determine equivalent fractions.

$\frac{5}{7} = \frac{\blacksquare}{14}$

Think: The denominator has been multiplied by 2, so multiply the numerator by 2. $2 \times 5 = 10$.

$\frac{5}{7} = \frac{15}{\blacksquare}$

Think: The numerator has been multiplied by 3, so multiply the denominator by 3. $3 \times 7 = 21$.

CLASS EXERCISES

What is the equivalent fraction?

1. $\frac{1}{5} = \frac{1 \times 2}{5 \times 2} = \frac{\blacksquare}{\blacksquare}$

2. $\frac{1}{2} = \frac{1 \times 8}{2 \times 8} = \frac{\blacksquare}{\blacksquare}$

3. $\frac{2}{3} = \frac{2 \times 3}{3 \times 3} = \frac{\blacksquare}{\blacksquare}$

4. $\frac{10}{15} = \frac{10 \times 5}{15 \times 5} = \frac{\blacksquare}{\blacksquare}$

5. $\frac{3}{10} = \frac{3 \times 4}{10 \times 4} = \frac{\blacksquare}{\blacksquare}$

6. $\frac{18}{24} = \frac{18 \times 3}{24 \times 3} = \frac{\blacksquare}{\blacksquare}$

PRACTICE

Use mental math to complete.

MENTAL MATH

7. $\frac{1}{8} = \frac{\blacksquare}{32}$ **8.** $\frac{1}{2} = \frac{5}{\blacksquare}$ **9.** $\frac{1}{5} = \frac{\blacksquare}{20}$ **10.** $\frac{4}{7} = \frac{16}{\blacksquare}$ **11.** $\frac{8}{12} = \frac{\blacksquare}{36}$

12. $\frac{5}{6} = \frac{\blacksquare}{24}$ **13.** $\frac{2}{11} = \frac{\blacksquare}{22}$ **14.** $\frac{8}{32} = \frac{16}{\blacksquare}$ **15.** $\frac{9}{27} = \frac{\blacksquare}{81}$ **16.** $\frac{1}{9} = \frac{\blacksquare}{18}$

17. $\frac{3}{7} = \frac{6}{\blacksquare}$ **18.** $\frac{7}{21} = \frac{\blacksquare}{105}$ **19.** $\frac{5}{9} = \frac{\blacksquare}{36}$ **20.** $\frac{2}{3} = \frac{18}{\blacksquare}$ **21.** $\frac{28}{40} = \frac{\blacksquare}{400}$

22. $\frac{20}{25} = \frac{\blacksquare}{125}$ **23.** $\frac{1}{6} = \frac{8}{\blacksquare}$ **24.** $\frac{15}{30} = \frac{\blacksquare}{90}$ **25.** $\frac{4}{24} = \frac{\blacksquare}{72}$ **26.** $\frac{13}{30} = \frac{39}{\blacksquare}$

27. $\frac{4}{7} = \frac{32}{\blacksquare}$ **28.** $\frac{3}{5} = \frac{\blacksquare}{20}$ **29.** $\frac{6}{9} = \frac{\blacksquare}{36}$ **30.** $\frac{5}{9} = \frac{10}{\blacksquare}$ **31.** $\frac{11}{20} = \frac{\blacksquare}{100}$

PROBLEM SOLVING APPLICATIONS
Using Mental Math

32. What are the people in the picture trying to do? To find
out, locate an equivalent fraction and write the letter.

W	K	A	O	L	P	J	C	Y	E	R	F
$\frac{2}{20}$	$\frac{2}{12}$	$\frac{4}{8}$	$\frac{8}{20}$	$\frac{2}{7}$	$\frac{5}{9}$	$\frac{7}{11}$	$\frac{1}{29}$	$\frac{1}{12}$	$\frac{15}{36}$	$\frac{24}{30}$	$\frac{3}{4}$

S	I	D	M	N	Q	B	U	T	G	H	V
$\frac{2}{6}$	$\frac{3}{8}$	$\frac{42}{60}$	$\frac{2}{3}$	$\frac{4}{20}$	$\frac{4}{7}$	$\frac{1}{8}$	$\frac{3}{75}$	$\frac{5}{13}$	$\frac{3}{21}$	$\frac{2}{9}$	$\frac{2}{8}$

FRACTIONS IN LOWEST TERMS

You can see that $\frac{4}{8}$ of the windows are open. You can write an equivalent fraction for $\frac{4}{8}$ by dividing the numerator and the denominator by the same number.

$$\frac{4}{8} = \frac{4 \div 2}{8 \div 2} = \frac{2}{4}$$

To write $\frac{4}{8}$ in **lowest terms** you can divide both terms of the fraction by 4, their greatest common factor (GCF).

$$\frac{4}{8} = \frac{4 \div 4}{8 \div 4} = \frac{1}{2}$$

CLASS EXERCISES

Complete.

1. $\frac{4}{6} = \frac{4 \div 2}{6 \div 2} = \frac{\blacksquare}{\blacksquare}$

2. $\frac{6}{9} = \frac{6 \div 3}{9 \div 3} = \frac{\blacksquare}{\blacksquare}$

3. $\frac{24}{32} = \frac{24 \div 8}{32 \div 8} = \frac{\blacksquare}{\blacksquare}$

4. $\frac{6}{24} = \frac{6 \div 6}{24 \div 6} = \frac{\blacksquare}{\blacksquare}$

5. $\frac{3}{15} = \frac{3 \div 3}{15 \div 3} = \frac{\blacksquare}{\blacksquare}$

6. $\frac{12}{16} = \frac{12 \div 4}{16 \div 4} = \frac{\blacksquare}{\blacksquare}$

7. **Think:** A fraction is written in lowest terms. What can you say about the numerator and the denominator?

PRACTICE

Write in lowest terms.

8. $\frac{8}{10}$ 9. $\frac{5}{25}$ 10. $\frac{20}{36}$ 11. $\frac{9}{12}$ 12. $\frac{28}{36}$ 13. $\frac{9}{15}$

14. $\frac{3}{6}$ 15. $\frac{2}{4}$ 16. $\frac{14}{21}$ 17. $\frac{9}{18}$ 18. $\frac{15}{24}$ 19. $\frac{7}{35}$

20. $\frac{8}{40}$ 21. $\frac{6}{15}$ 22. $\frac{8}{24}$ 23. $\frac{6}{10}$ 24. $\frac{5}{36}$ 25. $\frac{9}{24}$

26. $\frac{7}{28}$ 27. $\frac{3}{9}$ 28. $\frac{8}{28}$ 29. $\frac{7}{21}$ 30. $\frac{8}{21}$ ★ 31. $\frac{108}{250}$

Write the answer.

32. 43×4.78 33. $6.72 \div 7$ 34. 307×15.08

35. $11.40 \div 4$ 36. 7.09×68 37. $2276.5 \div 29$

MIXED REVIEW

PROBLEM SOLVING APPLICATIONS
Using Fractions in Lowest Terms

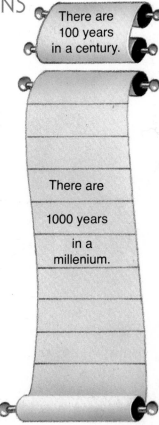

There are 100 years in a century.

There are 1000 years in a millenium.

Franklin D. Roosevelt was president of the United States for 12 years. This amount of time is $\frac{12}{100}$ or $\frac{3}{25}$ of a century.

Write the number of years as a fraction of a century. Write your answer in lowest terms.

38. 20 years   39. 90 years   40. 50 years

41. 75 years   42. 5 years   43. 22 years

44. 84 years   45. 35 years   46. 38 years

Write the number of years as a fraction of a millennium. Write your answer in lowest terms.

47. 300 years   48. 250 years   49. 60 years

50. 700 years   51. 800 years   52. 500 years

53. 650 years   54. 125 years   55. 435 years

★ 56. What fraction of a millennium is a century?

COMPARING AND ORDERING FRACTIONS

It's easy to compare $\frac{2}{5}$ and $\frac{3}{5}$ because they have the same denominator.

$2 < 3$, so $\frac{2}{5} < \frac{3}{5}$

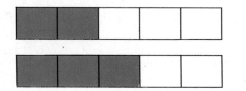

$\frac{2}{5} < \frac{3}{5}$

It's not as easy to compare $\frac{2}{3}$ and $\frac{3}{4}$ because they have different denominators. Find the LCM of the denominators. Since 12 is the LCM of 3 and 4, it's the **least common denominator** (LCD) of $\frac{2}{3}$ and $\frac{3}{4}$.

Write equivalent fractions with a denominator of 12.

Compare the fractions.

$$\frac{2}{3} = \frac{8}{12} \qquad \frac{3}{4} = \frac{9}{12}$$

$$\frac{8}{12} < \frac{9}{12}, \text{ so } \frac{2}{3} < \frac{3}{4}$$

You can order fractions by comparing them in pairs. For example, put $\frac{5}{6}, \frac{3}{4},$ and $\frac{2}{3}$ in order from least to greatest.

$$\frac{5}{6} = \frac{10}{12} \qquad \frac{3}{4} = \frac{9}{12} \qquad \frac{2}{3} = \frac{8}{12}$$

Since $\frac{8}{12} < \frac{9}{12} < \frac{10}{12}$, the order from least to greatest is $\frac{2}{3}, \frac{3}{4}, \frac{5}{6}$.

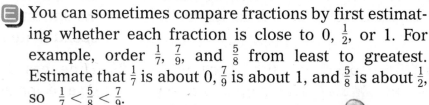

You can sometimes compare fractions by first estimating whether each fraction is close to 0, $\frac{1}{2}$, or 1. For example, order $\frac{1}{7}, \frac{7}{9},$ and $\frac{5}{8}$ from least to greatest. Estimate that $\frac{1}{7}$ is about 0, $\frac{7}{9}$ is about 1, and $\frac{5}{8}$ is about $\frac{1}{2}$, so $\frac{1}{7} < \frac{5}{8} < \frac{7}{9}$.

CLASS EXERCISES

Find the LCD of the pair of fractions. Use it to write the equivalent fractions. Then write < or > to compare the fractions.

1. $\frac{1}{3}$ and $\frac{3}{8}$ **2.** $\frac{5}{6}$ and $\frac{7}{10}$ **3.** $\frac{2}{5}$ and $\frac{8}{15}$ **4.** $\frac{3}{4}$ and $\frac{5}{12}$

PRACTICE

Write < or > to compare the fractions.

5. $\frac{5}{9}$ ▦ $\frac{2}{9}$　　**6.** $\frac{5}{16}$ ▦ $\frac{3}{4}$　　**7.** $\frac{7}{9}$ ▦ $\frac{2}{3}$　　**8.** $\frac{5}{9}$ ▦ $\frac{7}{18}$　　**9.** $\frac{3}{7}$ ▦ $\frac{14}{35}$

10. $\frac{4}{5}$ ▦ $\frac{3}{4}$　　**11.** $\frac{7}{10}$ ▦ $\frac{2}{3}$　　**12.** $\frac{5}{6}$ ▦ $\frac{8}{9}$　　**13.** $\frac{3}{7}$ ▦ $\frac{5}{21}$　　**14.** $\frac{2}{3}$ ▦ $\frac{3}{5}$

15. $\frac{5}{8}$ ▦ $\frac{2}{3}$　　**16.** $\frac{11}{12}$ ▦ $\frac{8}{9}$　　**17.** $\frac{7}{18}$ ▦ $\frac{5}{12}$　　**18.** $\frac{2}{9}$ ▦ $\frac{1}{6}$　　**19.** $\frac{6}{25}$ ▦ $\frac{1}{4}$

Estimate to write the fractions in order from least to greatest.

ESTIMATE

20. $\frac{7}{12}, \frac{2}{15}, \frac{99}{100}$　　　**21.** $\frac{14}{15}, \frac{9}{20}, \frac{1}{11}$　　　**22.** $\frac{2}{27}, \frac{13}{15}, \frac{20}{43}$

23. $\frac{1}{19}, \frac{6}{13}, \frac{37}{39}$　　　**24.** $\frac{4}{9}, \frac{4}{5}, \frac{1}{11}$　　　**25.** $\frac{17}{20}, \frac{25}{49}, \frac{1}{16}$

PROBLEM SOLVING APPLICATIONS
Using Comparisons

Solve.

26. Alex and Charlie shared a bucket of clams. Alex ate $\frac{1}{2}$ of the clams and Charlie ate $\frac{3}{8}$. Who ate more?

27. Ellen spent $\frac{2}{3}$ of an hour baking and $\frac{7}{8}$ of an hour watching television. On which activity did she spend more time?

28. Sal cooked $\frac{1}{4}$ of a box of spaghetti on Monday and $\frac{1}{3}$ of a box on Saturday. On which day did he cook more spaghetti?

29. Ming has 2 tofu salad recipes. One recipe uses $\frac{3}{5}$ of a package of tofu. The other uses $\frac{2}{3}$ of a package. Which recipe uses less tofu?

30. April has 0.4 kg of rice. She wants to serve 8 people. About how much rice will each person get?

31. Two vegetable recipes serve 8 people. Which one is more economical: the one that uses $\frac{1}{2}$ box of broccoli and $\frac{1}{3}$ package of carrots or the one that uses $\frac{3}{8}$ box of broccoli and $\frac{2}{9}$ package of carrots?

PROBLEM SOLVING
Strategy: Reading Information
from a Graph

1. Understand
2. Plan
3. Work
4. Answer/ Check

The students are studying the size of insects. They recorded the measurements on a bar graph. The graph makes it easy to picture and compare the lengths.

You can read the graph and use the information to solve problems. Look at the left side of the graph. The vertical scale shows the names of the insects measured. Find "flea" on the scale. Look at the right end of the bar beside "flea."

Look down from the end of the bar to the horizontal scale that shows lengths in fractions of an inch. The bar for "flea" ends at the $\frac{1}{8}$-inch mark. So, the recorded measurement for the flea is $\frac{1}{8}$ in.

The end of the bar for the red ant is closer to $\frac{1}{8}$ than $\frac{3}{16}$. You estimate that the red ant is about $\frac{1}{8}$ in. long.

LENGTH OF INSECTS

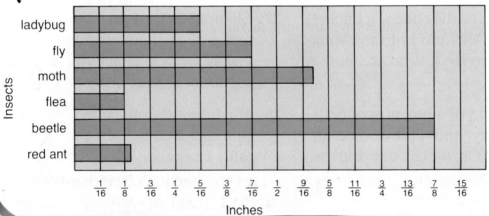

CLASS EXERCISES

Use the graph above to solve.

1. How many kinds of insects did the students measure?

2. On which scale are the lengths shown?

3. How long is the ladybug?

4. What insect is $\frac{7}{16}$ in. long?

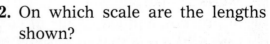

PRACTICE

Use the bar graph about insects to answer the questions.

5. What insect is the longest?

6. What insect is the shortest?

7. Which is longer, the moth or the fly?

8. Which is longer, the red ant or the ladybug?

9. Estimate the length of the moth.

10. Estimate about how much longer the moth is than the fly.

The class measured the rainfall for a week. They recorded what they learned on the bar graph at the right. Use it to answer the question.

11. What does the left scale show? bottom scale?

12. How much rain fell on Monday? Write your answer as it appears on the graph and then in lowest terms.

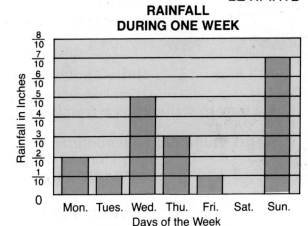

RAINFALL DURING ONE WEEK

13. Which two days had the same amount of rain? how much?

CHECKPOINT 1

Write all the factors. Then write the GCF. *(pages 212–219)*

1. 14 and 20　　**2.** 4 and 5

3. 12 and 24　　**4.** 21 and 49

Write an equivalent fraction.
(pages 220–225)

5. $\frac{8}{9} = \frac{\blacksquare}{18}$　　　　**6.** $\frac{2}{3} = \frac{\blacksquare}{21}$

7. $\frac{10}{15} = \frac{\blacksquare}{3}$　　**8.** $\frac{14}{35} = \frac{\blacksquare}{5}$

Order the fractions from least to greatest. *(pages 226–227)*

9. $\frac{1}{2}, \frac{2}{3}, \frac{3}{8}$　　**10.** $\frac{2}{5}, \frac{2}{7}, \frac{9}{10}, \frac{1}{2}$

Use the rainfall graph above to answer the question.
(pages 228–229)

11. Which day had $\frac{5}{10}$ in. of rain?

Extra Practice on page 434

FRACTIONS AND MIXED NUMBERS

A fraction greater than 1 may be written as a **mixed number,** that is, a whole number and a fraction.

The diagram shows that $2\frac{3}{4}$ is $\frac{11}{4}$.

To change a fraction greater than 1 to a mixed number, divide.

1   and   1   and $\frac{3}{4}$ ⇨ $2\frac{3}{4}$

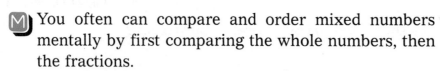

$\frac{11}{4}$ ⇨ $4\overline{)11}$ ⇨ $2\frac{3}{4}$ — remainder

$\dfrac{-8}{3}$ — divisor

$\frac{4}{4}$ and $\frac{4}{4}$ and $\frac{3}{4}$ ⇨ $\frac{11}{4}$

Here's how to write $2\frac{3}{4}$ as a fraction.

Step 1 Multiply the denominator by the whole number. $2 \times 4 = 8$

Step 2 Add the numerator to the product. $8 + 3 = 11$

Step 3 Write the sum over the denominator. $\frac{11}{4}$

 You often can compare and order mixed numbers mentally by first comparing the whole numbers, then the fractions.

Write in order from least to greatest. $3\frac{1}{4}$, $2\frac{4}{5}$, $2\frac{1}{4}$

Since $3 > 2$, $3\frac{1}{4}$ is the greatest.   Since $\frac{4}{5} > \frac{1}{4}$, $2\frac{4}{5} > 2\frac{1}{4}$.

The order from least to greatest is $2\frac{1}{4}$, $2\frac{4}{5}$, $3\frac{1}{4}$.

CLASS EXERCISES

Complete.

1.

$2\frac{1}{3} = \frac{\blacksquare}{3}$

2.

$2\frac{1}{2} = \frac{\blacksquare}{2}$

3.

$\frac{31}{6} = \blacksquare\frac{1}{6}$

Write the quotient as a mixed number. Write the fraction in lowest terms.

4. $4\overline{)9}$ **5.** $4\overline{)13}$ **6.** $6\overline{)26}$ **7.** $9\overline{)39}$ **8.** $5\overline{)47}$ **9.** $8\overline{)79}$

PRACTICE

Write as a mixed number or a whole number.

10. $\frac{11}{6}$ **11.** $\frac{8}{8}$ **12.** $\frac{26}{5}$ **13.** $\frac{35}{1}$ **14.** $\frac{32}{4}$ **15.** $\frac{23}{8}$

16. $\frac{17}{11}$ **17.** $\frac{22}{7}$ **18.** $\frac{40}{8}$ **19.** $\frac{51}{8}$ **20.** $\frac{41}{7}$ **21.** $\frac{37}{3}$

Write as a fraction.

22. $2\frac{1}{2}$ **23.** $3\frac{1}{5}$ **24.** $2\frac{2}{3}$ **25.** $6\frac{1}{7}$ **26.** $8\frac{1}{2}$ **27.** $8\frac{3}{4}$

28. $4\frac{4}{5}$ **29.** $4\frac{1}{8}$ **30.** $6\frac{1}{3}$ **31.** $7\frac{1}{2}$ **32.** $1\frac{3}{7}$ **33.** $7\frac{1}{10}$

Arrange the numbers in order from least to greatest.

34. $4\frac{7}{9}, 2\frac{1}{2}, 3\frac{1}{4}, 5\frac{7}{9}, 2\frac{1}{3}$ **35.** $7\frac{6}{7}, 5\frac{2}{3}, 7\frac{2}{5}, 6\frac{8}{9}, 7\frac{3}{4}$

MENTAL MATH

PROBLEM SOLVING APPLICATIONS
Using Fractions

Solve.

36. Gary needs 14 orange halves to make desserts. How many whole oranges does he need?

37. Ibuto had two and five eighths apples to share with his friends. How many eighths did he have?

38. Lola had two mushroom-cheese pies. She cut each one into eighths. To how many people could she serve one slice?

39. Alice made up a recipe for a fruit drink. Rewrite the amounts using mixed numbers whose fractions are in lowest terms.

$\frac{5}{3}$ c lemon juice $\frac{14}{4}$ c orange juice

$\frac{7}{4}$ c grape juice $\frac{12}{8}$ c apple juice

FRACTIONS AND DECIMALS

Barbara spent three tenths of an hour taking care of her tropical fish. You can write three tenths as a fraction or as a decimal.

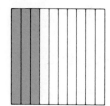

$\frac{3}{10} = 0.3$

When fractions have denominators that are powers of 10, you can easily write them as decimals. Tenths, hundredths, thousandths, and so on can be written as decimals or as fractions with denominators that are powers of 10.

Look at these examples.

NUMBER	FRACTION	DECIMAL
7 tenths	$\frac{7}{10}$	0.7
5 hundredths	$\frac{5}{100}$	0.05
135 thousandths	$\frac{135}{1000}$	0.135
6 and 2 tenths	$6\frac{2}{10}$ or $\frac{62}{10}$	6.2

CLASS EXERCISES

Complete.

1. $\frac{3}{10} = 0.\blacksquare$

2. $\frac{31}{100} = 0.\blacksquare\blacksquare$

3. $\frac{315}{1000} = 0.\blacksquare\blacksquare\blacksquare$

4. $4\frac{5}{1000} = 4.\blacksquare\blacksquare\blacksquare$

5. $0.7 = \frac{\blacksquare}{10}$ $0.17 = \frac{\blacksquare\blacksquare}{100}$ $0.017 = \frac{\blacksquare\blacksquare}{1000}$ $1.7 = \blacksquare\frac{\blacksquare}{10}$

6. $0.38 = \frac{\blacksquare\blacksquare}{100}$ $0.308 = \frac{\blacksquare\blacksquare\blacksquare}{1000}$ $3.08 = \blacksquare\frac{\blacksquare}{100}$ $38.03 = \blacksquare\frac{\blacksquare}{100}$

7. Think: How does the number of decimal places in the decimal compare with the number of zeros in the denominator of the fraction?

PRACTICE

Write as a decimal.

8. $\frac{5}{10}$ **9.** $\frac{68}{100}$ **10.** $\frac{3}{100}$ **11.** $\frac{124}{1000}$ **12.** $\frac{7}{1000}$ **13.** $5\frac{3}{10}$

14. $4\frac{37}{100}$ **15.** $9\frac{371}{1000}$ **16.** $4\frac{7}{100}$ **17.** $8\frac{67}{1000}$ **18.** $7\frac{18}{100}$ **19.** $5\frac{92}{1000}$

Write as a fraction or a mixed number.

20. 0.1   **21.** 0.09   **22.** 0.803   **23.** 0.01   **24.** 0.66   **25.** 0.107

26. 3.15   **27.** 5.73   **28.** 7.5   **29.** 4.003   **30.** 2.017   **31.** 9.783

PROBLEM SOLVING APPLICATIONS
Using Money

Write the amount of money as a fraction and as a decimal part of a dollar.

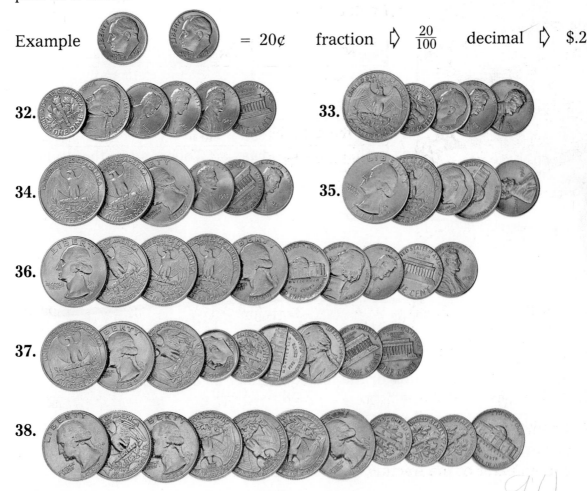

Example ... = 20¢   fraction ⇨ $\frac{20}{100}$ decimal ⇨ $.20

32.

33.

34.

35.

36.

37.

38.

WRITING FRACTIONS
AS DECIMALS

Terry ordered $\frac{3}{4}$ lb of cheese. The reading on the scale was 0.75 lb. Did Terry get what she ordered? To find out, change the fraction to a decimal by dividing.

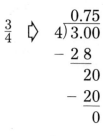

$$\frac{3}{4} \implies 4\overline{\smash{)}3.00}$$
$$\begin{array}{r} 0.75 \\ 4\overline{\smash{)}3.00} \\ -\ 2\ 8 \\ \hline 20 \\ -\ 20 \\ \hline 0 \end{array}$$

Remember, $\frac{3}{4}$ means $3 \div 4$.

Since $\frac{3}{4} = 0.75$, Terry got the amount she ordered.

You can divide to write mixed numbers as decimals, too. Here's how to write $2\frac{4}{5}$ as a decimal.

First write the fraction as a decimal.

$$\frac{4}{5} \implies 5\overline{\smash{)}4.0}$$
$$\begin{array}{r} 0.8 \\ 5\overline{\smash{)}4.0} \end{array}$$

Then add the whole number and the decimal.

$$2 + 0.8 = 2.8$$

You may have to divide to more than one decimal place with some fractions by writing extra zeros in the dividend.

CLASS EXERCISES

Complete. Write the fraction or the mixed number as a decimal.

1. $\frac{1}{5} \implies 5\overline{\smash{)}1.0}$

2. $\frac{3}{5} \implies 5\overline{\smash{)}3.0}$

3. $\frac{1}{4} \implies 4\overline{\smash{)}1.00}$

4. $\frac{3}{8} \implies 8\overline{\smash{)}3.000}$

5. $\frac{3}{4} \implies 4\overline{\smash{)}3.00}$ $2\frac{3}{4} = 2.\blacksquare\blacksquare$

6. $\frac{9}{20} \implies 20\overline{\smash{)}9.00}$ $2\frac{9}{20} = 2.\blacksquare\blacksquare$

PRACTICE

Write as a decimal. Use zeros in as many places as you need to complete the division.

7. $\frac{1}{2}$ **8.** $\frac{2}{5}$ **9.** $\frac{1}{8}$ **10.** $\frac{8}{20}$ **11.** $\frac{16}{25}$ **12.** $\frac{9}{40}$

13. $\frac{7}{16}$ **14.** $2\frac{3}{4}$ **15.** $3\frac{7}{8}$ **16.** $1\frac{9}{10}$ **17.** $8\frac{7}{50}$ **18.** $6\frac{5}{16}$

19. $6\frac{7}{25}$ **20.** $9\frac{19}{20}$ **21.** $5\frac{1}{32}$ **22.** $8\frac{17}{20}$ **23.** $\frac{9}{64}$ ★ **24.** $3\frac{48}{625}$

Estimate the answer.

25. 11.12×47.3 **26.** $104.6 - 78.364$ **27.** $68.2 + 9.5$

28. 951.3×5.1 **29.** $3.9\overline{)23.2}$ **30.** $39 - 19.0128$

31. $12.6\overline{)411.03}$ **32.** $1.01 + 0.9$ **33.** 0.908×2.307

MIXED REVIEW

PROBLEM SOLVING APPLICATIONS
Writing Decimals

Write the fraction or the mixed number as a decimal.

34. It took Jamie half an hour to shampoo his dog.

35. Jackie spent $2\frac{3}{4}$ h shopping for bargains.

36. Pete ate $\frac{9}{10}$ of a pound of grapes before his mother put them away.

37. Lisa walked a quarter of the way to school before she remembered she forgot to bring her homework.

38. Eartha ran $6\frac{3}{10}$ mi last week.

39. Terry spent three and a half dollars at the grocery store.

REPEATING DECIMALS

When you write a fraction as a decimal and have no remainder, the quotient is a **terminating decimal**.

$$\frac{1}{5} \quad \Rightarrow \quad 5)\overline{1.0} \quad = 0.2$$

Sometimes, no matter how many zeros you write in the dividend, the division just keeps on going. When the same numbers repeat in the quotient, you have a **repeating decimal**.

$$\frac{4}{11} \quad \Rightarrow \quad 11)\overline{4.0000} \quad = 0.3636\ldots \quad \Rightarrow \quad 0.\overline{36}$$

```
      0.3636...
11) 4.0000
   - 3 3
     ----
      70
   - 66
     ----
      40
    - 33
      ----
      70
```

> The bar in $0.\overline{36}$ means the digits 3 and 6 keep repeating

Sometimes, only some of the numbers repeat. For example, $\frac{7}{12} = 0.58333\ldots = 0.58\overline{3}$.

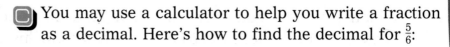 You may use a calculator to help you write a fraction as a decimal. Here's how to find the decimal for $\frac{5}{6}$:

$$\boxed{5} \ \boxed{\div} \ \boxed{6} \ \boxed{=} \quad 0.833333$$

To the nearest hundredth, $\frac{5}{6}$ is 0.83.

CLASS EXERCISES

Complete. Is the quotient a terminating or a repeating decimal? Write *T* or *R*.

1. $20)\overline{9.00} \quad = 0.4\blacksquare$

2. $3)\overline{1.00} \quad = 0.3\blacksquare$

3. $11)\overline{8.000} \quad = 0.72\blacksquare$

4. $25)\overline{17.00} \quad = 0.6\blacksquare$

Write the repeating decimal using a bar.

5. $0.444\ldots$

6. $0.451451451\ldots$

7. $0.68666\ldots$

PRACTICE

Write as a decimal. Use a bar to show the repeating part of the decimal.

8. $\frac{2}{3}$ **9.** $\frac{5}{11}$ **10.** $\frac{5}{9}$ **11.** $\frac{13}{15}$ **12.** $\frac{7}{9}$ **13.** $\frac{7}{18}$

14. $\frac{17}{30}$ **15.** $\frac{11}{12}$ **16.** $\frac{16}{9}$ **17.** $\frac{11}{6}$ **18.** $\frac{21}{22}$ ★ **19.** $\frac{1}{7}$

Write the fractions as decimals. Round to the nearest hundredth. You may wish to use a calculator. Then write < or > to compare the numbers.

CALCULATOR

20. $\frac{4}{11}$ ▨ $\frac{1}{3}$ **21.** $\frac{3}{11}$ ▨ $\frac{7}{18}$ **22.** $\frac{19}{24}$ ▨ $\frac{7}{9}$

23. $\frac{12}{17}$ ▨ $\frac{9}{13}$ **24.** $\frac{27}{35}$ ▨ $\frac{33}{59}$ **25.** $\frac{115}{168}$ ▨ $\frac{246}{275}$

Write the fractions in order from least to greatest. A calculator may be helpful.

★ **26.** $\frac{23}{24}$, $\frac{35}{37}$, $\frac{22}{27}$, $\frac{28}{31}$ ★ **27.** $\frac{16}{9}$, $\frac{51}{37}$, $\frac{39}{25}$, $\frac{31}{18}$

PROBLEM SOLVING APPLICATIONS
Choosing the Operation

Solve.

28. Brandon bought a model for his collection. If the model cost $5.89 and the tax was $.27, what was the total cost?

29. Brandon used 0.25 L of paint to complete his largest model. He used another 0.3 L of paint to complete some smaller models. How much paint did he use in all?

30. One of the car models is 14.5 cm long and 7 cm high. Brandon wants to build another model that is 3 times as long and 2 times as high. What will be the length and the height of the new model?

★ **31.** A ship model is 0.45 m long and 19 cm high. If you build a model that has triple the length and height, how much longer (in centimeters) will the length be than the height?

$5.89
plus tax

PROBLEM SOLVING
Strategy: Interpreting Answers

1. Understand
2. Plan
3. Work
4. Answer/Check

Compare the four problems below. Notice how common sense tells you how to interpret the quotient and the remainder in each case.

Case I   Ignore the remainder.

There are 150 pencils for 60 students. How many pencils does each student get?

$$\begin{array}{r} 2 \text{ R30} \\ 60\overline{)150} \end{array}$$

Answer: 2 pencils

Case II   Write the quotient as a mixed number.

A movie is 150 minutes long. How many hours is this?

$$\begin{array}{r} 2\frac{1}{2} \\ 60\overline{)150} \end{array}$$

Answer: $2\frac{1}{2}$ hours

Case III   Round the quotient up.

There is room for 60 people on a boat. How many boats are needed for 150 people?

$$\begin{array}{r} 2 \text{ R30} \\ 60\overline{)150} \end{array}$$

Answer: 3 boats

Case IV   Write the quotient as a decimal.

It costs $150 for 60 gerbils. How much does 1 gerbil cost?

$$\begin{array}{r} \$2.50 \\ 60\overline{)\$150.00} \end{array}$$

Answer: $2.50 per gerbil

CLASS EXERCISES

Which case describes the quotient? Write *I*, *II*, *III*, or *IV*. Then solve.

1. A crafts worker gets $4 for every key chain sold. How many key chains must be sold to earn $25?

2. A gymnast did 12 flips in 30 seconds. What was the time for 1 flip if each took the same time?

3. It costs $450 for 20 basketballs. How much does 1 basketball cost?

4. Each bag holds 10 peanuts. How many bags can you fill from a bowl containing 257 peanuts?

PRACTICE

Solve.

5. The Fit-for-Life Health Club ordered 298 sweat shirts. The bill was $1639. How much did each shirt cost?

6. Robin swam 20 km in 8 days. She swam the same distance each day. How far did she swim each day?

7. The aerobics instructor has 950 wristbands to give to 308 students. If each student gets the same number of bands, how many does each get?

8. The Olympic Shoe Company ships aerobics shoes in boxes of 25. How many boxes are needed to fill an order for 480 shoes?

9. The health club tennis pro ordered 45 cans of tennis balls. If he sells the same number of cans for each of 7 days, how many cans will he sell each day?

10. The chef at the health club cafeteria made 74 L of vegetable soup. How many 0.24 L servings can be made from this amount?

Write a reasonable problem for the division.

★ 11. $8)\overline{98}$ gives $12\frac{1}{4}$

Answer: $12\frac{1}{4}$ mi

★ 12. $28)\overline{4225}$ gives 150 R25

Answer: 151 cartons

CHECKPOINT 2

Write as a mixed number or whole number. *(pages 230–231)*

1. $\frac{14}{6}$

2. $\frac{28}{7}$

Write as a fraction or mixed number. *(pages 232–237)*

3. 0.04

4. 4.51

Write as a decimal. Use a bar if the decimal repeats.

5. $\frac{4}{10}$ 6. $\frac{1}{8}$ 7. $4\frac{1}{5}$ 8. $\frac{2}{3}$

Solve. *(pages 238–239)*

9. Ari ran 12 km in 5 h of practice. He ran the same distance each hour. How far did he run in an hour?

Extra Practice on page 434

Is the first number divisible by the second? Write *yes* or *no*. *(pages 212–213)*

1. 15; 2   **2.** 20; 2   **3.** 27; 9   **4.** 750; 5

Write the LCM of the numbers. *(pages 214–215)*

5. 2 and 4   **6.** 5 and 15   **7.** 4 and 5   **8.** 6 and 9

Write the common factors for the pair of numbers.
Then write the GCF. *(pages 216–217)*

9. 18 and 48   **10.** 65 and 39   **11.** 30 and 80   **12.** 28 and 70

Is the number prime or composite? Write *P* or *C*. *(pages 218–219)*

13. 17   **14.** 34   **15.** 29   **16.** 51

Write the equivalent fraction. *(pages 220–225)*

17. $\frac{1}{4} = \frac{}{28}$ **18.** $\frac{5}{9} = \frac{}{54}$ **19.** $\frac{41}{60} = \frac{}{600}$ **20.** $\frac{5}{16} = \frac{}{64}$

Order the fractions from least to greatest. *(pages 226–227)*

21. $\frac{4}{9}, \frac{2}{3}, \frac{1}{4}$ **22.** $\frac{3}{4}, \frac{2}{5}, \frac{5}{8}, \frac{3}{10}$ **23.** $\frac{5}{12}, \frac{3}{7}, \frac{1}{6}, \frac{1}{2}$

Write as a mixed number. *(pages 230–231)*

24. $\frac{15}{7}$ **25.** $\frac{23}{4}$ **26.** $\frac{11}{8}$ **27.** $\frac{59}{6}$

Write as a fraction. *(pages 232–233)*   Write as a decimal. *(pages 234–237)*

28. 0.03   **29.** 0.88   **30.** $6\frac{4}{5}$ **31.** $\frac{7}{9}$

Use the bar graph to solve.
(pages 228–229, 238–239)

32. Which one of Sandra's activities takes about 30 minutes?

33. How many hours does Sandra spend ice skating?

Extra Practice on page 435

SANDRA'S ACTIVITIES

MATHEMATICS and ART

Artists study the shape of an object from all sides before drawing it to find the view that is most pleasing to the eye.

DO YOU HAVE AN ANGLE?

1. The first two pictures represent different pitchers. The third picture represents the same pitcher as one of the first two. Which one does it represent? Explain how you know.

2. Which of the two pitchers above do you think is more interesting? Draw it from a different direction.

A still life is a group of objects such as pottery and books. Imagine that you are viewing the still life from different directions. Draw the still life as you would see it from the given direction.

3. the left side

4. the right side

Enrichment

People have studied numbers and their special properties for centuries. Numbers that form patterns are particularly interesting. Do you remember the triangular numbers and the square numbers?

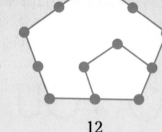

1. Here are the first 3 pentagonal numbers. What is the next pentagonal number?

1   5   12

2. Leonard of Pisa (often called Fibonacci) is remembered for this pattern of numbers: 1, 1, 2, 3, 5, 8, 13, . . . (The next term is the sum of the two previous terms). Name the next eight Fibonacci numbers.

3. Consider 4 Fibonacci numbers in a row at the right. Multiply the two outside numbers. Multiply the two middle numbers. What is the difference between the two products? Try this with four other Fibonacci numbers in a row. Is the difference always one?

3	5	8	13

$$3 \times 13 = 39$$
$$5 \times 8 = 40$$
$$40 - 39 = 1$$

4. Consider 3 Fibonacci numbers in a row at the right. Multiply the first and the last numbers. Square the middle number. What is the difference? Try this with other examples.

3	5	8

$$3 \times 8 = 24$$
$$5^2 = 25$$
$$25 - 24 = 1$$

SPECIAL NUMBERS

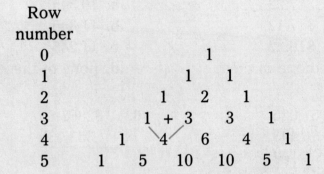

5. Blaise Pascal (1623–1662) is remembered for the following pattern of numbers which he studied a great deal. It is known as Pascal's Triangle even though people knew about it before Pascal was born!

Row
number

0					1				
1				1		1			
2			1		2		1		
3		1 +	3		3		1		
4	1		4	6		4		1	
5	1	5	10	10	5	1			

Each number is determined by the sum of the two numbers above it.

Copy and complete the next five rows of Pascal's Triangle.

6. What is the sum of the numbers in each row of Pascal's Triangle? Can you predict the sum of the numbers in row 11?

7. What are the numbers in the diagonal column of this Pascal's Triangle? Describe the pattern in the shaded diagonal column.

8. Determine the sum of the columns shown in this Pascal's Triangle. What numbers are these sums?

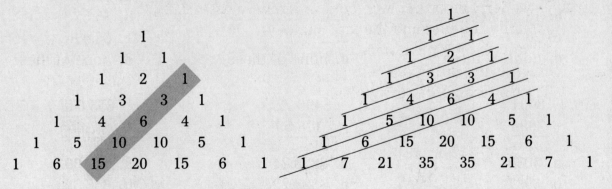

★9. Study Pascal's Triangle. Make a list of other patterns you discover.

CUMULATIVE REVIEW

Choose the correct answer. Write *a*, *b*, *c*, or *d*.

Find the answer.

1.
```
   76
   52
+  13
```
a. 131
b. 141
c. 142
d. none of these

2.
```
  $9.34
+  7.88
```
a. $17.22
b. $17.12
c. $16.22
d. none of these

3.
```
   6565
+  4780
```
a. 10,345
b. 11,345
c. 11,245
d. none of these

4.
```
  47,739
+  9,406
```
a. 57,135
b. 56,145
c. 56,245
d. none of these

5.
```
  51,025
   6,443
+    707
```
a. 58,275
b. 58,165
c. 58,175
d. none of these

6.
```
  $2862.89
+  3537.36
```
a. $6400.25
b. $6400.15
c. $6399.25
d. none of these

Find the answer.

7.
```
   54
-  36
```
a. 90
b. 18
c. 28
d. none of these

8.
```
   921
-  787
```
a. 234
b. 134
c. 144
d. none of these

9.
```
  $6.04
-   .57
```
a. $6.57
b. $5.57
c. $5.47
d. none of these

10.
```
   8031
-  2994
```
a. 5037
b. 6037
c. 5047
d. none of these

11.
```
  $496.72
-  178.59
```
a. $328.24
b. $328.23
c. $318.13
d. none of these

12.
```
  653,048
-   7,655
```
a. 645,393
b. 646,393
c. 655,393
d. none of these

Find the answer.

13.
    9.168
  + 61.359

   a. 71.527
   b. 70.527
   c. 70.517
   d. none of these

14.
    2.074
  + 8.74

   a. 10.714
   b. 10.724
   c. 10.814
   d. none of these

15.
    6.1
  + 32.95

   a. 39.95
   b. 38.05
   c. 39.05
   d. none of these

16.
    8.3
  − 6.8

   a. 1.5
   b. 2.5
   c. 2.1
   d. none of these

17.
   15.07
  − 4.642

   a. 11.338
   b. 11.428
   c. 11.432
   d. none of these

18.
    0.9
  − 0.0056

   a. 0.8944
   b. 0.9056
   c. 0.8954
   d. none of these

Solve.

19. Ken buys a baseball mitt for $17.98, a cap for $6.99, and a shirt for $11.99. How much change should he receive from 2 twenty-dollar bills?

   a. $5.04   **b.** $4.04
   c. $3.04   **d.** none of these

20. Ken wants to buy a baseball bat that costs $16.95. He has saved $6.00. How long will it take him to save the rest of the money if he saves $2.00 each week?

   a. 6 weeks   **b.** 5 weeks
   c. 4 weeks   **d.** none of these

LANGUAGE and VOCABULARY REVIEW

Use one of the terms to complete.

repeating decimal   terminating decimal   square
hexagon   multiples   factors   mixed number

1. When you divide to name a fraction as a decimal and have no remainder, the quotient is a __?__.

2. A rhombus with four right angles is a __?__.

3. The numeral $5\frac{3}{8}$ is an example of a __?__.

4. A __?__ is a polygon with six sides.

5. The numbers 6, 12, 18, and 24 are __?__ of 6.

PLANNING A PROGRAM

Programmers are problem solvers. When they are given a problem, they use many steps to develop a plan for solving it.

Here are the steps for planning a program to find the area of a right triangle or a rectangle.
• *Write what the computer will do:* Find the area of a right triangle or rectangle.
• *Write what is known:* Area is the surface inside the figures.

The formula for a right triangle is $A = (b \times h) \div 2$ and for a rectangle is $A = l \times w$.
• *Decide what you will tell the computer:* If there are three sides, three measures, and one right angle, then use $A = (b \times h) \div 2$. If there are four sides, four measures, and four right angles, then use $A = l \times w$.
• *Write a plan or a flowchart:* Test the flowchart. Write what the computer will do.

1. [square: 5, 5]   2. [right triangle: 3, 5, 4]

3. [triangle: 8, 8, 8]   4. [parallelogram: 5, 7]

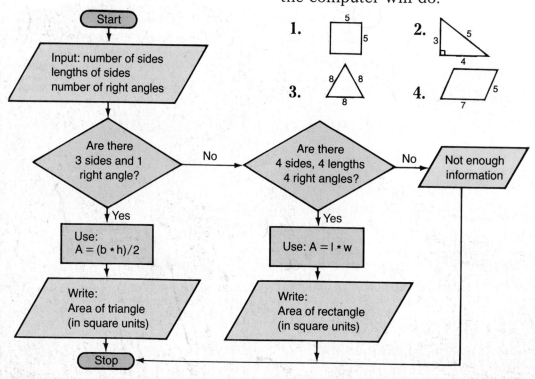

If weaving a carpet requires 100 spools of yarn and 60 have been used, what fraction of the carpet remains to be completed?

9

ADDITION AND SUBTRACTION OF FRACTIONS

USING AN INCH RULER

You can use an inch ruler to measure and draw line segments. Each inch unit can be divided into smaller units to make measuring more precise.

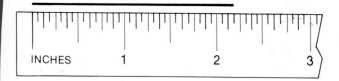

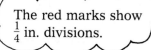

The red marks show $\frac{1}{4}$ in. divisions.

To the nearest $\frac{1}{4}$ in., the line segment is $2\frac{1}{4}$ in. long.

The red marks show $\frac{1}{8}$ in. divisions.

To the nearest $\frac{1}{8}$ in., the line segment is $1\frac{6}{8}$ in. long.

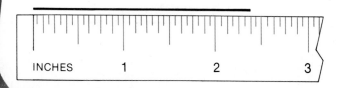

The red marks show $\frac{1}{16}$ in. divisions.

To the nearest $\frac{1}{16}$ in., the line segment is $2\frac{6}{16}$ in. long.

CLASS EXERCISES

Measure the segment to the nearest $\frac{1}{4}$ in.

1.   2.   3.   4.

Measure the segment to the nearest $\frac{1}{8}$ in. and $\frac{1}{16}$ in.

5.   6.   7.   8.

PRACTICE

Measure the segment to the nearest $\frac{1}{4}$ in., $\frac{1}{8}$ in., and $\frac{1}{16}$ in.

9.   **10.**   **11.**   **12.** ——

Draw a segment with the given length.

13. $2\frac{5}{8}$ in.   **14.** 6 in.   **15.** $2\frac{3}{4}$ in.   **16.** $3\frac{7}{8}$ in.   **17.** $5\frac{1}{4}$ in.

18. $1\frac{1}{16}$ in.   **19.** $4\frac{7}{16}$ in.   **20.** $3\frac{1}{4}$ in.   **21.** $\frac{7}{8}$ in.   ★ **22.** $4\frac{11}{32}$ in.

PROBLEM SOLVING APPLICATIONS
Estimating Lengths

Estimate the length of the segment in inches. Record your estimate. Then measure and record the length to the nearest $\frac{1}{8}$ in. Use the chart at the right to rate your estimate. Write *A*, *B*, or *C* to tell how close your estimate is to the actual measure.

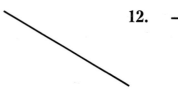

A ⇨ within 1 in.
B ⇨ within 2 in.
C ⇨ within 3 in.

23. ————————————————

24. ——————————————————

25. ——————————————————

26. ——————————————

★ **27.** ——————————

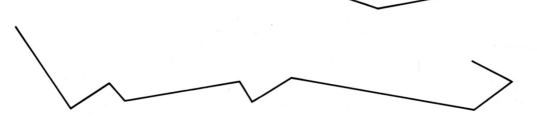

★ **28.**

PROBLEM SOLVING
Strategy: Estimating with Fractions and Mixed Numbers

1. Understand
2. Plan
3. Work
4. Answer / Check

Lily helped her father measure the perimeter of their backyard. The lengths of the sides of the yard are $53\frac{1}{2}$ ft, $48\frac{1}{3}$ ft, $42\frac{5}{6}$ ft, and $17\frac{3}{8}$ ft. If Lily walks around the edge of the yard, about how many feet will she walk?

The problem asks you to estimate the perimeter. To do this, round each mixed number to the nearest whole number. Then add the rounded lengths.

Follow these rules to round mixed numbers:

- If the fractional part is equal to or greater than $\frac{1}{2}$, round up to the next whole number.

- If the fractional part is less than $\frac{1}{2}$, round down by dropping the fraction.

To estimate the perimeter of the backyard, **think:**

$53\frac{1}{2}$ ft ⟶ Round up for $\frac{1}{2}$ ⟶ about 54 ft
$48\frac{1}{3}$ ft ⟶ $\frac{1}{3} < \frac{1}{2}$, round down ⟶ about 48 ft
$42\frac{5}{6}$ ft ⟶ $\frac{5}{6} > \frac{1}{2}$, round up ⟶ about 43 ft
$17\frac{3}{8}$ ft ⟶ $\frac{3}{8} < \frac{1}{2}$, round down ⟶ about 17 ft

$54 + 48 + 43 + 17 = 162$ Lily will walk about 162 ft.

CLASS EXERCISES

Round to the nearest whole number.

1. $1\frac{3}{5}$ **2.** $\frac{7}{8}$ **3.** $16\frac{1}{12}$ **4.** $7\frac{5}{8}$ ft   **5.** $11\frac{2}{5}$ lb

6. Think: If you have $12\frac{1}{2}$ ft of rope and use $4\frac{7}{8}$ ft of it, about how many feet are left?

7. Think: You have $7\frac{5}{8}$ yd of blue fabric and $3\frac{1}{3}$ yd of yellow fabric. Is this more than 12 yd?

PRACTICE

Estimate to solve the problem.

8. Clare's fruit punch recipe calls for $4\frac{1}{2}$ c of orange juice, $7\frac{1}{3}$ c of cranberry juice, and $\frac{5}{8}$ c of lemon juice. About how many cups of juice will Clare need for the punch?

9. Art Brown drove $3\frac{7}{10}$ mi to the hardware store and another $2\frac{4}{10}$ mi to the grocery store. Then he drove $2\frac{1}{10}$ mi back home. About how many miles did he drive in all?

10. Bernie wants to double the amount of punch that Clare made in Exercise 8. About how many cups of each kind of juice will he need?

11. Each time Angela cuts the grass she uses $\frac{4}{5}$ gal of gasoline. If she has 5 gal, about how many times can she cut the grass?

12. Sean's pet cat, Ringo, eats $\frac{3}{4}$ can of cat food a day. About how many cans does Ringo eat in a week?

13. Clara rode her bike $1\frac{1}{4}$ mi a day for 3 days and $2\frac{7}{8}$ mi a day for the next 4 days. About how many miles did Clara ride in all?

★ 14. Arman built a doghouse. Each of the 4 sides of the house and each of the 2 sides of the roof needed $6\frac{5}{6}$ ft of lumber. About how much lumber did he use in all?

★ 15. Lin-Tao found 5 cartons of juice in the refrigerator, each about $\frac{1}{5}$ empty. If she needs about 4 cartons of juice for breakfast, does she have enough?

Name the least common multiple of the pair of numbers.

16. 12 and 8

17. 6 and 10

18. 4 and 12

19. 10 and 16

20. 5 and 4

21. 12 and 10

22. 7 and 6

23. 10 and 15

24. 16 and 24

MIXED REVIEW

ADDING AND SUBTRACTING FRACTIONS

To add fractions with the same denominator, add the numerators and write the sum over the same denominator. Write the sum in lowest terms.

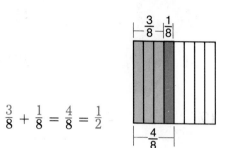

$$\frac{3}{8} + \frac{1}{8} = \frac{4}{8} = \frac{1}{2}$$

$$\begin{array}{r} \frac{3}{8} \\ + \frac{1}{8} \\ \hline \frac{4}{8} = \frac{1}{2} \end{array}$$

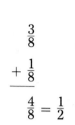

To subtract fractions with the same denominator, subtract the numerators and write the difference over the same denominator. Write the difference in lowest terms.

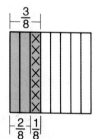

$$\frac{3}{8} - \frac{1}{8} = \frac{2}{8} = \frac{1}{4}$$

$$\begin{array}{r} \frac{3}{8} \\ - \frac{1}{8} \\ \hline \frac{2}{8} = \frac{1}{4} \end{array}$$

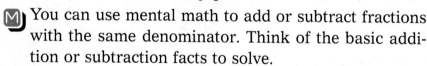

Ⓜ You can use mental math to add or subtract fractions with the same denominator. Think of the basic addition or subtraction facts to solve.

CLASS EXERCISES

What sum or difference of fractions does the picture show?

1.

2.

3.

PRACTICE

Add or subtract. Write the sum or difference in lowest terms. Use mental math.

4. $\frac{1}{4} + \frac{3}{4}$

5. $\frac{2}{10} + \frac{3}{10}$

6. $\frac{5}{8} - \frac{2}{8}$

7. $\frac{11}{12} - \frac{7}{12}$

8. $\frac{5}{7} + \frac{2}{7}$

9. $\frac{3}{4} - \frac{1}{4}$

10. $\frac{4}{5} - \frac{2}{5}$

11. $\frac{5}{8} + \frac{1}{8}$

12. $\frac{5}{6} - \frac{1}{6}$

13. $\frac{5}{12} + \frac{5}{12}$

14. $\frac{9}{10} - \frac{3}{10}$

15. $\frac{6}{7} - \frac{2}{7}$

16. $\begin{array}{r} \frac{13}{16} \\ - \frac{7}{16} \end{array}$

17. $\begin{array}{r} \frac{3}{8} \\ + \frac{3}{8} \end{array}$

18. $\begin{array}{r} \frac{1}{5} \\ + \frac{2}{5} \end{array}$

19. $\begin{array}{r} \frac{17}{24} \\ - \frac{7}{24} \end{array}$

20. $\begin{array}{r} \frac{1}{6} \\ + \frac{1}{6} \end{array}$

21. $\begin{array}{r} \frac{19}{20} \\ - \frac{3}{20} \end{array}$

22. $\begin{array}{r} \frac{7}{12} \\ + \frac{1}{12} \end{array}$

23. $\begin{array}{r} \frac{13}{18} \\ - \frac{5}{18} \end{array}$

24. $\begin{array}{r} \frac{7}{12} \\ - \frac{5}{12} \end{array}$

25. $\begin{array}{r} \frac{3}{20} \\ + \frac{9}{20} \end{array}$

26. $\begin{array}{r} \frac{7}{15} \\ - \frac{2}{15} \end{array}$

27. $\begin{array}{r} \frac{3}{10} \\ - \frac{1}{10} \end{array}$

PROBLEM SOLVING APPLICATIONS
Choosing the Operation

Solve.

28. Tammy ate $\frac{1}{4}$ of a sandwich. Todd ate $\frac{3}{4}$ of the same sandwich. How much of the sandwich did they eat in all? How much more of the sandwich did Todd eat than Tammy?

29. Tim used $\frac{3}{4}$ c of flour to make dinner rolls. The batter was too thin, so he added $\frac{1}{4}$ c more flour. How much flour did he use in all?

30. Randy walks $\frac{3}{10}$ mi to school. Chris walks $\frac{8}{10}$ mi. Who walks farther? How much farther?

★ 31. Nelly jogged $\frac{7}{10}$ mi, walked $\frac{5}{10}$ mi, ran $\frac{3}{10}$ mi, walked another $\frac{7}{10}$ mi, then jogged $\frac{6}{10}$ mi. How many miles did she travel in all?

ADDING FRACTIONS: DIFFERENT DENOMINATORS

To add fractions with different denominators, first write equivalent fractions with a common denominator. Then add these fractions. Write the sum in lowest terms if you need to.

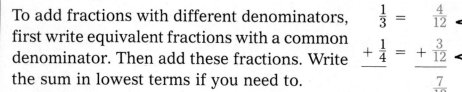

$$\frac{1}{3} = \frac{4}{12}$$
$$+\frac{1}{4} = +\frac{3}{12}$$
$$\frac{7}{12}$$

12 is the least common denominator (LCD).

To see that this is true, look at the egg cartons.

Each blue part shows $\frac{1}{3}$ or $\frac{4}{12}$.

Each red part shows $\frac{1}{4}$ or $\frac{3}{12}$.

$\frac{1}{3} + \frac{1}{4} = \frac{7}{12}$

The commutative, associative, and zero properties you learned for addition of whole numbers also apply to fractions. For example:

$$\frac{1}{3} + \frac{3}{8} = \frac{3}{8} + \frac{1}{3} \qquad \left(\frac{1}{8} + \frac{3}{16}\right) + \frac{1}{2} = \frac{1}{8} + \left(\frac{3}{16} + \frac{1}{2}\right) \qquad \frac{3}{7} + 0 = \frac{3}{7}$$

CLASS EXERCISES

Complete the sums pictured. Write the sum in lowest terms.

1.

$\frac{1}{6} + \frac{1}{3} = $ ▨

$\frac{1}{3} + \frac{1}{6} = $ ▨

2.

$\frac{1}{2} + \frac{1}{3} = $ ▨

$\frac{1}{3} + \frac{1}{2} = $ ▨

3.

$\frac{1}{6} + \frac{1}{4} = $ ▨

$\frac{1}{4} + \frac{1}{6} = $ ▨

What is the LCD of the pair of fractions?

4. $\frac{1}{2}, \frac{1}{5}$ **5.** $\frac{1}{6}, \frac{1}{9}$ **6.** $\frac{1}{4}, \frac{1}{10}$ **7.** $\frac{1}{4}, \frac{1}{8}$ **8.** $\frac{1}{8}, \frac{1}{12}$

PRACTICE

Add. Write the sum in lowest terms.

(9.) $\frac{1}{6}$ **10.** $\frac{1}{3}$ **11.** $\frac{1}{4}$ **12.** $\frac{1}{6}$ **13.** $\frac{1}{8}$ **14.** $\frac{3}{7}$

$+\frac{1}{2}$ $+\frac{1}{8}$ $+\frac{1}{5}$ $+\frac{1}{4}$ $+\frac{1}{2}$ $+\frac{1}{3}$

15. $\frac{2}{3}$ **16.** $\frac{1}{6}$ **17.** $\frac{3}{7}$ **18.** $\frac{1}{6}$ **19.** $\frac{3}{4}$ **20.** $\frac{1}{8}$

$+\frac{1}{5}$ $+\frac{3}{8}$ $+\frac{1}{2}$ $+\frac{4}{5}$ $+\frac{1}{10}$ $+\frac{5}{12}$

21. $\frac{3}{4} + \frac{1}{10}$ **22.** $\frac{4}{9} + \frac{2}{5}$ **23.** $\frac{5}{12} + 0$ **24.** $\frac{5}{9} + \frac{3}{8}$

25. $\frac{7}{10} + \frac{1}{8}$ **26.** $\frac{3}{8} + \frac{1}{4}$ **27.** $\frac{7}{10} + \frac{1}{6}$ **(28.)** $\frac{7}{10} + \frac{3}{20}$

★ **29.** $\frac{1}{2} + \frac{1}{6} + \frac{1}{8}$ ★ **30.** $\frac{2}{5} + \frac{1}{3} + \frac{2}{15}$ ★ **31.** $\frac{1}{9} + \frac{2}{3} + \frac{1}{5}$

PROBLEM SOLVING APPLICATIONS
Nonroutine Problems

Use the rules for Fraction Toss to find out who won the game.

32. Amy

Brad

33. Kara

Ryan

FRACTION TOSS RULES

1. Toss the fraction cubes.
2. Write a fraction for each shaded part.
3. Add the fractions.
4. The player with the highest score wins.

★ **34.** Jennifer

Shawn

★ **35.** Phillip

Kathryn

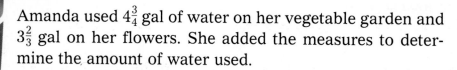

ADDING MIXED NUMBERS

Amanda used $4\frac{3}{4}$ gal of water on her vegetable garden and $3\frac{2}{3}$ gal on her flowers. She added the measures to determine the amount of water used.

Write equivalent fractions with a common denominator.	Add the fractions. Then add the whole numbers.	Rename $\frac{17}{12}$.
$4\frac{3}{4} = 4\frac{9}{12}$	$4\frac{3}{4} = 4\frac{9}{12}$	$7\frac{17}{12} = 7 + 1\frac{5}{12} = 8\frac{5}{12}$
$+\ 3\frac{2}{3} = +\ 3\frac{8}{12}$	$+\ 3\frac{2}{3} = +\ 3\frac{8}{12}$	
	$7\frac{17}{12}$	

Amanda used $8\frac{5}{12}$ gal of water.

CLASS EXERCISES

Complete.

1. $2\frac{1}{4} = 2\frac{\blacksquare}{8}$

2. $3\frac{1}{5} = 3\frac{\blacksquare}{15}$

3. $5\frac{1}{6} = 5\frac{\blacksquare}{18}$

4. $4\frac{3}{4} = 4\frac{\blacksquare}{20}$

5. $6\frac{5}{4} = 7\frac{\blacksquare}{4}$

6. $3\frac{8}{7} = 4\frac{\blacksquare}{7}$

7. $8\frac{5}{3} = 9\frac{\blacksquare}{3}$

8. $4\frac{10}{7} = \blacksquare\frac{3}{7}$

9. **Think:** What steps would you use to rename $3\frac{7}{6}$?

PRACTICE

Add. Write the sum in lowest terms.

10. $\quad 4\frac{1}{4}$
$\quad +\ 3\frac{1}{4}$

11. $\quad 3\frac{1}{5}$
$\quad +\ 2\frac{3}{5}$

12. $\quad 4\frac{5}{7}$
$\quad +\ 1\frac{4}{7}$

13. $\quad 1\frac{1}{4}$
$\quad +\ 1\frac{5}{8}$

14. $\quad 6\frac{2}{3}$
$\quad +\ 4\frac{1}{4}$

15. $8\frac{5}{6} + 3\frac{5}{8}$ **16.** $7\frac{4}{9} + 3\frac{1}{6}$ **17.** $3\frac{1}{3} + 3\frac{4}{5}$ **18.** $8\frac{13}{25} + 9\frac{11}{20}$

19. $3\frac{1}{5} + 2\frac{7}{10}$ **20.** $4\frac{1}{3} + 1\frac{1}{8}$ **21.** $6\frac{4}{5} + 4\frac{2}{3}$ **22.** $5\frac{3}{4} + 8\frac{1}{2}$

23. $5\frac{5}{6} + 4\frac{5}{12}$ **24.** $\frac{11}{12} + 5\frac{1}{4}$ ★ **25.** $3\frac{1}{2} + 5\frac{2}{3} + 7\frac{7}{8}$ ★ **26.** $7\frac{9}{10} + 2\frac{2}{5} + 6\frac{3}{8}$

PROBLEM SOLVING APPLICATIONS
Using Information from a Chart

Solve.

27. How much fabric do you need to make a throw pillow and a wall hanging?

28. How much fabric do you need to make a sofa cover and a window shade?

29. How much fabric do you need to make a floor pillow and a window shade?

★ **30.** How much fabric do you need to make two window shades, a sofa cover, and a wall hanging?

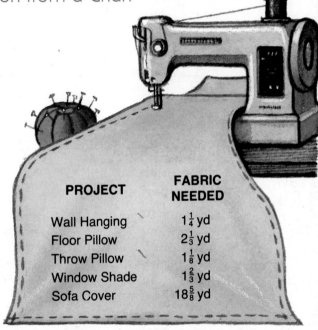

PROJECT	FABRIC NEEDED
Wall Hanging	$1\frac{1}{4}$ yd
Floor Pillow	$2\frac{1}{3}$ yd
Throw Pillow	$1\frac{1}{8}$ yd
Window Shade	$1\frac{2}{3}$ yd
Sofa Cover	$18\frac{5}{8}$ yd

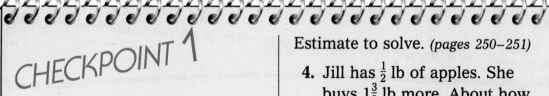

CHECKPOINT 1

Measure to the nearest $\frac{1}{4}$ in.
(pages 248–249)

1. _____

2. _____

3. _____

Estimate to solve. *(pages 250–251)*

4. Jill has $\frac{1}{2}$ lb of apples. She buys $1\frac{3}{8}$ lb more. About how many pounds does she have in all?

Write the answer in lowest terms.
(pages 252–257)

5. $\frac{5}{16} + \frac{2}{16}$ **6.** $\frac{7}{8} - \frac{3}{8}$

7. $\frac{1}{10} + \frac{2}{5}$ **8.** $5\frac{1}{3} + 1\frac{5}{12}$

Extra Practice on page 436

SUBTRACTING FRACTIONS: DIFFERENT DENOMINATORS

MARY $\frac{4}{5}$ mile

KEVIN $\frac{1}{2}$ mile

Look at the picture. Who walked farther, Mary or Kevin? How much farther?

You can determine how much farther Mary walked by subtracting.

Write equivalent fractions with a common denominator.

$$\frac{4}{5} = \frac{8}{10}$$
$$-\frac{1}{2} = -\frac{5}{10}$$

Now subtract the numerators.

$$\frac{4}{5} = \frac{8}{10}$$
$$-\frac{1}{2} = -\frac{5}{10}$$
$$\frac{3}{10}$$

The difference is in lowest terms.

Mary walked $\frac{3}{10}$ mi farther than Kevin.

CLASS EXERCISES

Complete.

1. $\frac{1}{3} = \frac{\blacksquare}{12}$
$-\frac{1}{4} = -\frac{\blacksquare}{12}$
$\frac{\blacksquare}{12}$

2. $\frac{2}{3} = \frac{\blacksquare}{12}$
$-\frac{1}{4} = -\frac{\blacksquare}{12}$
$\blacksquare$

3. $\frac{3}{4} = \frac{\blacksquare}{20}$
$-\frac{1}{5} = -\frac{\blacksquare}{20}$
$\blacksquare$

4. $\frac{7}{8} = \frac{\blacksquare}{24}$
$-\frac{1}{6} = -\frac{\blacksquare}{24}$
$\blacksquare$

5. Think: Explain the steps you would use to subtract $\frac{2}{3}$ from $\frac{7}{9}$.

PRACTICE

Subtract. Write the difference in lowest terms.

6. $\dfrac{1}{2}$ **7.** $\dfrac{7}{8}$ **8.** $\dfrac{2}{3}$ **9.** $\dfrac{5}{12}$ **10.** $\dfrac{1}{2}$ **11.** $\dfrac{4}{10}$
$-\dfrac{2}{7}$ $-\dfrac{5}{6}$ $-\dfrac{1}{9}$ $-\dfrac{1}{8}$ $-\dfrac{1}{3}$ $-\dfrac{1}{4}$

12. $\dfrac{7}{9}$ **13.** $\dfrac{8}{9}$ **14.** $\dfrac{2}{5}$ **15.** $\dfrac{3}{4}$ **16.** $\dfrac{5}{6}$ **17.** $\dfrac{4}{5}$
$-\dfrac{1}{2}$ $-\dfrac{5}{6}$ $-\dfrac{1}{4}$ $-\dfrac{1}{8}$ $-\dfrac{1}{4}$ $-\dfrac{3}{4}$

18. $\dfrac{5}{6} - \dfrac{3}{10}$ **19.** $\dfrac{3}{4} - \dfrac{1}{12}$ **20.** $\dfrac{1}{4} - \dfrac{1}{12}$ **21.** $\dfrac{7}{9} - \dfrac{7}{12}$

22. $\dfrac{4}{5} - \dfrac{1}{2}$ **23.** $\dfrac{9}{10} - \dfrac{3}{4}$ **24.** $\dfrac{3}{5} - \dfrac{2}{15}$ **25.** $\dfrac{1}{2} - \dfrac{2}{9}$

Determine the area. Use $\pi \approx 3.14$.

**MIXED
REVIEW**

26. Rectangle   **27.** Square   **28.** Circle
$l = 5.2$ m $s = 12.5$ cm $r = 7.8$ mm
$w = 3.4$ m

PROBLEM SOLVING APPLICATIONS
Choosing the Operation

Solve.

29. Paul rode his bike $\frac{1}{2}$ mi to the store and $\frac{3}{8}$ mi to Lori's house. How far did Paul ride his bike?

30. Tasha's house is $\frac{1}{8}$ mi from school. Mica's house is $\frac{1}{2}$ mi from school. Who lives farther from school? how much farther?

31. Herman lives $\frac{7}{8}$ mi from the library. If he walks for $\frac{1}{5}$ mi and meets a friend, how much farther do they have to walk to reach the library?

32. At the Brace School $\frac{2}{5}$ of the students ride the bus to school and $\frac{1}{2}$ of the students walk. What fraction of the students use other forms of transportation?

SUBTRACTING MIXED NUMBERS WITHOUT RENAMING

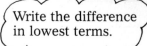

To subtract mixed numbers without renaming, subtract the fractions first, then the whole numbers. Write the difference in lowest terms.

Subtract $1\frac{4}{9}$ from $3\frac{7}{9}$.

Subtract the fractions.

$$3\frac{7}{9}$$
$$-1\frac{4}{9}$$
$$\overline{\frac{3}{9}}$$

Subtract the whole numbers.

$$3\frac{7}{9}$$
$$-1\frac{4}{9}$$
$$\overline{2\frac{3}{9} = 2\frac{1}{3}}$$

> Write the difference in lowest terms.

Subtract $1\frac{1}{8}$ from $4\frac{5}{6}$.

Write equivalent fractions with a common denominator.

$$4\frac{5}{6} = 4\frac{20}{24}$$
$$-1\frac{1}{8} = -1\frac{3}{24}$$

Subtract the fractions.

$$4\frac{5}{6} = 4\frac{20}{24}$$
$$-1\frac{1}{8} = -1\frac{3}{24}$$
$$\overline{\frac{17}{24}}$$

Subtract the whole numbers.

$$4\frac{5}{6} = 4\frac{20}{24}$$
$$-1\frac{1}{8} = -1\frac{3}{24}$$
$$\overline{3\frac{17}{24}}$$

 To estimate $4\frac{5}{6} - 1\frac{1}{8}$, **think:** $5 - 1 = 4$.

CLASS EXERCISES

Complete. Write the difference in lowest terms.

1.
$$2\frac{3}{8}$$
$$-1\frac{1}{8}$$
$$\overline{1\frac{\blacksquare}{8} = 1\frac{\blacksquare}{4}}$$

2.
$$5\frac{3}{5} = 5\frac{\blacksquare}{\blacksquare}$$
$$-2\frac{1}{10} = -2\frac{\blacksquare}{\blacksquare}$$
$$\overline{\blacksquare\frac{\blacksquare}{\blacksquare} = \blacksquare\frac{\blacksquare}{\blacksquare}}$$

3.
$$12\frac{5}{6} = 12\frac{\blacksquare}{\blacksquare}$$
$$-3\frac{2}{9} = -3\frac{\blacksquare}{\blacksquare}$$
$$\overline{\blacksquare\frac{\blacksquare}{\blacksquare}}$$

PRACTICE

Subtract. Write the answer in lowest terms.

4. $6\frac{5}{7}$
$- 4\frac{3}{7}$

5. $5\frac{1}{2}$
$- 2\frac{1}{5}$

6. $8\frac{3}{4}$
$- 2\frac{3}{8}$

7. $4\frac{13}{16}$
$- 1\frac{9}{16}$

8. $5\frac{5}{6}$
$- 4\frac{1}{3}$

9. $16\frac{7}{10}$
$- 5\frac{4}{15}$

10. $11\frac{5}{6}$
$- 3\frac{1}{6}$

11. $15\frac{3}{4}$
$- 8\frac{3}{5}$

12. $9\frac{9}{10}$
$- 7\frac{3}{4}$

13. $8\frac{2}{3}$
$- 4\frac{5}{8}$

14. $4\frac{7}{10} - 3\frac{3}{10}$

15. $2\frac{1}{2} - 1\frac{1}{3}$

16. $3\frac{3}{4} - 2\frac{1}{6}$

17. $4\frac{5}{7} - 1\frac{2}{7}$

Estimate, then subtract. Is the estimated difference a little less, a little more, or about the same as the actual difference?

ESTIMATE

18. $5\frac{3}{4} - 1\frac{1}{2}$

19. $7\frac{2}{3} - 2\frac{2}{5}$

20. $8\frac{5}{6} - 2\frac{1}{6}$

21. $26\frac{1}{2} - 12\frac{2}{5}$

22. $13\frac{7}{8} - 9\frac{5}{6}$

23. $50\frac{3}{10} - 24\frac{1}{12}$

PROBLEM SOLVING APPLICATIONS
Writing Reasonable Answers

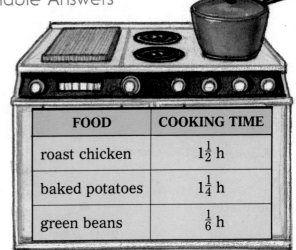

Barney is making supper. He wants everything to be ready at the same time. The table shows the cooking time for each food. Solve.

24. How long after the chicken is started should the potatoes go into the oven?

25. How long after the chicken is started should the green beans start cooking?

FOOD	COOKING TIME
roast chicken	$1\frac{1}{2}$ h
baked potatoes	$1\frac{1}{4}$ h
green beans	$\frac{1}{6}$ h

26. Barney needs $\frac{1}{3}$ h to clean and cut the green beans. How much time will it take him to prepare and cook the green beans?

★ **27.** Barney wants to allow $\frac{1}{3}$ h for the chicken to cool before serving supper. What time should he start cooking to serve supper at 7:15 P.M.?

SUBTRACTING MIXED NUMBERS WITH RENAMING

You may need to rename a mixed number before you can subtract. Look at the following examples.

To subtract $2\frac{1}{4}$ from 6, you first think of 6 as $5 + 1$. Then write 6 as $5\frac{4}{4}$.

$$6 = 5 + 1 = 5\frac{4}{4}$$

Now you can subtract.

$$\begin{array}{r} 6 = 5\frac{4}{4} \\ -\ 2\frac{1}{4} = -\ 2\frac{1}{4} \\ \hline 3\frac{3}{4} \end{array}$$

To subtract $2\frac{3}{4}$ from $5\frac{1}{4}$, you need to rename $5\frac{1}{4}$ since $\frac{3}{4} > \frac{1}{4}$. First rewrite 5 as $4\frac{4}{4}$. Then add $\frac{1}{4}$.

$$5\frac{1}{4} = 4\frac{4}{4} + \frac{1}{4} = 4\frac{5}{4}$$

Now you can subtract.

$$\begin{array}{r} 5\frac{1}{4} = 4\frac{5}{4} \\ -\ 2\frac{3}{4} = -\ 2\frac{3}{4} \\ \hline 2\frac{2}{4} = 2\frac{1}{2} \end{array}$$

 To solve $6 - 2\frac{1}{4}$ mentally, you can use the count on method. Begin at $2\frac{1}{4}$. Add $\frac{3}{4}$ to get 3, then add 3 to get 6. Altogether you added 3 and $\frac{3}{4}$, so $3\frac{3}{4}$ is the difference.

CLASS EXERCISES

Complete.

1. $4 = 3\frac{\blacksquare}{5}$

2. $6 = 5\frac{\blacksquare}{4}$

3. $2 = 1\frac{\blacksquare}{6}$

4. $5 = 4\frac{\blacksquare}{3}$

5. $2\frac{1}{5} = 1\frac{\blacksquare}{5}$

6. $8\frac{2}{5} = 7\frac{\blacksquare}{5}$

7. $19\frac{1}{8} = 18\frac{\blacksquare}{8}$

8. $6\frac{1}{7} = 5\frac{\blacksquare}{7}$

9. Think: How would you use mental math to subtract $3\frac{1}{2}$ from 6?

PRACTICE

Subtract. Write the answer in lowest terms.

10. 4
$-2\frac{2}{3}$

11. $8\frac{1}{4}$
$-3\frac{3}{4}$

12. $7\frac{2}{5}$
$-3\frac{4}{5}$

13. 6
$-\frac{3}{8}$

14. $9\frac{2}{9}$
$-6\frac{5}{9}$

15. 17
$-1\frac{1}{3}$

16. $9\frac{2}{5}$
$-3\frac{4}{5}$

17. $22\frac{1}{8}$
$-19\frac{7}{8}$

18. $63\frac{1}{9}$
$-20\frac{7}{9}$

19. $4\frac{10}{21}$
$-2\frac{15}{21}$

20. $15\frac{1}{3}$
$-10\frac{2}{3}$

21. $10\frac{4}{9}$
$-7\frac{7}{9}$

22. $8\frac{2}{5}$
$-6\frac{4}{5}$

23. $6\frac{3}{8}$
$-3\frac{5}{8}$

24. 8
$-\frac{6}{7}$

25. $7 - 4\frac{1}{2}$

26. $5\frac{1}{6} - 3\frac{5}{6}$

27. $10\frac{1}{8} - 3\frac{5}{8}$

28. $15\frac{8}{15} - 8\frac{14}{15}$

Subtract using mental math. Write the answer in lowest terms.

29. $6 - 1\frac{1}{4}$

30. $10 - 3\frac{5}{6}$

31. $8\frac{1}{2} - 6$

MENTAL MATH

32. $8\frac{1}{3} - 6\frac{2}{3}$

33. $2\frac{5}{12} - 1\frac{11}{12}$

34. $17 - 3\frac{7}{10}$

PROBLEM SOLVING APPLICATIONS
Mental Math, Paper and Pencil

Tell whether you would choose mental math or paper and pencil to solve. Write *M* or *P*. Then solve.

35. Dan made 16 sandwiches for a party. Wendy made $3\frac{1}{2}$ more sandwiches before the guests arrived. How many sandwiches did they have at the start of the party?

36. Laura made 3 servings of Spinach Surprise. The surprise was that only $1\frac{1}{8}$ servings of the casserole were eaten. How many servings did Laura have left over?

37. Jan bought $3\frac{1}{4}$ lb of cheese. She used $2\frac{3}{4}$ lb for dessert. She used the rest to make baked macaroni. How much was used for the macaroni?

★ 38. Three people each brought 3 L of juice to a party. If $5\frac{1}{4}$ L of juice was used and they shared equally what was left over, how many liters did each person take home?

SUBTRACTING MIXED NUMBERS

Fred tries to practice the guitar for $2\frac{1}{2}$ h each day. Yesterday he practiced for only $1\frac{3}{4}$ h. Subtract to see how much longer he should have practiced.

First write equivalent fractions with a common denominator. Notice that you can't subtract the fractions.

$$2\frac{1}{2} = \quad 2\frac{2}{4}$$
$$-1\frac{3}{4} = -1\frac{3}{4}$$

Think of $2\frac{2}{4}$ as $1 + \frac{4}{4} + \frac{2}{4}$.
Rename $2\frac{2}{4}$ as $1\frac{6}{4}$.

Now you can subtract.

$$2\frac{1}{2} = \quad 2\frac{2}{4} = \quad 1\frac{6}{4}$$
$$-1\frac{3}{4} = -1\frac{3}{4} = -1\frac{3}{4}$$
$$\frac{3}{4}$$

Fred should have practiced $\frac{3}{4}$ h longer.

It's easy to add or subtract with fractions on a calculator when the denominators are 10. For example, to subtract $1\frac{6}{10}$ from $2\frac{5}{10}$, enter 2.5 ⊟ 1.6 ⊜. The display will show ⌈ 0.9 ⌉.

CLASS EXERCISES

What is the equivalent fraction?

1. $4\frac{1}{6} = 4\frac{\blacksquare}{12}$

2. $5\frac{1}{5} = 5\frac{\blacksquare}{15}$

3. $9\frac{3}{4} = 9\frac{\blacksquare}{12}$

4. $2\frac{4}{7} = 2\frac{\blacksquare}{21}$

5. $7\frac{2}{5} = 6\frac{\blacksquare}{10}$

6. $8\frac{4}{5} = 7\frac{\blacksquare}{20}$

7. $3\frac{2}{5} = 2\frac{\blacksquare}{25}$

8. $6\frac{4}{5} = 5\frac{\blacksquare}{35}$

9. **Think:** Explain the steps you would use to subtract $1\frac{1}{2}$ from $4\frac{1}{4}$.

PRACTICE

Subtract. Write the answer in lowest terms.

10. $8\frac{1}{4}$ **11.** $4\frac{3}{8}$ **12.** $5\frac{1}{2}$ **13.** 8 **14.** $7\frac{3}{10}$

    $-\,6\frac{1}{2}$ $-\,2\frac{5}{6}$ $-\,\frac{2}{3}$ $-\,4\frac{2}{3}$ $-\,3\frac{3}{5}$

15. $6\frac{2}{3}$ **16.** $9\frac{1}{6}$ **17.** 5 **18.** $10\frac{5}{12}$ **19.** $2\frac{1}{4}$

    $-\,2\frac{3}{4}$ $-\,5\frac{4}{9}$ $-\,\frac{3}{4}$ $-\,3\frac{2}{3}$ $-\,\frac{3}{5}$

20. $7\frac{2}{5} - 2\frac{1}{2}$ **21.** $8 - 4\frac{5}{8}$ **22.** $9\frac{2}{7} - 4\frac{2}{3}$ **23.** $16 - \frac{3}{8}$

24. $10 - 4\frac{1}{5}$ **25.** $3\frac{1}{3} - \frac{7}{8}$ **26.** $14\frac{1}{7} - 6\frac{3}{4}$ **27.** $12 - 3\frac{2}{7}$

Subtract. Write the answer in decimal form. You may wish to use a calculator.

CALCULATOR

28. $3\frac{3}{10} - 1\frac{8}{10}$ **29.** $6\frac{3}{10} - \frac{9}{10}$ **30.** $14\frac{7}{10} - 11\frac{3}{10}$

31. $21\frac{7}{10} - 9\frac{9}{10}$ ★ **32.** $1\frac{1}{2} - \frac{7}{10}$ ★ **33.** $6\frac{2}{5} - 3\frac{9}{10}$

PROBLEM SOLVING APPLICATIONS
Using Information from a Table

Bob Nolan's piano students keep a record of how long they practice each week. Here is last week's record. Use the information to solve.

STUDENT	PRACTICE TIME
Tony	$5\frac{3}{4}$ h
Sarah	$6\frac{1}{2}$ h
Marianna	7 h
Valdez	$4\frac{2}{3}$ h

34. How much longer did Marianna practice than Valdez?

35. What is the difference in practice times for Sarah and Tony?

36. Marianna practiced $6\frac{3}{4}$ h this week. How long did she practice in the last 2 weeks?

37. Valdez should practice for $5\frac{1}{2}$ h each week. If he had practiced for another 45 min would he have reached his goal?

PROBLEM SOLVING
Strategy: Simplifying the Problem

1. Understand
2. Plan
3. Work
4. Answer/Check

Sometimes a math problem looks more difficult than it is. If you rewrite the problem using only the important information and substitute simpler numbers you may be able to decide more easily what to do.

Original Problem

A volunteer worked in the forest $6\frac{1}{2}$ h on the first day and $4\frac{3}{4}$ h on each of the next two days. How many hours did she work during the three days?

Simpler Problem

A volunteer worked 7 h, then 5 h, and then 5 h more. How many hours did she work in all?

You can see by reading the simpler problem that you can add the hours worked each day to find the answer. Go back to the original problem. Add.

$$6\frac{1}{2} + 4\frac{3}{4} + 4\frac{3}{4} = 16$$

A volunteer worked 16 h during the three days.

CLASS EXERCISES

Use the simpler problem to plan how to solve the original problem. Then solve the problem.

Original Problem

1. The eruptions of Mount St. Helens leveled forest land that was about 18.6 km wide and 32.15 km long. Estimate the area of forest land destroyed.

2. About 2,000,000 trees were planted on 5000 sections to replace those destroyed by Mount St. Helens. About how many trees per section were planted?

Simpler Problem

The land was about 19 km wide and 32 km long. Estimate the area.

About 2000 trees were planted on 5 sections. About how many trees were planted on each section?

PRACTICE

Write a simpler problem. Use it to solve the original problem.

3. The Forest Service reports that 4986 black-tailed deer, 1487 elk, 215 black bears, 15 mountain goats, and about 27,000 grouse were lost on Mount St. Helens. About how many animals is this?

4. Bart hauled sandbags weighing $75\frac{1}{2}$ lb, and Jenna hauled portable water tanks weighing $89\frac{3}{4}$ lb. How much more weight did Jenna haul?

5. The eruptions of Mount St. Helens created many new lakes and ponds. A channel 885.7 m long was dug in just 14 weeks to prevent one new lake from overflowing. About how many meters were dug each week?

6. Scientists estimate that the rocks and mud that filled Spirit Lake will raise the water level about 114.82 m. The water level of the lake was about 959.40 m before the eruptions. About how many meters will the new level be?

7. Geologists continue to take measurements to predict future eruptions. A circular warning zone with a radius of 49.5 km surrounds Mount St. Helens. What is the area of the warning zone? Use $\pi \approx 3.14$.

★ 8. The loggers helping to save the lumber around Mount St. Helens earned $11.80 per hour plus $6.00 per day for hazardous duty. How much was earned by a logger who worked $8\frac{1}{2}$ h per day for 14 days?

CHECKPOINT 2

Subtract. Write the answer in lowest terms. (pages 258–265)

1. $\frac{3}{5} - \frac{2}{15}$

2. $\frac{7}{9} - \frac{1}{3}$

3. $9\frac{3}{4} - 1\frac{1}{4}$

4. $6\frac{5}{8} - 1\frac{1}{2}$

5. $8 - 2\frac{2}{5}$

6. $7\frac{1}{2} - 5\frac{3}{4}$

Solve. (pages 266–267)

7. Lucille bought $13\frac{7}{8}$ ft of wood molding for some windows. She used all but $1\frac{3}{4}$ ft of it. How much molding was used?

Extra Practice on page 436

Measure the segment to the nearest $\frac{1}{4}$ in., $\frac{1}{8}$ in., and $\frac{1}{16}$ in. *(pages 248–249)*

1. _____

2. _____

3. _____

Estimate. *(pages 250–251)*

4. Eva walked along the beach for $\frac{3}{4}$ h, along the boardwalk for $\frac{2}{3}$ h, and in town for $1\frac{1}{4}$ h. About how long did Eva walk in all?

5. Brooks jogs $3\frac{5}{8}$ mi each day. About how far does Brooks jog in one week?

Add or subtract. Write the answer in lowest terms. *(pages 252–257)*

6. $\frac{7}{18}$
$+\frac{5}{18}$

7. $\frac{9}{10}$
$-\frac{5}{10}$

8. $\frac{1}{8}$
$+\frac{7}{12}$

9. $\frac{2}{4}$
$-\frac{1}{5}$

10. $5\frac{3}{8} + 4\frac{5}{6}$

11. $6\frac{2}{3} + 2\frac{3}{7}$

12. $9\frac{1}{5} + 9\frac{1}{4}$

13. $7\frac{11}{25} + 3\frac{7}{10}$

Write the answer in lowest terms. *(pages 258–265)*

14. $\frac{7}{10} - \frac{2}{3}$

15. $9\frac{5}{6} - 7\frac{1}{4}$

16. $8 - 5\frac{5}{8}$

17. $10\frac{1}{3} - 4\frac{5}{6}$

Write a simpler problem. Use it to solve the original problem. *(pages 266–267)*

18. Doug lives $8\frac{1}{2}$ blocks from school. On Monday he ran $3\frac{1}{4}$ blocks and walked the rest of the distance. How far did he walk?

19. Members of the Hiking Club walked $14\frac{1}{2}$ mi on Friday and $11\frac{5}{8}$ mi on Sunday. How many miles did they hike in all?

Extra Practice on page 437

MATHEMATICS and PHYSICAL EDUCATION

Measurements in track and field competition in the U.S. are usually made in customary units.

In a quarter-mile relay, each of four runners runs an equal leg.

1. What fraction of a mile does each runner in a quarter-mile relay run?

2. There are 1760 yd in a mile. Is each leg of the quarter-mile relay more than or less than 100 yd?

3. One runner runs one leg of a quarter-mile relay. A second runner runs the 220 yd dash. Who runs farther?

HOW LONG IS A LEG?

In the long jump, the length of a jump is measured from the take-off line to the closest point in the landing area touched by the jumper.

4. A jumper jumped $5\frac{3}{4}$ in. before the take-off line. If his jump is measured from the take-off line as 9 ft $8\frac{3}{4}$ in., how far did he actually jump?

5. A jumper's feet touched the ground 10 ft 11 in. from the take-off line, but her hand touched 2 ft $9\frac{1}{2}$ in. closer to the line. What will be the recorded length of her jump?

269

Enrichment

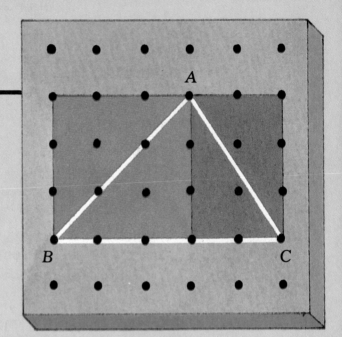

You can use a geoboard or dot paper to find the area of a polygon in many different ways.

- You can sometimes use a formula.
- You can count all of the whole units inside the polygon, and then put the partial units together to form whole units.
- You can sometimes add or subtract using shapes whose area is easier to figure.

For example:

For △ ABC, **think:** The area of the red square is 9 square units. The area of the blue rectangle is 6 square units. The area of △ ABC is half of the red square plus half of the blue rectangle: $7\frac{1}{2}$ square units.

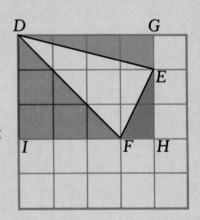

For △ DEF, **think:** The area of DGHI is 12. If you subtract the area of the red triangle $(4\frac{1}{2})$, the blue triangle (1), and the green triangle (2), then what is left will be the area of △ DEF, that is, $4\frac{1}{2}$ square units.

Find the area of the polygon.

1.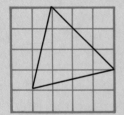

2.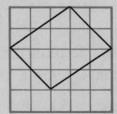

3.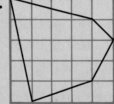

AREA ON A GEOBOARD

Using a geoboard or dot paper, make a polygon that has the given area.

4. 2 square units

5. $3\frac{1}{2}$ square units

6. 7 square units

7. $10\frac{1}{2}$ square units

A man by the name of Pick discovered a simple formula for determining the area of any shape on a geoboard or dot paper. For this formula consider a point to be the intersection of two grid lines.

If b is the number of points on the boundary of the shape, and i is the number of points inside the shape, then $A = \frac{b}{2} + i - 1$.

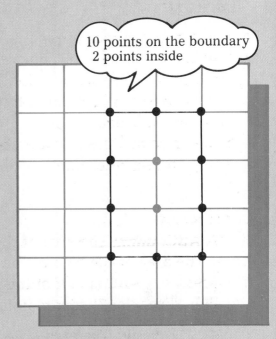

10 points on the boundary
2 points inside

For the rectangle on the right, $b = 10$ and $i = 2$, so $A = \frac{10}{2} + 2 - 1 = 6$ square units.

Use Pick's formula to determine the area of the shape.

8.

9.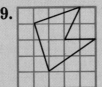

10.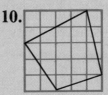

11. Think: Pick's formula involves only whole numbers and halves. Is it possible to have a shape on a geoboard whose area is $4\frac{1}{3}$ square units?

12. Think: The smallest shape you can show on a geoboard would have an area of $\frac{1}{2}$ square unit. What would this shape have to be? The area of the whole geoboard is 25 square units. Do you think it is possible to show a figure on the geoboard whose area is either a whole number or a whole number and a half for all possibilities between $\frac{1}{2}$ and 25?

CUMULATIVE REVIEW

Choose the correct answer. Write *a, b, c,* or *d.*

Which is the best estimate?

1. 5.2
×3.4

a. 24
b. 20
c. 15
d. 150

2. $21.55
×6.7

a. $140
b. $120
c. $210
d. $14

3. 28.9
×1.78

a. 28
b. 30
c. 60
d. 280

Find the answer.

4. 8.4
×7.3

a. 6.132
b. 61.32
c. 60.32
d. none of these

5. 0.9
×155.6

a. 14.004
b. 1400.4
c. 140.04
d. none of these

6. 0.08
×0.006

a. 48
b. 0.048
c. 0.0048
d. none of these

Find the answer. If necessary, round to the nearest hundredth.

7. 7)25.76

a. 3.68
b. 36.8
c. 368
d. none of these

8. 42)7.955

a. 0.0185
b. 0.19
c. 1.85
d. none of these

9. 0.039)0.2886

a. 74
b. 7.4
c. 0.74
d. none of these

Find the matching measure.

10. 23.1 cm

a. 231 km
b. 2.31 m
c. 231 mm
d. none of these

Which is the best estimate?

11. 6.71)34.8

a. 50
b. 5
c. 0.5
d. 500

Find the reasonable answer.

12. The Klines live 63 km from their mountain cabin. They drive about 0.5 of the way before they stop for lunch. About how many kilometers do they drive before lunch?

a. about 3.0 km
b. about 30 km
c. about 300 km
d. about 62.5 km

13. A bowl of soup costs $1.75 and a sandwich costs $2.40. The Klines order 4 bowls of soup and 4 sandwiches. About how much do they pay in all?

a. about $16.00
b. about $24.00
c. about $30.00
d. about $12.00

Find the circumference.

14. Circle
$d = 3.6$ mm

a. 12.304 mm
b. 11.304 mm
c. 11.404 mm
d. none of these

Find the area.

15. Rectangle
$l = 7.4$ m
$w = 5.2$ m

a. 38.48 m^2
b. 384.8 m^2
c. 39.48 m^2
d. none of these

16. Right Triangle
$b = 28$ cm
$h = 19$ cm

a. 532 cm^2
b. 266 cm^2
c. 276 cm^2
d. none of these

LANGUAGE and VOCABULARY REVIEW

Choose the correct word or words to complete.

1. In a fraction the (numerator, denominator) represents the total number of parts in a whole unit.

2. The (least common multiple, greatest common factor) of 3 and 4 is 12.

3. Numbers which divide a number with no remainder are called (factors, multiples).

4. When you divide the numerator and the denominator of a fraction by their greatest common factor, the fraction is in (prime factorization, lowest terms).

5. An (isosceles triangle, right triangle) has two sides of equal length and two angles of equal measure.

COMPUTER
LITERACY

SPREADSHEETS

An **electronic spreadsheet** is a program that keeps a record of earnings, expenses, and savings.

The spreadsheet looks like a chart. It has columns labeled with letters. The rows are labeled with numbers. The boxes in each column and each row are called **cells.**

The spreadsheet below shows earnings of four softball teammates. They are saving to buy uniforms. Cell B2 shows that Bill earned $12.00 mowing lawns.

	A	B	C	D	E	F
1		BILL	MARY	STAN	ADA	TOTAL
2	LAWN MOWING	$12.00	$12.00	$ 7.00	$00.00	?
3	BABY SITTING	$ 9.00	$ 7.00	$13.00	$10.00	$39.00
4	YARD CLEANING	$00.00	$ 5.00	$11.00	$10.00	$26.00
5	RECYCLING	$ 4.00	$00.00	$ 6.00	$ 5.00	$15.00
6	DOG WALKING	$00.00	$ 4.00	$00.00	$00.00	$ 4.00
7	TOTAL SAVINGS	?	?	?	?	?

Use the spreadsheet. Solve.

1. What is shown in B1?

2. What amount is in E3?

3. Which cell shows how much Stan earned cleaning yards?

4. Which cell shows the total earned for lawn mowing?

5. How much more must Mary earn to equal the amount Stan earned?

6. Complete the spreadsheet.

The umbrellas form a design when seen from above. Half of 1200 umbrellas in a display are red, and $\frac{1}{3}$ are yellow. How many are red? How many are yellow?

10

MULTIPLICATION AND DIVISION OF FRACTIONS

MULTIPLYING FRACTIONS
AND WHOLE NUMBERS

You can think of multiplying a fraction and a whole number in different ways. For example:

You can think of $3 \times \frac{1}{2}$ as repeated addition.

$$3 \times \frac{1}{2} = \frac{1}{2} + \frac{1}{2} + \frac{1}{2} = \frac{3}{2} = 1\frac{1}{2}$$

You can think of $\frac{1}{2} \times 3$ as $\frac{1}{2}$ of 3.

$$\frac{1}{2} \times 3 = 3 \div 2 = 1\frac{1}{2}$$

To multiply a fraction and a whole number, first multiply the numerator of the fraction by the whole number. Then write the product over the denominator.

$$5 \times \frac{1}{4} = \frac{5 \times 1}{4} = \frac{5}{4} = 1\frac{1}{4}$$ $$5 \times \frac{3}{4} = \frac{5 \times 3}{4} = \frac{15}{4} = 3\frac{3}{4}$$

 You can multiply a fraction and a whole number on a calculator.

$$5 \times \frac{3}{4} \quad \Diamond \quad 5 \boxed{\times} 3 \boxed{\div} 4 \boxed{=} \; 3.75$$

Think: Are $3\frac{3}{4}$ and 3.75 equal?

Complete.

1. $\frac{1}{5} \times 10 = \frac{\blacksquare \times 10}{5} = \frac{\blacksquare}{5} = \blacksquare$

$10 \times \frac{1}{5} = \frac{\blacksquare \times 1}{5} = \frac{\blacksquare}{5} = \blacksquare$

2. $\frac{1}{8} \times 9 = \frac{1 \times \blacksquare}{8} = \frac{\blacksquare}{8} = 1\frac{\blacksquare}{8}$

$9 \times \frac{1}{8} = \frac{\blacksquare \times 1}{8} = \frac{\blacksquare}{8} = 1\frac{\blacksquare}{8}$

3. $6 \times \frac{1}{4} = \frac{\blacksquare}{4} = 1\frac{\blacksquare}{4} = 1\frac{\blacksquare}{2}$

$\frac{1}{4} \times 6 = \frac{\blacksquare}{4} = 1\frac{\blacksquare}{4} = 1\frac{\blacksquare}{2}$

4. $5 \times \frac{1}{7} = \frac{\blacksquare}{7}$

$\frac{1}{7} \times 5 = \frac{\blacksquare}{7}$

5. $\frac{2}{3} \times 12 = \frac{\blacksquare \times 12}{3} = \frac{\blacksquare}{3} = \blacksquare$

$12 \times \frac{2}{3} = \frac{\blacksquare \times 2}{3} = \frac{\blacksquare}{3} = \blacksquare$

6. $15 \times \frac{3}{5} = \frac{\blacksquare \times 3}{5} = \frac{\blacksquare}{5} = \blacksquare$

$\frac{3}{5} \times 15 = \frac{3 \times \blacksquare}{5} = \frac{\blacksquare}{5} = \blacksquare$

PRACTICE

Multiply. Write the product in lowest terms.

7. $8 \times \frac{1}{11}$ **8.** $4 \times \frac{5}{6}$ **9.** $4 \times \frac{4}{7}$ **10.** $\frac{5}{8} \times 7$ **11.** $\frac{5}{12} \times 3$

12. $15 \times \frac{4}{5}$ **13.** $\frac{6}{7} \times 8$ **14.** $9 \times \frac{1}{4}$ **15.** $5 \times \frac{2}{3}$ **16.** $\frac{1}{6} \times 12$

17. $\frac{1}{3} \times 7$ **18.** $\frac{3}{4} \times 10$ **19.** $6 \times \frac{2}{3}$ **20.** $6 \times \frac{3}{10}$ **21.** $\frac{5}{9} \times 6$

22. $6 \times \frac{4}{5}$ **23.** $\frac{2}{3} \times 7$ **24.** $\frac{7}{8} \times 11$ **25.** $\frac{3}{4} \times 16$ **26.** $\frac{9}{10} \times 15$

27. $12 \times \frac{1}{8}$ **28.** $\frac{4}{5} \times 30$ **29.** $\frac{7}{12} \times 54$ **30.** $33 \times \frac{2}{9}$ **31.** $65 \times \frac{3}{10}$

★ **32. Think:** When Inez multiplied $\frac{5}{6}$ and 30, she pressed
5 ÷ 6 × 30 and got an answer of 24.999999. When
Albert worked out the same problem, he pressed
5 × 30 ÷ 6 and got 25. Why are their answers
different?

CALCULATOR

PROBLEM SOLVING APPLICATIONS
Choosing the Operation

Solve.

33. Ramon owns a Courser II that
has an 18 gal tank. He now has $2\frac{1}{2}$
gal of gasoline in his car. How
much more gasoline is needed to
fill the tank?

34. Monica's car has a 24 gal tank.
How many gallons are in the tank
when the gauge points to $\frac{1}{2}$?

35. Fern had a flat tire after driving $\frac{2}{3}$
of the distance to the beach. If the
total distance is 6 mi, how far did
Fern drive before she had the flat
tire?

★ **36.** The Chins own a Sphinx RX7
that has a 20 gal tank. How much
gasoline is needed to fill the tank
if the gauge reads $\frac{1}{8}$ full?

MULTIPLYING FRACTIONS

Each of the sections A, B, and C is $\frac{1}{3}$ of the parking lot. Spaces for the handicapped occupy $\frac{1}{2}$ of Section A. What part of the lot is for the handicapped? Multiply to find out.

$\frac{1}{3}$

3 equal sections means each section is $\frac{1}{3}$ of the lot.

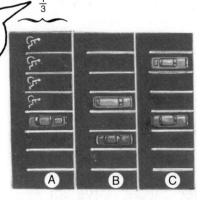

$\frac{1}{2}$ of $\frac{1}{3}$

$\frac{1}{2}$ of $\frac{1}{3}$ is $\frac{1}{6}$.

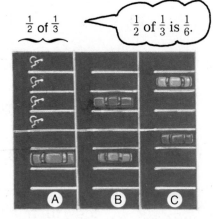

To multiply two fractions, you multiply the numerators and then multiply the denominators.

$$\frac{\text{numerator} \times \text{numerator}}{\text{denominator} \times \text{denominator}} \qquad \frac{1}{2} \times \frac{1}{3} = \frac{1 \times 1}{2 \times 3} = \frac{1}{6}$$

Spaces for the handicapped occupy $\frac{1}{6}$ of the lot.

 You can use mental math to multiply most fractions. Here's how to multiply $\frac{1}{3} \times \frac{7}{8}$.

Think: $1 \times 7 = 7$
$3 \times 8 = 24$
$\frac{1}{3} \times \frac{7}{8} = \frac{7}{24}$

basic facts

PARKING ONLY

CLASS EXERCISES

Complete.

1.
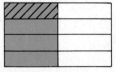

$\frac{1}{4} \times \frac{1}{2} = \frac{\blacksquare}{8}$

2.

$\frac{3}{4} \times \frac{1}{2} = \frac{\blacksquare}{8}$

3.

$\frac{3}{5} \times \frac{1}{3} = \frac{\blacksquare}{15}$

4.

$\frac{5}{6} \times \frac{3}{4} = \frac{\blacksquare}{24}$

PRACTICE

Multiply. Write the product in lowest terms.

5. $\frac{1}{3} \times \frac{1}{5}$ **6.** $\frac{1}{2} \times \frac{1}{8}$ **7.** $\frac{1}{5} \times \frac{1}{4}$ **8.** $\frac{1}{3} \times \frac{1}{7}$ **9.** $\frac{1}{6} \times \frac{1}{3}$

10. $\frac{7}{8} \times \frac{3}{4}$ **11.** $\frac{5}{8} \times \frac{1}{6}$ **12.** $\frac{2}{9} \times \frac{2}{3}$ **13.** $\frac{1}{7} \times \frac{7}{8}$ **14.** $\frac{5}{6} \times \frac{7}{10}$

15. $\frac{4}{5} \times \frac{2}{3}$ **16.** $\frac{3}{4} \times \frac{5}{8}$ **17.** $\frac{7}{12} \times \frac{2}{5}$ **18.** $\frac{1}{2} \times \frac{5}{16}$ **19.** $\frac{3}{10} \times \frac{5}{8}$

20. $\frac{3}{4} \times \frac{4}{9}$ **21.** $\frac{7}{12} \times \frac{4}{5}$ **22.** $\frac{4}{5} \times \frac{7}{11}$ **23.** $\frac{2}{3} \times \frac{3}{7}$ **24.** $\frac{8}{19} \times \frac{2}{3}$

25. $\frac{3}{5} \times \frac{9}{11}$ **26.** $\frac{8}{15} \times \frac{3}{4}$ **27.** $\frac{7}{9} \times \frac{6}{13}$ **28.** $\frac{4}{11} \times \frac{3}{4}$ **29.** $\frac{15}{38} \times \frac{2}{3}$

★ **30. Think:** *True* or *false:* The product of two fractions less than one will be less than either factor. Give an example.

Use mental math to name the product.

31. $\frac{7}{8} \times \frac{1}{6}$ **32.** $\frac{1}{4} \times \frac{5}{6}$ **33.** $\frac{2}{3} \times \frac{7}{9}$ **34.** $\frac{4}{9} \times \frac{2}{7}$

MENTAL MATH

PROBLEM SOLVING APPLICATIONS
Using Fractions

Derek needs to make only half the amount of Yogurt Dip that the recipe makes. Use the recipe at the right to solve the problem.

35. How much of each ingredient should Derek use?

36. How much dip will half the recipe make?

37. Does the recipe use more yogurt than cottage cheese?

★ **38.** Derek used $\frac{1}{2}$ of the dip he made. What fraction of the original recipe is the remaining dip?

Yogurt Dip for Vegetables

$\frac{1}{2}$ c cottage cheese

$\frac{1}{3}$ c yogurt

$\frac{1}{4}$ c chopped walnuts

$\frac{1}{2}$ teaspoon lemon juice

1 tablespoon chopped parsley

$\frac{1}{2}$ clove minced garlic

Mix well. Chill for 2 hours.
Makes about 1 c.

MULTIPLYING FRACTIONS

You already have learned how to multiply fractions and then write the product in lowest terms.

$$\frac{4}{9} \times \frac{3}{5} = \frac{4 \times 3}{9 \times 5} = \frac{12}{45} = \frac{4}{15}$$

Sometimes you can simplify the multiplication of fractions by using a shortcut. You can look for common factors of the numerators and denominators. In the example below, 3 is the greatest common factor (GCF) of the numerator 3 and the denominator 9. So, first divide the numerator and the denominator by 3, and then multiply.

$$\frac{4}{9} \times \frac{3}{5} = \frac{4}{\overset{}{9}} \times \frac{\overset{1}{3}}{5} = \frac{4}{15}$$

$9 \div 3 = 3$ $\qquad 3 \div 3 = 1$

CLASS EXERCISES

Describe in words how you would use the shortcut to simplify the multiplication.

1. $\frac{5}{12} \times \frac{8}{13}$ **2.** $\frac{3}{10} \times \frac{7}{9}$ **3.** $\frac{8}{10} \times \frac{5}{9}$ **4.** $\frac{1}{6} \times \frac{3}{5}$ **5.** $\frac{7}{10} \times \frac{15}{49}$

Complete.

6. $\frac{2}{3} \times \frac{5}{6} = \frac{2}{3} \times \frac{5}{\underset{3}{\cancel{6}}} = \blacksquare$ **7.** $\frac{3}{4} \times \frac{2}{5} = \frac{3}{\underset{2}{\cancel{4}}} \times \frac{\overset{1}{\cancel{2}}}{5} = \blacksquare$ **8.** $\frac{7}{10} \times \frac{8}{21} = \frac{\overset{1}{\cancel{7}}}{\underset{5}{\cancel{10}}} \times \frac{\overset{4}{\cancel{8}}}{\underset{3}{\cancel{21}}} = \blacksquare$

Complete. Simplify before you multiply.

9. $\frac{3}{4} \times \frac{8}{9} = \blacksquare$ **10.** $\frac{8}{15} \times \frac{5}{6} = \blacksquare$ **11.** $\frac{2}{3} \times \frac{5}{8} = \blacksquare$ **12.** $\frac{5}{6} \times \frac{1}{10} = \blacksquare$

PRACTICE

Multiply. Write the product in lowest terms.

13. $\frac{4}{9} \times \frac{3}{2}$ **14.** $\frac{15}{8} \times \frac{2}{7}$ **15.** $\frac{4}{9} \times \frac{5}{6}$ **16.** $\frac{3}{10} \times \frac{5}{7}$ **17.** $\frac{5}{6} \times \frac{2}{3}$

18. $\frac{3}{2} \times \frac{7}{9}$ **19.** $\frac{7}{10} \times \frac{5}{8}$ **20.** $\frac{4}{5} \times \frac{5}{8}$ **21.** $\frac{7}{8} \times \frac{9}{4}$ **22.** $\frac{2}{9} \times \frac{3}{4}$

23. $\frac{4}{3} \times \frac{6}{7}$ **24.** $\frac{9}{20} \times 4$ **25.** $\frac{7}{9} \times \frac{3}{4}$ **26.** $\frac{5}{6} \times \frac{8}{15}$ **27.** $\frac{9}{16} \times \frac{8}{9}$

28. $\frac{8}{3} \times \frac{5}{12}$ **29.** $\frac{3}{8} \times \frac{4}{7}$ **30.** $\frac{1}{2} \times \frac{3}{10}$ **31.** $\frac{7}{12} \times \frac{3}{8}$ **32.** $\frac{9}{7} \times \frac{4}{15}$

Complete. Write <, >, or =.

13-22

MIXED REVIEW

33. $\frac{3}{5} \,\blacksquare\, \frac{2}{3}$ **34.** $\frac{9}{2} \,\blacksquare\, \frac{9}{3}$ **35.** $\frac{12}{18} \,\blacksquare\, \frac{2}{3}$

36. $\frac{1}{4} \,\blacksquare\, 0.25$ **37.** $\frac{5}{3} \,\blacksquare\, \frac{8}{5}$ **38.** $4\frac{2}{5} \,\blacksquare\, 4\frac{1}{3}$

39. $2.017 \,\blacksquare\, 2.107$ **40.** $0.319 \,\blacksquare\, 0.32$ **41.** $0.102 \,\blacksquare\, 0.099$

PROBLEM SOLVING APPLICATIONS
Using Formulas with Fractions

When you want to know the temperature but don't have a thermometer, try listening to the crickets. The number of times they chirp in a minute and the following formula can give you a good idea of the temperature. Here's how to use the formula.

Let t = degrees Celsius
     n = number of chirps per minute

Then $t = \left(\frac{n}{4} + 8\right) \times \frac{5}{9}$

Suppose $n = 100$

Then $t = \left(\frac{100}{4} + 8\right) \times \frac{5}{9}$

$= 33 \times \frac{5}{9}$

$= \frac{165}{9} = 18\frac{1}{3} \approx 18°C$

Find t for the value of n. Round to the nearest degree.

42. 120   **43.** 160   **44.** 200   **45.** 220   **46.** 227   **47.** 155

MULTIPLYING MIXED NUMBERS

Mansun grew a pumpkin that weighed $5\frac{1}{4}$ lb. Kimberly grew one that weighed $2\frac{2}{3}$ times as much. How many pounds did Kimberly's pumpkin weigh?

To multiply $5\frac{1}{4}$ by $2\frac{2}{3}$, first write the mixed numbers as fractions.

$$5\frac{1}{4} = \frac{21}{4} \qquad 2\frac{2}{3} = \frac{8}{3}$$

Then simplify, if possible, before multiplying.

$$5\frac{1}{4} \times 2\frac{2}{3} = \frac{21}{4} \times \frac{8}{3} = \frac{\overset{7}{21} \times \overset{2}{8}}{\underset{1}{4} \times \underset{1}{3}} = \frac{14}{1} = 14$$

Kimberly's pumpkin weighed 14 lb.

 The properties of multiplication that you learn for whole numbers apply to fractions. For example you can use the distributive property and mental math to multiply a mixed number by a whole number.

$$\begin{aligned}
\textbf{Think:} \quad 4 \times 3\frac{1}{5} &= 4 \times \left(3 + \frac{1}{5}\right) \\
&= \left(4 \times 3\right) + \left(4 \times \frac{1}{5}\right) \\
&= 12 + \frac{4}{5} \\
&= 12\frac{4}{5}
\end{aligned}$$

CLASS EXERCISES

What is the value of the numerator?

1. $1\frac{1}{2} = \frac{\blacksquare}{2}$ **2.** $3\frac{1}{4} = \frac{\blacksquare}{4}$ **3.** $6\frac{2}{5} = \frac{\blacksquare}{5}$ **4.** $7\frac{3}{8} = \frac{\blacksquare}{8}$ **5.** $2\frac{1}{6} = \frac{\blacksquare}{6}$

6. $4\frac{3}{8} = \frac{\blacksquare}{8}$ **7.** $5\frac{2}{7} = \frac{\blacksquare}{7}$ **8.** $3\frac{2}{5} = \frac{\blacksquare}{5}$ **9.** $4\frac{1}{8} = \frac{\blacksquare}{8}$ **10.** $1\frac{2}{3} = \frac{\blacksquare}{3}$

PRACTICE

Multiply. Write the product in lowest terms.

11. $1\frac{1}{4} \times \frac{2}{3}$ **12.** $1\frac{1}{9} \times \frac{3}{5}$ **13.** $\frac{3}{7} \times 2\frac{1}{3}$ **14.** $\frac{2}{3} \times 1\frac{1}{2}$ **15.** $1\frac{3}{10} \times 2\frac{1}{2}$

16. $1\frac{5}{6} \times 1\frac{1}{2}$ **17.** $1\frac{1}{3} \times 2\frac{1}{4}$ **18.** $1\frac{1}{5} \times 3\frac{1}{3}$ **19.** $1\frac{1}{2} \times 8$ **20.** $1\frac{1}{6} \times 4$

21. $4\frac{1}{6} \times 2\frac{2}{5}$ **22.** $2\frac{4}{7} \times 10\frac{1}{2}$ **23.** $1\frac{3}{4} \times 2\frac{5}{6}$ **24.** $2\frac{1}{3} \times 1\frac{1}{4}$ **25.** $1\frac{3}{8} \times 2\frac{2}{5}$

26. $3\frac{3}{4} \times 1\frac{7}{10}$ **27.** $1\frac{1}{6} \times 1\frac{4}{5}$ ★ **28.** $12\frac{3}{4} \times 6\frac{4}{9}$ ★ **29.** $5\frac{5}{8} \times 9\frac{3}{10}$ ★ **30.** $2\frac{5}{12} \times 3\frac{3}{10}$

Use mental math to multiply. Write the product in lowest terms.

MENTAL MATH

31. $3 \times 2\frac{1}{3}$ **32.** $5 \times 2\frac{1}{6}$ **33.** $0 \times 3\frac{3}{4}$

34. $3 \times 5\frac{1}{2}$ **35.** $8 \times 1\frac{3}{4}$ **36.** $1 \times 18\frac{2}{9}$

PROBLEM SOLVING APPLICATIONS
Simplifying the Problem

Tell whether you would choose mental math or paper and pencil to solve the problem. Write *M* or *P*. Then solve.

37. Jim can weed $3\frac{1}{2}$ rows in his garden in 1 h. At this rate how many rows can he weed in $2\frac{1}{4}$ h?

38. Mabel worked in her garden for $1\frac{1}{2}$ h each day for 2 weeks. How many hours did she work in all?

39. Steve ordered $2\frac{1}{4}$ dozen tomato plants. Only $1\frac{2}{3}$ dozen plants were delivered. How many plants were not delivered?

★ **40.** May grew 37 pumpkins. She used 8 to bake bread and 12 as gifts. She entered 5 in a "perfect pumpkin" contest. Then she sold the rest for $2.50 each. How much did she earn?

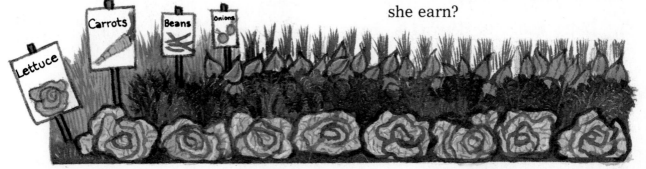

PROBLEM SOLVING

Strategy: Multi-Step Problems

To solve some problems, several steps may be needed.

Ron will use $\frac{1}{4}$ c milk and $2\frac{1}{2}$ c flour to bake one loaf of bread. He has $\frac{2}{3}$ c milk and 8 c flour. How much more milk and flour does he need to bake four loaves of bread?

Step 1 *Multiply* to determine the amount of milk needed.

$$4 \times \frac{1}{4} = 1$$

Step 2 *Multiply* to determine the amount of flour needed.

$$4 \times 2\frac{1}{2} = \overset{2}{\cancel{4}} \times \frac{5}{\underset{1}{\cancel{2}}} = 10$$

Step 3 *Subtract* to determine how much more milk and flour Ron needs.

milk: $1 - \frac{2}{3} = \frac{1}{3}$ flour: $10 - 8 = 2$

Ron needs $\frac{1}{3}$ c more milk and 2 c more flour.

CLASS EXERCISES

Complete to tell the operation used. Then solve.

There are 24 marbles. One fourth of them are red. There are 2 more green than red marbles. The rest are blue. How many marbles are blue?

1. __?__ 24 and $\frac{1}{4}$ to determine the number of red marbles.
2. __?__ ____ and ____ to determine the number of green marbles.
3. __?__ ____ and ____ to determine the number of red and green marbles.
4. __?__ ____ from ____ to determine the number of blue marbles.
5. ____ marbles are blue.

PRACTICE

Solve.

6. Tom had $4\frac{3}{4}$ yd of material. He used $\frac{1}{2}$ of the material to make a costume for the class play. He used another $\frac{3}{4}$ yd each to make 2 hats. How much material did he have left?

7. Ramon bought 14 chairs and 3 tables. He put 3 chairs at one table. He put twice as many chairs at the second table as the first. How many chairs did he put at the third table?

8. Leo's driveway is 14.7 m long. He wants to plant 2 rows of flowers along one length of it and 3 rows along the other length. How many meters long are the rows of flowers altogether?

9. Doris sold 12 subscriptions to Sports Review. One fourth of the people paid $7.60 each for 12 issues. The rest paid $12.40 each for 24 issues. How much money did Doris collect for the subscriptions?

10. Dee ordered 13 packs of paper clips for $.87 per pack, 10 boxes of erasers for $2.60 per box, and 3 boxes of pencils for $2 per box. How much did the order cost in all?

★ 11. Suppose you buy a $150 coat. You pay $35 down and agree to pay 6 monthly installments of $22.92 each. How much more do you pay for the coat on the installment plan?

CHECKPOINT 1

Multiply. Write the answer in lowest terms. *(pages 276–283)*

1. $3 \times \frac{1}{6}$

2. $\frac{1}{8} \times \frac{1}{3}$

3. $\frac{5}{8} \times \frac{9}{10}$

4. $\frac{5}{6} \times \frac{3}{10}$

5. $1\frac{3}{8} \times \frac{2}{3}$

6. $5\frac{2}{5} \times 1\frac{1}{3}$

Solve. *(pages 284–285)*

7. The sixth grade class is raising money at a car wash. They charge $1.50 to wash a standard size car and $1.25 for a compact size car. How much money will they earn if they wash 6 standard size cars and 15 compact size cars?

Extra Practice on page 438

DIVIDING A WHOLE NUMBER BY A FRACTION

Alvin is serving $\frac{1}{2}$ of a grapefruit to each of his friends. If he has 3 grapefruits, how many friends can he serve?

Here is one way to picture the problem:

Divide 3 grapefruits into halves. How many halves are there?

6 halves

There are 6 halves in 3 grapefruits so, $3 \div \frac{1}{2} = 6$.
Alvin can serve 6 friends.

Two numbers whose product is 1 are called **reciprocals.**

$2 \times \frac{1}{2} = 1$, so 2 and $\frac{1}{2}$ are reciprocals.

Instead of dividing by $\frac{1}{2}$, you can multiply by 2.

$3 \div \frac{1}{2} = 6$ $\qquad$ $3 \times 2 = 6$

Dividing by a number gives the same result as multiplying by the reciprocal of the number.

CLASS EXERCISES

What is the reciprocal of the number?

1. $\frac{1}{3}$ $\qquad$ **2.** $\frac{1}{4}$ $\qquad$ **3.** $\frac{1}{5}$ $\qquad$ **4.** $\frac{5}{6}$ $\qquad$ **5.** $\frac{7}{8}$ $\qquad$ **6.** $\frac{5}{9}$

Complete.

7.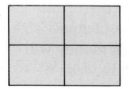

How many $\frac{1}{4}$'s are in 2? ▨

$2 \div \frac{1}{4} = 2 \times$ ▨ $=$ ▨

8.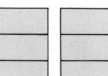

How many $\frac{2}{3}$'s are in 4? ▨

$4 \div \frac{2}{3} = 4 \times \frac{▨}{▨} =$ ▨

PRACTICE

Divide. Write the quotient in lowest terms.

9. $2 \div \frac{1}{3}$ **10.** $8 \div \frac{3}{5}$ **11.** $5 \div \frac{1}{4}$ **12.** $7 \div \frac{1}{7}$ **13.** $1 \div \frac{1}{10}$

14. $4 \div \frac{2}{5}$ **15.** $8 \div \frac{3}{7}$ **16.** $2 \div \frac{1}{9}$ **17.** $18 \div \frac{5}{4}$ **18.** $8 \div \frac{4}{5}$

19. $9 \div \frac{3}{10}$ **20.** $6 \div \frac{2}{7}$ **21.** $3 \div \frac{2}{3}$ **22.** $4 \div \frac{3}{4}$ **23.** $6 \div \frac{2}{5}$

24. Think: If there are 4 halves in 2, how many halves are there in 4?

★ **25. Think:** Compare $6 \div \frac{2}{3}$ and $6 \div \frac{3}{2}$. Draw a picture to show your results.

★ **26. Think:** *True* or *false:* When you divide a whole number by a fraction less than one, the quotient will always be greater than the dividend.

Round the number to the nearest tenth.

27. 3.63   **28.** 0.75   **29.** 8.629   **30.** 1.414

MIXED REVIEW

Round the number to the nearest hundredth.

31. 1.772   **32.** 8.645   **33.** 5.6663   **34.** 2.098

PROBLEM SOLVING APPLICATIONS
Choosing the Operation

Solve.

35. For a salad, Norma used $\frac{1}{2}$ c of cherries, $\frac{3}{4}$ c of sliced bananas, and $1\frac{5}{8}$ c of melon. How many cups of fruit did she use in all?

36. There are 8 c of detergent in a bottle of Brite-O. Each load of wash requires $\frac{1}{4}$ c. How many loads can you do with 1 bottle?

37. Alberto baked 2 loaves of bread. He cut each loaf into sixths. How many pieces does he have?

★ **38.** Tina bought $3\frac{1}{2}$ ft of ribbon. She used $\frac{1}{3}$ of it to decorate a package. How many feet did she have left?

DIVIDING A FRACTION BY A WHOLE NUMBER

After dinner $\frac{3}{4}$ of Mai's carrot cake was left. She decided to share it equally with her neighbor. She divided $\frac{3}{4}$ by 2. How much of the cake did her neighbor receive?

To divide a fraction by a whole number, first write the reciprocal of the whole number divisor. Then multiply.

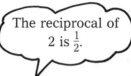

The reciprocal of 2 is $\frac{1}{2}$.

$$\frac{3}{4} \div 2 = \frac{3}{4} \times \frac{1}{2} = \frac{3}{8}$$

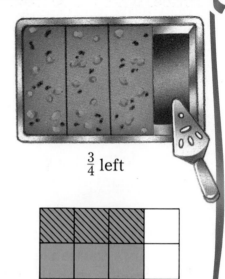

$\frac{3}{4}$ left

Her neighbor received $\frac{3}{8}$ of the cake.

$$\frac{3}{4} \div 2 = \frac{3}{8}$$

If you know the decimal equivalent of a fraction, you can use a calculator to divide. Your answer will be a whole number or a decimal. Here is the example above solved on a calculator.

$$0.75 \div 2 = 0.375$$

Think: Are $\frac{3}{8}$ and 0.375 equal?

CLASS EXERCISES

What is the reciprocal of the number?

1. 6 **2.** 8 **3.** 11 **4.** 5 **5.** 2 **6.** 26

Complete. Write the quotient in lowest terms.

7.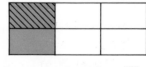

$\frac{1}{3} \div 2 = \frac{1}{3} \times \frac{1}{2} = $ ▨

8.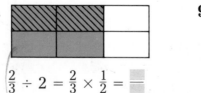

$\frac{2}{3} \div 2 = \frac{2}{3} \times \frac{1}{2} = $ ▨

9.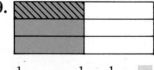

$\frac{1}{2} \div 3 = \frac{1}{2} \times \frac{1}{3} = $ ▨

PRACTICE

Divide. Write the quotient in lowest terms.

10. $\frac{1}{2} \div 2$ **11.** $\frac{3}{5} \div 3$ **12.** $\frac{5}{6} \div 2$ **13.** $\frac{1}{3} \div 4$ **14.** $\frac{5}{8} \div 5$

15. $\frac{1}{2} \div 4$ **16.** $\frac{1}{3} \div 3$ **17.** $\frac{2}{5} \div 4$ **18.** $\frac{3}{4} \div 6$ **19.** $\frac{1}{8} \div 2$

20. $\frac{3}{4} \div 4$ **21.** $\frac{4}{9} \div 4$ **22.** $\frac{9}{10} \div 3$ **23.** $\frac{2}{3} \div 3$ **24.** $\frac{6}{7} \div 2$

25. $\frac{1}{6} \div 2$ **26.** $\frac{4}{5} \div 8$ **27.** $\frac{1}{3} \div 5$ **28.** $\frac{5}{8} \div 2$ **29.** $\frac{2}{3} \div 6$

30. $\frac{1}{8} \div 6$ **31.** $\frac{3}{7} \div 4$ **32.** $\frac{2}{9} \div 5$ **33.** $\frac{4}{5} \div 12$ **34.** $\frac{6}{11} \div 10$

35. Think: When you divide a fraction by a whole number will the quotient be less than or greater than the dividend?

36. Think: Does $2 \div \frac{1}{4}$ give the same result as 2×4?

37. Think: Does $\frac{1}{3} \div 4$ give the same result as $3 \times \frac{1}{4}$?

Divide. Write the answer as a decimal and as a fraction.

38. $\frac{1}{2} \div 8$ **39.** $\frac{1}{4} \div 5$ **40.** $\frac{3}{4} \div 3$ **41.** $\frac{3}{10} \div 6$

CALCULATOR

PROBLEM SOLVING APPLICATIONS
Mental Math or Paper and Pencil

Tell whether you would choose mental math or paper and pencil to solve. Write *M* or *P*. Then solve.

42. Ossie spent $58.50 for a radio. Later, he spent $14.63 for repairs. About what fraction of the cost of the radio were repairs?

43. Jeff had a piece of wood that was $\frac{3}{5}$ ft long. He cut it into 4 equal pieces. What was the length of each piece?

44. Boyd, Rico, and Lolo each buy $\frac{3}{4}$ lb of grapes. Together they eat $\frac{1}{2}$ of the grapes. How many pounds of grapes do they have left?

★ 45. Regina gave $\frac{2}{5}$ of her money to her family. She divided the rest into two portions. What fraction of the total is each portion?

DIVIDING A FRACTION BY A FRACTION

The Sleep-Tight Pillow Company ordered $\frac{9}{10}$ t of feathers. If each delivery truck can carry $\frac{1}{6}$ t of feathers, how many trucks will be needed to ship the order?

Divide $\frac{9}{10}$ by $\frac{1}{6}$. To divide a fraction by a fraction, multiply by the reciprocal of the divisor.

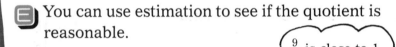

$$\frac{9}{10} \div \frac{1}{6} = \frac{9}{10} \times \frac{6}{1} = \frac{9 \times \overset{3}{\cancel{6}}}{\underset{5}{\cancel{10}} \times 1} = \frac{27}{5} = 5\frac{2}{5}$$

A total of 6 trucks will be needed.

E You can use estimation to see if the quotient is reasonable.

$\frac{9}{10}$ is close to 1.

For $\frac{9}{10} \div \frac{1}{6}$, think $\frac{9}{10} \times 6 \ \Rightarrow\ 1 \times 6 = 6$.

Since you rounded $\frac{9}{10}$ up, the actual quotient is less than 6. The answer $5\frac{2}{5}$ is reasonable.

CLASS EXERCISES

What is the reciprocal of the number?

1. $\frac{2}{3}$ 2. $\frac{3}{5}$ 3. $\frac{7}{8}$ 4. $\frac{7}{5}$ 5. $\frac{8}{13}$ 6. $\frac{11}{12}$

Complete. Write the quotient in lowest terms.

7. $\frac{1}{2} \div \frac{4}{5} = \frac{1}{2} \times \rule{1cm}{0.4cm} = \rule{1cm}{0.4cm}$

8. $\frac{3}{5} \div \frac{2}{3} = \frac{3}{5} \times \rule{1cm}{0.4cm} = \rule{1cm}{0.4cm}$

9. $\frac{5}{8} \div \frac{3}{4} = \frac{5}{8} \times \rule{1cm}{0.4cm} = \rule{1cm}{0.4cm}$

10. $\frac{1}{6} \div \frac{2}{5} = \frac{1}{6} \times \rule{1cm}{0.4cm} = \rule{1cm}{0.4cm}$

PRACTICE

Divide. Write the quotient in lowest terms.

11. $\frac{3}{4} \div \frac{1}{2}$ **12.** $\frac{1}{6} \div \frac{5}{9}$ **13.** $\frac{2}{3} \div \frac{1}{5}$ **14.** $\frac{1}{5} \div \frac{4}{5}$ **15.** $\frac{3}{4} \div \frac{2}{3}$

16. $\frac{2}{9} \div \frac{4}{3}$ **17.** $\frac{5}{6} \div \frac{7}{12}$ **18.** $\frac{1}{2} \div \frac{1}{3}$ **19.** $\frac{2}{5} \div \frac{9}{5}$ **20.** $\frac{3}{10} \div \frac{2}{5}$

21. $\frac{5}{12} \div \frac{1}{4}$ **22.** $\frac{7}{8} \div \frac{7}{6}$ **23.** $\frac{9}{10} \div \frac{5}{6}$ **24.** $\frac{8}{15} \div \frac{2}{3}$ **25.** $\frac{16}{9} \div \frac{3}{4}$

26. $3 \div \frac{9}{4}$ **27.** $\frac{1}{25} \div \frac{7}{5}$ **28.** $\frac{2}{5} \div \frac{1}{3}$ **29.** $\frac{5}{9} \div \frac{10}{27}$ **30.** $\frac{7}{12} \div \frac{21}{4}$

★ **31. Think:** Since $\frac{5}{8} < \frac{2}{3}$, will $\frac{5}{8} \div \frac{2}{3}$ be greater than or less than one?

★ **32. Think:** Since $\frac{3}{5} > \frac{1}{4}$, will $\frac{3}{5} \div \frac{1}{4}$ be greater than or less than one?

Divide. Then estimate the quotient to check the reasonableness of your answer.

ESTIMATE

33. $\frac{6}{5} \div \frac{7}{8}$ **34.** $\frac{4}{5} \div \frac{1}{3}$ **35.** $\frac{4}{5} \div \frac{1}{5}$ **36.** $\frac{8}{9} \div \frac{4}{8}$

PROBLEM SOLVING APPLICATIONS
Choosing the Operation

Solve.

37. The Sleep-Tight workers loaded a total of $\frac{7}{10}$ t of feathers on to 2 trucks. The same amount was put on each truck. What amount of feathers was loaded onto each truck?

38. A pillow stuffer worked for $8\frac{1}{2}$ h on Monday. He worked for 4 h on Tuesday. How many hours did he work in all during these 2 days?

★ **39.** Sleep-Tight's first robot could stitch 25 small or 16 large pillow covers in 1 h. Its new robot can stitch $1\frac{1}{2}$ times as many pillow covers as the first robot. How many more large pillow covers can the new robot stitch in an 8 h day than the first robot?

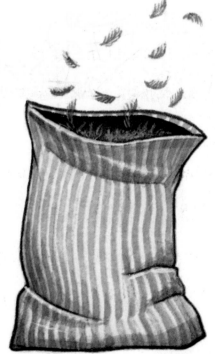

DIVIDING WITH MIXED NUMBERS

Jacob can complete a model ship in about $6\frac{1}{2}$ h. He works on his model for $1\frac{1}{4}$ h each day. At this rate, how many days should it take him to complete the model?

Divide $6\frac{1}{2}$ by $1\frac{1}{4}$.

Write the mixed numbers as fractions and multiply by the reciprocal of the divisor.

$$6\frac{1}{2} \div 1\frac{1}{4} = \frac{13}{2} \div \frac{5}{4}$$

> The reciprocal of $\frac{5}{4}$ is $\frac{4}{5}$.

$$= \frac{13}{2} \times \frac{4}{5}$$

$$= \frac{13 \times \overset{2}{\cancel{4}}}{\underset{1}{\cancel{2}} \times 5} = \frac{26}{5} = 5\frac{1}{5}$$

Jacob will need a little more than 5 days to complete the model.

When dividing fractions, here is a way to test whether you have used the reciprocal of the correct number. In the example above, the dividend $6\frac{1}{2}$ is greater than the divisor $1\frac{1}{4}$, so you can estimate that a reasonable answer must be greater than 1. If by mistake you had used the reciprocal of $6\frac{1}{2}$, your answer would have been less than 1.

CLASS EXERCISES

Write the mixed number as a fraction. What is the reciprocal of the fraction?

1. $2\frac{2}{5}$ **2.** $3\frac{1}{4}$ **3.** $1\frac{1}{10}$ **4.** $4\frac{5}{6}$ **5.** $2\frac{9}{10}$ **6.** $5\frac{3}{5}$

PRACTICE

Divide. Write the quotient in lowest terms.

7. $\frac{2}{3} \div 3\frac{2}{3}$ **8.** $\frac{1}{8} \div 3\frac{1}{5}$ **9.** $7 \div 1\frac{1}{8}$ **10.** $4\frac{1}{2} \div 6$

11. $3\frac{1}{5} \div \frac{2}{3}$ **12.** $9\frac{2}{5} \div \frac{1}{2}$ **13.** $5\frac{1}{2} \div \frac{1}{2}$ **14.** $8\frac{1}{6} \div 7$

15. $11\frac{1}{3} \div 2\frac{1}{2}$ **16.** $9\frac{2}{3} \div 4\frac{1}{5}$ **17.** $7\frac{1}{2} \div 3$ **18.** $\frac{3}{4} \div 2\frac{3}{4}$

19. $5 \div 1\frac{2}{3}$ **20.** $8\frac{2}{3} \div 6\frac{1}{4}$ **21.** $9\frac{2}{3} \div 8$ **22.** $4\frac{7}{9} \div 5\frac{2}{3}$

23. $4\frac{7}{8} \div 5\frac{3}{4}$ **24.** $2\frac{1}{8} \div 6\frac{3}{8}$ **25.** $1\frac{7}{10} \div 1\frac{3}{5}$ **26.** $6\frac{5}{12} \div 3\frac{3}{10}$

Estimate whether the quotient will be greater than 1 or less than 1. Write *greater* or *less*.

ESTIMATE

27. $2\frac{1}{3} \div 1\frac{1}{4}$ **28.** $\frac{7}{8} \div 1\frac{1}{6}$ **29.** $3\frac{1}{2} \div 3\frac{1}{4}$

30. $2\frac{7}{8} \div \frac{9}{4}$ **31.** $4\frac{1}{3} \div 4\frac{1}{2}$ **32.** $8\frac{5}{8} \div 10$

33. $3\frac{7}{12} \div 3\frac{4}{5}$ **34.** $1\frac{1}{7} \div \frac{4}{5}$ **35.** $4\frac{1}{4} \div \frac{3}{8}$

PROBLEM SOLVING APPLICATIONS
Simplifying the Problem

Solve.

36. Ben has $9\frac{1}{3}$ ft of wool yarn to dye. He wants to dye equal lengths of the yarn in 3 colors. How much yarn will be of each color?

37. Karim pours $\frac{2}{3}$ qt of blue paint into a bucket. He wants to add half as much red paint. How much red paint does he need?

38. Dede has $4\frac{2}{3}$ yd of cord to make a clothesline. She uses $2\frac{3}{4}$ yd. How much cord is left?

★ **39.** Rhonda has rectangular ceramic tiles with lengths of $1\frac{7}{8}$ in., $\frac{1}{2}$ in., $1\frac{1}{8}$ in., and $\frac{1}{4}$ in., all with a height of 1 in. How can she arrange them to make one rectangle 2 in. high?

PROBLEM SOLVING
Strategy: Working Backwards

1. Understand
2. Plan
3. Work
4. Answer/Check

Mei-hua worked 3 days last week. On Wednesday she worked 2 h more than on Monday, and on Friday she worked twice as many hours as on Wednesday. If she worked 8 h on Friday, how many hours did Mei-hua work in all?

You can work backwards to solve this problem by using the last fact given. Recall that addition and subtraction are opposite operations, as are multiplication and division.

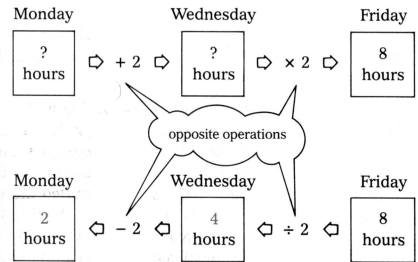

Monday		Wednesday		Friday
? hours	⇨ + 2 ⇨	? hours	⇨ × 2 ⇨	8 hours

opposite operations

Monday		Wednesday		Friday
2 hours	⇦ − 2 ⇦	4 hours	⇦ ÷ 2 ⇦	8 hours

Mei-hua worked 2 h on Monday, 4 h on Wednesday, and 8 h on Friday. She worked 14 h all week.

CLASS EXERCISES

Work backwards to complete.

1. ▦ $\xrightarrow{+\,5}$ ▦ $\xrightarrow{\div\,6}$ 3

2. ▦ $\xrightarrow{\times\,4}$ ▦ $\xrightarrow{+\,6}$ ▦ $\xrightarrow{-\,8}$ 34

3. ▦ $\xrightarrow{-\frac{1}{2}}$ ▦ $\xrightarrow{\times\frac{3}{4}}$ $\frac{9}{8}$

4. ▦ $\xrightarrow{+\$10}$ ▦ $\xrightarrow{-\,\$17.50}$ ▦ $\xrightarrow{\div\,2}$ $6.25

PRACTICE

Solve.

5. Anna withdrew some money from the bank. She spent $6.95 on a cassette and twice that amount on two records. Afterwards she had $19.15 left. How much money did she start with?

6. Simon noted that the money he earned gardening doubled each day for 5 consecutive days. If he earned $40 on the fifth day, how much did he earn in all?

7. Leroy and Jana made stuffed celery sticks. Each kept half of the sticks. After Leroy gave 12 to his mother, and shared the rest equally with two friends, Leroy had 8 sticks. How many sticks did they make in all?

8. Hal Allen had 21 rulers at the end of the day. He recalls giving out 14, getting back 12, then giving out 17 again, and getting back 18. How many rulers did he have at the beginning of the day?

★ 9. Justine baby-sat for 4 consecutive Saturdays. She earned as much the third Saturday as she did the second and fourth Saturdays combined. She earned half as much the first Saturday as the third Saturday. If she earned $20 the third Saturday, how much did she earn in all?

★10. Sunny Sports Inc. doubled its profits in its second year. The next year the profits were halved, but in the fourth year the profits tripled those of the second year. In the fifth year, the profits were two thirds those of the fourth year. If the profits in the fifth year were $80,000, how does this compare with the first year's profits?

CHECKPOINT 2

Divide. Write the answer in lowest terms. *(pages 286–293)*

1. $4 \div \frac{1}{5}$

2. $\frac{2}{3} \div 7$

3. $\frac{2}{3} \div \frac{8}{9}$

4. $2\frac{1}{3} \div 1\frac{1}{8}$

Solve. *(pages 294–295)*

5. Loretta made yogurt on Monday, Friday, and Sunday. Each time she doubled the previous amount. If she made $4\frac{1}{2}$ qt on Sunday, how many quarts did she make in all?

Extra Practice on page 438

Multiply. Write the answer in lowest terms. *(pages 276–283)*

1. $8 \times \frac{7}{12}$

2. $\frac{3}{10} \times 45$

3. $\frac{7}{8} \times \frac{4}{9}$

4. $\frac{5}{11} \times \frac{3}{7}$

5. $\frac{13}{6} \times \frac{3}{4}$

6. $7 \times 4\frac{1}{6}$

7. $1\frac{3}{8} \times \frac{6}{7}$

8. $5\frac{1}{4} \times 8\frac{4}{9}$

9. $\frac{4}{15} \times 50$

10. $\frac{12}{17} \times \frac{2}{36}$

11. $6\frac{4}{5} \times 1\frac{3}{7}$

12. $2\frac{1}{4} \times 2\frac{8}{9}$

Solve. *(pages 284–285)*

13. Lizzie bought a 10-speed bicycle for $180 and 2 spare tires for $17.58 each. How much did the bicycle and the tires cost Lizzie?

14. Dan's Window Service charges $5.00 to clean a small window and $7.50 to clean a large window. How much will it cost to clean a house with 12 small windows and 5 large ones?

Divide. Write the answer in lowest terms. *(pages 286–293)*

15. $6 \div \frac{9}{10}$

16. $18 \div \frac{2}{9}$

17. $\frac{2}{3} \div 5$

18. $\frac{4}{7} \div .16$

19. $\frac{7}{8} \div \frac{3}{4}$

20. $\frac{1}{10} \div \frac{18}{25}$

21. $5\frac{5}{6} \div 7$

22. $2\frac{1}{12} \div 9\frac{1}{3}$

23. $27 \div \frac{1}{2}$

24. $\frac{6}{11} \div 36$

25. $9\frac{4}{5} \div 7\frac{1}{3}$

26. $2\frac{1}{7} \div 3\frac{3}{7}$

Solve. *(pages 294–295)*

27. Janet made bran muffins. She gave half of them to Martha. Martha shared the muffins equally with two friends. How many muffins did Janet make if Martha and her friends each got 6 muffins?

28. Marty bought a T-shirt for $4.99 and a pair of jeans that cost three times the price of the T-shirt. He had $14.52 left after paying the bill. How much money did Marty have to start with?

Extra Practice on page 439

MATHEMATICS and SCIENCE

The life expectancy of a person is about 70 years. The typical life spans of different living things vary. For example:

Alligator	55 years	Mouse	3 years
Dolphin	65 years	Owl	24 years
Horse	30 years	Rabbit	12 years
Hippopotamus	40 years	Rhinoceros	70 years

WHAT DO YOU EXPECT?

1. Write a fraction comparing a rhinoceros's typical life span with a person's.

2. Name two animals whose life spans are between $\frac{2}{5}$ and $\frac{3}{5}$ as long as a rhinoceros's.

3. Which animal has an expected life span $\frac{12}{35}$ as long as a person's?

4. A tortoise lives about $1\frac{3}{7}$ as long as a person. An ostrich lives about $\frac{1}{2}$ as long as a tortoise. What is an ostrich's life span?

★**5.** A mayfly's life span is about $\frac{1}{1095}$ as long as a mouse's. Express the mayfly's life span to the closest unit of time.

Enrichment

A Greek mathematician named Pythagoras proved a very interesting relationship among the sides of right triangles.

In a right triangle, the longest side is called the **hypotenuse**. The other sides are called **legs**.

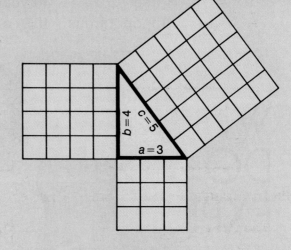

If you count the squares drawn on each side of the triangle, you'll find that the sum of the squares on the legs is equal to the square on the hypotenuse.

In this triangle
$$a^2 + b^2 = c^2$$
$$3^2 + 4^2 = 5^2$$
$$9 + 16 = 25$$

What is the length of the hypotenuse in the right triangle?

1.

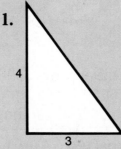

4

3

2.

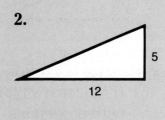

5

12

THE
PYTHAGOREAN
THEOREM

3.

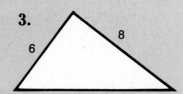

6

8

Write an equation you can use to find the missing number. Then solve the equation.

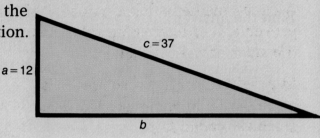

$c = 37$

$a = 12$

b

Example.

$$a^2 + b^2 = c^2$$
$$(12)^2 + b^2 = (37)^2$$
$$144 + b^2 = 1369$$
$$b^2 = 1225$$
$$b = 35$$

4.

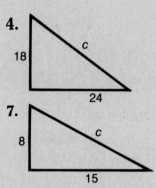

18

c

24

5.

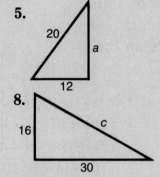

20

a

12

6.

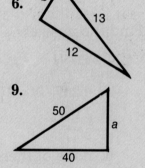

b

13

12

7.

8

c

15

8.

16

c

30

9.

50

a

40

Is the triangle a right triangle? Write *yes* or *no*.

10.

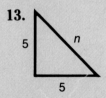

3.7

1.2

3.5

11.

2.5

4.0

2.4

12.

3.0

1.6

3.4

Use the table to find n to the nearest hundredth.

13.

5

n

5

14.

2

n

1

15.

3

n

2

16.

7

n

4

n^2	n
5	2.236
10	3.162
11	3.317
13	3.606
25	5
40	6.325
42	6.481
44	6.633
50	7.071
65	8.062

Choose the correct answer. Write *a*, *b*, *c*, or *d*.

Find the answer.

1. 17.2
$\times$5.8

    a. 99.76
    b. 98.76
    c. 98.66
    d. none of these

2. 3.367
$\times$10.19

    a. 3430.973
    b. 343.0973
    c. 34.30973
    d. none of these

3.   0.08
$\times$0.406

    a. 3.248
    b. 0.3248
    c. 0.03248
    d. none of these

Find the answer.

4. $13\overline{)26.91}$

    a. 0.207
    b. 2.07
    c. 20.7
    d. none of these

5. $0.7\overline{)6.167}$

    a. 0.881
    b. 8.81
    c. 88.1
    d. none of these

6. $0.058\overline{)0.5452}$

    a. 9.4
    b. 0.94
    c. 0.094
    d. none of these

Find the GCF of the numbers.

7. 18 and 22

    a. 2
    b. 6
    c. 11
    d. none of these

8. 38 and 76

    a. 2
    b. 19
    c. 38
    d. none of these

9. 48 and 64

    a. 12
    b. 16
    c. 48
    d. none of these

Compare the fractions.

10. $\frac{7}{12}$ ▢ $\frac{6}{10}$

    a. >
    b. <
    c. =
    d. none of these

11. $\frac{2}{3}$ ▢ $\frac{26}{39}$

    a. >
    b. <
    c. =
    d. none of these

12. $\frac{8}{9}$ ▢ $\frac{5}{6}$

    a. >
    b. <
    c. =
    d. none of these

Rename the fraction as a mixed number.

13. $\frac{38}{7}$

   a. $5\frac{3}{7}$

   b. $5\frac{2}{7}$

   c. $5\frac{1}{7}$

   d. none of these

14. $\frac{49}{5}$

   a. $9\frac{1}{5}$

   b. $9\frac{2}{5}$

   c. $9\frac{3}{5}$

   d. none of these

15. $\frac{26}{8}$

   a. $3\frac{5}{8}$

   b. $3\frac{1}{4}$

   c. $4\frac{1}{4}$

   d. none of these

Use the bar graph to solve Exercises 16 and 17.

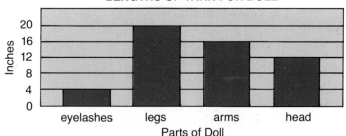

16. Which part of the yarn doll has the longest piece of yarn?

   a. eyelash

   b. head

   c. legs

   d. none of these

17. How long is each piece of yarn that is used for a doll's arms?

   a. $1\frac{1}{2}$ feet

   b. $1\frac{1}{3}$ feet

   c. $1\frac{2}{3}$ feet

   d. none of these

LANGUAGE and VOCABULARY REVIEW

Write *true* or *false*. If you write false, correct the sentence by replacing the underlined word.

1. A <u>line segment</u> has one endpoint.

2. Two intersecting lines that form right angles are <u>perpendicular</u>.

3. <u>Parallel</u> lines cross each other.

4. A <u>plane</u> is a set of points extending without end on a flat surface.

5. An <u>acute</u> angle measures more than 90°.

PRINT

Computer programs are written in special languages. One programming language is BASIC (Beginners All Purpose Symbolic Instruction Code). When you write a program in BASIC, you use line numbers, statements, and commands.

Line numbers tell the computer the order for following instructions. It is convenient to number lines by tens so you can add lines anywhere in a program.

Statements are special words in a program that make up instructions. Statements always have line numbers.

Commands are words that tell the computer to do something. Commands do not have line numbers.

The program below uses the **PRINT** statement.
PRINT with quotation marks displays exactly what is between the quotation marks. PRINT without quotation marks displays a number or an arithmetic answer.

PROGRAM   **OUTPUT**

The semicolon makes the computer show more than one output on a line.

```
10 PRINT "MULTIPLY"
20 PRINT "5*6"
30 PRINT 5*6; " APPLES"
40 END
```

Press ENTER or RETURN after each line.

```
MULTIPLY
5*6
30 APPLES
```

Type the command RUN to tell the computer to process the program.

Write the output.

1.
```
10 PRINT "DISTANCE"
20 PRINT 125-19;
30 PRINT " MILES"
40 END
```

2.
```
10 PRINT "TRY THIS"
20 PRINT "56 + 104 IS ";
30 PRINT 56+104
40 END
```

The monument at Mt. Rushmore is about 70 times life-size. Abraham Lincoln actually was over 6 ft tall. About how tall would a Mt. Rushmore-sized Abraham Lincoln stand?

RATIO, PROPORTION, PERCENT

303

RATIOS

Angela took a survey in her class. She learned that 2 people had pet turtles and 3 people had pet rabbits.

Angela used a ratio to compare the numbers of pets. A **ratio** is the quotient of two numbers and is used to compare one number with the other. The ratio of turtles to rabbits is 2 to 3.

You can write a ratio in different ways. You read all of these ratios as *two to three:*

$$2 \text{ to } 3 \qquad 2 : 3 \qquad \frac{2}{3}$$

To compare two measurements, use the same unit for both. To compare the mass of a 0.5 kg notebook with the mass of a 12 g pencil, first rename 0.5 kg as 500 g. Then write the ratio of their masses.

$$500 \text{ to } 12 \qquad 500 : 12 \qquad \frac{500}{12} \text{ or } \frac{125}{3}$$

When a ratio is written as a fraction, you can write it in lowest terms. The ratios $\frac{500}{12}$ and $\frac{125}{3}$ are equivalent.

CLASS EXERCISES

For each picture, write the ratio as a fraction in lowest terms.

1.

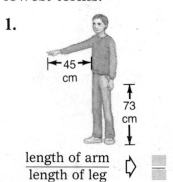

45 cm

73 cm

$\dfrac{\text{length of arm}}{\text{length of leg}}$ ⇨ ▦

2.

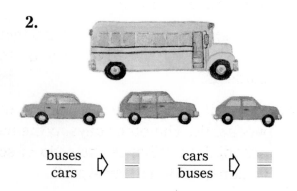

$\dfrac{\text{buses}}{\text{cars}}$ ⇨ ▦ $\dfrac{\text{cars}}{\text{buses}}$ ⇨ ▦

PRACTICE

Write the ratio as a fraction. Then write it in lowest terms.

3. 5 to 15   **4.** 8 to 12   **5.** 9 to 3   **6.** 12 : 15   **7.** 24 : 16

Write the ratio as a fraction in lowest terms to compare the numbers in the table below.

BRANDON SCHOOL TALENT SHOW

ACTS	Singing	Dancing	Gymnastics	Magic	Musical
NUMBER	5	3	4	2	6

8. gymnastics acts to dancing acts   **9.** magic acts to gymnastic acts

10. gymnastics acts to all acts   **11.** magic acts to dancing acts

12. dancing acts to musical acts   **13.** magic acts to singing acts

14. singing acts to musical acts   **15.** musical acts to all acts

Exercises 16–20 refer to a rectangle. Write the ratio of length to width as a fraction in lowest terms.

	16.	**17.**	**18.**	★ **19.**	★ **20.**
LENGTH	5 m	18 cm	2 m	0.1 m	0.05 m
WIDTH	3 m	15 cm	16 cm	8 cm	1.5 cm

PROBLEM SOLVING APPLICATIONS
Using Ratios

Solve. Write the ratio as a fraction in lowest terms.

21. Sofia spent an hour studying for a history test and 25 min studying for a math quiz. Write a ratio to compare study time for history with study time for math.

22. Swandon School has 250 students and 15 teachers. What is the ratio of teachers to students?

★ **23.** In April there were 6 vacation days and 4 weekends. The other days in the month were school days. What is the ratio of school days to non-school days in April?

RATES

A **rate** is a ratio that compares different kinds of quantities.

Suppose Todd can paint 9 signs in 3 hours. You can say he paints at the rate of 9 signs in 3 hours.

To find the rate per hour, or **unit rate,** write an equivalent ratio with a denominator of 1.

$$\text{signs} \longrightarrow \frac{9}{3} = \frac{3}{1} \longleftarrow \text{hours}$$

Todd paints at the rate of 3 signs per hour. You can also write this rate as 3 signs/hour.

Think: What does km/h mean?

CLASS EXERCISES

Complete.

1. $\frac{24}{8} = \frac{\blacksquare}{1}$

2. $\frac{10}{5} = \frac{\blacksquare}{1}$

3. $\frac{12}{3} = \frac{\blacksquare}{1}$

4. $\frac{20}{4} = \frac{\blacksquare}{1}$

5. $\frac{165}{5} = \frac{\blacksquare}{1}$

6. $\frac{216}{3} = \frac{\blacksquare}{1}$

7. $\frac{36}{9} = \frac{\blacksquare}{1}$

8. $\frac{132}{6} = \frac{\blacksquare}{1}$

Complete the table.

9.

DOLLARS EARNED	$48.50	?	?	?
NUMBER OF DAYS	1	2	5	10

10.

REVOLUTIONS	$33\frac{1}{3}$	?	?	?	?
MINUTES	1	2	7	10	25

PRACTICE

Write the unit rate.

11. 10 eggs for 5 omelets

12. 850 km in 10 h

13. $36 in 9 h

14. 500 words in 25 min

15. 120 books in 5 boxes

16. $72 for 12 kg

17. 50 fish for 25 people **18.** $2275 for 7 months **19.** 540 words in 9 min

20. $2.42 for 11 stamps **21.** 1200 chairs in 50 rows **22.** 2250 m in 15 min

---

Write the answer. Write quotients as decimals to the nearest tenth.

MIXED REVIEW

23. 463
×9

24. 876
×27

25. 3.65
×65

26. 2.837
×0.8

27. 8)685

28. 86)4265

29. 0.3)5.88

PROBLEM SOLVING APPLICATIONS
Multi-Step Problems

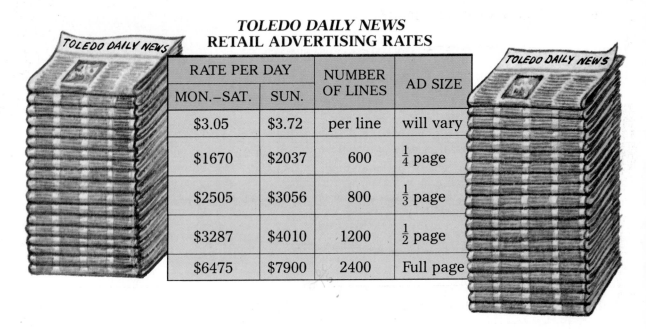

TOLEDO DAILY NEWS
RETAIL ADVERTISING RATES

RATE PER DAY		NUMBER OF LINES	AD SIZE
MON.–SAT.	SUN.		
$3.05	$3.72	per line	will vary
$1670	$2037	600	$\frac{1}{4}$ page
$2505	$3056	800	$\frac{1}{3}$ page
$3287	$4010	1200	$\frac{1}{2}$ page
$6475	$7900	2400	Full page

Use the table to solve.

30. You want to run a 555-line ad on Monday. Is it cheaper to buy a $\frac{1}{4}$-page ad or to pay by the line?

31. Waverly Cinema is running a $\frac{1}{2}$-page ad on Friday, Saturday, and Sunday. What is the cost?

32. The weekly advertising budget for Cameraland is $8500. Will a $\frac{1}{3}$-page ad on Sunday, Monday, and Saturday fit in the budget?

★ **33.** The Jog Shop is running a 68-line ad on Tuesday, Thursday, and Friday, and a $\frac{1}{2}$-page ad on Saturday. How much will this cost?

PROPORTIONS

Penny played the game of Tagalong against her computer. Penny won 8 games out of 24. At this rate, how many times can Penny expect to win if she plays 48 games?

You can write a proportion to solve this problem. A **proportion** is an equation stating that two ratios or rates are equivalent. To find the value of n in the proportion below, find a fraction equivalent to $\frac{8}{24}$ with 48 as the denominator.

wins $\longrightarrow$ games $\longrightarrow$ $\frac{8}{24} = \frac{n}{48}$ $\frac{8}{24} = \frac{8 \times 2}{24 \times 2} = \frac{16}{48}$ so $n = 16$

If Penny continues to win at the same rate, she can expect to win 16 times in 48 games.

You can estimate to check that your solution to a proportion is reasonable.

$$\frac{12}{5} = \frac{m}{30} \quad \Rightarrow \quad m = 72$$

Think: $12 > 5$, so m should be greater than 30. Is it?

CLASS EXERCISES

Are the ratios equivalent? Write *yes* or *no*.

1. 2 to 4
6 to 12

2. 3 to 5
12 to 15

3. 10 to 4
40 to 16

4. 8 to 18
24 to 54

Complete.

5. $\frac{4}{6} = \frac{n}{18}$ $\Rightarrow$ $\frac{4}{6} = \frac{4 \times 3}{6 \times 3} = \frac{\blacksquare}{18}$, so $n = \blacksquare$.

6. $\frac{8}{14} = \frac{32}{n}$ $\Rightarrow$ $\frac{8}{14} = \frac{8 \times 4}{14 \times \blacksquare} = \frac{32}{\blacksquare}$, so $n = \blacksquare$.

7. $\frac{7}{10} = \frac{x}{30}$ $\Rightarrow$ $\frac{7}{10} = \frac{7 \times 3}{10 \times 3} = \frac{\blacksquare}{30}$, so $x = \blacksquare$.

8. $\frac{9}{13} = \frac{27}{x}$ $\Rightarrow$ $\frac{9}{13} = \frac{9 \times 3}{13 \times 3} = \frac{27}{\blacksquare}$, so $x = \blacksquare$.

PRACTICE

Solve.

9. $\frac{3}{10} = \frac{6}{n}$

10. $\frac{3}{6} = \frac{n}{36}$

11. $\frac{9}{2} = \frac{a}{20}$

12. $\frac{16}{8} = \frac{4}{b}$

13. $\frac{15}{2} = \frac{150}{m}$

14. $\frac{9}{12} = \frac{3}{n}$

15. $\frac{15}{8} = \frac{30}{n}$

16. $\frac{3}{8} = \frac{a}{24}$

17. $\frac{30}{35} = \frac{6}{y}$

18. $\frac{2}{7} = \frac{x}{35}$

19. $\frac{5}{17} = \frac{20}{a}$

20. $\frac{24}{64} = \frac{3}{n}$

★ 21. **Think:** Is the ratio 5 to 2 the same as $2\frac{1}{2}$ to 1?

★ 22. **Think:** Is the ratio $3\frac{1}{3}$ to 1 the same as 10 to 3?

Write R if the solution to the proportion is reasonable. If it
is not reasonable write the correct value.

ESTIMATE

23. $\frac{6}{2} = \frac{a}{8}$ $a = 4$

24. $\frac{15}{20} = \frac{45}{x}$ $x = 60$

25. $\frac{17}{9} = \frac{n}{36}$ $n = 68$

26. $\frac{7}{11} = \frac{28}{w}$ $w = 44$

PROBLEM SOLVING APPLICATIONS
Choosing a Strategy

Solve.

27. Ivy Pierce earned $6.40 from selling 8 loaves
of bread. How much can she earn from selling
24 loaves of bread?

28. Todd MacDonald needs 3 horses to pull each
wagon. How many horses does he need to pull
6 wagons?

29. Jon Strauss bought 6 peaches at 3 for $.89. He
also bought a dozen eggs for $1.06. How much
did he spend?

★ 30. Elizabeth has only ivy, fern, palm, and fig
plants. The ratio of ivy plants to ferns is 3 to 5.
The ratio of ferns to palms is 2 to 4. The ratio
of ivy plants to figs is 2 to 5. There are 6 ivy
plants. How many plants does Elizabeth have
in all?

CROSS MULTIPLYING

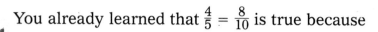

You already learned that $\frac{4}{5} = \frac{8}{10}$ is true because

$$\frac{4 \times 2}{5 \times 2} = \frac{8}{10}.$$

Ⓜ It also happens that $\frac{4}{5} = \frac{8}{10}$ is true because the cross products, 4×10 and 5×8, are equal. You can use mental math to cross multiply and check whether two ratios are equivalent.

Look at these examples. The symbol $\overset{?}{=}$ is used here to ask whether the two ratios are equivalent.

$$\frac{2}{3} \overset{?}{\times} \frac{4}{6} \qquad\qquad \frac{8}{10} \overset{?}{\times} \frac{12}{18}$$

$$2 \times 6 \overset{?}{=} 3 \times 4 \qquad\qquad 8 \times 18 \overset{?}{=} 10 \times 12$$

$$12 \overset{?}{=} 12 \text{ True.} \qquad\qquad 144 \overset{?}{=} 120 \text{ False.}$$

The ratios $\frac{2}{3}$ and $\frac{4}{6}$ are equivalent. The ratios $\frac{8}{10}$ and $\frac{12}{18}$ are not equivalent.

Cross multiplying is another way to solve a proportion.

$$\frac{4}{2} \overset{}{\times} \frac{n}{9} \qquad 2 \times n = 4 \times 9$$
$$2 \times n = 36$$
$$n = 36 \div 2 = 18$$

> $2 \times 18 = 36$
> so $n = 18$

CLASS EXERCISES

Complete. Are the ratios equivalent? Write *yes* or *no*.

1. $\frac{2}{6} \overset{?}{=} \frac{3}{9}$ $2 \times 9 = \blacksquare$
$6 \times 3 = \blacksquare$

2. $\frac{6}{8} \overset{?}{=} \frac{8}{12}$ $6 \times 12 = \blacksquare$
$8 \times 8 = \blacksquare$

3. $\frac{6}{4} \overset{?}{=} \frac{15}{10}$ $6 \times 10 = \blacksquare$
$4 \times 15 = \blacksquare$

Complete to solve the proportion.

4. $\frac{6}{10} = \frac{n}{25}$ $10 \times n = 6 \times 25$
$10 \times n = 150$
$n = 150 \div 10 = \blacksquare$

5. $\frac{6}{8} = \frac{21}{y}$ $6 \times y = 8 \times 21$
$6 \times y = 168$
$y = 168 \div \blacksquare = \blacksquare$

PRACTICE

Cross multiply to solve the proportion.

6. $\frac{1}{4} = \frac{n}{28}$

7. $\frac{7}{8} = \frac{b}{32}$

8. $\frac{8}{6} = \frac{20}{a}$

9. $\frac{9}{w} = \frac{12}{4}$

10. $\frac{12}{8} = \frac{z}{18}$

11. $\frac{y}{50} = \frac{30}{75}$

12. $\frac{8}{a} = \frac{14}{7}$

13. $\frac{18}{15} = \frac{30}{e}$

14. $\frac{12}{b} = \frac{54}{45}$

15. $\frac{h}{27} = \frac{42}{54}$

16. $\frac{5}{10} = \frac{24}{m}$

17. $\frac{20}{16} = \frac{n}{44}$

18. $\frac{20}{c} = \frac{30}{21}$

19. $\frac{12}{7} = \frac{48}{d}$

20. $\frac{15}{33} = \frac{10}{f}$

21. $\frac{44}{77} = \frac{a}{56}$

Use mental math to determine whether the ratios are equivalent. Write *yes* or *no*.

22. $\frac{4}{3}, \frac{8}{7}$

23. $\frac{5}{25}, \frac{10}{100}$

24. $\frac{2.3}{23} = \frac{1}{10}$

MENTAL MATH

PROBLEM SOLVING
Mental Math or Paper and Pencil

Tell whether you would choose mental math or paper and pencil. Write *M* or *P*. Then solve.

25. If it is about $2\frac{1}{2}$ in. from Uba to Crystal City on the map, how many miles would this be?

26. Norbert is about 150 mi from Trimtown. About how many inches apart would Norbert be from Trimtown on the map?

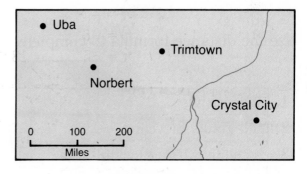

27. Paul took a nap from 1:15 P.M. to 3:05 P.M. He went to bed at 10:35 that night and arose at 6:10 the next morning. How much time did he spend sleeping in all?

28. A pool is being filled at the rate of 200 L of water every 25 min. About how long will it take to add 10,000 L of water?
Hint: $\frac{200}{25} = \frac{10,000}{n}$

29. Randy's heart beats 145 times in 2 min. About how many times does it beat in 30 min?
Hint: $\frac{145}{2} = \frac{n}{30}$

★ **30.** Suppose your watch gains 4 s every 8 h. How many minutes will it gain in a week?

1. Understand
2. Plan
3. Work
4. Answer/Check

PROBLEM SOLVING
Strategy: Using Formulas

You can solve problems involving rates by using a rule called a **formula.** A formula is a rule that is written with symbols.

A passenger train travels between two towns at a rate of 95 km/h. It takes 3 h to travel from one town to the other. How far apart are the towns?

Use the formula: distance = rate × time

$$D = r \times t$$

Here the rate (r) is 95 km/h and the time (t) is 3 h.

$$
\begin{aligned}
D &= r \times t \\
&= 95 \times 3 \\
&= 285
\end{aligned}
$$

The towns are 285 km apart.

CLASS EXERCISES

Use the distance formula to complete the table.

		r (km/h)	t (hours)	r × t
1.	jet cruising	950	3	?
2.	6th grader bicycling	16	4.5	?
3.	satellite orbiting Earth	27,400	2.8	?
4.	housefly flying	8	0.25	?
5.	gazelle running	65.5	0.75	?

PRACTICE

Solve.

6. A car is traveling at the rate of 80 km/h. How far will it travel in half an hour?

7. A rainstorm is moving at 35 km/h. At this rate, how far will the storm travel in 4.5 h?

8. A small sailboat traveling at the rate of 21 km/h crossed a lake in 14 min. How far across is the lake?

9. The three-toed sloth is one of the slowest-moving land animals. It travels at the rate of about 2.4 m/min. At this rate, how far can it travel in one hour?

Use the formula to solve.

10. Eddie took a taxi to the airport located 12 km from his home. What was the fare?

★ 11. A construction worker 120 m above the ground accidentally dropped his apple. How long did it take the apple to reach the ground?

(fare)   distance (km)
$f = \$1.75 + (\$1.50 \times d)$

distance (m)   time (seconds)
$d = 4.8 \times t^2$

CHECKPOINT 1

Compare the figures. Write a ratio as a fraction in lowest terms. (*pages 304–305*)

◯ ◯ ◯ △ △ ⬡ ⬡

1. ◯ to △   2. △ to ⬡

Write the unit rate. (*pages 306–307*)

3. $80 for 5 books

4. 75 km in 25 min

Solve. (*pages 308–311*)

5. $\frac{6}{24} = \frac{n}{48}$

6. $\frac{3}{7} = \frac{12}{n}$

7. $\frac{x}{18} = \frac{12}{36}$

8. $\frac{16}{x} = \frac{8}{3}$

Solve. (*pages 312–313*)

9. A car travels at about 85 km/h for 5 hours. About how far will it have gone?

Extra Practice on page 440

MEANING OF PERCENT

Percent is a form of ratio and compares a number to 100. The symbol % is read *percent* and means *per hundred*.

Each of the units below has 100 parts. You can use a percent to tell how much of each unit is shaded.

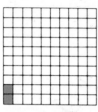

2 out of 100
2%

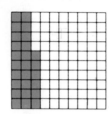

26 out of 100
26%

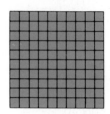

100 out of 100
100%

 What do you see when you mentally picture a wall 100% painted? a sandwich 100% eaten?

CLASS EXERCISES

What percent of the unit is shaded?

1. 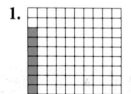   **2.** 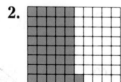   **3.** 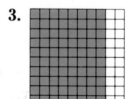   **4.**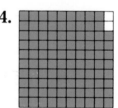

Write the percent.

5. 9 out of 100

6. 10 out of 100

7. 16 out of 100

8. 99 out of 100

9. 43 out of 100

10. 75 out of 100

11. 95 out of 100

12. 25 out of 100

13. 50 out of 100

14. 75 out of 100

15. 1 out of 100

16. 0 out of 100

17. Think: Is 4 out of 100 equivalent to 40%?

PRACTICE

For each unit, tell what percent is blue, what percent is green, and what percent is not shaded.

18.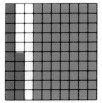

19.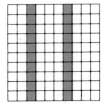

20.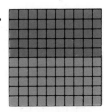

21.

22.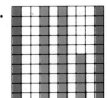

23.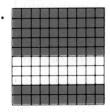

24. Describe what you see when you mentally picture 1% of 100 pennies.

25. Describe what you see when you mentally picture 50% of a door in glass.

MENTAL MATH

PROBLEM SOLVING APPLICATIONS
Writing Percents

The chart at the right shows the favorite sports of 100 students. Use the chart to solve.

26. How many of the 100 students named soccer as their favorite sport? What percent is this amount?

27. What percent of the students named football as their favorite sport? baseball?

★ **28.** How much greater is the percent who named baseball as their favorite sport than the percent who named hockey?

FAVORITE SPORTS

47	Baseball
16	Soccer
29	Football
8	Hockey

FRACTIONS AND PERCENTS

The Smithfield Light Bulb Company estimates that 94 out of every 100 bulbs it makes will last for 1000 h.

You can write *94 out of 100* as a fraction or as a percent.

$$\frac{94}{100} = 94 \text{ percent} = 94\%$$

These examples show how to write a fraction as a percent.

- When the denominator is 100, just write the numerator with a percent symbol.

$$\frac{9}{100} = 9\% \qquad \frac{47}{100} = 47\%$$

- When the denominator is not 100, first write an equivalent fraction with a denominator of 100. Then write the new numerator with a percent symbol.

$$\frac{1}{5} = \frac{20}{100} = 20\%$$

You can also write a percent as a fraction. These examples show how to write a percent as a fraction in lowest terms.

$$31\% = \frac{31}{100} \qquad 80\% = \frac{80}{100} = \frac{4}{5} \qquad 5\% = \frac{5}{100} = \frac{1}{20}$$

CLASS EXERCISES

What is the percent?

1. $\frac{67}{100} = $ ▢%

2. $\frac{7}{10} = \frac{▢}{100} = $ ▢%

3. $\frac{4}{5} = \frac{▢}{100} = $ ▢%

Complete. Write the fraction in lowest terms.

4. $11\% = \frac{▢}{100}$

5. $40\% = \frac{▢}{100} = \frac{▢}{▢}$

6. $85\% = \frac{▢}{100} = \frac{▢}{▢}$

7. $7\% = \frac{▢}{▢}$

8. $90\% = \frac{▢}{▢}$

9. $4\% = \frac{▢}{▢}$

PRACTICE

Write as a percent.

10. $\frac{17}{100}$ **11.** $\frac{8}{10}$ **12.** $\frac{1}{2}$ **13.** $\frac{43}{50}$ **14.** $\frac{1}{25}$ **15.** $\frac{3}{5}$

16. $\frac{19}{20}$ **17.** $\frac{47}{100}$ **18.** $\frac{7}{25}$ **19.** $\frac{1}{20}$ **20.** $\frac{11}{20}$ **21.** $\frac{14}{25}$

Write as a fraction in lowest terms.

22. 10%   **23.** 57%   **24.** 75%   **25.** 6%   **26.** 1%   **27.** 72%

28. 2%   **29.** 65%   **30.** 67%   **31.** 39%   **32.** 84%   **33.** 35%

34. Think: What whole number is 100% equal to?   ★ **35. Think:** What mixed number is 150% equal to?

Write <, >, or = to compare.

36. 0.09 ▨ 0.109   **37.** $\frac{7}{8}$ ▨ $\frac{2}{3}$ **38.** 2.10 ▨ 2.0987

39. $\frac{1}{3}$ ▨ $\frac{3}{9}$ **40.** 0.48 ▨ $\frac{12}{25}$ **41.** 0.9856 ▨ 1.03

MIXED REVIEW

PROBLEM SOLVING APPLICATIONS
Using Percents

Solve.

42. In a survey $\frac{3}{5}$ of the people interviewed said they listened to the radio for at least 45 minutes per day. What percent of the people is this amount?

44. Write and solve a problem whose answer is 50%.

★ **45.** Jed asked his classmates what percent of their allowances they spent on food. The table shows their responses. What percent said they spent 25% on food?

43. At Research Co., 15% of the employees work part-time. What fraction of the employees work part-time?

HOW ALLOWANCES ARE SPENT

Number of Students	8	4	6	2
Percent Spent on Food	15%	25%	35%	50%

DECIMALS AND PERCENTS

You can write a decimal as a percent.

0.27 is read *27 hundredths*.
You write the percent as 27%.

Thus, "27 out of 100" can be shown as a fraction, as a decimal, or as a percent. Sometimes you may need to write a decimal first in order to write a percent.

Fraction	To write the fraction as a decimal, divide.	To write the decimal as a percent, move the decimal point 2 places to the right, and write the percent symbol.
$\frac{7}{8}$	$8\overline{)7.000}$ 0.875	$0.875 = 87.5\%$

If a fraction names a repeating decimal, you may round to name a percent. You may use a calculator to help you write percents.

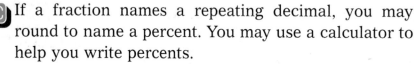

$\frac{8}{11}$ ⟹ $8 \div 11 = 0.7272727$ ⟹ $0.727 = 72.7\%$

Round to thousandths

You can also change a percent to a decimal.

$$31\% = \frac{31}{100} = 0.31 \qquad 8\% = \frac{8}{100} = 0.08$$

CLASS EXERCISES

Complete to write the decimal as a percent.

1. $0.63 = \frac{}{100} = \%$

2. $0.05 = \frac{}{100} = \%$

3. $0.45 = \frac{}{100} = \%$

Complete to write the percent as a decimal.

4. $38\% = \frac{}{100} = 0.$

5. $2\% = \frac{}{100} = 0.$

6. $93\% = \frac{}{100} = 0.$

7. Think: How do you change 28% to a decimal?

PRACTICE

Write as a percent.

8. 0.23 **9.** 0.3 **10.** 0.15 **11.** 0.03 **12.** 0.485

13. 0.8 **14.** 0.827 **15.** 0.12 **16.** 0.1 **17.** 0.09

18. 0.07 **19.** 0.111 **20.** 0.60 **21.** 0.79 ★ **22.** 0.003

Write as a decimal.

23. 42% **24.** 55% **25.** 8% **26.** 97% **27.** 2%

28. 37.5% **29.** 84.7% **30.** 1.8% **31.** 16.4% **32.** 2.5%

33. 1.5% **34.** 79% **35.** 7.5% ★ **36.** 245% ★ **37.** 0.9%

Write as a decimal, then as a percent. Round repeating decimals to the nearest thousandth. You may wish to use a calculator.

CALCULATOR

38. $\frac{3}{4}$ **39.** $\frac{1}{8}$ **40.** $\frac{4}{9}$ **41.** $\frac{5}{18}$

42. $\frac{5}{11}$ **43.** $\frac{3}{8}$ **44.** $\frac{8}{9}$ **45.** $\frac{5}{6}$

46. $\frac{11}{15}$ **47.** $\frac{17}{20}$ **48.** $\frac{1}{7}$ **49.** $\frac{15}{13}$

PROBLEM SOLVING APPLICATIONS
Nonroutine Problems

The flag at the right is a whole unit. Write a fraction, a decimal, and a percent for the given part.

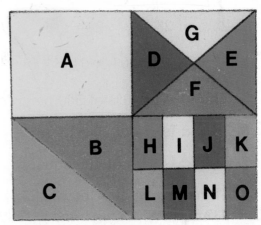

50. A **51.** B

52. G **53.** M

54. B + C **55.** A + B + C

56. E + G **57.** H + I

★ **58.** C + G ★ **59.** A + B + F

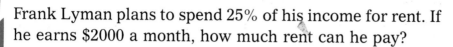

A PERCENT OF A NUMBER

Frank Lyman plans to spend 25% of his income for rent. If he earns $2000 a month, how much rent can he pay?

You can find 25% of $2000 in two ways.

Write the percent as a fraction. Then multiply.

Write the percent as a decimal. Then multiply.

$$25\% = \frac{25}{100} \text{ or } \frac{1}{4}$$

$$25\% = 0.25$$

$$\frac{1}{4} \times 2000 = \frac{2000}{4} = 500$$

$$\begin{array}{r} \$2000 \\ \times 0.25 \\ \hline 10000 \\ 40000 \\ \hline \$500.00 \end{array}$$

He can afford to pay $500 a month for rent.

🔲 You can use a calculator to find a percent of a number. Round money to the nearest cent.

7% of $23.98 ▷ 0.07 ⊠ 23.98 🟰 1.6786 ▷ $1.68

CLASS EXERCISES

Complete.

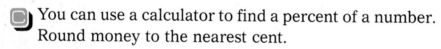

1. 25% of 28 = $\frac{1}{4} \times 28 = $ ▨

2. 46% of 57 = 0.46 × 57 = ▨

3. 3% of 64 = 0.03 × 64 = ▨

4. 20% of 55 = $\frac{1}{5} \times 55 = $ ▨

5. **Think:** Will 40% of 500 be greater than or less than 250?

6. **Think:** Is 6% of 100 the same as 60% of 10?

7. **Think:** Is 25% of 100 equal to 10% of 250?

8. **Think:** Since 10% of $32.50 is $3.25, what is 20% of $32.50?

PRACTICE

Use a fraction or a decimal to find the number.

9. 19% of 72   **10.** 20% of 25   **11.** 5% of 26   **12.** 25% of 40

13. 2% of 87   **14.** 6% of 47   **15.** 32% of 54   **16.** 73% of 58

17. 10% of 90   **18.** 11% of 94   **19.** 75% of 80   **20.** 35% of 82

21. 4% of 26   **22.** 50% of 22   **23.** 95% of 53   **24.** 28% of 64

Write < or > to compare the numbers.

25. 3% of 345 ▨ 5% of 325   **26.** 45% of 67 ▨ 50% of 58

27. 18% of 27 ▨ 62% of 48   **28.** 75% of 49 ▨ 80% of 62

Write the answer rounded to the nearest cent. A calculator will be helpful.

CALCULATOR

29. 4% of $95.98   **30.** 13% of $45.70   **31.** 47% of $36.01

32. 28% of $119   **33.** 87% of $69.23   **34.** 99% of $80.10

PROBLEM SOLVING APPLICATIONS
Using Percents

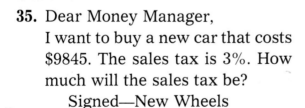

Suppose you write a newspaper column that answers people's questions about money. How would you answer the letter? If necessary, round your answer to the nearest cent.

35. Dear Money Manager,
I want to buy a new car that costs $9845. The sales tax is 3%. How much will the sales tax be?
Signed—New Wheels

36. Dear Money Manager,
I want to buy a house that costs $78,500. The down payment is 20%. How much will the down payment be?
Signed—House Hunter

37. Dear Money Manager,
I found a bookstore that gives 15% off the regular price of all books. How much can I save on a book that usually costs $15.98?
Signed—Book Lover

★ **38.** Dear Money Manager,
Last month I saw a telescope that cost $387.50. Since then, the price has increased 7%. How much will it cost now?
Signed—Star Gazer

ONE NUMBER AS A PERCENT OF ANOTHER

For her social studies class, Myra surveyed 20 people. She found that 7 of them were against Clear City's park proposal. What percent of the people surveyed were against the proposal?

Follow these steps to write one number as a percent of another.

Write a fraction.	Write an equivalent fraction with a denominator of 100.	Write the fraction as a percent.
$\frac{7}{20}$	$\frac{7}{20} = \frac{n}{100} = \frac{35}{100}$	$\frac{35}{100} = 35\%$

Since 7 is 35% of 20, 35% of the people surveyed were against the proposal.

 You can also estimate one number as a percent of another. Since 9 is close to half of 20, 9 is about 50% of 20. Since 14 is close to one fourth of 60, 14 is about 25% of 60.

CLASS EXERCISES

Complete.

1. $\frac{3}{20} = \frac{n}{100}$ $\qquad$ $\frac{9}{20} = \frac{y}{100}$ $\qquad$ $\frac{13}{20} = \frac{a}{100}$

3 is ▦% of 20. $\qquad$ 9 is ▦% of 20. $\qquad$ 13 is ▦% of 20.

2. $\frac{8}{50} = \frac{n}{100}$ $\qquad$ $\frac{42}{50} = \frac{a}{100}$ $\qquad$ $\frac{33}{50} = \frac{y}{100}$

8 is ▦% of 50. $\qquad$ 42 is ▦% of 50. $\qquad$ 33 is ▦% of 50.

3. $\frac{18}{200} = \frac{a}{100}$ $\qquad$ $\frac{46}{200} = \frac{n}{100}$ $\qquad$ $\frac{74}{200} = \frac{y}{100}$

18 is ▦% of 200. $\qquad$ 46 is ▦% of 200. $\qquad$ 74 is ▦% of 200.

PRACTICE

Write the number as a percent of 25.

4. 4   **5.** 10   **6.** 12   **7.** 21   **8.** 17   **9.** 8

Write the number as a percent of 50.

10. 7   **11.** 16   **12.** 30   **13.** 28   **14.** 45   **15.** 5

Write the number as a percent of 200.

16. 8   **17.** 26   **18.** 42   **19.** 130   **20.** 198   **21.** 125

Write the number as a percent of 300.

22. 3   **23.** 48   **24.** 75   **25.** 180   **26.** 273   **27.** 200

Tell whether the first number is about *25%, 50%,* or *100%* of the second number.

28. 19, 40   **29.** 86, 88   **30.** 19, 79   **31.** 95, 403

32. 59, 63   **33.** 1098, 2200   **34.** 603, 598   **35.** 1800, 7700

ESTIMATE

PROBLEM SOLVING APPLICATIONS
Writing Equations

Solve.

36. Paula found that 6 of the first 24 people she asked did not plan to vote. What percent did not plan to vote?

37. In Exercise 36, what percent did plan to vote?

38. Supporters of the park proposal raised $2100 to campaign for its passage. They spent about 25% of this on posters. About how much was spent on posters?

★ **39.** Gavin found that of the 24 people he surveyed, 9 people planned to vote for the proposal and 65% of the 24 planned to vote against it. What was wrong with Gavin's findings?

PROBLEM SOLVING
Using Percents

The Thrifty Travel Agency often gives a certain percent off the cost of a trip to attract customers. The decrease in the price is called the **discount**. Here is how to find the final cost of a $325 trip with a 20% discount.

Write the percent as a decimal.	Multiply the full cost by the decimal.	Subtract the amount of the discount from the full cost.
20% = 0.20	$325 ×0.20 $65.00	$325.00 − 65.00 $260.00

Some calculators have a percent key, $\boxed{\%}$. You can use it to find a discount or a markup.

The regular price of a river cruise is $125. What is the final cost with a 10% discount?

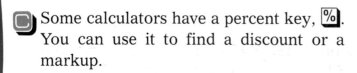

The final cost is $112.50.

CRUISE THE MISSISSIPPI

NOW AT 10% OFF

CLASS EXERCISES

Here are some of the other specials that Thrifty Travel has listed. Find the amount of the discount.

1. 10% discount on a $45 bus trip to Houston

2. 20% discount on a $277 one way flight to Miami

3. 5% discount on a $75 round trip train fare

4. 15% discount on a $400 weekend summer cruise

5. Sam got a 10% discount on a $600 ski trip. Sue paid $550 for the same trip. Explain the steps you would take to figure whose trip was the best buy.

PRACTICE

Day-by-Day Discount put discount tags on some items for a sale. How much would a customer pay for each item?

6.
$419.75
20% off

7.
$269.25
20% off

8.
$57.50
12% off

9.
$24.00
15% off

10.
$89.50
10% off

11.
$69.80
30% off

Which is the better buy?

12. A $60 jacket at a 20% discount or the same jacket reduced by $15?

13. A $15 dinner reduced by $3 or a $10 dinner at 25% off?

14. A $4.50 ticket to a ballgame reduced by a dollar or the same ticket reduced by 20%?

15. A $120 camera at a 20% discount or a $140 camera at a 30% discount?

CHECKPOINT 2

Write as a percent. *(pages 314–319)*

1. 3 out of 100   **2.** 37 out of 100

3. $\frac{18}{100}$ **4.** $\frac{15}{20}$

5. 0.87   **6.** 0.09

What is the percent of the number? *(pages 320–321)*

7. 60% of 50   **8.** 20% of 18

Write the number as a percent of 40. *(pages 322–323)*

9. 8   **10.** 10   **11.** 20

Find the final cost. *(pages 324–325)*

12. 15% discount on a $500 weekend boat rental

13. 25% discount on $65 hiking boots

Extra Practice on page 440

CHAPTER 11 TEST

Write the ratio as a fraction in lowest terms. *(pages 304–305)*

1. 48 to 4   **2.** 3 : 36

Write the unit rate. *(pages 306–307)*

3. $112 for 14 kg

4. 2030 books on 70 shelves

Cross multiply to solve. *(pages 308–311)*

5. $\frac{16}{a} = \frac{56}{49}$ **6.** $\frac{b}{11} = \frac{30}{6}$ **7.** $\frac{33}{27} = \frac{c}{36}$ **8.** $\frac{20}{64} = \frac{25}{d}$

Use the formula distance *(D)* = rate *(r)* × time *(t)* to solve. *(pages 312–313)*

9. A truck travels at a rate of 75 km/h. How far will the truck travel in 15 min?

10. A cheetah travels at a rate of 70 mi/h. At this rate how long will it take a cheetah to travel 245 mi?

Find the percent. *(pages 314–319)*

11. 18 out of 100   **12.** 67 out of 100   **13.** $\frac{1}{4}$ **14.** $\frac{13}{20}$

15. $\frac{14}{25}$ **16.** 0.23   **17.** 0.70   **18.** 0.877

Use a fraction to find the number. *(pages 320–321)*

19. 22% of 46   **20.** 35% of 52

Use a decimal to find the number. *(pages 320–321)*

21. 7% of 81   **22.** 84% of 63

Write the number as a percent of 400. *(pages 322–323)*

23. 4   **24.** 68   **25.** 236   **26.** 392

Find the final cost. *(pages 324–325)*

27. 20% discount on an $85 jacket

28. 15% markup on a $12 record album

Extra Practice on page 441

MATHEMATICS and GEOGRAPHY

The National Census Bureau counts America's population every ten years. The chart shows data from the 1950 and the 1980 censuses.

1950		1980	
Total population:	151,326,000	Total population:	226,505,000
Northeast	26%	Northeast	22%
North Central	29%	North Central	26%
South	31%	South	33%
West	13%	West	19%

WHERE WERE YOU IN 1980?

1. To the nearest tenth, what percent did the nation's population grow from 1950 to 1980?

2. Which region grew at the fastest rate during the three decades?

3. Has any region's population actually decreased?

4. Would the Northeast and the North Central regions combined have accounted for more than half of the country's population in 1950? in 1980?

5. In 1980, the populations of two regions were in the ratio 3:2. Which regions were they?

Enrichment

Look at the problem to the right to see why mathematics is sometimes called the study of patterns.

How many squares of all sizes can you find in figure ABCD?

You could try counting all the squares. Since this would be boring and confusing, try looking for a pattern.

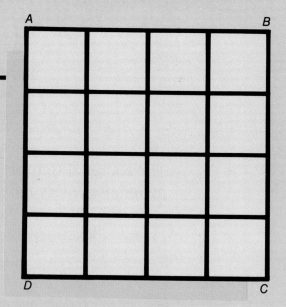

There is only 1 square in this diagram. It has a side with a length of 1 unit.

In this diagram, there are several squares.

1^2 1   square has a side 2 units long.
2^2 $+4$ squares have a side 1 unit long.
      5   or $1^2 + 2^2$ squares

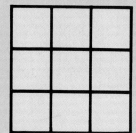

There are even more squares in this diagram.

1^2 1   square has a side 3 units long.
2^2 4   squares have a side 2 units long.
     $+9$ squares have a side 1 unit long.
3^2 14   or $1^2 + 2^2 + 3^2$ squares

Now you can tell how many squares are in figure ABCD above.

PATTERNS

$1^2 + 2^2 + 3^2 + 4^2 = 1 + 4 + 9 + 16 = 30$ squares

Use the pattern above. How many squares are in a diagram of the given size?

1. 5 by 5   **2.** 6 by 6   **3.** 8 by 8   **4.** 10 by 10   **5.** 15 by 15

To make the pattern of squares shown, draw a square whose sides are 1 cm long in the bottom left-hand corner of a sheet of paper.

Now double each side and draw another square. Then make a square with sides 3 cm long, 4 cm long, and so on.

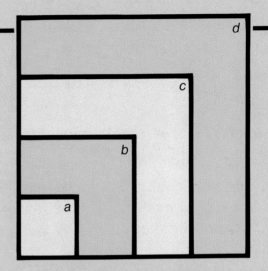

Your pattern will look like the one above, but with more squares.

Copy and complete the table.

SQUARE	LENGTH OF SIDE	AREA
a	1 cm	1 cm²
b	2 cm	4 cm²
6. c	3 cm	?
7. d	4 cm	?
8. e	5 cm	?
9. f	6 cm	?

10. The lengths of the sides of squares a, b, c, and d increase by 1 unit each time. How do the areas of the squares increase?

Can the following pattern be made using squares drawn so that the sides increase by 1 unit each time?

11.   12.   13.   14.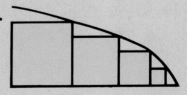

329

Choose the correct answer. Write *a*, *b*, *c*, or *d*.

Choose the matching description.

1.

2.

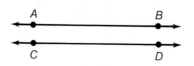

3.

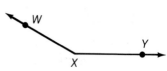

a. line	**a.** intersecting lines	**a.** right angle
b. angle	**b.** parallel lines	**b.** obtuse angle
c. ray	**c.** perpendicular lines	**c.** acute angle
d. none of these	**d.** none of these	**d.** none of these

Choose the name of the described figure.

4. a quadrilateral with exactly one pair of opposite sides parallel
  a. rhombus
  b. trapezoid
  c. rectangle
  d. none of these

5. a polygon with 6 sides, 6 vertexes, and 9 diagonals
  a. pentagon
  b. octagon
  c. hexagon
  d. none of these

6. a triangle with 2 sides the same and 2 angles the same
  a. isosceles triangle
  b. right triangle
  c. equilateral triangle
  d. none of these

Find the GCF.

7. 16 and 28
  a. 2
  b. 4
  c. 7
  d. none of these

8. 30 and 120
  a. 120
  b. 15
  c. 30
  d. none of these

Find the prime factorization.

9. 180
  a. $9 \times 2 \times 10$
  b. $2 \times 2 \times 3 \times 3 \times 5$
  c. $3 \times 3 \times 2 \times 5$
  d. none of these

Find the number to make the fractions equivalent.

10. $\frac{4}{9} = \frac{\blacksquare}{81}$
  a. 36
  b. 18
  c. 9
  d. none of these

11. $\frac{3}{17} = \frac{\blacksquare}{85}$
  a. 34
  b. 15
  c. 12
  d. none of these

12. $\frac{18}{21} = \frac{\blacksquare}{7}$
  a. 6
  b. 14
  c. 3
  d. none of these

Use the graph to answer the question.

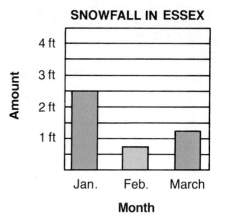

SNOWFALL IN ESSEX

13. About how many inches of snow fell in Feb.?

　a. 1 in.
　b. 6 in.
　c. 9 in.
　d. none of these

14. About how many feet of snow fell in all three months?

　a. $4\frac{1}{2}$ ft　**b.** $4\frac{1}{4}$ ft
　c. $3\frac{3}{4}$ ft
　d. none of these

Find the answer.

15. $\frac{15}{19} - \frac{8}{19}$

　a. $\frac{19}{7}$　**b.** $\frac{7}{19}$

　c. $\frac{24}{19}$
　d. none of these

16. $9\frac{3}{4} + 2\frac{5}{6}$

　a. $11\frac{7}{12}$　**b.** $12\frac{7}{12}$

　c. $11\frac{8}{10}$
　d. none of these

17. $6\frac{2}{3} + 4\frac{3}{8}$

　a. $11\frac{1}{24}$　**b.** $10\frac{1}{24}$

　c. $10\frac{5}{11}$
　d. none of these

Find the answer.

18. $\frac{5}{8} - \frac{3}{5}$

　a. $\frac{2}{3}$　**b.** $\frac{8}{13}$

　c. $\frac{1}{40}$
　d. none of these

19. $7 - \frac{3}{10}$

　a. $7\frac{7}{10}$　**b.** $7\frac{3}{10}$

　c. $6\frac{7}{10}$
　d. none of these

20. $12\frac{1}{6} - 6\frac{8}{9}$

　a. $6\frac{5}{18}$　**b.** $5\frac{5}{18}$

　c. $6\frac{9}{15}$
　d. none of these

LANGUAGE and VOCABULARY REVIEW

Copy the words on your paper. Write the letter of the matching description next to the word.

1. proportion

2. rate

3. vertex

4. polygon

5. quadrilateral

A. the common endpoint formed by two rays

B. a simple, closed figure formed by joining three or more line segments

C. a ratio that compares different kinds of quantities

D. a simple, closed figure with four sides

E. an equation that shows two ratios are equivalent

PROGRAMS WITH VARIABLES

You can use variables with the
LET and INPUT statements.

LET *D* = 4   INPUT *P*

variable

The **LET** statement assigns a value to the letter on the left side of the equals sign.

The **INPUT** statement makes the computer ask for data. A question mark shows on the screen. The computer waits for data to be typed in before it goes to the next line of the program.

Roberto wrote a program that finds the amount saved on items for sale at 15% off. He used LET and INPUT statements.

PROGRAM

OUTPUT

```
10 PRINT "BIG SALE TODAY"
20 PRINT "SAVE 15%"
30 LET D = 0.15
40 PRINT "TYPE IN PRICE OF ITEM"
50 INPUT P
60 PRINT "$"; P * D; " SAVED ON ITEM"
70 END
RUN
```

```
BIG SALE TODAY
SAVE 15%
TYPE IN PRICE OF ITEM
? 5.00
$.75 SAVED ON ITEM
```

P stands for price. The value for P can change each time the program is used. Roberto's first item of data for P was $5.00.

Write the output. In Exercises 2 and 3 use 7 as the INPUT.

1.
```
10 PRINT "ADD"
20 PRINT "3 NUMBERS"
30 LET M = 21
40 LET H = 14
50 LET A = 10
60 PRINT M + H + A
```

2.
```
10 PRINT "HOW MANY DAYS"
20 PRINT "IN A WEEK";
30 INPUT D
40 PRINT D; " DAYS"
50 END
```

3.
```
10 LET T = 2
20 PRINT "DOUBLE"
30 INPUT N
40 PRINT N * T
50 END
```

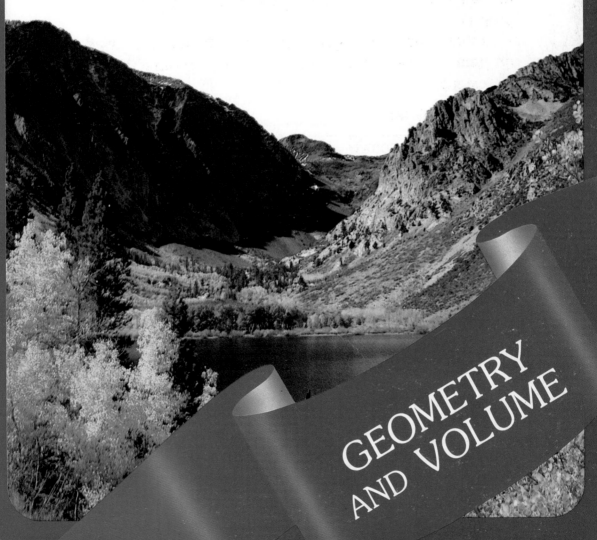

Do you think it's possible for two lakes to have the same surface area and contain different amounts of water? Draw a sketch to illustrate your answer.

12

GEOMETRY AND VOLUME

SYMMETRY

If you can fold a figure so that both halves fit exactly on one another, the figure is **symmetrical.** The fold is called a **line of symmetry.**

Some figures have more than one line of symmetry.

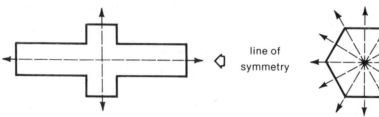

line of symmetry

Some figures have no lines of symmetry.

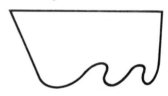

 To decide whether a figure has a line of symmetry, mentally picture it folded over in different ways.

CLASS EXERCISES

Is the fold a line of symmetry? Write *yes* or *no*.

1. 2. 3.  4.

Describe the position of the line of symmetry.

5.   6.   7.   8.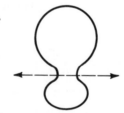

PRACTICE

Copy the figure. Draw all the lines of symmetry. If there are none, write *none*.

9.

10.

11.

12.

13.

14.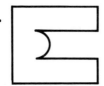

15.

16.

17.

18.

19.

20.

21.

22.

23.

24.

PROBLEM SOLVING APPLICATIONS
Drawing a Diagram

Draw the polygon.

25. A polygon that has only 1 line of symmetry.

26. A polygon that has 2 and only 2 lines of symmetry.

27. A polygon that has 4 and only 4 lines of symmetry.

28. A polygon that has no lines of symmetry.

Write *true* or *false*.

29. An equilateral triangle has 3 lines of symmetry.

30. An isosceles triangle has 2 lines of symmetry.

31. A regular hexagon has 6 lines of symmetry.

32. A rhombus that isn't a square has no lines of symmetry.

SLIDES, FLIPS, TURNS

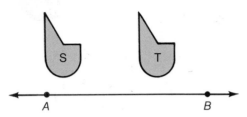

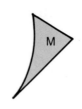

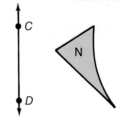

If you **slide** Figure S along $\overrightarrow{AB}$, it will fit on Figure T.

If you **flip** Figure M over $\overleftrightarrow{CD}$, it will fit on Figure N.

If you **turn** Figure E one 90° ⤸ turn around P, it will fit on Figure F.

If you **turn** Figure E two 90° ⤸ turns around P, it will fit on Figure G.

If you **turn** Figure E three 90° ⤸ turns around P, it will fit on Figure H.

 You can mentally picture how a figure will look after a slide, a flip, or a turn. How will Figure Q look after you:

slide it along $\overrightarrow{AB}$?

flip it over $\overleftrightarrow{CD}$?

turn it 90° ⤸ around the lower right corner?

Picture:

Picture:

Picture:

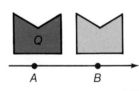

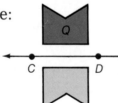

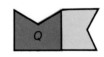

CLASS EXERCISES

Will Figure X fit on Figure Y if you slide it along $\overrightarrow{AB}$? if you flip it over $\overleftrightarrow{CD}$? Answer *yes* or *no*.

1.

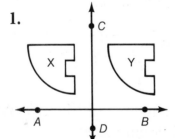

2.

3.

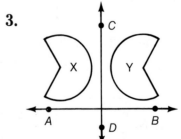

PRACTICE

Draw Figure Q as it will look after it is flipped over $\overleftrightarrow{CD}$.

4.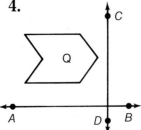

5.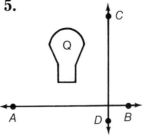

6.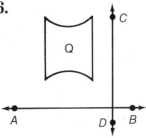

7–9. Draw Figure Q in Exercises 4–6 as it will look after it is flipped over $\overleftrightarrow{AB}$.

10–12. Draw Figure Q in Exercises 4–6 as it will look after it is flipped over $\overleftrightarrow{CD}$ and then over $\overleftrightarrow{AB}$.

Describe Figure K as it will look after two 90° ⤳ turns.

13.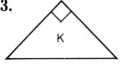

14.

15.

16.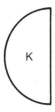

17–20. Draw Figure K in Exercises 13–16 as it will look after it is turned four 90° ⤳ turns.

PROBLEM SOLVING APPLICATIONS
Logical Thinking

Solve.

21. The letters E and B look the same if you flip them over horizontal line AB. Write five other examples.

22. The word BED looks the same if you flip it over horizontal $\overleftrightarrow{AB}$. Write two other examples.

23. The letter M looks the same if you flip it over vertical line CD. Write five other examples.

24. The word MUM looks the same if you flip it over vertical line CD. Write two other examples.

CONGRUENCE

If you slide △ABC along $\overleftrightarrow{XY}$, it will fit on △DEF. If you flip △BEG over $\overleftrightarrow{MN}$, it will fit on △ATR. Figures that are the same size and shape are **congruent**.

$$\triangle ABC \cong \triangle DEF \qquad \triangle BEG \cong \triangle ATR$$

read, *is congruent to*

Corresponding or matching parts of congruent figures are congruent. For example, for △BEG and △ATR:

$$\overline{BE} \cong \overline{AT} \qquad \overline{EG} \cong \overline{TR} \qquad \overline{BG} \cong \overline{AR}$$
$$\angle B \cong \angle A \qquad \angle E \cong \angle T \qquad \angle G \cong \angle R$$

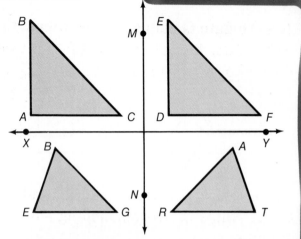

CLASS EXERCISES

Which figures are congruent to the first figure? Choose from *a, b, c,* and *d.*

1.   **a.**   **b.**   **c.**   **d.**

2.   **a.**   **b.**   **c.**   **d.**

Complete to show which parts of △RUT are congruent to parts of △FOX.

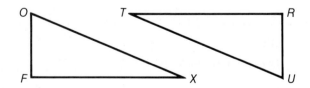

3. $\overline{FO} \cong$ ▨   **4.** $\overline{OX} \cong$ ▨   **5.** $\overline{FX} \cong$ ▨

6. $\angle O \cong$ ▨   **7.** $\angle F \cong$ ▨   **8.** $\angle X \cong$ ▨

PRACTICE

Are the figures congruent? Write *yes* or *no*. If congruent, write *slide, flip,* or *turn* to indicate how the first figure relates to the second figure.

9. **10.** **11.**

Quadrilateral *BARK* ≅ quadrilateral *LIME*. Name the corresponding side or angle.

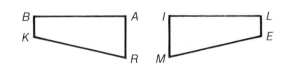

12. $\overline{BA}$ **13.** $\overline{ME}$ **14.** $\overline{AR}$ **15.** $\overline{LE}$

16. $\angle B$ **17.** $\angle E$ **18.** $\angle R$ **19.** $\angle I$

Write <, >, or = to compare the products.

20. 2^3 ▨ 3^2 **21.** 4^3 ▨ 8^2 **22.** 9^3 ▨ 3^5 **23.** 6^2 ▨ 2^4

MIXED REVIEW

24. 11^2 ▨ 5^3 **25.** 12^2 ▨ 6^3 **26.** 2^8 ▨ 16^2 **27.** 1.8^3 ▨ 2.4^2

PROBLEM SOLVING APPLICATIONS
Nonroutine Problems

Solve.

28. I am one of two acute angles in a right triangle. I am congruent to the other acute angle. How many degrees do I measure?

29. The two other angles of a triangle are congruent. I measure 80°. How many degrees does each congruent angle measure?

★ **30.** Arrange 7 points so that you can have 6 line segments with 3 points on each segment.

★ **31.** You have 6 toothpicks of equal length. How can you make four equilateral triangles without altering the toothpicks in any way?

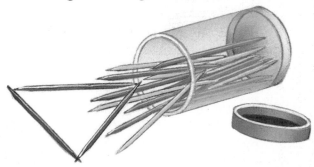

SIMILAR FIGURES

Two figures that are the same shape but not necessarily the same size are **similar figures.**

When two figures are similar, corresponding angles are congruent and ratios of corresponding sides are equivalent.

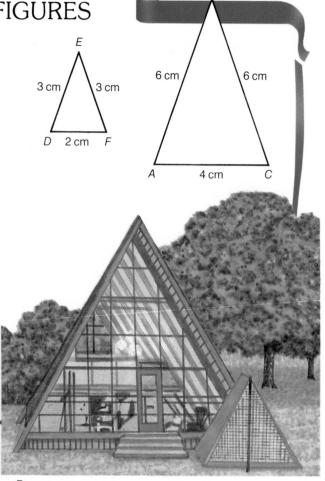

$$\angle D \cong \angle A, \ \angle E \cong \angle B, \ \angle F \cong \angle C$$

$$\frac{DE}{AB} = \frac{3}{6} = \frac{1}{2}, \ \frac{EF}{BC} = \frac{3}{6} = \frac{1}{2}, \ \frac{DF}{AC} = \frac{2}{4} = \frac{1}{2}$$

So, $\triangle DEF \sim \triangle ABC$.

read, *is similar to*

CLASS EXERCISES

Complete. Use $\triangle ARM$ and $\triangle OPT$.

1. $\angle A \cong$ ▨

2. $\angle M \cong$ ▨

3. $\angle R \cong$ ▨

4. $\dfrac{RA}{PO} = \dfrac{▨}{▨} = \dfrac{▨}{▨}$

5. $\dfrac{AM}{OT} = \dfrac{▨}{▨} = \dfrac{▨}{▨}$

6. $\dfrac{RM}{PT} = \dfrac{▨}{▨} = \dfrac{▨}{▨}$

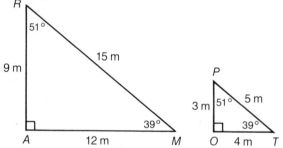

7. Are all of the corresponding angles of rectangle *BARN* and rectangle *OWLS* congruent?

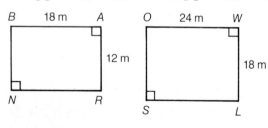

8. $\dfrac{BN}{OS} = \dfrac{▨}{▨} = \dfrac{▨}{▨}$

9. $\dfrac{BA}{OW} = \dfrac{▨}{▨} = \dfrac{▨}{▨}$

Write *true* or *false*.

10. $\triangle ARM \sim \triangle OPT$

11. $\triangle ARM \cong \triangle OPT$

12. quadrilateral *BARN* $\sim$ quadrilateral *OWLS*

PRACTICE

Are the figures similar? Write *yes* or *no*.

13.

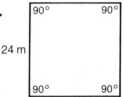 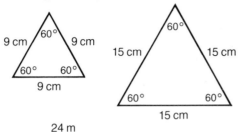

14.

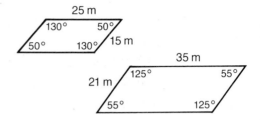

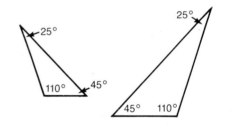

15.

24 m square with 90° angles, 24 m side; 15 m square with 90° angles, 15 m side

16.

Two triangles with angles 25°, 110°, 45°

Write *true* or *false*.

17. Any two triangles are similar.

18. Any two squares are similar.

19. Any two circles are similar.

20. Any two rectangles are similar.

21. Congruent figures are also similar.

22. Similar figures are also congruent.

PROBLEM SOLVING APPLICATIONS
Drawing a Diagram

Solve.

23. Phil broke an equilateral triangle on his mobile. The triangle measured 6 cm on each side. He wants to replace it with a similar triangle $1\frac{1}{2}$ times larger. How long should the sides of the new piece be?

24. Jill made a new square piece for her mobile. The sides of the new piece are half as long as an existing 5 cm square. What is the perimeter of the new square?

25. A mobile has two similar right triangles. The angles of the larger triangle measure 90°, 30°, and 60°. What are the angles of the smaller triangle?

26. A rectangular piece of Phil's mobile is 3 cm wide by 4 cm high. If he wants to use a similar rectangular piece that is 9 cm wide, what should the height of the piece be?

SCALE DRAWING

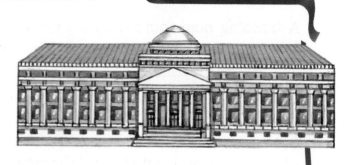

This drawing shows rooms with the same shape as the real museum rooms, but smaller in size. The ratio of the size in the drawing to the actual size is called the **scale.** A drawing made using a scale is called a **scale drawing.**

The scale of the measurements in the drawing to the actual measurements is 1 cm to 4 m. You can determine the actual size of the East Wing by solving the proportions using cross multiplication.

width: $\frac{1 \text{ cm}}{4 \text{ m}} \diagup\!\!\!\!\diagdown \frac{13 \text{ cm}}{w \text{ m}}$ ⇨ $w = 4 \times 13$
$\qquad\qquad\qquad\qquad\quad = 52$ m

length: $\frac{1 \text{ cm}}{4 \text{ m}} \diagup\!\!\!\!\diagdown \frac{18 \text{ cm}}{l \text{ m}}$ ⇨ $l = 4 \times 18$
$\qquad\qquad\qquad\qquad\quad = 72$ m

The East Wing is 52 m wide and 72 m long.

Ⓜ When one number in a proportion is 1, as in the examples above, it is easy to solve the proportion using mental math.

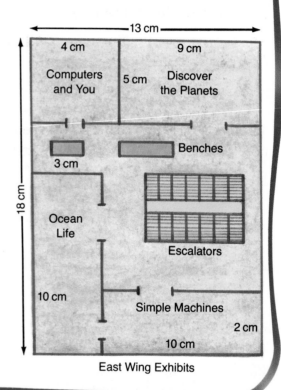

East Wing Exhibits

CLASS EXERCISES

Use the scale drawing above. Solve to find the actual size.

1. Computers and You
   length: $\frac{1}{4} = \frac{5}{l}$ width: $\frac{1}{4} = \frac{4}{w}$

2. Simple Machines
   length: $\frac{1}{4} = \frac{2}{l}$ width: $\frac{1}{4} = \frac{10}{w}$

3. Discover the Planets
   length: $\frac{1}{4} = \frac{5}{l}$ width: $\frac{1}{4} = \frac{9}{w}$

4. Ocean Life
   length: $\frac{1}{4} = \frac{10}{l}$ width: $\frac{1}{4} = \frac{3}{w}$

5. **Think:** Is a scale drawing similar to the actual area it represents? Is it congruent?

PRACTICE

A building plan is drawn with a scale of 2 cm to 15 m.
Determine the actual length of the building using the scale
on the plan.

6. 4 cm   **7.** 1 cm   **8.** 10 cm   **9.** 9.5 cm   **10.** 12.6 cm

A plan for hiking trails is drawn with a scale of 1 cm to
2 km. Use mental math to find the actual length of the trail
using the scale on the plan.

MENTAL MATH

11. 1 cm   **12.** 3 cm   **13.** 1.2 cm   **14.** 0.5 cm

PROBLEM SOLVING APPLICATIONS
Using Scale Drawings

The dinosaur models at the museum are built with a scale
of 5 cm to 2 m. What was the actual size of the dinosaur?

15.

75 cm

Diplodocus

16.

19 cm

Triceratops

17.

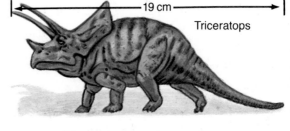

Ceratorsaurus

15 cm

18.

Stegosaurus

9 cm

19. The actual length of an Iguano-
don skeleton is 9 m. How long
would the scale model be?
(Use the scale above.)

★ **20.** The actual mass of an Apato-
saurus (Brontosaurus) is estimated at 36 t. Using a scale of 1 kg to
5 t, what would the mass of the
model be?

PROBLEM SOLVING
Strategy: Logical Thinking

Logical thinking is often used in problem solving. A chain of observations and careful reasoning can lead to a solution. Looking for patterns is an important part of logical thinking.

What do you think comes next in this pattern?

Logic probably tells you that the next figure should be , since it appears that the figure is being turned 90° each time.

CLASS EXERCISES

What probably comes next in the pattern? Write *a* or *b*.

1.
   a.   b.

2.
   a.   b.

3.
   a.   b.

PRACTICE

What comes next in the pattern?

4.

5. A∀BᗺC

6. 1, 12, 123, 1234

7. 1568, 5681, 6815

8.

9.

10.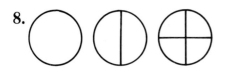

11. 135, 153, 315, 351

12.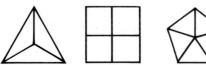

★ **13.** Study the figures carefully to discover the pattern. Continue the pattern until you can do no more.

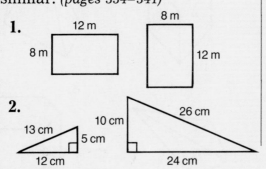

CHECKPOINT 1

Write *C* if the figures are congruent. Write *S* if they are similar. *(pages 334–341)*

1.

12 m
8 m

8 m
12 m

2.

13 cm
10 cm
5 cm
12 cm

26 cm
24 cm

Solve. *(pages 342–343)*

3. A building plan is drawn with a scale of 1.5 cm to 9 m. What is the actual length of a 4.5 cm length in the drawing?

4. Draw what comes next. *(pages 344–345)*

Extra Practice on page 442

PRISMS AND PYRAMIDS

Three-dimensional figures are called **space figures.** A **prism** is a space figure with 5 or more surfaces, or **faces.** Two of the faces, called **bases,** must be congruent and parallel. The prism below has 6 vertexes, 5 faces, and 9 edges.

a triangular prism

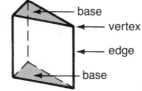
base — vertex — edge — base

A **pyramid** has 4 or more faces. Only one is called the base. The pyramid below has 4 vertexes and 4 faces.

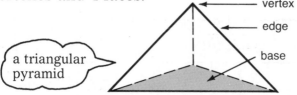
a triangular pyramid — vertex — edge — base

Prisms and pyramids are named according to the shapes of their bases.

CLASS EXERCISES

Is the figure a prism or a pyramid?

1.

2.

3.

4.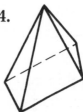

5.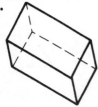

6.

7.

8.

PRACTICE

Use the figure to complete the table.

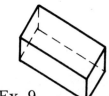

Ex. 9

Ex. 10

Ex. 11

Ex. 12

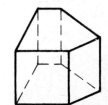

Ex. 13

Ex. 14

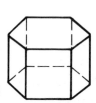

Ex. 15

Ex. 16

	V = number of vertexes	F = number of faces	E = number of edges	V + F	(V + F) − E
9.	?	?	?	?	?
10.	?	?	?	?	?
11.	?	?	?	?	?
12.	?	?	?	?	?
13.	?	?	?	?	?
14.	?	?	?	?	?
15.	?	?	?	?	?
16.	?	?	?	?	?

PROBLEM SOLVING APPLICATIONS
Using Visual Images

Imagine you fold the pattern along the dotted line. What figure do you form? Choose the letter to match the figure with its name.

A. triangular prism
B. square pyramid
C. cube
D. triangular pyramid
   (sometimes called a tetrahedron)

17.

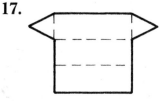

18.

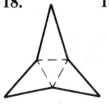

19.

VOLUME OF A
RECTANGULAR PRISM

The **volume (V)** of a figure is the amount of space it contains. Cubic units are used to measure volume.

You can use the following formula to find the volume of a rectangular prism.

Volume = length × width × height

$$V = l \times w \times h$$

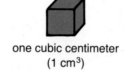

one cubic centimeter
(1 cm³)

Here's how to use the formula to find the volume of the rectangular prism at the right.

$$V = 4 \times 2 \times 3$$
$$= 8 \times 3$$
$$= 24$$

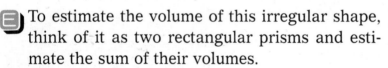

width   4 cm
3 cm
height
2 cm
length

The volume is 24 cm³.

Since a cube is a rectangular prism with all edges the same length, you can use this formula for its volume.

$$V = s \times s \times s = s^3$$

s
s
s

 To estimate the volume of this irregular shape, think of it as two rectangular prisms and estimate the sum of their volumes.

$$V \approx (5 \times 2 \times 2) + (2)^3$$
$$\approx 28$$

The volume is about 28 cm³.

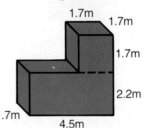

1.7m   1.7m
1.7m
2.2m
1.7m   4.5m

CLASS EXERCISES

What is the volume if the edges have the given lengths?

1. ⌐8

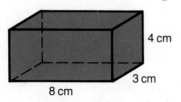

4 cm
3 cm
8 cm

$$V = \boxed{} \times \boxed{} \times \boxed{} = \boxed{} \text{ cm}^3$$

2.

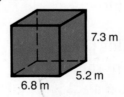

7.3 m
5.2 m
6.8 m

$$V = \boxed{} \times \boxed{} \times \boxed{} = \boxed{} \text{ m}^3$$

PRACTICE

What is the volume if the edges have the given lengths?

3. AB = 18 cm
   BC = 9 cm
   CD = 7 cm

4. AB = 15 cm
   BC = 8 cm
   CD = 6 cm

5. AB = 9 m
   BC = 5 m
   CD = 4 m

6. AB = 2.0 m
   BC = 1.1 m
   CD = 0.9 m

7. AB = 0.42 m
   BC = 0.32 m
   CD = 0.09 m

8. AB = 16.2 m
   BC = 12.6 m
   CD = 10.0 m

Estimate the volume of the figure.

9.
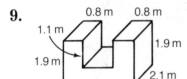

10.
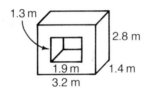

ESTIMATE

PROBLEM SOLVING APPLICATIONS
Using Formulas

Use the picture at the right. Solve. Which formula did you use?

11. How many square meters of carpet will the library need?

12. How many cubic meters of space are there to be heated?

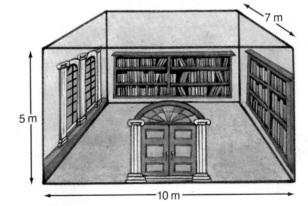

Complete.

13. If the length and width of a room are doubled, the number of cubic meters to be heated is ▨ times as great.

14. Double the length, width, and height of a room. The volume of space to heat becomes ▨ times as great.

★ **15.** Suppose a library is built in the shape of a cube. About what would the dimensions be for the library to have about the same volume as the one shown above?

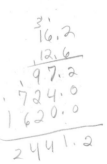

CYLINDERS, CONES, SPHERES

Every point on a **sphere** is the same distance from the center. The distance from the center to any point on the sphere is called the *radius*. A sphere is perfectly round.

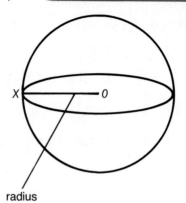

radius

A **cone** has one circular base and one vertex.

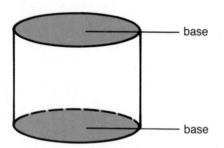

base

base

vertex

base

A **cylinder** has two circular bases that are congruent and parallel.

CLASS EXERCISES

Name the shape that is most like the figure.

1.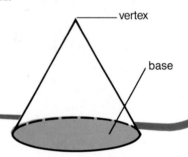

2.

3.

4.

5.

6.

7.

8. Think: How is a cylinder like a prism? How is a cone like a pyramid?

PRACTICE

Complete.

9. A cone has ▨ flat surface(s) and ▨ curved surface(s).

10. A cylinder has ▨ flat surface(s) and ▨ curved surface(s).

11. A sphere has ▨ flat surface(s).

12. A cylinder has ▨ vertex(es).

13. A cone has ▨ vertex(es).

14. A sphere has ▨ vertex(es).

Write the answer in lowest terms.

15. $\frac{1}{2} + \frac{1}{3}$

16. $\frac{1}{2} - \frac{1}{3}$

17. $\frac{3}{4} - \frac{1}{8}$

18. $\frac{7}{10} - \frac{1}{2}$

19. $\frac{7}{12} + \frac{3}{4}$

20. $2\frac{2}{3} + \frac{5}{8}$

21. $3\frac{9}{10} - \frac{5}{6}$

22. $3\frac{8}{9} + 1\frac{5}{12}$

MIXED REVIEW

PROBLEM SOLVING APPLICATIONS
Choosing Mental Math or a Calculator

Tell whether you would choose mental math or a calculator to solve the problem. Write *M* or *C*. Then solve.

Suppose an ant travels the dashed-line path in the figure. What figure is made by the ant's path?

23.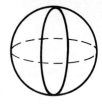

24.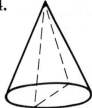

25.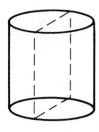

★ **26.** The volume of a cube is 11,390,625 cm³. What is the length of each edge?

★ **27.** A rectangular prism has a volume of 27,000 cm³. Determine the dimensions of two different prisms that could have this volume.

VOLUME OF A CYLINDER

What is the volume of the jar? You can use the formula for the volume of a cylinder to find out.

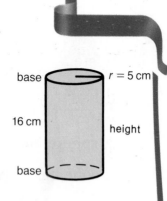

base $r = 5$ cm

16 cm   height

base

Volume (V) = area of base (B) × height (h)

The base is a circle.

Remember, the area of a circle is $\pi \times r^2$ and $\pi \approx 3.14$.

$V = B \times h$
$\approx (3.14 \times 5^2) \times 16$
$\approx 78.5 \times 16$
≈ 1256

The jar has a volume of about 1256 cm³.

Some calculators have a special key for π. You can use this key to determine the volume of a cylinder.

Think: Why will your answers be a little different from those obtained using 3.14 for π?

In the example above, press

$\boxed{\pi}$ $\boxed{\times}$ 5 $\boxed{\times}$ 5 $\boxed{\times}$ 16 $\boxed{=}$ $\boxed{1256.6371}$

round to 1257 cm³

CLASS EXERCISES

Complete.

1. $B = 15$ cm², $h = 10$ cm
   $V = $ ▨ $\times$ ▨ $=$ ▨ cm³

2. $B = 20$ cm², $h = 5$ cm
   $V = $ ▨ $\times$ ▨ $=$ ▨ cm³

3. $B = 8$ cm², $h = 16$ cm
   $V = $ ▨ $\times$ ▨ $=$ ▨ cm³

4. $r = 10$ cm, $h = 40$ cm
   $V \approx 3.14 \times$ ▨² $\times$ ▨ $\approx$ ▨ cm³

5. $r = 2$ m, $h = 10$ m
   $V \approx 3.14 \times$ ▨² $\times$ ▨ $=$ ▨ m³

6. $r = 5$ cm, $h = 11$ cm
   $V \approx 3.14 \times$ ▨² $\times$ ▨ $\approx$ ▨ cm³

PRACTICE

Determine the volume of a cylinder with the given area of the base (B) and the height (h).

7. $B = 20$ cm²
$h = 10$ cm

8. $B = 30$ cm²
$h = 10$ cm

9. $B = 20$ cm²
$h = 4$ cm

10. $B = 15.8$ cm²
$h = 6.5$ cm

11. $B = 0.9$ cm²
$h = 1.6$ cm

12. $B = 22.5$ cm²
$h = 3.6$ cm

Determine the volume of a cylinder with the given radius (r) and height (h). Use $\pi \approx 3.14$.

13. $r = 5$ cm
$h = 20$ cm

14. $r = 10$ cm
$h = 8$ cm

15. $r = 20$ cm
$h = 15$ cm

16. $r = 25$ cm
$h = 9$ cm

17. $r = 8$ m
$h = 10$ m

18. $r = 6$ m
$h = 7$ m

Estimate which will hold more water, cylinder A or cylinder B? You may use a calculator to determine the volume.

 CALCULATOR

19.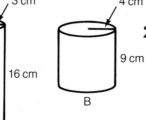

20.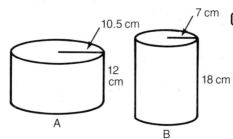

PROBLEM SOLVING
Using Formulas

Use the picture to solve.

21. What is the circumference of the base of the tank?

22. What is the area of one of the bases of the tank?

23. What is the volume of water the tank will hold?

★ **24.** What is the volume of the tank in cubic centimeters?

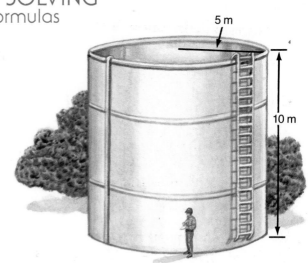

SURFACE AREA OF A RECTANGULAR PRISM

How much paper is needed to wrap the gift?

The figure below shows how the gift box would look if it were unfolded and placed on a flat surface.

To find the **surface area** of a rectangular prism, add the areas of the faces.

Face	$l \times w$		Area (cm^2)
A	20×18	=	360
B	12×18	=	216
C	20×18	=	360
D	12×18	=	216
E	12×20	=	240
F	12×20	=	+240
	Surface area	⇨	1632 cm^2

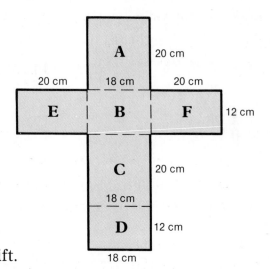

It takes 1632 cm^2 of paper to wrap the gift.

CLASS EXERCISES

1. ⌐-⎤

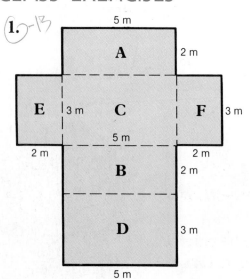

Complete to find the surface area.

Face	$l \times w$		Area
A	2×5	=	▦
B	2×5	=	▦
C	3×5	=	▦
D	▦ $\times$ ▦	=	▦
E	▦ $\times$ ▦	=	▦
F	▦ $\times$ ▦	=	+▦
	Surface area	⇨	▦ m^2

PRACTICE

What is the surface area?

2.

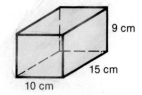

9 cm
15 cm
10 cm

3.

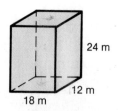

24 m
12 m
18 m

4.

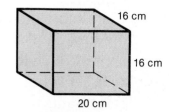

16 cm
16 cm
20 cm

5.

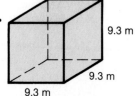

9.3 m
9.3 m
9.3 m

6.

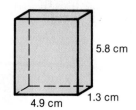

5.8 cm
1.3 cm
4.9 cm

7.

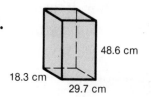

48.6 cm
18.3 cm
29.7 cm

Solve.

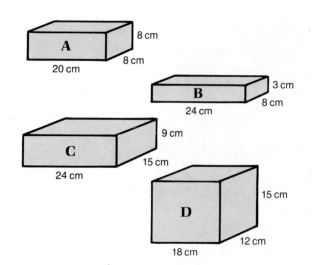

A — 8 cm, 8 cm, 20 cm

B — 3 cm, 8 cm, 24 cm

C — 9 cm, 15 cm, 24 cm

D — 15 cm, 12 cm, 18 cm

8. Boxes A and B have the same surface area, 576 cm². Which box has a greater volume?

9. Boxes C and D have the same volume, 3240 cm³. Which box has a greater surface area?

10. Think: If two cubes have the same volume must they also have the same surface area?

PROBLEM SOLVING APPLICATIONS
Choosing a Formula

A standard water polo pool is a rectangular prism 30 m by 20 m and about 2 m deep. Use this information to solve.

11. What is the volume of the pool?

12. What is the surface area of the walls and the floor of the pool?

13. If the walls and the floor of the pool are to be painted and 1 can of paint will cover 30 m², how many cans of paint are needed?

PROBLEM SOLVING
Strategy: Drawing a Picture

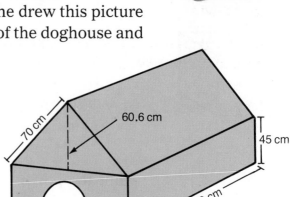

1. Understand
2. Plan
3. Work
4. Answer/ Check

You have learned how to use formulas to find the perimeter, the area, and the volume of different figures. Sometimes it's difficult to decide which formula to use to solve a problem. Drawing a picture can often help you decide.

Jenny wants to build a doghouse. She drew this picture to help her determine the surface area of the doghouse and how much plywood she needs.

$$2 \times (70 \times 100) = 14,000 \quad \text{(roof)}$$
$$2 \times (45 \times 100) = 9,000 \quad \text{(sides)}$$
$$2 \times (45 \times 70) = 6,300 \quad \text{(front and back)}$$
$$2 \times (\tfrac{1}{2} \times 70 \times 60.6) = \underline{4,242} \quad \text{(triangles)}$$
$$33,542$$

Jenny needs 33,542 cm², or about 3.35 m², of wood to build the doghouse. One sheet of plywood has an area of about 3 m². Jenny decides to buy two sheets.

CLASS EXERCISES

Draw a picture. Tell whether area, volume, perimeter, or surface area is needed in each situation.

1. Lea wants to put wall-to-wall carpeting in the dining room.

2. Dale needs to fill some square containers with sand.

3. Liz needs to buy fencing to put around a section of the yard.

4. Sam plans to wallpaper his kitchen.

PRACTICE

Draw a picture to help you solve the problem.

5. Jim Grey wants to run an electric wire around his pasture to keep the cows in. If the pasture is rectangular, 120 yd by 180 yd, how much wire does he need?

6. The Greys' yard is a square that is 120 ft on a side. The house is 30 ft by 36 ft. If the rest of the yard is grass, how much does Shirley Grey have to mow?

7. Eve Grey is spraying a field 560 ft wide by 720 ft long. The sprayer is 8 ft wide. About how many lengthwise passes across the field will she make to spray the whole field?

8. A farm silo is cylindrical with a cone on top. Suppose the cylinder is 40 ft tall and has a radius of 12 ft. If the volume of the cone is 1206 ft^3, what is the volume of the silo?

9. Tom is going to paint the porch walkway. It is L-shaped, 12 ft wide at each end and 24 ft long on each of the two outer sides. What is the area of the walkway?

10. The Greys have a shed that is 24 ft wide by 12 ft tall. If the shed has a volume of at least 9000 ft^3, what would be the minimum length of the shed?

★11. The Greys' goat is tied to the corner of the barn. The barn is 30 ft wide and 40 ft long. The rope tied to the goat is 30 ft long. Over how much area can the goat graze?

★12. The Grey children are covering an empty oatmeal container with colored paper to make a bank. They made a 3-piece pattern of the surface area of the cylindrical container. What were the shapes of the 3 pieces?

CONSTRUCTIONS

You know how to use a ruler to draw segments of a given length and how to use a protractor to draw angles of a given size. A compass may be used to draw circles or parts of circles, called **arcs.** With a ruler and a compass you can construct many figures.

Follow the steps below to construct a circle with a center at C and a radius of 1 in. You'll need a compass and a ruler.

Step 1
Set your compass to an opening of 1 in.

1 inch

Step 2
Draw point C with a pencil.

• C

Step 3
Place the point of the compass on C. Rotate the compass to draw the circle.

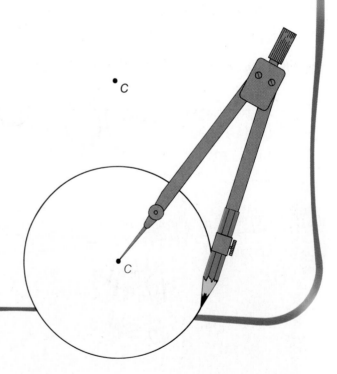

C

CLASS EXERCISES

Follow the steps to make the figure.

1. Construct a circle with center at P and a radius of 3 in.

2. Construct a circle with center at O and a radius of $2\frac{1}{2}$ in.

PRACTICE

3. Follow these steps to draw a line perpendicular to a given line.

   a. Draw $\overleftrightarrow{AB}$. Mark a point P on the line.

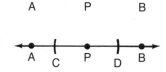

   b. Place the point of the compass on P. Make two arcs intersecting $\overleftrightarrow{AB}$ at C and D.

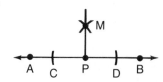

   c. With the compass opened to more than half of the distance between C and D, make two arcs above $\overleftrightarrow{AB}$ using C and D as centers. Label the intersecting point M.

   d. Draw $\overleftrightarrow{MP}$. $\overleftrightarrow{MP}$ is perpendicular to $\overleftrightarrow{AB}$.

   e. Use your protractor to check.

4. Draw $\overleftrightarrow{AB}$ and pick two points on the line. Follow the steps in Exercise 3 to construct two lines perpendicular to $\overleftrightarrow{AB}$ through each of the two points. Are the new lines parallel to each other?

★ 5. Use your compass to copy the design at the right.

CHECKPOINT 2

1. What is the volume? *(pages 346–353)*

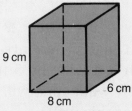

9 cm
6 cm
8 cm

2. Find the surface area of the figure above. *(pages 354–355)*

Draw a picture. Tell whether *area* or *perimeter* is needed. *(pages 356–357)*

3. Sean wants to carpet his room.

Use a compass and a ruler to construct the following. *(pages 358–359)*

4. A circle with a radius of 2 in.

5. $\overleftrightarrow{CD} \perp \overleftrightarrow{AB}$.

Extra Practice on page 442

Are the figures congruent or similar? If congruent, write *slide, flip,* or *turn* to indicate how the first figure relates to the second. *(pages 334–341)*

1.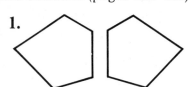

2.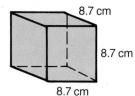

8 m / 5 m   15 m / 24 m

3.

15 cm / 15 cm   5 cm / 5 cm

A building plan is drawn with a scale of 1.5 cm to 7 m. Find the actual length of the building using the scale. *(pages 342–343)*

4. 3 cm   **5.** 9 cm   **6.** 7.5 cm   **7.** 19.5 cm

Find the volume of the rectangular prism. *(pages 346–349)*

8. l = 22 cm
 w = 8 cm
 h = 7 cm

9. l = 3.4 m
 w = 2.6 m
 h = 1.5 m

Find the volume of the cylinder. (Use $\pi \approx 3.14$) *(pages 350–353)*

10. B = 29 mm^2
 h = 18 mm

11. r = 6 m
 h = 12 m

Find the surface area. *(pages 354–355)*

12.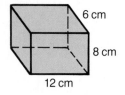

6 cm / 8 cm / 12 cm

13.

8.7 cm / 8.7 cm / 8.7 cm

14.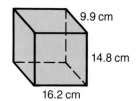

9.9 cm / 14.8 cm / 16.2 cm

Draw the next figure. *(pages 344–345)*

15.

Draw a picture. Solve. *(pages 356–357)*

16. A wall measures 28 ft wide by 12 ft high. There are 2 windows, each 3 ft wide by 5 ft high. How much wallpaper will you use to paper this wall?

Use a compass and a ruler to construct the following. *(pages 358–359)*

17. A circle with a radius of 3 in.

18. $\overleftrightarrow{DE} \perp \overleftrightarrow{FG}$

Extra Practice on page 443

MATHEMATICS and
HOME ECONOMICS

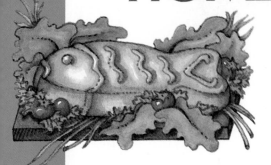

A recipe is a list of ingredients and directions for preparing food. Here is Pierre's recipe for salmon paté that he uses at his restaurant. *Paté* is a French word for a pasty meat, cheese, or fish dish. Paté tastes good on crusty French bread.

CAN YOU EQUAL THIS?

Salmon Paté

3		$7\frac{3}{4}$ oz cans flaked salmon
2	c	mashed potatoes
$\frac{1}{2}$	c	yogurt
$2\frac{1}{8}$	T	capers
$2\frac{1}{2}$	T	lemon juice
$1\frac{7}{8}$	T	green peppers, chopped
$\frac{1}{2}$	T	parsley, finely chopped
$\frac{1}{4}$	t	pepper

Mix all ingredients. Refrigerate for at least 4 h.

Use the recipe and the table of equivalents to answer the question.

1. How many ways of measuring can you find on the recipe?

2. Write 32 tablespoons using cups.

3. Write 4 teaspoons using tablespoons.

4. Is there more parsley or yogurt in the recipe?

5. Are there more than or less than 3 cups of salmon in the recipe?

6. Order the ingredients from the least amount to the greatest.

7. Pierre only has one can of salmon, so he has to make less salmon paté. Do you think he should use less than or more than 1 c of potatoes? 1 T of lemon juice? $\frac{1}{2}$ T green peppers?

Table of Equivalents
T tablespoon
c cup
t teaspoon
1 c = 16 T
1 c = 8 oz
3 t = 1 T

Enrichment

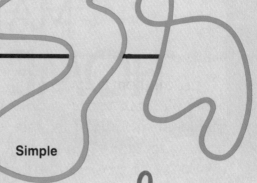

Topology is a branch of mathematics that involves looking at the properties of figures that stay the same after the shape has been stretched, bent, or twisted, but not cut. Here are some simple ideas about curves that come under the heading of topology.

Simple

- Closed curves start and end at the same point and can be drawn without lifting your pencil off the paper.
- A closed curve has an inside and an outside.
- Simple closed curves do not cross themselves.

CLOSED CURVES

OPEN CURVES

Write *true* or *false*.

1. All polygons are simple closed curves.

2. A circle is not a simple closed curve.

3. A simple closed curve separates the points of a plane into 3 sets: points inside the curve, points outside the curve, and points on the curve itself.

4. A closed curve is simple if you can join any two points inside the curve without crossing the curve itself.

Which figure does not belong? Why?

5. a. 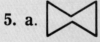   b.   c.   d.

6. a.    b.   c.   d.

7. a. 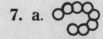   b.

c.   d.

IDEAS IN TOPOLOGY

362

A mathematician by the name of Jordon discovered a simple idea to determine whether a given point was inside or outside a simple closed curve. He picked a point outside the curve and joined it to the given point. If the segment crossed the curve an odd number of times, the point was inside; if it crossed an even number of times, the point was outside.

8. Is point *B* inside or outside the simple closed curve?

Copy the figures. Then write *yes* or *no*.

9. Can you connect each house with each utility without any lines crossing?

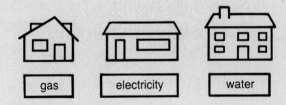

gas   electricity   water

Can you draw lines connecting 1 with 1, 2 with 2, and 3 with 3 without crossing any lines?

10.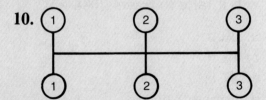

11.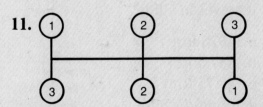

Choose the correct answer. Write *a, b, c,* or *d*.

Find the answer.

1. $\frac{5}{7} \times \frac{21}{40}$

    a. $\frac{26}{47}$ **b.** $\frac{3}{8}$ **c.** $\frac{4}{7}$
    d. none of these

2. $1\frac{1}{5} \times 10$

    a. $\frac{3}{25}$ **b.** 12   **c.** $1\frac{1}{2}$
    d. none of these

3. $7\frac{7}{8} \times 8\frac{2}{9}$

    a. $15\frac{9}{17}$ **b.** $56\frac{9}{17}$ **c.** $64\frac{3}{4}$
    d. none of these

Find the answer.

4. $\frac{2}{3} \div 6$

    a. 4   **b.** $\frac{1}{9}$ **c.** $\frac{1}{12}$
    d. none of these

5. $\frac{9}{10} \div \frac{3}{5}$

    a. $1\frac{1}{2}$ **b.** $\frac{27}{50}$ **c.** $\frac{12}{15}$
    d. none of these

6. $5\frac{1}{4} \div 4\frac{3}{12}$

    a. $9\frac{1}{2}$ **b.** $1\frac{4}{17}$ **c.** $1\frac{5}{16}$
    d. none of these

Find the rate.   Complete.

7. $5400 for 8 months

    a. $575 per month
    b. $625 per month
    c. $675 per month
    d. none of these

8. 9828 words on 39 pages

    a. 250 words per page
    b. 252 words per page
    c. 262 words per page
    d. none of these

9. $\frac{24}{72} = \frac{16}{n}$

    a. 24
    b. 36
    c. 48
    d. none of these

Solve.

10. A hurricane is moving at a rate of 65 km/h. At that rate, how far will it travel in 7.5 h?

    a. 4875 km
    b. 487.5 km
    c. 48.75 km
    d. none of these

11. A truck travels at a rate of 72 km/h. At that rate, how long will it take to travel 2088 km?

    a. 29 h
    b. 28 h
    c. 27 h
    d. none of these

Find the number.

12. 8% of 46

   a. 3.78
   b. 36.8
   c. 3.68
   d. none of these

13. 57% of 142

   a. 81.94
   b. 80.84
   c. 80.94
   d. none of these

14. 93% of 93

   a. 93.93
   b. 86.49
   c. 86.93
   d. none of these

Find the number as a percent of 225.

15. 27

   a. 12%
   b. 10%
   c. 9%
   d. none of these

16. 216

   a. 94%
   b. 95%
   c. 96%
   d. none of these

17. 162

   a. 50%
   b. 72%
   c. 75%
   d. none of these

Find the final cost.

18. 25% discount on a $490 stereo

   a. $367.50   **b.** $467.50
   c. $122.50   **d.** none of these

19. 15% markup on a $230 radio

   a. $264.50   **b.** $195.50
   c. $34.50   **d.** none of these

LANGUAGE and VOCABULARY REVIEW

Use the words to complete each sentence. Write the words on your paper.

formula   prism   scale   Venn diagram
percent   prime number   pyramid   fraction

1. A __?__ shows the relationship of measurements in a drawing to actual measurements.

2. A ratio that compares a number with 100 is a __?__.

3. A __?__ has only two factors.

4. A cube is a rectangular __?__.

5. You can use a __?__ to find the volume of a cylinder.

6. A __?__ has four or more faces and has only one base.

7. A __?__ compares part of a unit with the whole unit.

IF . . . THEN, GOTO

Christine wrote a program for a guessing game. She wants her friend to guess the secret number, 14. Christine used the IF . . . THEN and GOTO statements in her program.

When Christine's friend types in a number, the computer compares it to 14.

PROGRAM

```
      ┌── 10 PRINT "TYPE IN A NUMBER"
      │   20 INPUT N
LOOP  │   30 IF N = 14 THEN 50
      └── 40 GOTO 10
          50 PRINT "YOU ARE A WINNER"
          60 END
```

IF . . . THEN makes the computer compare the number.

```
        IF N = 14 THEN 50
```

When the number is 14, the computer goes to line 50. When the number is not 14, the computer goes to the next line. A loop makes the computer repeat lines in a program. You can use **GOTO** to make the computer loop. GOTO 10 makes the computer keep returning to line 10 until Christine's friend types in 14.

This is the output when the number is 14.

```
TYPE IN A NUMBER
14
YOU ARE A WINNER
```

Write the output for two loops.

1. Use 31 and 16 for T.

```
10 PRINT "PICK A NUMBER"
20 INPUT T
30 IF T < 20 THEN 60
40 PRINT T; " IS MORE THAN 20"
50 GOTO 10
60 PRINT T; " IS LESS THAN 20"
70 GOTO 10
80 END
```

2. Use 123 and 609 for R.

```
10 PRINT "CHOOSE A ROOM NUMBER"
20 INPUT R
30 IF R > 502 THEN 60
40 PRINT R; " IS ON FLOOR 1"
50 GOTO 10
60 PRINT R; " IS ON FLOOR 2"
70 END
```

A cube has 6 sides, each a different color. Two of the colors are red and yellow. How many sides are either yellow or red? neither yellow nor red?

STATISTICS AND PROBABILITY

RANGE AND MODE

MINT COIN SHOP CUSTOMER COUNT

| DAY | WEEK OF | |
	APR. 3	APR. 10
Mon.	36	42
Tues.	39	49
Wed.	63	91
Thurs.	86	91
Fri.	91	102

The owner of a coin shop kept track of the number of customers who came in. During the first two weeks in April, the numbers varied from 36 to 102. Numbers in a set such as this are called **data.**

The **range** of the data is the difference between the greatest and the least numbers.

$$102 - 36 = 66$$ range

The **mode** is 91 because that number appears most often. If no number appears more than once, there is no mode. If two or more numbers appear the same number of times and more often than any of the other numbers, then there is more than one mode.

 You can use mental math to find the mode of data such as 6, 12, 10, 10, 4, 8, 9, 6.

Think: There are two 6's. There are two 10's. There is only one of each of the other numbers. So, 6 and 10 are both modes. You may also be able to use mental math to name the range.

CLASS EXERCISES

Complete.

1. data: 13, 15, 16, 16, 19
   range: 19 − 13 = ▨
   mode: ▨

2. data: 87, 91, 94, 94, 94
   range: 94 − 87 = ▨
   mode: ▨

3. data: 59, 63, 57, 65, 58, 64
   range: 65 − ▨ = ▨
   mode: ▨

4. data: 125, 136, 136, 172, 134
   range: ▨ − 125 = ▨
   mode: ▨

5. **Think:** If the coin shop owner plans to close one extra day a week, which day should it be?

PRACTICE

Write the range and the mode.

6. 17, 12, 18, 21, 23, 29, 18

7. 41, 56, 28, 35, 44, 41

8. 76, 74, 61, 92, 73, 78, 85

9. 271, 258, 316, 294, 271

10. 9, 7, 6, 8, 6, 11, 7

11. 36, 29, 42, 36, 38, 36, 40

12. 150, 162, 158, 156, 160, 156

13. 1.8, 2.3, 1.5, 1.7, 2.0, 1.7

The table shows the savings of five families for three months. Use mental math for Exercises 14–17.

MENTAL MATH

14. For January, what is the range? the mode?

15. For February, what is the range? the mode?

16. For the Corcorans, what is the range? the mode?

17. What is the range for January, February, and March combined?

18. For the Johnsons, Riveras, and Takases combined what is the range of the total savings?

MONTHLY SAVINGS

FAMILY	JAN.	FEB.	MAR.
Johnsons	$100	$200	$ 75
Riveras	$212	$280	$125
Takases	$400	$200	0
Corcorans	$ 75	$ 30	$175
Roeschs	0	$180	$175

19. For the three months what is the total savings?

PROBLEM SOLVING APPLICATIONS
Mental Math, Paper and Pencil, or Calculator

Tell whether you would choose mental math, paper and pencil, or a calculator to solve the problem. Write *M*, *P*, or *C*. Then solve.

20. Sandra has the following Lincoln Head pennies: 1950, 1950, 1953, 1954, 1955, 1957, 1959, and 1959. What is the range of dates on the coins? What is the mode?

21. Randall paid $.75 for a Lincoln Head penny, $1.78 for a Buffalo nickel, $14.76 for an Indian Head penny, and $.97 for a Roosevelt dime. How much did he spend in all?

MEAN AND MEDIAN

The table below shows the prices of several 10-speed bikes. One way to describe the data is to say that they range from $109 to $249.

Another way to describe the data is to give their **average,** or **mean.** To find the average price of the bikes, divide the sum of the prices by the number of bikes.

10-SPEED BICYCLES

BRAND	PRICE
Scruffy	$109
Pedal-Up	$249
Roller	$169
Run Around	$175
Grand Sport	$220

Add the prices.

$$\begin{array}{r} \$109 \\ 249 \\ 169 \\ 175 \\ +\ 220 \\ \hline \$922 \end{array}$$

Divide the sum by the number of addends.

$$5)\overline{\begin{array}{c}\$184.40 \\ \$922.00\end{array}}$$

The average price for the five bikes is $184.40.

 You can use a calculator to find the mean of a set of data. Add the data. Then divide by the number of items in the data.

The middle number in an ordered set of data is called the **median.** When there are two middle numbers, find their mean.

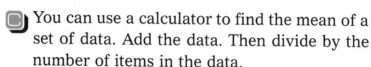

$109, $169, $175, $220, $249
$\uparrow$
median

$46, 48, 50, 52, 56, 65 \quad \diamondsuit \quad \dfrac{50+52}{2} = 51$
$\uparrow$
median

CLASS EXERCISES

Complete. Round decimals to the nearest tenth if necessary.

1. data: 5, 6, 7, 8, 9
mean: ▨ ÷ 5 = ▨
median: ▨

2. data: 125, 133, 134
mean: ▨ ÷ 3 = ▨
median: ▨

3. data: 75, 80, 90, 95
mean: ▨ ÷ 4 = ▨
median: ▨ ÷ 2 = ▨

4. data: 136, 142, 140
mean: ▨ ÷ 3 = ▨
median: ▨

PRACTICE

CALCULATOR

Write the mean and the median. Round the mean to the nearest whole number. You may wish to use a calculator to find the mean.

5. 21, 19, 17, 11, 24, 16

6. 18, 27, 31, 14, 27

7. 78, 45, 39, 62, 70

8. 39, 47, 51, 49, 42, 50, 50, 45

9. 1.5, 2.8, 1.9, 2.5

10. 8.39, 8.21, 8.26, 8.24

11. 8.62, 7.99, 8.43, 7.86, 8.04

12. 3.5, 3.7, 4.2, 4.6, 3.8, 4.5

Write the standard form.

MIXED REVIEW

13. twenty-seven thousand, three hundred fifty

14. 6 million, 8 hundred four thousand, ninety-two

15. seventy-five and sixty-nine hundredths

16. one and five hundred eight thousandths

17. fifty-two ten thousandths

PROBLEM SOLVING APPLICATIONS
Using Information from a Chart

Use the information in the chart to write the mean and the median for the type of fish. Round the mean to the nearest whole number.

AQUALAND • INVENTORY CONTROL
FISH SALES WEEK OF JAN. 6

TYPE	MON.	TUES.	WED.	THURS.	FRI.	SAT.
Bettas	8	3	15	6	4	7
Guppies	12	50	35	48	22	61
Angelfish	16	23	28	15	26	37
Mollies	6	3	0	10	12	8

18. Bettas

19. Angelfish

20. Guppies

21. Mollies

22. What was the total number of fish sold on Wednesday?

23. Write a fraction and a decimal, rounded to the nearest hundredth, to show what part of Saturday's sales were Mollies.

DOUBLE BAR GRAPHS

Video City offered a $5.00 discount on any video game purchased with a coupon in February. The manager made a **double bar graph** to compare sales with the coupon and without the coupon.

By reading the numbers on the vertical scale, you can see that in the first week 80 games were sold without a coupon and 75 games were sold with a coupon.

Note that in the fourth week the number of games sold without coupons was between 60 and 65. You can estimate that about 63 games were sold without coupons.

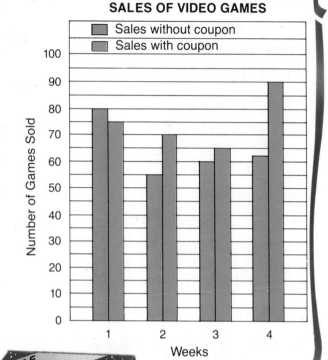

SALES OF VIDEO GAMES

Use the graph above to answer the question.

1. How many games were sold with a coupon in the third week?

2. In which week were the most games sold without a coupon?

3. What was the range of sales without the coupon?

4. In which weeks were the total sales greater than 130 games?

5. What was the total number of games sold for the month with a coupon?

6. What was the mean number of games sold each week without a coupon?

7. **Think:** How does the double bar graph help you compare the data?

PRACTICE

Use the graph to answer the question.

During the first semester about how many attended the workshop?

8. dramatics   **9.** science

10. computer   **11.** cooking

Estimate the total number that attended workshops.

12. first semester   **13.** second semester

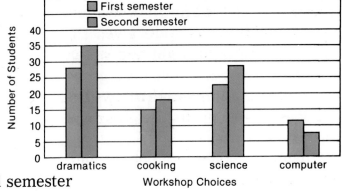

AFTER SCHOOL WORKSHOP ATTENDANCE

First semester
Second semester

Number of Students

Workshop Choices: dramatics, cooking, science, computer

What was the difference in attendance between first and second semester for the workshop?

14. dramatics   **15.** cooking   **16.** science   **17.** computer

18. What was the mean number of students that took cooking for the two semesters?

19. Which workshops had more than 15 students attending the second semester?

PROBLEM SOLVING APPLICATIONS
Drawing a Double Bar Graph

Draw a double bar graph to compare the data in the table.

20.   **MAYFAIR MOVIE ATTENDANCE**

TIME	SUN.	MON.	TUES.	WED.	THURS.	FRI.	SAT.
Afternoon	335	127	142	111	231	488	561
Evening	1086	792	641	374	398	1288	1575

For data like this use a scale of 100 or 200 and estimate the height of each bar.

21. WANDA'S WEEKLY TEST SCORES

SUBJECT	WEEK					
	1	2	3	4	5	6
Math	90	72	93	84	81	93
Spelling	94	86	73	86	90	95

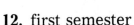

Use a scale of 10.

DOUBLE LINE GRAPHS

The makers of Allegrow Plant Food tried an experiment. For six weeks they measured the growth of two sets of plants. Both sets were given the same amount of sunlight and water, but one set was also given Allegrow.

The **double line graph** shows the changes in the plants' heights over the six-week period.

By the third week, the plants with Allegrow had grown about 2.4 cm. Those without Allegrow had grown about 1.5 cm.

Shana used the graph to compare the heights. For the third week, she estimated the heights as 2.5 cm with Allegrow and 1.5 cm without. The plants with Allegrow grew about 1 cm more by the third week.

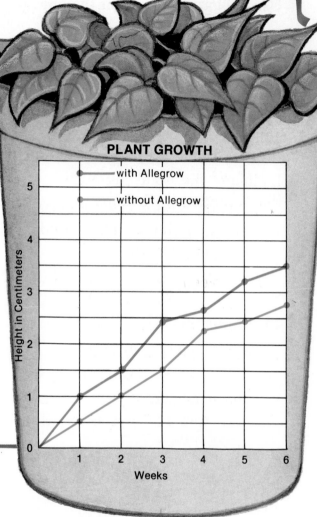

PLANT GROWTH

CLASS EXERCISES

Use the graph above to answer Exercises 1–8.

What was the difference in growth between the sets of plants for the week?

1. week 2   **2.** week 1   **3.** week 4   **4.** week 5   **5.** week 6

6. In which week did the plants with Allegrow grow the most? the least?

7. What was the total growth after six weeks for the plants with Allegrow? without Allegrow?

8. During which week was the amount of growth the same for both sets of plants?

9. Think: How is a double line graph like a double bar graph?

PRACTICE

Use the graph to answer the question.

10. Were more deliveries made at 12 noon on Saturday or on Sunday?

11. At which time were the greatest number of deliveries made on Saturday? on Sunday?

12. About how many deliveries were made on Saturday in all? on Sunday?

13. Between which two times was the change in the number of deliveries the greatest on Saturday? on Sunday?

14. How many more deliveries were made at 6 P.M. on Sunday than at 6 P.M. on Saturday?

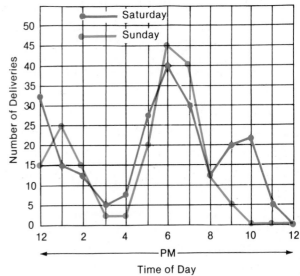

FOOD-ON-THE-MOVE DELIVERIES

15. Food-on-the-Move wants to close at 10 P.M. About how many deliveries would it lose on Saturday?

PROBLEM SOLVING APPLICATIONS
Drawing a Double Line Graph

AGE	HEIGHT (cm)	
	Milton	Marge
9	130	132
10	135	139
11	141	147
12	146	149
13	152	152
14	158	156
15	165	160
16	170	164
17	170	167

Milton and Marge kept a record of their heights on nine birthdays. Draw a double line graph to show their growth. Let the horizontal scale represent their ages.

16. What was the range of Milton's height for the nine years?

17. Between which two birthdays did Marge grow the most?

18. Between which two birthdays did Milton grow the least?

CIRCLE GRAPHS

The Clover Grove School raised $5500 at its annual fair. The **circle graph** shows the percent of the money raised from each activity.

How much money was raised from entertainment?

$$45\% \text{ of } 5500 = 0.45 \times \$5500$$
$$= \$2475$$

Of the $5500 raised at the fair, $2475 was from entertainment.

CLOVER GROVE FUND RAISING

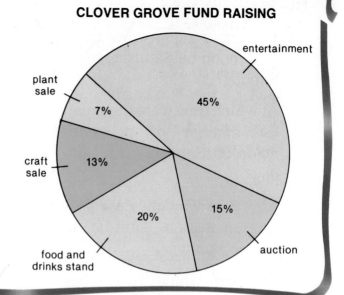

CLASS EXERCISES

Use the graph above to answer the question.

1. How much money was raised by the plant sale?

2. Which activity raised the most money? the least?

3. What percent of the money was raised from the craft sale?

4. Was more money raised by the auction or the craft sale?

5. How much money was raised by the auction and the craft sale combined?

6. How much more money was raised by the craft sale than the plant sale?

7. What is the sum of the percents on the graph?

8. **Think:** To find the total amount of money raised by the plant sale and the craft sale combined, would you get the correct answer if you added the two percents first and then multiplied to find the answer?

PRACTICE

The graph for Exercises 9–12 shows what percent of the town's $100,000 community development budget was spent on each item. Use it to answer the question.

9. What percent was spent on the senior and youth centers?

10. What percent was spent on parks and parades?

11. How much more money was spent on parks than on publicity?

12. How much was spent on publicity, parades, and street cleaning combined?

13. Copy and complete the graph. Show how much the Orlandos spent on each item.

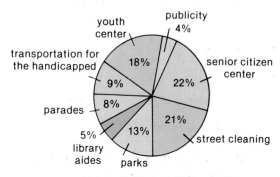

COMMUNITY BUDGET

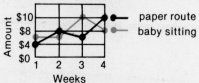

ORLANDO'S CAMPING BUDGET: $400

tents: 50%
sleeping bags: 25%
backpacks: 15%
cooking gear: 10%

CHECKPOINT 1

Write the range, mode, mean, and median. *(pages 368–371)*

1. 9, 5, 7, 9, 6, 3, 4, 8

Use the graph to answer the question. *(pages 372–377)*

JUANITA'S EARNINGS

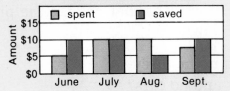

2. How much more did Juanita save than she spent in June?

BRIAN'S EARNINGS

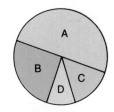

3. About how much did Brian earn in the 4 weeks?

Use the information in Exercise 13 above to answer the question.

4. If the Orlandos had $300 to spend on camping gear, how much would they spend on tents?

Extra Practice on page 444

PROBLEM SOLVING
Strategy: Open-Ended Problems

1. Understand
2. Plan
3. Work
4. Answer/Check

Tim counted 42 wheels in a parking lot for cars and motorcycles. What possible combinations of vehicles could he have seen?

Some problems may have more than one solution. Making a table and looking for a pattern often helps in solving such a problem.

CARS (4 WHEELS)	MOTORCYCLES (2 WHEELS)
10	1
9	3
8	5
7	7
6	9
5	11
4	13
3	15
2	17
1	19
0	21

$(4 \times 10) + (2 \times 1) =$
$40 + 2 =$
42 wheels

The table shows all possible combinations of cars and motorcycles that Tim could have seen.

CLASS EXERCISES

Use the table above to answer the question.

1. Is there only 1 correct solution to the problem?

2. Suppose Tim saw 4 cars. How does that change the problem?

3. Suppose Tim saw at least 11 motorcycles. How does that change the problem?

4. Suppose Tim saw at most 6 cars. How does that change the problem?

5. **Think:** Could Tim have seen all cars and no motorcycles? Could he have seen all motorcycles and no cars?

6. **Think:** If Tim had counted 52 wheels, what is the maximum number of cars that could have been in the lot?

PRACTICE

Solve.

7. At a school play, $100 was collected in one evening. Tickets were $2 for children and $3 for adults. If the number of children who attended was between 19 and 30, what possible combinations of children and adults attended?

8. You have exactly six coins in your pocket. Their value is $.75. What might the coins be?

9. Using 6 darts, determine at least three different ways of scoring 200 on this target.

10. For the triangle below to be "magic" the sum of the 3 numbers on each side must be the same. Find 2 solutions using different numbers in each circle for this triangle.

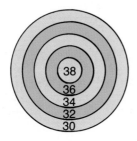

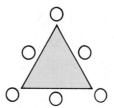

11. Herman built a rectangular pen with an area of 48 m^2 in his back yard. What are the possible dimensions of Herman's pen? (Assume the lengths of the sides are whole numbers.)

12. Juan Ortega is driving from Nome to Numb. What are the possible routes he could take?

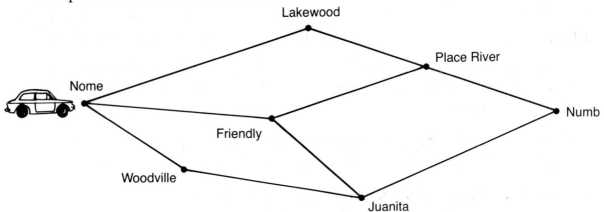

PROBABILITY

When you toss a coin, there are two possible **outcomes**, both equally likely. There is 1 chance in 2 of the outcome being a head. The **probability** of a head is 1 out of 2 or $\frac{1}{2}$. The probability of a tail is also $\frac{1}{2}$.

The spinner is equally likely to stop on any of the 6 equal-size sections. There are 3 chances in 6 of landing on a star. The probability of this event, $P(\bigstar)$, is given by the following ratio.

$$P(\bigstar) = \frac{\text{number of} \bigstar \text{ outcomes}}{\text{number of possible outcomes}}$$

$$P(\bigstar) = \frac{3}{6} = \frac{1}{2}$$

The spinner has 3 sections with a star and 2 sections with a triangle. Since there are 5 sections in all with a star or a triangle, $P(\bigstar \text{ or } \blacktriangle) = \frac{5}{6}$.

The probability of an impossible event is 0. Since there are no circles on the spinner, the probability of landing on a circle is 0. The probability of an event that must occur is 1.

Think: $P(\bigstar \text{ or } \blacktriangle \text{ or } \blacksquare) = ?$

CLASS EXERCISES

Complete.

	ACTIVITY	POSSIBLE OUTCOMES	PROBABILITY
1.	Tossing a number cube	1 2 3 4 5 6	$P(4) = \frac{\blacksquare}{6}$
2.	Spinning a spinner	☆, △, △, ○, ■, ■, ■, ■	$P(☆) = \frac{\blacksquare}{8} = \frac{\blacksquare}{2}$ $P(△) = \frac{\blacksquare}{\blacksquare} = \frac{\blacksquare}{4}$

PRACTICE

There are 3 green, 7 red, and 2 yellow marbles in a jar. They are all the same size and shape. You choose a marble without looking. Write the probability of the outcome.

3. green   **4.** red   **5.** yellow   **6.** purple   **7.** red or green

Daisy invited 18 people to a party. The guests included 4 cousins, 2 aunts, 10 friends, and 2 uncles. All are equally likely to arrive first. Write the probability that the first guest to arrive is the following.

8. a cousin   **9.** a friend   **10.** an uncle   **11.** a nephew

A letter from the word ENGINEER is chosen without looking. Write the probability of the outcome.

12. E   **13.** N   **14.** E or R   **15.** a vowel   **16.** a consonant

---

Write the answer in lowest terms.

17. $\frac{3}{7} + \frac{3}{8}$ **18.** $\frac{3}{7} \times \frac{3}{8}$ **19.** $\frac{2}{3} \times \frac{9}{10}$ **20.** $\frac{2}{5} + \frac{1}{4}$

MIXED REVIEW

21. $\frac{3}{4} + \frac{1}{12}$ **22.** $\frac{5}{8} + \frac{1}{3}$ **23.** $\frac{7}{8} \times \frac{4}{8}$ **24.** $\frac{3}{10} + \frac{3}{4}$

PROBLEM SOLVING APPLICATIONS
Using Probability

Solve.

25. The Franklin School sold 348 raffle tickets to raise money for playground equipment. Jack Marcos bought 5 tickets. Is it more likely that he will win the prize, or not win the prize?

26. There are 67 books on a library shelf. Of the 67 books, 29 include pictures. If you choose a book without looking, are you more likely to choose one with pictures, or one without pictures?

27. The 1000th customer at Maxie's will get $5\frac{1}{2}$ times the amount of money he or she has. Bea has $10.75. How much could she win?

★ **28.** In Exercise 25, how many tickets would Jack Marcos have to buy to be more likely to win than not win? to be sure of winning?

PROBABILITY

Room 18 had to assign jobs and parts for the class play. The 16 jobs and 16 parts for the play were written on slips of paper and put into two boxes. Without looking, everyone drew a slip from each box.

JOBS	NUMBER
MAKE POSTERS	2
MAKE COSTUMES	6
MAKE SETS	6
MAKE TICKETS	2
TOTAL JOBS	16

PARTS	NUMBER
BUS DRIVER	1
PASSENGERS	10
STREET SIGNS	3
HORSES	2
TOTAL PARTS	16

Suppose you are the first person to choose.
The probability of choosing *make posters* is $\frac{2}{16}$.
The probability of choosing *passenger* is $\frac{10}{16}$.

$$P \text{ (make posters and passenger)} = \frac{2}{16} \times \frac{10}{16} = \frac{20}{256} = \frac{5}{64}$$

The choice of a slip from the first box has no effect on the choice from the second box. The events are **independent.** You can use this formula to find the probability that two independent events will occur.

$$P(A \text{ and } B) = P(A) \times P(B)$$

CLASS EXERCISES

Suppose you pick a marble, without looking, from each container. The table shows the possible outcomes.

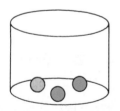 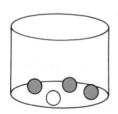

OUTCOME TABLE

Write the probability.

1. A yellow and a green marble
2. 2 marbles
3. A blue and a white marble
4. A yellow and a white marble
5. A blue and a green marble
6. 2 yellow marbles

PRACTICE

The Bright family wrote their choices for pets and pet names on slips of paper. The 5 choices for each were put into two boxes. Suppose a slip is drawn, without looking, from each box. Write the probability of the outcome.

7. a hamster named Spike

8. a fish named Axlerod

9. a turtle named Rover

10. a cat named Rascal

11. a dog named Clementine

12. a dog named Belle

13. a gerbil named Caesar

14. a fish named Spike

PETS

| Dog |
| Cat |
| Hamster |
| Fish |
| Dog |

NAMES

| Axelrod |
| Spike |
| Rascal |
| Clementine |
| Belle |

PROBLEM SOLVING APPLICATIONS
Using Mental Math or Pencil and Paper

Tell whether you would choose mental math or paper and pencil to solve the problem. Write *M* or *P*. Then solve.

15. At a party there are 3 blue hats, 2 white hats, and 1 green hat left in a box. In another box there are 2 horns, 2 rattles, and 2 noisemakers. What is the probability that the next person who arrives will choose, without looking, a blue hat and a horn?

16. At the party there are 6 door prizes worth $40 each. The probability of winning a door prize is $\frac{1}{50}$. How much would Erna win if she won 2 of the prizes?

★ 17. At the party there are 6 boys, 6 girls, and 3 adults. They play a game blindfolded during which people are picked and asked questions. What is the probability that the first three picked will be an adult, a boy, then a girl? (*Hint:* After an adult is picked, how many people are left?)

USING PROBABILITY

There are three books on the librarian's desk. Suppose that the books are equally likely to be fiction or nonfiction. What is the probability that exactly two of the books are nonfiction?

You may draw a **tree diagram** to show all the possibilities.

The diagram shows that there are 8 possible outcomes. Of these, 3 outcomes have exactly two books that are nonfiction.

(F,N,N) (N,F,N) (N,N,F)

The probability that exactly two of the books are nonfiction is 3 out of 8.

$P(\text{exactly 2 nonfiction books}) = \frac{3}{8}$

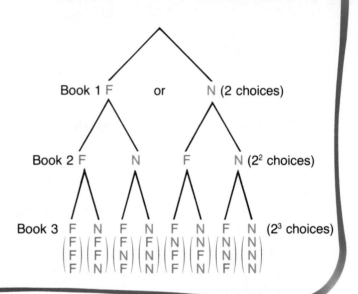

CLASS EXERCISES

Two students will each win a watch. Each watch is either a sports watch (S) or a calculator watch (C). The chances of winning either are equally likely. The diagram shows the possible outcomes. Use it to answer the question.

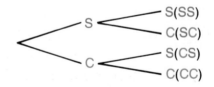

1. How many possible outcomes are there?   **2.** Explain the meaning of SS.

3. What is the probability that both students will win calculator watches?

4. What is the probability that at least one student will win a sports watch?

PRACTICE

Copy and complete the tree diagram. Use it to answer.

5. Two cats are waiting for suppers of fish or eggs. The chances of either meal are equally likely. What is the probability that only one cat gets fish?

6. What is the probability that both cats get fish?

7. What is the probability that neither cat gets fish?

8. Compare: P(both fish), P(both eggs).

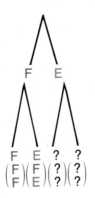

PROBLEM SOLVING APPLICATIONS
Logical Thinking

Solve.

9. Four people enter a cafeteria. They have a choice between the regular line or the soup-and-salad line. What is the probability that exactly 3 of the 4 will select the soup-and-salad line?

10. Three people are waiting for either an up or a down elevator. The chances of either are equally likely. What is the probability that all 3 people are waiting for a down elevator?

11. The Taylors chose the name for their third child by letting their oldest child pick from A without looking, and their middle child pick from B without looking. What are the chances the baby was named Esther Louise?

A	B
Ann	Lola
Bonita	Clair
Esther	Kathryn
	Louise

★ 12. You are going to flip 5 coins. Since it is equally likely that you will get a head or a tail, what is the probability that you will get:

a. all heads?

b. all tails?

c. 1 head, 4 tails?

d. 1 tail, 4 heads?

e. 2 heads, 3 tails?

f. 2 tails, 3 heads?

PROBLEM SOLVING
Strategy: Sampling and Estimating

Porpoise Publications developed a magazine called *Persnickety*. They took a survey and projected that 13% of the population would buy it. How many copies should be shipped to a chain of stores that serves 250,000 people?

If the survey sample is correct, 13% of the 250,000 people are likely to buy the magazine.

$$13\% = 0.13$$
$$0.13 \times 250,000 = 32,500$$

About 32,500 copies of the magazine should be shipped.

It is sometimes convenient to use ratios instead of percents to make predictions.

In Center City, the ratio of those who vote to those who are eligible to vote is usually 3:5. If there are 80,000 eligible voters, about how many do you expect to vote in the next election?

About $\frac{3}{5}$ of the eligible voters will vote.

$$\frac{3}{5} \times 80,000 = 48,000$$

You would expect that about 48,000 people will vote.

CLASS EXERCISES

Solve.

1. In a survey of pet food buyers, 20% chose Spunky Mix as their pets' favorite brand. Of 100,000 pet food buyers, how many would you expect to choose Spunky Mix?

2. The ratio of students who walk to school to the total student population at the Stuart School is about 2:3. If there are 450 students enrolled, how many of them do you expect to walk to school?

PRACTICE

Solve.

3. The ratio of jazz records to pop records sold in one city is 3:5. The city's music store buys a total of 256,000 of the two kinds of records each year. How many of these should be pop?

4. An analyst found that about 16% of fresh fruit gets spoiled before it is sold. The Market Basket buys 3500 kg of peaches. About how many kilograms can they expect to discard due to spoilage?

5. Of 300 people surveyed, 48 liked Whirlwind Window Wash better than other brands. If a store has 88 customers in a week who will buy window cleaner, how many can be expected to buy Whirlwind?

6. On an assembly line, 400 television sets were checked for defects. Of those checked, 32 had defects. What percent were not defective? If a store orders 150 sets, how many of the sets can they expect to be free of defects?

★ 7. To estimate the number of deer in a wildlife preserve, a zoologist captured 75 deer. She then marked and released them. A week later she captured 25 deer and found that 3 of them were marked. How many deer should she estimate are in the forest?

CHECKPOINT 2

Solve. *(pages 378–379)*

1. You have $.83 in coins. What might the coins be?

Solve. *(pages 380–383)*

2. A box has 2 red, 2 blue, and 3 white marbles. If you pick a marble without looking, what is the probability of choosing a red marble? a white marble?

Solve. *(pages 384–385)*

3. Three people are waiting at a bus stop where 2 different buses stop. What is the probability that 2 people are waiting for the same bus?

Solve. *(pages 386–387)*

4. The ratio of small cars to all the cars in a parking lot is 2:7. If there are 560 cars in the lot how many do you expect to be small cars?

Extra Practice on page 444

Write the range, mode, median, and mean. *(pages 368–371)*

1. 138, 150, 146, 144, 148, 144

2. 2.6, 3.1, 2.3, 2.2, 2.8

Use the graph to answer the question. *(pages 372–377)*

3. What was the total number of computers sold in Week 2?

5. How many houses did Herb clean in 4 weeks?

4. What was the mean number of all computers sold in 3 weeks?

6. What was the range of houses cleaned by the Helpers?

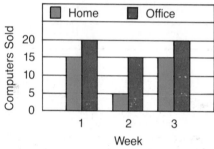

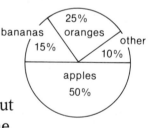

The circle graph shows the percent of 500 items sold at a fruit stand.

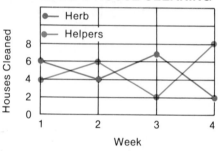

7. How many apples were sold? oranges?

A letter from the word MISSISSIPPI is chosen without looking. Write the probability of the following outcome. *(pages 380–383)*

8. S

9. M

10. a vowel

11. a consonant

Suppose you choose a marble from each jar. Write the probability of the following outcome. *(pages 384–385)*

12. 2 blue marbles

13. 1 blue and 1 white marble

Solve. *(pages 378–379, 386–387)*

14. You have exactly 6 coins in your pocket. Their value is $.95. What might the coins be?

15. The ratio of trail bikes to all bikes sold each month is 5:8. Jo's Bike Store orders 480 bikes. How many of these are trail bikes?

Extra Practice on page 445

MATHEMATICS and THE LIBRARY

A school library kept a record of book circulation over the course of a week. The chart shows four kinds of books and how frequently they were borrowed.

	MON.	TUES.	WED.	THURS.	FRI.	TOTAL
Mystery	23	16	19	11	30	99
Animals	25	12	17	15	32	101
Crafts	3	0	2	1	5	11
Science	15	8	14	8	18	63
Total	66	36	52	35	85	274

WILL YOU CHECK IT OUT?

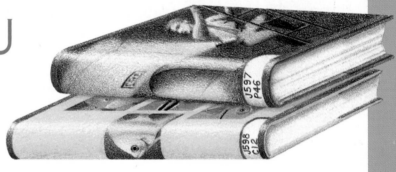

1. To the nearest whole number, what was the mean number of books borrowed on each of the five days?

2. Which kind of book had the greatest range of borrowings over the course of the week? the least?

3. What percent of books borrowed on Tuesday were mysteries? What percent of science books borrowed during the week were borrowed on Friday? (Round to the nearest hundredth)

★4. If the library were to buy 100 new books of these four kinds in proportion to their popularity, how many of each would be bought?

Enrichment

Benjamin Arthur Raymond Turner wants to use his initials for a 4-letter code for his savings account. How many different combinations are possible if each letter is used only once?

You can list all the possible ways of writing the initials.

BART	BATR	BRAT	BRTA	BTRA	BTAR
TBRA	TBAR	TABR	TARB	TRAB	TRBA
ATBR	ATRB	ABTR	ABRT	ARBT	ARTB
RATB	RABT	RTAB	RTBA	RBTA	RBAT

Think: What pattern did Ben follow while listing the letters? Since this is a lot of work, let's look at the problem in another way.

With 1 initial there is only 1 possible code.
With 2 initials there are 2 possible codes. $2 \times 1 = 2$
With 3 initials there are 6 possible codes. $3 \times 2 \times 1 = 6$
With 4 initials there are 24 possible codes. $4 \times 3 \times 2 \times 1 = 24$

Use a pattern like the one above to solve the problem.

1. How many different radio stations can be identified using the call letters K, L, and M. Assume the letters can't be repeated.

2. How many different 6-digit license plate numbers can be made with 4, 7, 3, 2, 8, and 9 if the digits can't be repeated?

3. In how many ways can Hugh, Shelly, Elliot, and Norma line up at the lunch counter?

4. How many different batting orders are possible for a baseball team with 9 players?

ARRANGEMENTS

Here's another way to look at the pattern you just used. Suppose there are *a* ways of doing one thing, *b* ways of doing a second thing, and *c* ways of doing a third thing. Then there are $a \times b \times c$ ways of doing the three things.

There are 15 people in a spelling contest. In how many different ways can 3 prizes be won if no one can win more than one prize? Here's how to use the rule.

There are 15 people who can win 1st prize.

After the 1st prize is won, there are 14 people who can win 2nd prize.

Then there are 13 people left to win 3rd prize.

Altogether, there are $15 \times 14 \times 13 = 2730$ ways to win the three prizes.

Solve.

5. Suppose you have 7 books on a shelf. How many ways can you choose 4 of the books?

6. Your new lock needs a combination. You can choose any 4-digit number using the digits from 1 through 9. How many choices do you have if no digits can be repeated? if some digits can be repeated?

7. Suppose you want to fly from Philadelphia to Kansas City and then take a bus to Pasadena. There are 3 different airlines and 4 different bus lines you can use. How many different ways can you make the round trip without using any plane or bus twice?

 # CUMULATIVE REVIEW

Choose the correct answer. Write *a*, *b*, *c*, or *d*.

Find the percent of the number.

1. 17% of 86

    a. 14.72
    b. 13.62
    c. 14.62
    d. none of these

2. 97% of 65

    a. 63.05
    b. 63
    c. 63.5
    d. none of these

3. 39% of 214

    a. 83.46
    b. 84.36
    c. 84.46
    d. none of these

Find the number as a percent of 215.

4. 43

    a. 2%
    b. 12%
    c. 20%
    d. none of these

5. 172

    a. 8%
    b. 80%
    c. 88%
    d. none of these

6. 129

    a. 6%
    b. 16%
    c. 66%
    d. none of these

Find the final cost.

7. 15% discount on a
$350 television set

    a. $52.50
    b. $297.50
    c. $298.50
    d. none of these

8. 20% discount on a
$48 jacket

    a. $38.40
    b. $9.40
    c. $57.40
    d. none of these

9. 12% markup on a
$575 sofa

    a. $69
    b. $644
    c. $506
    d. none of these

Solve.

A building plan is drawn with a scale of 2 cm to 27 m. Find
the actual length of the building for the length used in the
drawing.

10. 3 cm

    a. 18 m
    b. 81 m
    c. 40.5 m
    d. none of these

11. 12 cm

    a. 27 m
    b. 54 m
    c. 324 m
    d. none of these

12. 8.6 cm

    a. 1161 m
    b. 116.1 m
    c. 11.61 m
    d. none of these

Find the volume.

13. rectangular prism
  $l = 3.0$ m $w = 2.1$ m
  $h = 1.9$ m
  a. 1197 m^3
  b. 119.7 m^3
  c. 11.97 m^3
  d. none of these

14. cylinder
  $B = 26.4$ cm^2
  $h = 2.8$ cm
  a. 73.82 cm^3
  b. 73.92 cm^3
  c. 74.92 cm^3
  d. none of these

15. cylinder
  $r = 7$ mm
  $h = 8$ mm
  a. 1406.72 mm^3
  b. 1230.88 mm^3
  c. 56 mm^3
  d. none of these

Find the surface area of the rectangular prism.

16. $l = 14$ m
  $w = 6$ m
  $h = 4$ m
  a. 336 m^2
  b. 164 m^2
  c. 328 m^2
  d. none of these

17. $l = 8.7$ m
  $w = 8.7$ m
  $h = 8.7$ m
  a. 454.14 m^2
  b. 52.2 m^2
  c. 26.1 m^2
  d. none of these

Solve.

18. The Griffins' property is a square that is 130 ft on each side. The house is 48 ft by 35 ft. How much of the yard is left for landscaping?

  a. $16,900$ ft^2 **b.** $15,220$ ft^2 **c.** 1680 ft^2 **d.** none of these

LANGUAGE and VOCABULARY REVIEW

Choose the correct word to complete each sentence. Write the word on your paper.

1. The amount of space a prism contains is its (surface area, volume).

2. An (equilateral, isosceles) triangle has exactly two equal sides and two equal angles.

3. Two figures that are the same shape but not necessarily the same size are (congruent, similar) figures.

4. The difference between the least and greatest numbers in a set of data is the (range, mean).

5. The (mode, median) is the middle number of an ordered set of data.

DEBUGGING

COMPUTER LITERACY

Abe wrote a program to find the average of his history grades. He estimated the average to be about 90. When the program gave an output of 204 he knew the answer was not reasonable.

Abe decided to check his program for mistakes. He used the BASIC command **LIST** to show the entire program on the screen. He checked line numbers, spelling, and operation signs. Then Abe remembered that the computer follows the order of operations when calculating. That is, working from left to right, the computer first does what is in parentheses; then it multiplies and divides; finally it adds and subtracts.

```
LIST
10 PRINT "AVERAGE IS:"
20 LET A=92
30 LET B=79
40 LET C=99
50 PRINT A+B+C/3
60 END


RUN
AVERAGE IS:
204
```

Abe found the error in line 50. He forgot the parentheses: 50 PRINT (A + B + C)/3. He corrected the error and got an output of 90.

Correct the program to get the given output.

Output:
```
THERE ARE
28
STUDENTS HERE
```

Output:
```
FIND
3
ERRORS
```

1. ```
PRINT "THERE ARE"
20 PRINT 10+4*2
30 PRINT "STUDENTS HERE"
END
```

2. ```
10 PRINT "FIND
20 PRINT A=12
30 PRINT A/2*2
40 PRINT "ERRORS"
50 END
```

When this ship is in the water, the draft marks on its hull show how deeply it's floating. If it floated 28 ft deep, then rose $8\frac{1}{2}$ ft, and then settled 9 ft deeper, how deeply would it float then?

B. T. ALASKA

14

INTEGERS AND GRAPHING

INTEGERS

Look at the number line. Numbers to the right of zero are called *positive*. Numbers to the left of zero are called *negative*. Two numbers that are the same distance from zero, but on opposite sides of zero are called **opposites.** Whole numbers and their opposites are called **integers.**

The integer ⁻5, read *negative five*, names the point 5 units to the left of zero. Its opposite is +5, read *positive five*.

The integer +4 names the point 4 units to the right of zero. Its opposite is ⁻4. You can write +4 without the + sign, as just 4.

M You can use mental math to find the opposite of an integer. Just picture the number with the opposite sign.

⁻6 ⇨ +6
+12 ⇨ −12

CLASS EXERCISES

What are the missing numbers?

1.

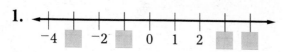

2.

3.

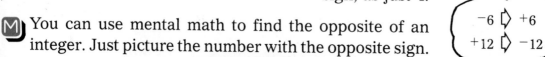

4.

PRACTICE

Complete.

5. ⁻15 is 15 units to the __?__ of zero.

6. 11 is 11 units to the __?__ of zero.

7. 7 is 7 units to the __?__ of zero.

8. ⁻8 is 8 units to the __?__ of zero.

9. The opposite of 9 is ▨.

10. The opposite of ⁻5 is ▨.

11. We read +8 as __?__.

12. We read ⁻1 as __?__.

13. Integers to the right of zero are __?__.

14. Integers to the left of zero are __?__.

Draw a number line. Locate the integer.

15. 7 units to the right of 0

16. 4 units to the left of zero

17. 2 units to the left of 0

18. 8 units to the right of zero

19. 6 units to the right of 1

20. 2 units to the left of $^-1$

21. 3 units to the left of $^-5$

22. 5 units to the right of 2

Write the integer between the two integers.

23. 5, 7   **24.** $^-8$, $^-10$ **25.** $^-1$, 1   **26.** 12, 14

27. $^-16$, $^-14$ **28.** $^-4$, $^-6$ **29.** 2, 4   **30.** $^-6$, $^-8$

Write the opposite of the integer.

31. $^-10$ **32.** 11   **33.** 2   **34.** $^-18$ **35.** $^-4$

36. 6   **37.** $^-7$ **38.** $^-15$ **39.** 14   **40.** 5

MENTAL MATH

PROBLEM SOLVING APPLICATIONS
Writing Reasonable Answers

Write an integer to name the number in the sentence. Then give its opposite.

41. The diver is 120 ft below sea level.

42. It was 20 s before liftoff.

43. The elevator is 2 floors below street level.

44. Today's temperature is 5° above zero.

45. The hiker traveled 14 km north.

Write an integer to show the final number.

46. Al received $10 for his birthday. He spent $3 on a new fish and $2 on art supplies.

47. Vicki went from the 3rd floor to the 2nd floor and then up 4 floors.

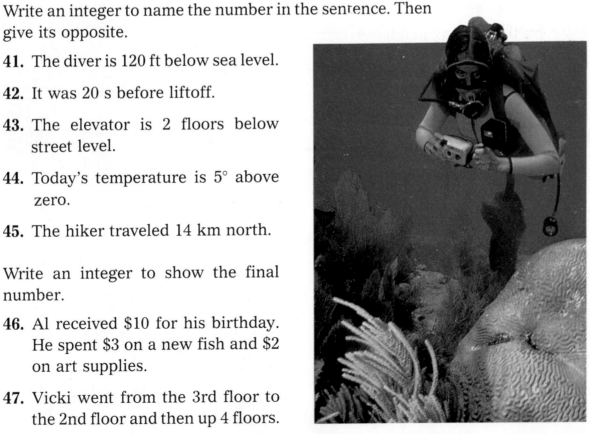

COMPARING INTEGERS

On Tuesday the temperature was 3°C. On Wednesday it was −5°C. On which day was it warmer?

You can compare integers by comparing their positions on a number line. The greater of two integers is always the one farther to the right.

3 is to the right of −5.

$$3 > -5$$
so 3°C > −5°C   It was warmer on Tuesday.

 You can use mental math to compare and order integers. Think of a number line. Negative integers are always to the left of positive integers. So, any negative integer is less than any positive integer. To compare and order 6, −4, and −12 from least to greatest, **think:** −12 is farthest to the left on a number line, and 6 is farthest to the right; −4 is between −12 and 6. Write −12, −4, 6.

CLASS EXERCISES

Write *right* or *left* to complete. Then write < or >.

1. −4 is to the _?_ of 9, so −4 ▢ 9

2. 3 is to the _?_ of −7, so 3 ▢ −7

3. −8 is to the _?_ of −1, so −8 ▢ −1

4. 5 is to the _?_ of −5, so 5 ▢ −5

5. −10 is to the _?_ of −12, so −10 ▢ −12

6. −6 is to the _?_ of −8, so −6 ▢ −8

7. 5 is to the _?_ of 0, so 5 ▢ 0

8. 2 is to the _?_ of 7, so 2 ▢ 7

9. **Think:** What whole number is neither positive nor negative?

PRACTICE

Write < or > to compare the integers.

10. ⁻9 ▮ 2　**11.** ⁻3 ▮ ⁻8　**12.** 4 ▮ ⁻4　**13.** ⁻7 ▮ ⁻3

14. 25 ▮ ⁻6　**15.** 45 ▮ 37　**16.** ⁻34 ▮ 13　**17.** 100 ▮ ⁻100

Write the integers in order from least to greatest.

18. ⁻5, 3, ⁻7, 4　　　　　**19.** ⁻3, ⁻8, 7, 0　　　　　**20.** ⁻8, ⁻10, ⁻4, 1, ⁻3

21. 10, ⁻6, 4, ⁻7, ⁻4　　　**22.** ⁻12, 5, 10, ⁻9, 2　　　**23.** 2, ⁻5, ⁻2, 0, ⁻11

24. Write the integers that are greater than ⁻4 and less than 2.

25. Write the integers that are less than ⁻2 and greater than ⁻10.

Complete by writing *greater* or *less*.

26. Any positive integer is ▮ than 0.　　**27.** Any negative integer is ▮ than 0.

28. Any positive integer is ▮ than any negative integer.

Solve the equation.

29. $19 + 6 = a$　　　**30.** $27 - 9 = b$　　　**31.** $n + 17 = 38$

32. $75 - d = 49$　　　**33.** $f - 68 = 0$　　　**34.** $g - 41 = 89$

PROBLEM SOLVING APPLICATIONS
Using Fahrenheit Scale

Solve.

35. On Sunday the temperature was ⁻5°F and on Monday it was ⁻10°F. On which day was the temperature lower?

36. The noontime temperatures for five days were 2°F, ⁻4°F, 16°F, ⁻8°F, and ⁻10°F. Order the temperatures from coldest to warmest.

★ **37.** On Monday it was ⁻8°F. On Tuesday the temperature increased 10 degrees. What was Tuesday's temperature?

★ **38.** How many degrees below freezing is ⁻10°F?

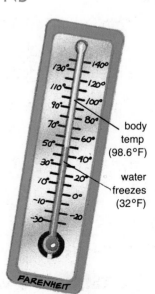

ADDING INTEGERS

The number line shows what happens when you add integers.

To add 6 and ⁻2 move from 0 to 6; then move 2 units to the left.

$$6 + {}^-2 = 4$$

To add ⁻8 and 5 move from 0 to ⁻8; then move 5 units to the right.

$$^-8 + 5 = {}^-3$$

When you add a number and its opposite the sum is 0.

$$4 + {}^-4 = 0 \qquad {}^-4 + 4 = 0$$

You can use the ⌀ key on a calculator to help you add integers. Here's how to calculate 5 + ⁻4:

5 ⊞ 4 ⌀ ⊟ [   ].

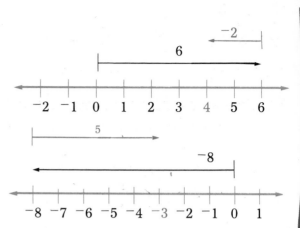

CLASS EXERCISES

Complete.

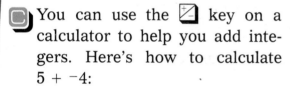

1.

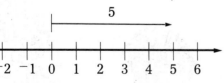

$$5 + {}^-3 = \blacksquare$$

2.

$$^-4 + {}^-2 = \blacksquare$$

3.

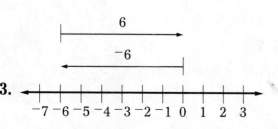

$$^-6 + 6 = \blacksquare$$

4.

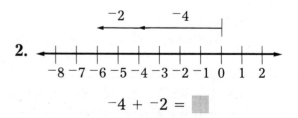
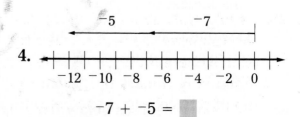

$$^-7 + {}^-5 = \blacksquare$$

PRACTICE

Add.

5. 4 + 5

6. $^-1 + {}^-8$

7. 13 + $^-9$

8. $^-11 + 5$

9. $^-3 + 12$

10. 6 + $^-11$

11. $^-14 + 9$

12. 15 + $^-8$

13. 2 + $^-5$

14. $^-5 + {}^-7$

15. $^-16 + 8$

16. 8 + $^-2$

17. Give an example to show that addition of integers is a commutative operation.

Add. Use a calculator if you have one.

CALCULATOR

18. $^-4 + 6 + {}^-8$

19. 12 + $^-5 + {}^-12$

20. $^-6 + {}^-2 + 8$

21. $^-12 + 5 + {}^-18$

22. $^-27 + {}^-56 + 42$

23. 16 + $^-88 + {}^-65$

PROBLEM SOLVING APPLICATIONS
Mental Math or Calculator

Tell whether you would choose mental math or a calculator to solve. Write *M* or *C*. Then solve.

24. In a board game, Kim earned $100 on one turn. On her next turn she lost $200. What was the total gain or loss after the two turns?

25. Clive wrote a check for $30. The next day he deposited $25 in his account. What was the gain or loss after the two transactions were made?

26. Ed Hill drove 300 km east. He then drove 800 km west. How far was Ed from his starting point?

★ **27.** The circumference of a round lake is 800.7 m. If Hal swims across at its widest point, how far will he swim?

★ **28.** Usually only about $\frac{1}{9}$ of an iceberg shows above the water. If the tip of an iceberg is 27 m above water, how many meters is it from the top of the iceberg to the bottom?

SUBTRACTING INTEGERS

The number line shows that $5 + {}^-2 = 3$. You also know that $5 - 2 = 3$, so $5 - 2 = 5 + {}^-2 = 3$.

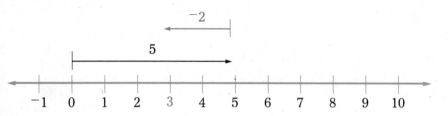

Subtracting an integer is the same as adding its opposite.

Here are more examples.

$${}^-4 - 5 = {}^-4 + {}^-5 = {}^-9 \qquad\qquad 3 - 5 = 3 + {}^-5 = {}^-2$$
$${}^-15 - {}^-6 = {}^-15 + 6 = {}^-9 \qquad\qquad 7 - {}^-3 = 7 + 3 = 10$$

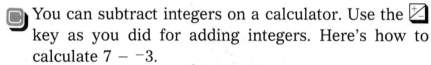 You can subtract integers on a calculator. Use the ⧄ key as you did for adding integers. Here's how to calculate $7 - {}^-3$.

$$7 \boxed{-} 3 \boxed{⧄} \boxed{=} 10.$$

CLASS EXERCISES

Complete.

1. $8 - 2 = 8 + \blacksquare = \blacksquare$ **2.** $1 - 2 = 1 + \blacksquare = \blacksquare$

3. ${}^-6 - {}^-4 = {}^-6 + \blacksquare = \blacksquare$ **4.** $2 - {}^-4 = 2 + \blacksquare = \blacksquare$

5. $10 - {}^-3 = 10 + \blacksquare = \blacksquare$ **6.** ${}^-10 - {}^-3 = {}^-10 + \blacksquare = \blacksquare$

7. $8 - 7 = 8 + \blacksquare = \blacksquare$ **8.** ${}^-8 - 7 = {}^-8 + \blacksquare = \blacksquare$

PRACTICE

Subtract.

9. $9 - 7$ **10.** $3 - {}^-6$ **11.** ${}^-16 - {}^-7$ **12.** ${}^-10 - {}^-5$

13. $13 - 9$ **14.** ${}^-8 - 4$ **15.** $11 - 5$ **16.** ${}^-2 - 8$

17. $^-12 - 6$ **18.** $1 - ^-3$ **19.** $7 - ^-8$ **20.** $^-17 - 8$

21. $^-6 - 2$ **22.** $0 - ^-5$ **23.** $14 - 5$ **24.** $18 - 10$

25. $^-12 - ^-12$ **26.** $0 - ^-8$ **27.** $14 - ^-7$ **28.** $^-21 - 21$

29. $100 - ^-99$ **30.** $^-65 - ^-25$ **31.** $50 - 49$ **32.** $33 - ^-22$

Add or subtract. You may wish to use a calculator.

33. $3 + ^-6 - ^-5$ **34.** $^-4 + ^-7 - ^-9$ **35.** $^-3 + 5 - 8$

36. $27 - ^-19 + ^-40$ **37.** $^-63 + 29 + ^-51$ **38.** $^-88 - ^-16 + 46$

CALCULATOR

PROBLEM SOLVING APPLICATIONS
Choosing a Strategy

Solve.

39. The temperature is $^-5°$ C. It becomes $7°$ colder. What is the new temperature?

40. The temperature was $8°$ C on Tuesday and $^-4°$ C on Wednesday. What was the change in temperature?

41. Two players are playing a game with a red number cube and a blue number cube. Numbers on the red cube are counted as negative points. Numbers on the blue cube are positive points. A throw of R5, B3 means $^-5 + 3$ or a score of $^-2$. The winner is the one with the greater total after 6 throws. Use the chart below to determine who wins the game.

PLAYER	1st Throw	2nd Throw	3rd Throw	4th Throw	5th Throw	6th Throw
1	R4, B5	R5, B2	R3, B3	R1, B5	R3, B5	R2, B6
2	R3, B1	R2, B6	R2, B5	R3, B2	R6, B2	R4, B1

★ **42.** A cube has the following faces: 3 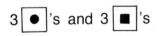's and 3 ■'s

Here are three views of the cube:

Determine the pattern that appears on the opposite face for a and for b.

a.   b.

1. Understand
2. Plan
3. Work
4. Answer/ Check

On a cold, windy day it often feels colder than it is because of the wind chill factor.

WIND CHILL CHART

Temperature (°C)	6	10	20	30	40	50	60
20	20	18	16	14	13	13	12
16	16	14	11	9	7	7	6
12	12	9	5	3	1	0	0
8	8	5	0	-3	-5	-6	-7
4	4	0	-5	-8	-11	-12	-13
0	0	-4	-10	-14	-17	-18	-19
-4	-4	-8	-15	-20	-23	-25	-26
-8	-8	-13	-21	-25	-29	-31	-32
-12	-12	-17	-26	-31	-35	-37	-39
-16	-16	-22	-31	-37	-41	-43	-45
-20	-20	-26	-36	-43	-47	-49	-51
-24	-24	-31	-42	-48	-53	-56	-58
-28	-28	-35	-47	-54	-59	-62	-64
-32	-32	-40	-52	-60	-65	-68	-70
-36	-36	-44	-57	-65	-71	-74	-77
-40	-40	-49	-63	-71	-77	-80	-83

Wind Speed (kilometers per hour)

Suppose the thermometer reading is -8°C and the wind speed is 10 km per hour. You can find how cold it feels by looking at the Wind Chill Chart.

- Find the wind speed of 10 km per hour.
- Then find -8°C.

With the wind chill factor, it feels like -13°C.

CLASS EXERCISES

Use the chart above. How cold will it feel on a day with the given temperature and wind speed?

1. Wind speed: 20 km per hour
   Temperature: -8°C

2. Wind speed: 10 km per hour
   Temperature: -24°C

3. Wind speed: 50 km per hour
   Temperature: -36°C

4. Wind speed: 30 km per hour
   Temperature: 20°C

What is the thermometer reading on the chart?

5. Wind speed: 30 km per hour
   Wind chill factor: -31°C

6. Wind speed: 60 km per hour
   Wind chill factor: -19°C

7. Wind speed: 40 km per hour
   Wind chill factor: -47°C

8. Wind speed: 10 km per hour
   Wind chill factor: 0°C

PRACTICE

Solve. Use the chart on page 404.

9. The captain of a fishing boat decides that his crew can't go out if the wind chill is ⁻35°C or below. The temperature is ⁻8°C. The wind speed is 30 km/h. Will the crew go out?

10. In Juneau, Alaska, the lowest temperature on a certain day was ⁻4°C. The highest temperature was 8° warmer. The wind speed was 30 km/h. How cold did it feel at the highest temperature?

11. Suppose the temperature was ⁻4°C. The wind speed changed from 10 km/h to 20 km/h. What was the change in how cold it felt?

12. On one day the temperature, with the wind chill, changed from ⁻35°C to ⁻47°C. The wind speed was 40 km/h. What was the actual change in temperature?

13. On Tuesday, the wind chill factor was ⁻8°C. The wind speed increased 10 km/h, and the wind chill factor became ⁻15°C. What was the thermometer reading?

★ 14. You're planning an ice skating party. You decide to go bowling if the wind chill drops below 0°C. The temperature is 4°C. The wind speed is 25 km/h. Will you go skating or bowling?

CHECKPOINT 1

Compare the integers. Write < or > to complete. (pages 396–399)

1. ⁻4 ■ ⁻5
2. 3 ■ ⁻2
3. 9 ■ 12
4. ⁻6 ■ 1

Add or subtract. (pages 400–403)

5. $2 + ^-1$
6. $^-5 + 3$
7. $^-4 + ^-6$
8. $7 + 5$

9. $3 - 2$
10. $7 - ^-4$
11. $^-2 - ^-5$
12. $^-8 - 2$

Solve. Use the chart on page 404. (pages 404–405)

13. The temperature was ⁻8°C. The wind speed dropped from 40 km/h to 10 km/h. How did that change the way the temperature felt?

Extra Practice on page 446

GRAPHING NUMBER PAIRS

You can use **ordered pairs** of integers to locate points on a grid.

To locate a point on a grid, start at 0. The first integer tells you to move right or left. The second tells you to move up or down.

 You can estimate the location of points using fractions in ordered pairs. The graph shows about where $(-1\frac{1}{2}, \frac{1}{4})$ is located.

The point (2, 5) is 2 units to the right and 5 units up.

The point (−3, −4) is 3 units to the left and 4 units down.

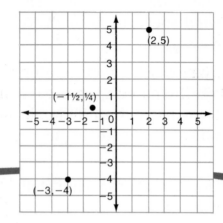

CLASS EXERCISES

What is the ordered pair for the directions?

1. to the right 5, then down 7

2. to the left 3, then down 8

3. to the left 8, then up 5

4. to the right 4, then up 2

5. to the right 0, then down 1

6. to the left 6, then up 6

PRACTICE

Write the letter for the ordered pair.

7. (−5, 3)

8. (7, 0)

9. (4, 1)

10. (−1, 7)

11. (−7, −4)

12. (6, −2)

13. (−3, −3)

14. (5, 3)

15. (−7, 1)

16. (2, −2)

17. (2, 6)

18. (−4, 1)

19. (−6, −5)

20. (3, −4)

21. (−4, −7)

22. (7, −6)

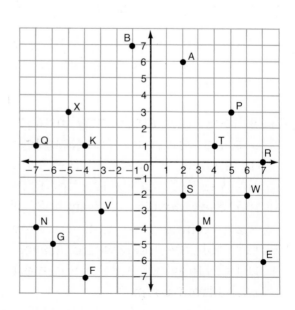

Write the ordered pair for the letter.

23. A	**24.** B
25. C	**26.** D
27. E	**28.** F
29. G	**30.** H
31. I	**32.** J
33. K	**34.** L
35. M	**36.** N
37. O	**38.** P

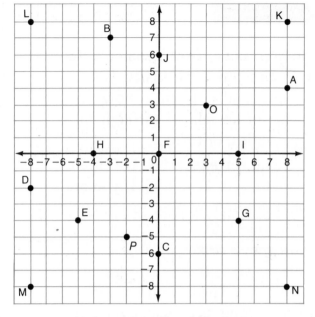

39. Locate each point on a grid. Join the points from K to Z in alphabetical order. What do you see?

$K\ (^-1,\ ^-7)$, $L\ (^-1,\ ^-6)$, $M\ (1,\ ^-6)$, $N\ (1,\ ^-7)$,

$O\ (3,\ ^-7)$, $P\ (2,\ ^-5)$, $Q\ (2,\ 5)$, $R\ (1,\ 6)$,

$S\ (1,\ 9)$, $T\ (0,\ 10)$, $U\ (^-1,\ 9)$, $V\ (^-1,\ 6)$,

$W\ (^-2,\ 5)$, $X\ (^-2,\ ^-5)$, $Y\ (^-3,\ ^-7)$, $Z\ (^-1,\ ^-7)$

Estimate to locate the point on a grid.

ESTIMATE

40. $A\ (3\frac{1}{2},\ 0)$ **41.** $B\ (2\frac{3}{4},\ 5\frac{1}{4})$ **42.** $C\ (3,\ ^-3\frac{1}{5})$

43. $E\ (^-1\frac{1}{3},\ ^-2)$ **44.** $H\ (^-3\frac{3}{4},\ ^-3\frac{3}{4})$ **45.** $F\ (2,\ ^-3\frac{4}{5})$

PROBLEM SOLVING APPLICATIONS
Nonroutine Problems

Solve.

46. A bookworm ate its way through a set of encyclopedias standing on a shelf. It began at the front cover of volume 1 and stopped at the back cover of volume 8. If each volume is 4 cm thick, how far did the bookworm travel? (*Hint:* On which side of volume 1 is the front cover?)

★ **47.** How quickly can you add all the numbers from 1 to 100? Even with a calculator it would take some time. A famous mathematician by the name of Karl Gauss (1777–1855) did it in a matter of seconds. See if you can determine his short cut.

GEOMETRY ON A GRID

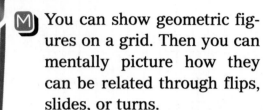

You can show geometric figures on a grid. Then you can mentally picture how they can be related through flips, slides, or turns.

The vertexes of △ *ABC* are at (⁻6, 6), (⁻8, 1), (⁻1, 3). If you add 9 to the first number in each pair you get (3, 6), (1, 1), (8, 3). These are the vertexes of a new triangle, △ *GHI*, that is congruent to the first. These figures show a slide along the horizontal number line.

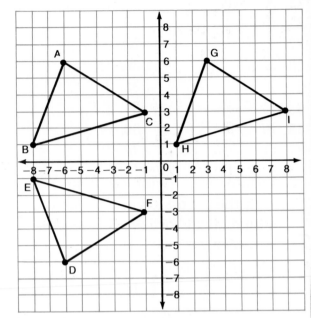

If you take the vertexes of △ *ABC* and use the opposite of the second number in each pair you get the following:

(⁻6, 6) ⟶ (⁻6, ⁻6)
(⁻8, 1) ⟶ (⁻8, ⁻1)
(⁻1, 3) ⟶ (⁻1, ⁻3)

These points are the vertexes of a new triangle, △ *DEF*, that is congruent to the first. This shows a flip over the horizontal number line.

CLASS EXERCISES

Copy the grid at the right. Then solve.

1. What are the ordered pairs for the vertexes of parallelogram *ABCD*?

2. Add ⁻7 to each second number of the ordered pairs in Exercise 1. Label your new parallelogram *EFGH*. Did you perform a slide or a flip?

3. Take the opposite of the first number in each ordered pair for the vertexes of *EFGH* in Exercise 2. Label your new parallelogram *JKLM*. Did you perform a slide or a flip?

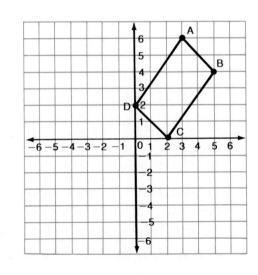

PRACTICE

Locate each point on a grid. Join the points in order and name the figure.

4. A (3, 3), B (‾3, 3), C (‾3, ‾3),
D (3, ‾3), A (3, 3)

5. E (‾3, ‾2), F (‾3, 5), G (4, ‾2),
E (‾3, ‾2)

6. H (0, 1), I (‾5, 1), J (‾5, 6),
K (0, 6), H (0, 1)

7. L (‾2, ‾2), M (3, ‾1), N (5, 4),
O (‾1, 6), P (‾4, 0), L (‾2, ‾2)

Show the figures on a grid. Tell whether the result is a slide or a flip.

MENTAL MATH

8. Join (‾2, ‾3), (‾6, ‾5), (‾4, ‾1). Make a new set of vertexes using the same first numbers and the opposites of the second numbers. Join these new points.

9. Join (3, 1), (6, 2), (5, 8), (2, 7). Make a new set of vertexes by adding ‾6 to the first number in each ordered pair. Join these new points.

Find the volume.

**MIXED
REVIEW**

10. Rectangular prism: $l = 20$ cm,
$w = 8$ cm, $h = 12$ cm

11. Cube: $s = 1.75$ m

PROBLEM SOLVING APPLICATIONS
Drawing a Diagram

Solve.

12. Three trained frogs are sitting on a grid at points E (3, 0), F (5, 4), and G (7, 0). At the sound of a whistle they move over 2 spaces to the left. Where are they now?

13. Four fleas are sitting on a grid at A (4, 8), B(‾4, 8), C (‾4, ‾2), and D (4, ‾2). Draw a grid and locate the fleas.

14. In Exercise 13, what shape is formed if the locations of the fleas are connected in order, A to B, B to C, C to D, and D to A?

15. An ant travels on a grid from (2, 0) to (2, 8) to (4, 0) and back to (2, 0). What is the shape of its path?

1. Understand
2. Plan
3. Work
4. Answer/ Check

PROBLEM SOLVING
Strategy: Logical Thinking

Turner, Zinkham, and Baez are a plumber, an electrician, and a gardener, but not necessarily in that order. Turner is neither the plumber nor the gardener. Zinkham is not the plumber. What is the occupation of each?

One way to solve a problem like this is to set up a chart. Then carefully read the problem, and write an X when a person cannot have a job.

Think: Turner is neither the plumber nor the gardener, so Turner is the electrician (✓).

Zinkham is neither the plumber nor the electrician, so Zinkham is the gardener (✓).

Then, Baez cannot be the gardener *or* the electrician. Baez must be the plumber (✓).

	P	E	G
Turner	X	✓	X
Zinkham	X	X	✓
Baez	✓	X	X

CLASS EXERCISES

Copy and complete the table. Then solve.

1. Carol, Joanna, and Su-Lin are wearing red, blue, and yellow sweaters, not necessarily in that order. Joanna is not wearing the red sweater. Carol is not wearing the red or the blue sweater. Who is wearing which sweater?

	R	B	Y
Carol			
Joanna			
Su-Lin			

PRACTICE

Solve.

2. Tom, Diana, and Harry have different sandwiches for lunch. One has meat, one has cheese, and one has cucumber. Tom does not have cheese or cucumber. Diana does not have cheese. Who has which sandwich?

3. Frieda, Sean, Ed, and Kente play first base, second base, shortstop, and third base on a softball team, but not necessarily in that order. Frieda and the third baseman come to the game with Kente. Sean and the shortstop are brothers. Kente, an only child, plays first base. Who plays at each position?

★ 4. You are running a single-elimination tennis tournament (which means when two players play, the winner goes on to play another match, the loser plays no more). If 256 people sign up for the tournament, how many matches must be held before the final winner is determined?

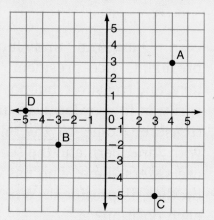

CHECKPOINT 2

1. Write the ordered pair for the letter. *(pages 406–407)*

Show the figure on a grid. Name the figure. *(pages 408–409)*

2. A (3, 1), B (5, 1), C (5, 3), D (3, 3)

Solve. *(pages 410–411)*

3. Ab, Eb, and Ib are a cook, a driver, and a nurse, not necessarily in that order. Ab is neither the cook nor the driver. Eb is not the driver. Who has each job?

Extra Practice on page 446

Write < or > to compare the integers. *(pages 398–399)*

1. ⁻8 ▨ 3 **2.** ⁻2 ▨ ⁻90 **3.** 36 ▨ ⁻4 **4.** ⁻200 ▨ 200

Write the answer. *(pages 400–403)*

5. ⁻17 + 9 **6.** ⁻7 + ⁻12 **7.** ⁻15 − ⁻6 **8.** 13 − ⁻4

9. ⁻23 − ⁻6 **10.** ⁻19 + ⁻19 **11.** ⁻11 − 11 **12.** ⁻10 + 10

Use the chart to answer the question. *(pages 404–405)*

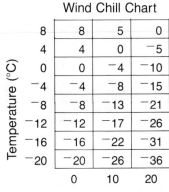

Wind Chill Chart

Temperature (°C)	0	10	20
8	8	5	0
4	4	0	⁻5
0	0	⁻4	⁻10
⁻4	⁻4	⁻8	⁻15
⁻8	⁻8	⁻13	⁻21
⁻12	⁻12	⁻17	⁻26
⁻16	⁻16	⁻22	⁻31
⁻20	⁻20	⁻26	⁻36

Wind Speed
(kilometers per hour)

13. One day the temperature was 4°C. The wind speed changed from 10 km/h to 20 km/h. What was the change in the wind chill factor?

14. On Monday the wind chill factor was ⁻26°C and the wind speed was 10 km/h. What was the temperature reading?

Locate each point on a grid. *(pages 406–409)*

15. A (⁻4, 5) **16.** B (⁻6, ⁻3) **17.** C (8, ⁻3) **18.** D (6, 5)

Solve. *(pages 410–411)*

19. Nellie Hurd, Debbie Costa, and Barbara Gallagher are a swimmer, a skater, and a jogger, but not necessarily in that order. Nellie is neither the swimmer nor the jogger. Debbie is not the jogger. What is the sport of each?

20. Fern, Dan, Ann, and Jane are president, vice president, secretary, and treasurer, but not necessarily in that order. Dan and the treasurer come to the meeting with Jane. Fern and the secretary are sisters. Jane, who has only a brother, is president. Who holds each position?

Extra Practice on page 447

MATHEMATICS and SOCIAL STUDIES

A *time line* is a form of number line in which the numbers are years. The more recent of two years is always the one to the right. The years labeled B.C. are like negative integers. The years starting with the year 1, which are sometimes labeled A.D., are like positive integers.

CAN YOU COUNT?

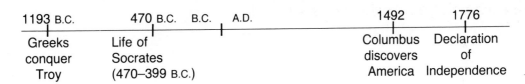

1193 B.C.	470 B.C.	B.C.	A.D.	1492	1776
Greeks conquer Troy	Life of Socrates (470–399 B.C.)			Columbus discovers America	Declaration of Independence

1. List the ten years preceding 5 B.C.

2. About how long was Socrates' life?

3. How many years after Columbus discovered America was the signing of the Declaration of Independence?

★**4.** About how many years have passed between the conquest of Troy and today? About what percent of that span is the age of the United States?

Enrichment

You have learned the following ideas that will help you determine how to multiply and divide with integers.

- Multiplication may be thought of as repeated addition.

- Division may be thought of as repeated subtraction.

- Multiplication and division are opposite operations.

- Number operations have certain properties.

Let's put these ideas to work. See if you can discover the rules for multiplying and dividing with integers.

Complete.

1. You know $4 \times 3 = 12$. What is $4 \times {}^-3$?
   $4 \times {}^-3 = {}^-3 + {}^-3 + {}^-3 + {}^-3 = \blacksquare$ $4 \times {}^-3 = \blacksquare$

2. You know $4 \times 3 = 3 \times 4$. If $4 \times {}^-3 = \blacksquare$, then ${}^-3 \times 4 = \blacksquare$

3. The distributive property says $a \times (b+c) = (a \times b) + (a \times c)$.

   a. ${}^-3 \times (4 + {}^-4) = {}^-3 \times \blacksquare$ b. ${}^-3 \times (4 + {}^-4) = ({}^-3 \times 4) + ({}^-3 \times {}^-4)$
   $\quad\quad = \blacksquare$ $\quad\quad\quad\quad = \blacksquare + ({}^-3 \times {}^-4)$

   Since the results of parts a and b are equal, what can you conclude about $({}^-3 \times {}^-4)$?

4. If you multiply positive or negative 3 and positive or negative 4, the result will be either 12 or ${}^-12$.
   $3 \times 4 = \blacksquare$ ${}^-3 \times 4 = \blacksquare$ $3 \times {}^-4 = \blacksquare$ ${}^-3 \times {}^-4 = \blacksquare$

MULTIPLYING AND DIVIDING INTEGERS

Write *positive* or *negative* to complete.

5. A positive number times a positive number is ____?____.

6. A positive number times a negative number is ____?____.

7. A negative number times a positive number is ____?____.

8. A negative number times a negative number is ____?____.

Complete.

9. $4 \times {}^-3 = {}^-12$ so ${}^-12 \div 4 = \blacksquare$ and ${}^-12 \div {}^-3 = \blacksquare$.

10. ${}^-4 \times {}^-3 = 12$ so $12 \div {}^-4 = \blacksquare$ and $12 \div {}^-3 = \blacksquare$.

11. You can think of ${}^-12 \div {}^-4$ as "How many ${}^-4$'s can you subtract from ${}^-12$?"

${}^-12 - {}^-4 = \blacksquare$ $\diamond$ ${}^-8 - {}^-4 = \blacksquare$ $\diamond$ ${}^-4 - {}^-4 = \blacksquare$

You can subtract ${}^-4$ from ${}^-12\ \blacksquare$ times, so ${}^-12 \div {}^-4 = \blacksquare$.

12. If you divide positive or negative 12 by positive or negative 4 the result will be either 3 or ${}^-3$.

$12 \div 4 = \blacksquare$ $12 \div {}^-4 = \blacksquare$ ${}^-12 \div 4 = \blacksquare$ ${}^-12 \div {}^-4 = \blacksquare$

Write positive or negative to complete.

13. A positive number divided by a positive number is ____?____.

14. A positive number divided by a negative number is ____?____.

15. A negative number divided by a positive number is ____?____.

16. A negative number divided by a negative number is ____?____.

Multiply or divide.

17. ${}^-6 \times 2$

18. ${}^-8 \times {}^-9$

19. $20 \times {}^-7$

20. ${}^-6 \times {}^-15$

21. ${}^-30 \div 6$

22. ${}^-42 \div {}^-6$

23. $54 \div {}^-9$

24. ${}^-96 \div {}^-12$

25. $({}^-9)^2$

26. ${}^-2.5 \times {}^-3$

27. $4.5 \div {}^-1.5$

28. ${}^-1 \times {}^-3 \times 2$

CUMULATIVE REVIEW

Choose the correct answer. Write *a*, *b*, *c*, or *d*.

Solve.

1. Sue is mowing a lawn 280 ft wide and 360 ft long. The lawn mower blade is 4 ft wide. How many lengthwise passes across the lawn must Sue make to mow the whole lawn?

a. 60   **b.** 90   **c.** 70
d. none of these

2. Al wants to build a rectangular storage bin 30 ft wide and 15 ft tall. If the bin is to have a volume of at least 8000 ft^3, about how long should the bin be?

a. 5 ft   **b.** 10 ft   **c.** 20 ft
d. none of these

Use the data to find the answer: 7.40, 6.77, 7.27, 6.64, 7.82

3. the range

a. 7.82   **b.** 6.64   **c.** 1.18
d. none of these

4. the mean

a. 35.9   **b.** 7.27   **c.** 7.18
d. none of these

Use the graph to find the answer.

5. How many parkas with hoods were sold on Saturday?

a. 4   **b.** 6   **c.** 9
d. none of these

6. How many parkas were sold in all?

a. 22   **b.** 23   **c.** 34
d. none of these

7. How much money was spent on costumes?

a. $21.60   **b.** $216.00   **c.** $226.00
d. none of these

8. How much more money was spent on props than on programs?

a. $120   **b.** $72   **c.** $48
d. none of these

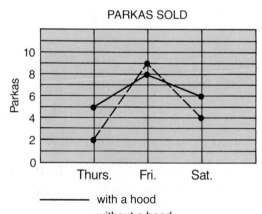

PARKAS SOLD

——— with a hood
– – – without a hood

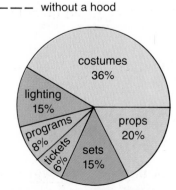

DRAMA CLUB BUDGET $600

A digit from the number 369,463,387 is chosen without looking. What will be the probability of the following outcome?

9. a three   **a.** $\frac{1}{9}$

                b. $\frac{2}{9}$

                c. $\frac{1}{3}$

                d. none of these

10. an odd number   **a.** 1

                        b. $\frac{1}{3}$

                        c. $\frac{5}{9}$

                        d. none of these

Solve.

11. At a sweater sale there are 10 green V-neck sweaters and 6 blue cardigan sweaters. If you choose a sweater without looking, what is the probability that you will choose a blue cardigan?

    a. $\frac{16}{16}$ **b.** $\frac{6}{12}$ **c.** $\frac{12}{16}$

    d. none of these

12. There are 3 people waiting to buy roses or tulips. The chances of buying either are equally likely. What is the probability that all the people are waiting to buy roses?

    a. $\frac{1}{3}$ **b.** 1   **c.** $\frac{1}{8}$

    d. none of these

LANGUAGE and VOCABULARY REVIEW

Write *true* or *false*. If you write false, correct the sentence by replacing the underlined word.

1. If you fold a figure so that both halves fit exactly on one another, the figure is <u>symmetrical</u>.

2. A <u>cone</u> has two circular bases that are congruent and parallel.

3. The <u>outcome</u> of a set of data is the difference between the greatest and the least numbers.

4. Whole numbers and their opposites are called <u>integers</u>.

5. A square is a <u>hexagon</u> with four right angles.

SIMULATION

A **simulation** is an imitation or a model of a situation. A computer can be programmed to display a model that can be changed easily. Suppose an architect is designing a house. A model of the house and the property is plotted on a screen. The architect can slide, rotate, or flip the model on the screen.

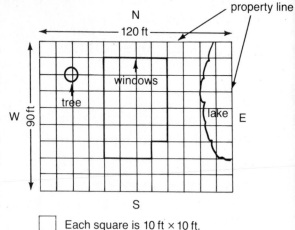

Each square is 10 ft × 10 ft.

The architect has three conditions to meet.

- Face the large windows toward the lake.
- Place a 20 ft yard on the north side.
- Save the old tree.

Use graph paper. Copy the property plan. Cut out an extra copy of the model of the house. Place the model in the position shown in the plan. Move it as directed.

1. Turn the model 90° to the right so that the windows face the lake.

2. Slide the model so that the distance from the north property line to the house is 20 ft.

3. Flip the model so that the open corner of the house will allow enough room for the tree. Check that all three conditions have been met.

4. Some simulations use a formula and a model. Suppose the architect wants the area of the house to show on the model. What formula could be used?

5. What is the area of the house?

TABLE OF MEASURES

Time

60 seconds (s) = 1 minute (min)	
60 minutes = 1 hour (h)	
24 hours = 1 day (d)	
7 days = 1 week	

$$\left.\begin{array}{l} 365 \text{ days} \\ 52 \text{ weeks} \\ 12 \text{ months} \end{array}\right\} = 1 \text{ year (y)}$$

10 years = 1 decade

100 years = 1 century

Metric

LENGTH

10 millimeters (mm) = 1 centimeter (cm)

10 centimeters = 1 decimeter (dm)

$$\left.\begin{array}{l} 10 \text{ decimeters} \\ 100 \text{ centimeters} \end{array}\right\} = 1 \text{ meter (m)}$$

10 meters = 1 dekameter (dam)

10 dekameters = 1 hectometer (hm)

$$\left.\begin{array}{l} 10 \text{ hectometers} \\ 1000 \text{ meters} \end{array}\right\} = 1 \text{ kilometer (km)}$$

AREA

100 square millimeters = 1 square centimeter

(mm^2)   (cm^2)

10,000 square centimeters = 1 square meter (m^2)

10,000 square meters = 1 hectare (ha)

VOLUME

1000 cubic millimeters = 1 cubic centimeter

(mm^3)   (cm^3)

1,000,000 cubic centimeters = 1 cubic meter (m^3)

MASS

1000 milligrams (mg) = 1 gram (g)

1000 grams = 1 kilogram (kg)

CAPACITY

1000 milliliters (mL) = 1 liter (L)

United States Customary

LENGTH

12 inches (in.) = 1 foot (ft)

$$\left.\begin{array}{l} 3 \text{ feet} \\ 36 \text{ inches} \end{array}\right\} = 1 \text{ yard (yd)}$$

$$\left.\begin{array}{l} 5280 \text{ feet} \\ 1760 \text{ yards} \end{array}\right\} = 1 \text{ mile (mi)}$$

AREA

144 square inches (in.^{2}) = 1 square foot (ft^2)

9 square feet = 1 square yard (yd^2)

4840 square yards = 1 acre (A)

VOLUME

1728 cubic inches = 1 cubic foot (ft^3)

27 cubic feet = 1 cubic yd (yd^3)

WEIGHT

16 ounces (oz) = 1 pound (lb)

2000 pounds = 1 ton (t)

CAPACITY

8 fluid ounces (fl oz) = 1 cup (c)

2 cups = 1 pint (pt)

2 pints = 1 quart (qt)

4 quarts = 1 gallon (gal)

FOR USE AFTER CHECKPOINT 1

Write the standard form. *(pages 2–3)*

1. 6 hundred 3   **2.** five thousand, two hundred six   **3.** three million, thirty

4. five million, two hundred sixty   **5.** 19 billion, 29 million, 147 thousand, 9

Complete. Write < or >. *(pages 4–5)*

6. 9111 ▨ 1999   **7.** 793 ▨ 794   **8.** 3704 ▨ 3740   **9.** 1911 ▨ 1191

10. 3099 ▨ 3999   **11.** 89,456 ▨ 98,517   **12.** 11,999 ▨ 1999

13. 3,874,603 ▨ 3,875,842

Round the number to its greatest place value. *(pages 6–9)*

14. 55   **15.** 6500   **16.** 84,602   **17.** 5,500,002   **18.** 968,238,518

Solve. *(pages 10–11)*

19. A theater sold 24,238 tickets last year and 24,382 tickets this year. In which year did it sell more tickets?

FOR USE AFTER CHECKPOINT 2

Estimate to the nearest millimeter and centimeter. Then measure. *(pages 12–13)*

1. _____   **2.** _____   **3.** _____

Choose the better estimate. Write *a* or *b*. *(pages 14–17)*

4. length of a camera
   a. 14 mm   **b.** 14 cm

5. length of a car
   a. 4 m   **b.** 4 cm

6. mass of an ice cube
   a. 50 kg   **b.** 50 g

Solve. *(pages 18–19)*

7. Is it cold enough for water to freeze? hot enough to boil?

Choose the best estimate. *(pages 20–23)*

8. height of a doorway
   a. 36 in.   **b.** 6 yd   **c.** 7 ft

9. weight of a shoe
   a. 1 lb   **b.** 1 oz   **c.** 20 lb

10. capacity of a soup bowl
   a. 2 c   **b.** 3 qt   **c.** 4 gal

11. length of a pencil
   a. 7 in.   **b.** 27 in.   **c.** 2 ft

EXTRA PRACTICE

FOR USE AFTER THE CHAPTER TEST

Write the standard form. *(pages 2–3)*

1. 6 million, 28 thousand, 432   **2.** 62 million, 216   **3.** 50,000 + 700 + 20 + 6

4. thirty million, eight   **5.** 2 million, 48 thousand   **6.** 9 billion, 400 thousand, 16

Complete. Write < or >. *(pages 4–5)*

7. 498 ▨ 501   **8.** 6792 ▨ 6972   **9.** 7500 ▨ 6989   **10.** 11,564 ▨ 11,546

11. 500,001 ▨ 501,000   **12.** 2,762,390 ▨ 986,999   **13.** 1,010,010 ▨ 1,009,090

Round to the place of the underlined digit. *(pages 6–9)*

14. 5̲6   **15.** 4̲621   **16.** 5̲099   **17.** 30̲,623

18. 10̲7,414   **19.** 604̲,290   **20.** 9̲48,000   **21.** 1̲,530,000

Solve. *(pages 10–11)*

22. Danny spent $7.39. Eli spent $7.93. Who spent more?

23. Susan ran 1875 m. To the nearest thousand, how far did she run?

Choose the better estimate. Write *a* or *b*.
(pages 12–17)

24. length of a pen
  a. 15 cm   **b.** 15 m

25. distance from Boston to Chicago
  a. 1600 m   **b.** 1600 km

26. amount of gas in a lawn mower
  a. 4 mL   **b.** 4 L

27. mass of a bag of potatoes
  a. 2 g   **b.** 2 kg

Choose the most likely temperature. Write *a*, *b*, or *c*.
(page 18–19)

28. an ice cube
  a. −10°C   **b.** 1°C   **c.** 20°C

29. hot soup
  a. 3°C   **b.** 20°C   **c.** 60°C

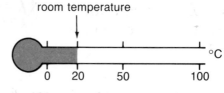

Choose the best estimate. Write *a*, *b*, or *c*. *(pages 20–23)*

30. height of a basketball hoop
  a. 10 yd   **b.** 10 ft   **c.** 48 in.

31. length of a pen
  a. 6 in.   **b.** 6 ft   **c.** 1 yd

FOR USE AFTER CHECKPOINT 1

Complete. *(pages 32–35)*

1. $6 - \blacksquare = 6$ 2. $7 - 7 = \blacksquare$ 3. $5 + \blacksquare = 12$ 4. $8 + \blacksquare = 8$

5. $3 + 8 = 11$, so $8 + \blacksquare = 11$ 6. $8 - 3 = 5$, so $3 + \blacksquare = 8$

Add. *(pages 36–37, 40–41)*

7. $\begin{array}{r} 61 \\ + 83 \\ \hline \end{array}$
8. $\begin{array}{r} 37{,}632 \\ + 68{,}969 \\ \hline \end{array}$
9. $\begin{array}{r} \$7253.16 \\ + \ \ 9478.08 \\ \hline \end{array}$
10. $\begin{array}{r} \$3.98 \\ .37 \\ + \ \ 1.38 \\ \hline \end{array}$

Estimate. *(pages 38–39)*

11. $\begin{array}{r} 685 \\ + \ \ 41 \\ \hline \end{array}$
12. $\begin{array}{r} \$.94 \\ + \ .61 \\ \hline \end{array}$
13. $\begin{array}{r} 13{,}894 \\ + \ \ 6{,}236 \\ \hline \end{array}$
14. $\begin{array}{r} \$4.09 \\ 8.32 \\ + \ \ .92 \\ \hline \end{array}$

15. $\$6.35 + \$8.98 + \$.66$ 16. $23 + 57 + 805 + 855$

Solve. *(pages 42–43)*

17. William bought items that cost $11.25, $5.29, $8.98, and $14.15. About how much did his purchases cost?

FOR USE AFTER CHECKPOINT 2

Estimate. *(pages 46–47)*

1. $\begin{array}{r} 964 \\ - 337 \\ \hline \end{array}$
2. $\begin{array}{r} 4282 \\ - 2739 \\ \hline \end{array}$
3. $\begin{array}{r} \$3.49 \\ - \ 2.26 \\ \hline \end{array}$
4. $\begin{array}{r} \$48.32 \\ - \ \ 6.81 \\ \hline \end{array}$

Subtract. *(pages 44–45, 48–51)*

5. $\begin{array}{r} \$8.19 \\ - \ 4.55 \\ \hline \end{array}$
6. $\begin{array}{r} 832 \\ - \ 85 \\ \hline \end{array}$
7. $\begin{array}{r} 2000 \\ - 1461 \\ \hline \end{array}$
8. $\begin{array}{r} 13{,}092 \\ - \ 5{,}738 \\ \hline \end{array}$

Solve. *(pages 52–53)*

9. How long does the woodworking activity take? the bird watching activity?

10. Which activity takes longer? how much longer?

Activity	Starting Time	Finishing Time
Bird watching	7:15 A.M.	9:30 A.M.
Woodworking	8:45 A.M.	10:00 A.M.

FOR USE AFTER THE CHAPTER TEST

Solve the equation. *(pages 32–35)*

1. $n - 0 = 7$ **2.** $x - 8 = 5$ **3.** $a + 5 = 5$ **4.** $10 - 0 = y$

Estimate the sum. *(pages 38–39)*

	5.	**6.**	**7.**	**8.**
	49	483	5559	$1.49
	+ 63	+ 241	+ 9143	2.15
				+ 8.75

Write the answer. *(pages 36–37, 40–41)*

9.	**10.**	**11.**	**12.**
36	$97.69	621,503	36,413
414	+ 2.42	47,881	2,102
62		+ 305	665
+ 582			+ 7,393

Solve. *(pages 42–43)*

13. Matthew's purchases cost $6.63, $.89, $8.15, and $5.98. Estimate the total cost of his purchases.

Estimate the difference. *(pages 46–47)*

14.	**15.**	**16.**	**17.**
73	3598	968	$52.39
− 19	− 1743	− 620	− 25.82

Write the answer. *(pages 44–45, 48–51)*

18.	**19.**	**20.**	**21.**
847	2767	8000	$900.00
− 329	− 893	− 1536	− 68.79

Use the chart to solve. *(pages 52–53)*

22. How long is the guitar concert? the piano concert?

23. How long after the guitar concert ends does the piano concert end?

Concert	Start	Finish
Guitar	7:30 P.M.	9:20 P.M.
Piano	7:45 P.M.	9:55 P.M.

FOR USE AFTER CHECKPOINT 1

Complete. *(pages 62–67)*

1. $3 \times 7 = 7 \times$ ▨   **2.** $(3 \times 5) \times 6 = 3 \times (5 \times$ ▨ $)$ **3.** $0 \times 7 =$ ▨

4. $9 \times$ ▨ $= 2 \times 9$ **5.** $(5 \times 3) \times 2 =$ ▨ $\times (3 \times 2)$ **6.** $8 \times 1 =$ ▨

7. $523 \times 10 =$ ▨   **8.** $2637 \times 9 =$ ▨   **9.** $3162 \times 100 =$ ▨

Estimate. *(pages 68–69)*

10. $\begin{array}{r} 22 \\ \times 5 \\ \hline \end{array}$ **11.** $\begin{array}{r} 47 \\ \times 63 \\ \hline \end{array}$ **12.** $\begin{array}{r} 302 \\ \times 93 \\ \hline \end{array}$ **13.** $\begin{array}{r} \$1.93 \\ \times 47 \\ \hline \end{array}$ **14.** $\begin{array}{r} 568 \\ \times 205 \\ \hline \end{array}$

Draw a picture to help you solve the problem. Then solve. *(pages 70–71)*

15. How many cuts does it take to cut a loaf of bread into 6 pieces?

16. A team's uniform will be chosen from a combination of 2 different styles of jerseys, 2 different pants, and 2 different hats. How many combinations are there?

FOR USE AFTER CHECKPOINT 2

Multiply. *(pages 72–75)*

1. 48×93 **2.** 78×945 **3.** $86 \times \$1.27$ **4.** 59×6429

5. $\begin{array}{r} 999 \\ \times 888 \\ \hline \end{array}$ **6.** $\begin{array}{r} 7839 \\ \times 75 \\ \hline \end{array}$ **7.** $\begin{array}{r} \$27.38 \\ \times 614 \\ \hline \end{array}$ **8.** $\begin{array}{r} 39{,}017 \\ \times 482 \\ \hline \end{array}$

Complete. *(pages 76–77)*

9. $9^3 =$ ▨ $\times$ ▨ $\times$ ▨   **10.** $6 \times 6 \times 6 \times 6 = 6^{▨}$ **11.** $5^3 =$ ▨

12. $2 \times 10^3 =$ ▨   **13.** $10{,}000 = 10^{▨}$ **14.** ▨ $\times 10^2 = 300$

Solve by trial and error. *(pages 78–79)*

15. Emily is 10 years older than Ellen. In 3 years, she will be 3 times as old as Ellen. How old is each now?

16. What is the greatest whole number you can multiply by 55 to get a product between 1100 and 1250?

FOR USE AFTER THE CHAPTER TEST

Write the answer. *(pages 62–67)*

1. 56	**2.** 364	**3.** 2802	**4.** 655	**5.** 4935
×7	×8	×4	×90	×50

Estimate. *(pages 68–69)*

6. 38	**7.** 57	**8.** 290	**9.** $4.15	**10.** 998
×19	×78	×12	×32	×99

Draw a picture to help you solve the problem. Then solve. *(pages 70–71)*

11. Bob has 3 pairs of pants and 3 shirts. How many different outfits does he have using 1 pair of pants and 1 shirt?

12. Joseph washes the dishes every third day and sets the table every fifth day. If he washes the dishes on Monday and sets the table on Wednesday, on what day will he have to do both jobs?

Write the answer. *(pages 72–75)*

13. 64	**14.** 328	**15.** 246	**16.** 7048	**17.** 8453
×36	×27	×77	×297	×8272

Write the product. *(pages 76–77)*

18. 4^2 **19.** 15^1 **20.** 9^3 **21.** 3^4 **22.** 8^2

Use trial and error to solve. *(pages 78–79)*

23. The product of 3 consecutive numbers is 9240. What are the numbers?

24. Maria bought a hat, a scarf, and a sweater. The hat cost twice as much as the scarf, the sweater cost twice as much as the hat. She spent $42 altogether. How much did each item cost?

425

CHAPTER 4   EXTRA PRACTICE

FOR USE AFTER CHECKPOINT 1

Solve. *(pages 88–89)*

1. $36 \div 9 = n$ **2.** $y \div 5 = 8$ **3.** $7 \times b = 42$ **4.** $z \times 6 = 54$

Write the answer. *(pages 90–93)*

5. $7\overline{)86}$ **6.** $5\overline{)337}$ **7.** $7\overline{)214}$ **8.** $5\overline{)305}$ **9.** $4\overline{)2817}$

Write an equation for the word sentence. Then solve. *(pages 94–95)*

10. A pound of tomatoes cost $1.12. How much do 3 pounds cost?

11. The 54 students in a gym class were divided into teams of 9 each. How many teams were there?

12. Ted earned $6.50 on Saturday and $7.25 on Sunday. How much did he earn altogether?

13. A cake which takes an hour to bake has been baking for 37 minutes. How much more time will it take?

FOR USE AFTER CHECKPOINT 2

Write the answer. *(pages 96–105)*

1. $30\overline{)265}$ **2.** $32\overline{)87}$ **3.** $24\overline{)461}$ **4.** $65\overline{)7936}$ **5.** $391\overline{)2304}$

Solve. *(pages 106–107)*

6. There were 11 players on each team. How many players were on 6 teams?

7. Donald weighs 102 lb. Michael weighs 111 lb. How much heavier is Michael than Donald?

8. Three pairs of tennis players shared 60 minutes of court time evenly. How much court time did each pair have?

9. Jody combined her collection of 37 stamps with Fred's collection of 43. How many stamps do they have altogether?

Estimate. *(pages 108–109)*

10. $7\overline{)356}$ **11.** $33\overline{)218}$ **12.** $42\overline{)1732}$ **13.** $41\overline{)2306}$ **14.** $740\overline{)489,023}$

FOR USE AFTER THE CHAPTER TEST

Solve. (*pages 88–89*)

1. $42 \div 7 = n$ 2. $a \div 7 = 9$ 3. $y \times 8 = 48$ 4. $9 \times b = 81$

Write the answer. (*pages 90–93*)

5. $2\overline{)457}$ 6. $7\overline{)856}$ 7. $6\overline{)6140}$ 8. $8\overline{)8087}$ 9. $9\overline{)9808}$

Match each problem with an equation. Then solve.
(*pages 94–95*)

10. Ned added 4 new minerals to his collection of 60. How many minerals are in his collection now?

11. There are 60 books equally piled on 4 shelves. How many books are on each shelf?

12. Of the 60 students in the 6th grade, 4 were absent. How many were present?

A. $60 \times 4 = n$

B. $60 \div 4 = x$

C. $60 - 4 = a$

D. $60 + 4 = b$

Write the answer. (*pages 96–105*)

13. $40\overline{)509}$ 14. $43\overline{)340}$ 15. $26\overline{)843}$ 16. $32\overline{)8427}$ 17. $327\overline{)90,325}$

Solve. (*pages 106–107*)

18. Peter and Wendy painted a picket fence together. Peter painted 37 of the 70 pickets. How many did Wendy paint?

19. The Tigers won the basketball game by 9 points. If they scored 28 points, how many points did their opponents score?

Estimate the quotient. (*pages 108–109*)

20. $183 \div 9$ 21. $476 \div 36$ 22. $4192 \div 557$ 23. $11,683 \div 253$

24. $429 \div 7$ 25. $8176 \div 91$ 26. $65,286 \div 72$ 27. $579,230 \div 813$

CHAPTER 5   EXTRA PRACTICE

FOR USE AFTER CHECKPOINT 1

Write the decimal. *(pages 118–121)*

1. 5 and 2 tenths   **2.** 4 tenths   **3.** 118 and 9 hundredths

4. 8 and 21 hundredths   **5.** 3251 ten-thousandths   **6.** 51 hundred-thousandths

Order from the least to the greatest. *(pages 122–123)*

7. 0.58, 0.85, 0.57, 0.157   **8.** 0.5, 0.495, 0.05, 0.945

9. 7.18, 6.18, 8.16, 8.76   **10.** 1.1, 1.01, 1.11, 0.11

Round to the nearest tenth, hundredth, and thousandth.
(pages 124–125)

11. 0.5921   **12.** 2.5185   **13.** 3.6098   **14.** 5.21645

15. 1.7852   **16.** 16.7019   **17.** 83.0191   **18.** 35.6152

Estimate the answer. *(pages 126–127)*

19. 392.23 + 502.9   **20.** 48.63 − 18.52   **21.** 78.1 + 5.003   **22.** 6008.638 − 43.66

FOR USE AFTER CHECKPOINT 2

Write *too much* or *too little information.*
Solve for too much. *(pages 128–129)*

1. Catherine bought a tennis racket for $39.95 and a pair of tennis shoes for $36.65. How much money did she have left?

2. Jan planted 18 tomato plants in each of 3 rows. Each plant was 4 in. tall. How many tomato plants did she plant?

Write the answer. *(pages 130–133)*

3. 3.92 + 4.84   **4.** 8.73 − 4.5   **5.** 4.900 + 8.613   **6.** 39.07 − 2.382

Complete. *(pages 134–135)*

	DATE	CHECK NUMBER	CHECKS OR DEPOSITS	AMOUNT OF CHECK	√	AMOUNT OF DEPOSIT	BALANCE
			BALANCE BROUGHT FORWARD →				1719 82
7.	3/1	216	Polly's Pet Shop	79 85			?
8.	3/12	217	Acme Barber Shop	6 75			?
9.	3/15		Deposit			351 16	?
10.	3/15	218	Clark's Drug Store	15 89			?
11.	3/20		Deposit			351 16	?

428

FOR USE AFTER THE CHAPTER TEST

Write the decimal. *(pages 118–121)*

1. 7 tenths   **2.** 7 and 31 hundredths   **3.** 428 thousandths

4. 9 and 8 thousandths   **5.** 53 ten-thousandths   **6.** 7 hundred-thousandths

Order the numbers from the least to the greatest.
(pages 122–123)

7. 7.6, 6.8, 8.7   **8.** 0.81, 0.18, 1.8   **9.** 3.03, 3.30, 3.003, 3.0303

10. 8.206, 8.2, 8.602, 8.205   **11.** 12.02, 1.202, 12.002, 12.20, 120.2

Estimate the sum or difference. *(pages 124–127)*

12.	**13.**	**14.**	**15.**	**16.**
5.3	0.77	5.295	$72.88	0.08
+ 2.8	− 0.43	− 3.57	+ 7.50	+ 0.14

Write *too much* or *too little information.*
Solve for too much. *(pages 128–129)*

17. Nellie bought 12 cans of cat food at $.33 a can, and a cat brush for $1.35. How much did she spend on cat food?

18. It cost Richard $12.53 to fill his tank with gasoline. How much did a gallon of gasoline cost?

19. Kirk bought a pen for $3.39. How much money did he receive from the cashier in change?

20. Steve spent 21 min walking to the store, 16 min at the store, and 17 min walking home. How many minutes did he spend walking?

Write the answer. *(pages 130–133)*

21.	**22.**	**23.**	**24.**	**25.**
3.4	8.03	92.458	39.07	78.01
+ 5.8	− 5.12	+ 0.931	− 2.382	− 44.253

Organize the information to solve the problem.
(pages 134–135)

26. Mary had a balance of $212.33. She deposited $230.00 and wrote checks for $218.20 and $47.50. What is her balance now?

27. Lucy had a balance of $415.15. She wrote a check for $330.00, and had a service charge of $5.00. What is her balance now?

CHAPTER 6   EXTRA PRACTICE

FOR USE AFTER CHECKPOINT 1

Estimate. *(pages 144–145)*

1. 486	**2.** 0.413	**3.** 9.21	**4.** 7.02	**5.** 655.3
×0.8	×78	×6.3	×4.98	×3.72

Write the answer. *(pages 146–151)*

6. 0.7	**7.** 0.9	**8.** 2.86	**9.** 0.01	**10.** 1.847
×6	×0.7	×3.1	×0.07	×0.015

Is the answer reasonable? Write *yes* or *no.*
(pages 152–153)

11. One ticket costs $5.75, so 5 tickets cost about $30.00.

12. One quart costs $.89, so 5 quarts cost $5.89.

Write the answer. *(pages 154–157)*

13. $150.5 \div 7$ **14.** $406.4 \div 16$ **15.** $657.6 \div 48$ **16.** 493.8×100 **17.** $6.78 \div 10$

FOR USE AFTER CHECKPOINT 2

Write the answer. If necessary, round to the nearest tenth. *(pages 158–163)*

1. $0.24\overline{)3.948}$ **2.** $1.35\overline{)0.999}$ **3.** $3.8\overline{)6.004}$ **4.** $4.3\overline{)11.567}$ **5.** $3.2\overline{)3.816}$

Complete. *(pages 164–167)*

6. 5.68 m = ▨ cm   **7.** 2.9 km = ▨ m   **8.** 1731 mL = ▨ L   **9.** 2.31 kg = ▨ g

Solve. *(pages 168–169)*

10. Barry ran 3.2 km on Monday, 4.3 on Tuesday, 1.9 on Wednesday, and 3.7 on Thursday. If his goal for the week is 15 km, how many more kilometers must he run?

11. Elsa wants to run 15 km over the course of 6 days. She has run 2.6 km each of the first 3 days. If she runs the same distance each day, what distance must she run on each of her last 3 days to meet her goal?

Estimate the quotient. *(pages 170–171)*

12. $4.8\overline{)34.97}$ **13.** $7.32\overline{)419.8}$ **14.** $9.94\overline{)5921.8}$ **15.** $19.3\overline{)61.45}$

FOR USE AFTER THE CHAPTER TEST

Estimate the product. *(pages 144–145)*

1. 468 ×9.3	**2.** 56.2 ×1.8	**3.** 80.36 ×2.4	**4.** 11.12 ×47.3	**5.** 951.3 ×5.1

Write the answer. *(pages 146–151)*

6. 4.08 ×9	**7.** 0.48 ×0.3	**8.** 0.82 ×0.64	**9.** 3.32 ×0.09	**10.** 0.036 ×0.5

Divide. Then round the quotient to the nearest tenth. *(pages 154–163)*

11. $6 \overline{)72.99}$ **12.** $2.4 \overline{)11.233}$ **13.** $0.35 \overline{)0.925}$ **14.** $0.21 \overline{)1.123}$

Complete. *(pages 164–167)*

15. 2.84 km = ▨ m   **16.** 0.6 L = ▨ mL   **17.** 5842 g = ▨ kg

Solve. Estimate to check the reasonableness of your answer. *(pages 152–153)*

18. A bus can carry a maximum of 67 passengers. What is the greatest number of passengers a fleet of 9 buses can carry?

19. The bus fare between two cities is $22.95. What is the total fare received from 52 passengers?

Solve. *(pages 168–169)*

20. Brad bought 2 pairs of socks for $1.95 each and a sweater for $14.65. How much change should he receive if he pays with two ten-dollar bills?

21. Holden exchanged a shirt that cost $13.50 for two shirts that cost $7.95 each. How much does he owe the store?

Estimate the quotient. *(pages 170–171)*

22. $6.6 \overline{)35.42}$ **23.** $18.9 \overline{)98.9}$ **24.** $12.4 \overline{)278.9}$ **25.** $4.9 \overline{)502.2}$

FOR USE AFTER CHECKPOINT 1

Name the figure. *(pages 180–183)*

1.

2.

3.

4.

Name the polygon. *(pages 184–189)*

5. 6. 7. 8.

Use the Venn diagram. Write *true* or *false*. *(pages 190–191)*

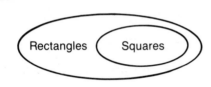

9. All squares are rectangles.

10. All rectangles are squares.

11. Some rectangles are squares.

FOR USE AFTER CHECKPOINT 2

Determine the perimeter or circumference. Use $\pi \approx 3.14$. *(pages 192–195)*

1.   6 cm   8 cm   2 cm   3 cm   9 cm

2.   56 mm   48 mm   39 mm

3.   4 m

4.   18 cm

Determine the area. *(pages 196–201)*

5. right triangle:
   $b = 50$ mm
   $h = 35$ mm

6. square:
   $s = 5.2$ m

7. circle:
   $r = 3$ in.
   (Use $\pi \approx 3.14$.)

8. rectangle:
   $l = 49$ m
   $w = 13$ m

Use a formula to solve. *(pages 202–203)*

9. Edna painted the ceiling of a square room whose sides measured 18 ft. How many square feet of ceiling did she paint?

10. Ralph is going to edge a circular flower garden with bricks. The diameter of the garden is 12 ft. How long will the border be?

EXTRA PRACTICE   CHAPTER 7

Name the figure. *(pages 180–183)*

1.

2.

3.

4.

Name the polygon. *(pages 184–189)*

5.

6.

7.

8.

Use the Venn diagram. Write *true* or *false*. *(pages 190–191)*

9. All triangles are quadrilaterals.

10. Some quadrilaterals are triangles.

11. No triangles are quadrilaterals.

Find the perimeter or circumference. Use $\pi \approx 3.14$. *(pages 192–195)*

12.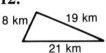
8 km   19 km   21 km

13.
37.2 m   37.2 m

14.
7 cm

15.
51 mm

Find the area. *(pages 196–201)*

16. rectangle:
$l = 28$ cm
$w = 17$ cm

17. right triangle:
$b = 16$ m
$h = 7$ m

18. square:
$s = 33$ in.

19. circle:
$r = 10$ ft
(use $\pi \approx 3.14$)

Use a formula to solve. *(pages 202–203)*

20. An airplane circles a control tower five miles away. How far does the airplane travel in one complete circle?

21. A football field is 360 ft long and 160 ft wide. How long is the chalk line that marks its sides and ends?

FOR USE AFTER CHECKPOINT 1

Is the first number divisible by the second? Write *yes* or
no. *(pages 212–213)*

1. 33; 3   **2.** 19; 2   **3.** 125; 5   **4.** 205; 10   **5.** 35,601; 9

Write the LCM of the numbers. *(pages 214–215)*

6. 8 and 12   **7.** 5 and 6   **8.** 2 and 10   **9.** 4 and 5   **10.** 4, 5, and 6

Write the GCF of the numbers. *(pages 216–217)*

11. 8 and 18   **12.** 7 and 11   **13.** 36 and 64   **14.** 56 and 98   **15.** 8 and 24

Is the number prime or composite? Write *P* or *C.*   *(pages 218–219)*

16. 19   **17.** 33   **18.** 27   **19.** 41   **20.** 50   **21.** 81

Write the equivalent fraction.   *(pages 220–225)*

22. $\frac{1}{8} = \frac{\blacksquare}{24}$ **23.** $\frac{5}{9} = \frac{\blacksquare}{36}$ **24.** $\frac{3}{4} = \frac{\blacksquare}{20}$ **25.** $\frac{4}{7} = \frac{\blacksquare}{21}$ **26.** $\frac{3}{5} = \frac{\blacksquare}{30}$

Order the fractions from the least to the greatest.   *(pages 226–227)*

27. $\frac{1}{2}, \frac{1}{4}, \frac{1}{3}$ **28.** $\frac{2}{3}, \frac{2}{7}, \frac{1}{2}, \frac{4}{5}$ **29.** $\frac{6}{7}, \frac{6}{8}, \frac{5}{8}, \frac{7}{9}$ **30.** $\frac{7}{10}, \frac{13}{20}, \frac{3}{4}, \frac{3}{5}$

Use the graph to answer.
(pages 228–229)

31. On which day did no rain fall?

32. Which day had between $\frac{1}{10}$ and $\frac{3}{10}$
in. of rain?

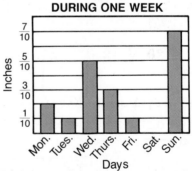

RAINFALL
DURING ONE WEEK

Inches

$\frac{7}{10}$
$\frac{5}{10}$
$\frac{3}{10}$
$\frac{1}{10}$

Mon. Tues. Wed. Thurs. Fri. Sat. Sun.
Days

FOR USE AFTER CHECKPOINT 2

Write as a mixed number.
(pages 230–231)

Write as a fraction or mixed number.
(pages 232–233)

1. $\frac{13}{6}$ **2.** $\frac{57}{4}$ **3.** $\frac{51}{7}$ **4.** 0.3   **5.** 0.001   **6.** 3.019

Write as a decimal. Use a bar if the decimal repeats.
(pages 234–237)

7. $\frac{9}{10}$ **8.** $\frac{4}{5}$ **9.** $\frac{7}{8}$ **10.** $\frac{2}{11}$ **11.** $\frac{7}{12}$ **12.** $\frac{9}{22}$

Solve.   *(pages 238–239)*

13. Each tent can accommodate 4 campers. How many
tents are needed for 19 campers?

FOR USE AFTER THE CHAPTER TEST

Write the common factors for the pair of numbers. Then write the GCF. *(pages 212–219)*

1. 6 and 21   **2.** 8 and 24   **3.** 10 and 35

4. 12 and 28   **5.** 13 and 39   **6.** 18 and 30

Write the equivalent fraction. *(pages 220–225)*

7. $\frac{2}{3} = \frac{\blacksquare}{6}$ **8.** $\frac{1}{2} = \frac{\blacksquare}{20}$ **9.** $\frac{3}{7} = \frac{\blacksquare}{49}$ **10.** $\frac{2}{3} = \frac{\blacksquare}{15}$ **11.** $\frac{4}{15} = \frac{\blacksquare}{45}$ **12.** $\frac{4}{9} = \frac{\blacksquare}{36}$

Order the fractions from the least to the greatest. *(pages 226–227)*

13. $\frac{3}{5}, \frac{7}{15}, \frac{3}{10}$ **14.** $\frac{7}{8}, \frac{5}{6}, \frac{7}{12}$ **15.** $\frac{4}{7}, \frac{1}{2}, \frac{3}{5}, \frac{2}{3}$ **16.** $\frac{5}{12}, \frac{13}{36}, \frac{7}{18}, \frac{5}{6}$ **17.** $\frac{5}{8}, \frac{2}{7}, \frac{3}{10}$

Write as a mixed number. *(pages 230–231)*

18. $\frac{15}{4}$ **19.** $\frac{33}{7}$ **20.** $\frac{17}{12}$ **21.** $\frac{14}{5}$ **22.** $\frac{10}{3}$ **23.** $\frac{20}{9}$

Write as a fraction or a mixed number. *(pages 232–233)*

24. 0.9   **25.** 0.07   **26.** 0.0021   **27.** 2.01   **28.** 3.889

Write as a decimal. Use a bar if the decimal repeats. *(pages 234–237)*

29. $\frac{1}{5}$ **30.** $\frac{3}{8}$ **31.** $\frac{5}{16}$ **32.** $\frac{1}{3}$ **33.** $\frac{7}{22}$ **34.** $\frac{23}{24}$

Use the bar graph to solve. *(pages 228–229)*

35. Order the days of the week from the most to the least rain.

36. If it had only rained $\frac{4}{10}$ in. on Sunday, which day would have been the rainest day?

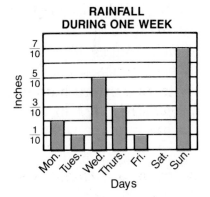

RAINFALL
DURING ONE WEEK

Solve. *(pages 238–239)*

37. A jug of fruit juice contains 12 servings. How many jugs should be bought to provide 55 servings?

38. Eleanor evenly divided 4 lb of birdseed between her 3 bird feeders. How much birdseed did she put in each feeder?

CHAPTER 9

EXTRA PRACTICE

Measure to the nearest $\frac{1}{16}$ in. *(pages 248–249)*

1. _____ 2. _____ 3. _____ 4. _____

Estimate to solve. *(pages 250–251)*

5. Gillian's car burns $1\frac{4}{5}$ gal of gas during her commute to and from work each day. About how many gallons are used for commuting during a five-day work week?

6. Peter hiked $2\frac{1}{3}$ mi up a mountain, $3\frac{3}{4}$ mi along a mountain ridge, and $4\frac{3}{5}$ mi back down to his starting point. About how far did he hike in all?

Write the answer in lowest terms. *(pages 252–257)*

7. $\frac{3}{11} + \frac{5}{11}$ 8. $\frac{15}{16} - \frac{5}{16}$ 9. $\frac{5}{9} - \frac{2}{9}$ 10. $\frac{1}{4} + \frac{7}{8}$ 11. $\frac{5}{16} + \frac{1}{8}$

12. $\frac{11}{21} + \frac{4}{7}$ 13. $3\frac{5}{6} + 2\frac{1}{4}$ 14. $1\frac{1}{2} + 6\frac{5}{7}$ 15. $1\frac{1}{8} + 2\frac{3}{4}$ 16. $2\frac{4}{5} + 1\frac{1}{3}$

Subtract. Write the answer in lowest terms. *(pages 258–265)*

1. $\frac{11}{12} - \frac{5}{6}$ 2. $\frac{2}{3} - \frac{1}{8}$ 3. $4\frac{5}{6} - 2\frac{1}{6}$ 4. $5\frac{9}{10} - 1\frac{3}{5}$ 5. $8\frac{7}{9} - 8\frac{1}{4}$

6. $7 - 3\frac{3}{8}$ 7. $10\frac{1}{4} - 3\frac{3}{4}$ 8. $5\frac{3}{8} - 1\frac{5}{6}$ 9. $7\frac{5}{9} - 2\frac{2}{3}$ 10. $7\frac{2}{7} - 3\frac{2}{3}$

Solve. *(pages 266–267)*

11. The traveler's suitcase weighed $35\frac{1}{2}$ lb, and her carry-on case weighed $12\frac{3}{4}$ lb. How much did her luggage weigh altogether?

12. A puppy weighed $5\frac{3}{4}$ lb. If her big brother weighed $7\frac{1}{8}$ lb, how much heavier was he than she?

13. Ella used $3\frac{3}{4}$ lb of a 5 lb bag of flour to bake bread. How much flour is left?

14. A basketball center is 6 ft $9\frac{1}{4}$ in. tall. This is $4\frac{3}{4}$ in. taller than a guard on the team. How tall is the guard?

FOR USE AFTER THE CHAPTER TEST

Measure the segment to the nearest $\frac{1}{4}$ in., $\frac{1}{8}$ in., and $\frac{1}{16}$ in. *(pages 248–249)*

1. _____ 2. _____ 3. _____

4. _____

Estimate to solve. *(pages 250–251)*

5. It takes Andrew $2\frac{1}{6}$ h to rake the lawn. This fall he raked the lawn twice. About how many hours did he spend raking?

6. Delmar lives $1\frac{7}{8}$ mi from school. About how far does he walk in five days to and from school?

7. Shelley earned $11.35 one Saturday morning. She earned $12.95 the next Saturday. About how much did she earn altogether?

8. Maria runs $2\frac{3}{4}$ mi a day. About how many miles would she run in 7 days?

Write the answer in lowest terms. *(pages 252–257)*

9. $\frac{1}{8} + \frac{5}{8}$
10. $\frac{2}{5} + \frac{1}{5}$
11. $\frac{7}{9} - \frac{4}{9}$
12. $\frac{6}{8} - \frac{1}{8}$
13. $\frac{1}{3} + \frac{5}{9}$

14. $\frac{3}{4} + \frac{1}{6}$
15. $\frac{3}{10} + \frac{1}{2}$
16. $\frac{5}{6} + \frac{1}{9}$
17. $3\frac{1}{4} + 2\frac{1}{3}$
18. $5\frac{5}{12} + 2\frac{7}{8}$

Write the answer in lowest terms. *(pages 258–265)*

19. $\frac{4}{7} - \frac{1}{2}$
20. $\frac{7}{8} - \frac{1}{4}$
21. $\frac{7}{9} - \frac{1}{3}$
22. $4\frac{8}{9} - 2\frac{5}{9}$
23. $7\frac{11}{12} - 3\frac{7}{8}$

24. $8\frac{3}{4} - 6\frac{2}{3}$
25. $5\frac{1}{6} - 2\frac{5}{6}$
26. $9 - 7\frac{3}{10}$
27. $4\frac{1}{3} - 2\frac{3}{5}$
28. $3\frac{3}{8} - 1\frac{2}{3}$

Write a simpler problem with simpler numbers. Use it to solve the original problem. *(pages 266–267)*

29. George had $4\frac{3}{4}$ lb of flour. He used $2\frac{3}{8}$ lb to make bread. How much flour did he have left?

30. Sheila has run $3\frac{1}{2}$ mi of a $6\frac{1}{5}$ mi-race. How much farther does she have to run?

FOR USE AFTER CHECKPOINT 1

Multiply. Write the product in lowest terms.   *(pages 276–283)*

1. $4 \times \frac{5}{8}$ **2.** $\frac{3}{7} \times 8$ **3.** $28 \times \frac{4}{7}$ **4.** $\frac{1}{3} \times \frac{4}{7}$ **5.** $\frac{5}{8} \times \frac{3}{4}$

6. $\frac{2}{3} \times \frac{5}{8}$ **7.** $\frac{7}{8} \times \frac{2}{5}$ **8.** $\frac{2}{3} \times \frac{7}{10}$ **9.** $\frac{8}{21} \times \frac{3}{10}$ **10.** $\frac{1}{5} \times \frac{15}{18}$

11. $\frac{9}{10} \times \frac{5}{6}$ **12.** $4 \times 1\frac{1}{4}$ **13.** $1\frac{3}{4} \times 2\frac{2}{5}$ **14.** $3\frac{1}{3} \times 4\frac{1}{4}$ **15.** $5\frac{1}{6} \times 1\frac{5}{7}$

Solve.   *(pages 284–285)*

16. Wilma has planted 6 rows of tomatoes. She plans to plant $\frac{1}{2}$ as many rows of lettuce as tomatoes, and twice as many rows of corn as tomatoes. How many rows will she have in her garden?

17. Lewis had two five-dollar bills. He spent $2.50 to see a movie and $6.98 for an inner tube for his bicycle. How much money did he have left?

18. A bus was carrying 24 riders. At the next stop, 8 riders got off and 13 got on. How many were on the bus then?

FOR USE AFTER CHECKPOINT 2

Divide. Write the quotient in lowest terms.
(pages 286–293)

1. $7 \div \frac{3}{5}$ **2.** $18 \div \frac{7}{10}$ **3.** $13 \div \frac{2}{10}$ **4.** $\frac{2}{3} \div 8$ **5.** $\frac{2}{9} \div 2\frac{1}{9}$

6. $\frac{1}{8} \div 5$ **7.** $\frac{2}{5} \div 7$ **8.** $\frac{2}{3} \div \frac{3}{4}$ **9.** $\frac{6}{7} \div \frac{7}{8}$ **10.** $\frac{1}{2} \div \frac{3}{8}$

11. $\frac{2}{5} \div \frac{4}{9}$ **12.** $2\frac{1}{7} \div \frac{3}{7}$ **13.** $\frac{1}{4} \div 1\frac{1}{2}$ **14.** $8\frac{2}{3} \div 5\frac{1}{4}$ **15.** $4\frac{7}{8} \div 3\frac{2}{3}$

Solve.   *(pages 294–295)*

16. The number of lily pads in a pond doubled every year. If there are 4096 lily pads in the pond this year, how many were there 3 years ago?

17. Lynn runs half as far on Wednesdays as on Mondays, and 3 times as far on Fridays as on Wednesdays. If she runs 6 km on Fridays, how far does she run on Mondays?

FOR USE AFTER THE CHAPTER TEST

Write the product in lowest terms.   *(pages 276–283)*

1. $\frac{2}{3} \times 5$ **2.** $\frac{7}{8} \times 9$ **3.** $6 \times \frac{4}{5}$ **4.** $\frac{5}{13} \times \frac{2}{5}$ **5.** $\frac{2}{3} \times \frac{7}{20}$

6. $1\frac{5}{6} \times 2$ **7.** $3\frac{3}{4} \times 4\frac{1}{4}$ **8.** $2\frac{2}{7} \times 1\frac{2}{5}$ **9.** $2\frac{5}{8} \times 1\frac{2}{3}$ **10.** $5\frac{1}{2} \times 4\frac{5}{8}$

11. $4\frac{1}{2} \times 2\frac{5}{8}$ **12.** $7\frac{1}{3} \times 6\frac{7}{8}$ **13.** $5\frac{1}{3} \times 6\frac{2}{7}$ **14.** $4\frac{2}{5} \times 2\frac{1}{2}$ **15.** $10\frac{2}{3} \times 7\frac{4}{5}$

Solve.   *(pages 284–285)*

16. James Murphy bought a refrigerator for $45.75 down and $37.50 a month for 12 months. How much did it cost?

17. Tim is applying finish on a gym floor that measures 90 ft by 50 ft. Each can of finish covers 450 ft². How many cans will he need?

18. Shireen bought 2 loaves of bread for $1.19 each and a container of milk for $.89. How much change did she receive from a five dollar bill?

Write the quotient in lowest terms.   *(pages 286–293)*

19. $8 \div \frac{4}{5}$ **20.** $14 \div \frac{6}{11}$ **21.** $\frac{5}{9} \div \frac{2}{3}$ **22.** $\frac{8}{9} \div \frac{4}{9}$ **23.** $\frac{4}{7} \div \frac{3}{5}$

24. $2 \div 3\frac{2}{3}$ **25.** $2\frac{3}{4} \div 1\frac{5}{8}$ **26.** $3\frac{1}{6} \div 1\frac{2}{3}$ **27.** $2\frac{1}{4} \div 1\frac{2}{5}$ **28.** $1 \div \frac{3}{8}$

29. $7\frac{1}{2} \div 5\frac{2}{3}$ **30.** $6\frac{1}{2} \div 4\frac{1}{3}$ **31.** $1\frac{1}{3} \div 6\frac{4}{5}$ **32.** $7\frac{1}{3} \div 4\frac{4}{5}$ **33.** $3\frac{3}{4} \div 4\frac{1}{2}$

Solve.   *(pages 294–295)*

34. A bake sale lasted 5 hours. Twice as much was earned each hour as the hour before. If the sale earned $80 in its last hour, how much did it earn altogether?

35. Edward bought a movie ticket for $4.50 and popcorn for $1.15. He still had $4.15. How much money did he begin with?

36. Kenji bought 12 cans of juice for $.49 each. Leo bought 2 cartons containing 6 cans each for $2.98 a carton. Who spent more?

FOR USE AFTER CHECKPOINT 1

Write a ratio as a fraction to compare the figures. *(pages 304–305)*

1. 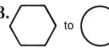 to

2. to

3. 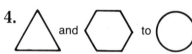 to

4. and to

Write the unit rate. *(pages 306–307)*

5. 54 bottles in 9 cartons   **6.** $56 in 7 h

7. $13.16 for 4 lb   **8.** 72 players on 8 teams

Solve. *(pages 308–311)*

9. $\frac{3}{5} = \frac{n}{20}$ **10.** $\frac{5}{9} = \frac{45}{b}$ **11.** $\frac{12}{19} = \frac{36}{x}$ **12.** $\frac{14}{a} = \frac{21}{45}$ **13.** $\frac{9}{81} = \frac{w}{9}$

Solve. *(pages 312–313)*

14. A car can travel 224 miles on 7 gallons of gasoline. How many miles can it travel per gallon?

15. Jeff walked 9 miles in 3 hours. How far did he walk in 1 hour?

FOR USE AFTER CHECKPOINT 2

Write as a percent. *(pages 314–319)*

1. $\frac{19}{100}$ **2.** $\frac{2}{10}$ **3.** $\frac{6}{20}$ **4.** 0.61   **5.** 0.5   **6.** 0.03

Determine the percent of the number. *(pages 320–321)*

7. 40% of 50   **8.** 5% of 40   **9.** 75% of 104   **10.** 98% of 500   **11.** 4% of 750

Write the number as a percent of 80. *(pages 322–323)*

12. 4   **13.** 40   **14.** 12   **15.** 80   **16.** 20   **17.** 60

Find the final cost. *(pages 324–325)*

18. 25% discount on a $60 coat   **19.** 30% discount on a $250 bicycle

20. 50% discount on a $19.98 watch   **21.** 20% discount on a $6.95 album

Write the ratio as a fraction in lowest terms.
(pages 304–305)

1. 5 to 25   **2.** 14:56   **3.** 8 to 28   **4.** 6:39   **5.** 3 to 81

Write the unit rate.   *(pages 306–307)*

6. 3 cans for $.87   **7.** 5 lb for $1.70

8. 750 words in 25 lessons   **9.** 1800 people in 75 rows

Cross multiply to solve.   *(pages 308–311)*

10. $\frac{15}{40} = \frac{3}{a}$ **11.** $\frac{x}{15} = \frac{18}{30}$ **12.** $\frac{28}{60} = \frac{n}{15}$ **13.** $\frac{17}{3} = \frac{51}{n}$

To solve, use this formula: distance (D) = rate (r) × time (t).
(pages 312–313)

14. A car travels at a rate of 55 miles per hour. How long will it take to travel 165 miles?

15. A long-distance runner ran 18 miles in 2 hours. At this rate, how long did it take him to run 3 miles?

Find the percent.   *(pages 314–319)*

16. 19 out of 100   **17.** 74 out of 100   **18.** $\frac{17}{10}$ **19.** $\frac{1}{5}$ **20.** $\frac{3}{25}$

21. $\frac{19}{50}$ **22.** 0.25   **23.** 0.76   **24.** 0.5   **25.** 0.98

Use a fraction to find the number.   *(pages 320–321)*

26. 20% of 93   **27.** 25% of 97   **28.** 5% of 46   **29.** 2% of 12

Use a decimal to find the number.   *(pages 320–321)*

30. 18% of 55   **31.** 13% of 90   **32.** 7% of 77   **33.** 26% of 99

Write the number as a percent of 200.   *(pages 322–323)*

34. 18   **35.** 120   **36.** 170   **37.** 46   **38.** 180   **39.** 48

Determine the final cost.   *(pages 324–325)*

40. 30% discount on a $120 coat   **41.** 40% markup on an $88 carpet

42. 60% discount on a $28 book   **43.** 15% markup on a $36 sweater

FOR USE AFTER CHECKPOINT 1

Write *C* if the figures are congruent. Write *S* if they are similar.   *(pages 334–341)*

1.   **2.** 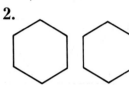   **3.** 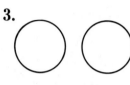   **4.**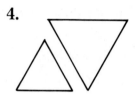

A building plan is drawn to the scale 1 cm to 5 m. Find the actual length of the building using the scale on the plan. *(pages 342–343)*

5. 2 cm   **6.** 6 cm   **7.** 10 cm   **8.** 50 cm   **9.** 4.2 cm

Draw what comes next.   *(pages 344–345)*

10. 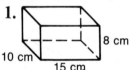   **11.**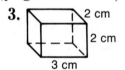

FOR USE AFTER CHECKPOINT 2

What is the volume? *(pages 346–353)*

1.   **2.**

What is the surface area? *(pages 354–355)*

3.   **4.**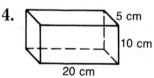

Draw a sketch. Tell whether area or perimeter is needed. *(pages 356–357)*

5. Jeremy plans to shingle a roof.

6. Linda is carpeting a floor.

7. Sean is going to coat a driveway with sealant.

8. Robert is going to plant a hedge around his yard.

Use a compass and a ruler to draw the following. *(pages 358–359)*

9. A circle with the center at *N* and a radius of 2 inches.

10. A circle with a diameter of 5 inches and a radius $\overline{CD}$.

11. $\overleftrightarrow{LM} \perp \overleftrightarrow{NM}$

12. $\overleftrightarrow{OP} \parallel \overleftrightarrow{QR}$

FOR USE AFTER THE CHAPTER TEST

Are the figures congruent or similar? If congruent, write *slide, flip,* or *turn* to indicate how the first figure relates to the second. *(pages 334–341)*

1.   2.   3.   4.

A building plan is drawn to the scale of 1 cm to 3 m. Find the actual length of the building using the scale on the plan. *(pages 342–343)*

   5. 4 cm   6. 3 cm   7. 7 cm   8. 5.5 cm   9. 0.5 cm

Find the volume of the rectangular prism. *(pages 346–349)*

10. $l = 12$ cm
    $w = 8$ cm
    $h = 5$ cm

11. $l = 64$ mm
    $w = 20$ mm
    $h = 35$ mm

Find the volume of the cylinder. *(pages 350–353)*

12. $B = 79$ cm^2
    $h = 2.7$ cm

13. $B = 28$ cm^2
    $h = 5$ cm

Find the surface area. *(pages 354–355)*

14.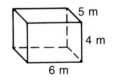

15.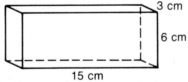

16.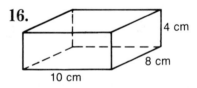

Draw the next figure. *(pages 344–345)*

17.

18.

Use a compass and a ruler to draw the following. *(pages 358–359)*

19. A circle with a diameter of 2 in.   20. $\overleftrightarrow{WX} \perp \overleftrightarrow{YZ}$

FOR USE AFTER CHECKPOINT 1

Write the range, mode, mean, and median. *(pages 368–371)*

1. 42, 45, 36, 29, 58, 42   **2.** 8.0, 8.5, 8.0, 8.8, 7.3   **3.** 98, 103, 72, 107, 86, 98

Use the graph to answer the questions. *(pages 372–377)*

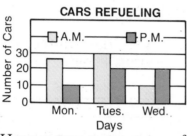

4. How many more cars refueled in the A.M. than in the P.M.?

5. What was the total amount collected in January?

A group of 60 students planted trees. The circle graph shows what percent of the students performed each task.

6. How many students dug holes?

7. How many watered the trees?

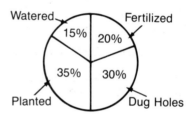

FOR USE AFTER CHECKPOINT 2

Solve. *(pages 380–385)*

1. You have 6 pennies in your pocket. Five are from the 1980's and one is dated 1976. You select one without looking. If all outcomes are equally likely, what is the probability that you select the 1976 penny?

A box containing letter tiles has 2 A's, 4 B's, 6 T's, and 12 M's. What is the probability of picking the following at random?

2. an *A*   **3.** a *B*   **4.** a *T*   **5.** an *M*

Solve. *(pages 378–379, 386–387)*

6. Children can ride a bus for $1.00. Adults pay $2.00. On one run, a bus collected $20.00 in fares. If no more than half of the passengers were children, what possible combinations of children and adults rode the bus?

7. Within a month, 12% of the customers at a restaurant returned. If 150 people dined at the restaurant on a given day, how many could be expected to eat there again within the next month?

FOR USE AFTER THE CHAPTER TEST

Write the range, mode, mean, and median. *(pages 368–371)*

1. 5, 10, 3, 12, 3, 14, 2   **2.** 9, 13, 7, 15, 10, 13, 17   **3.** 33, 17, 24, 48, 17, 16, 69

Use the graph to answer the questions. *(pages 372–377)*

4. How many people attended the 7:00 show on Monday?

5. What was the mean number of people attending the four shows?

6. How much gas was sold on the third day?

7. What was the range in the amount of gas sold?

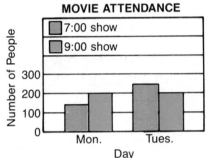

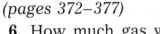
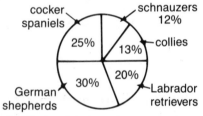

The circle graph shows the percent by breed of 200 dogs entered in a dog show.

8. How many Labrador retrievers were entered?

9. Which breed was represented by the most dogs? the fewest?

A letter is chosen, without looking, from the word *PARALLELOGRAM*. Write the probability of the outcome. *(pages 380–385)*

10. the letter *A*   **11.** the letter *L*   **12.** a vowel   **13.** a consonant

Suppose you pick a marble, without looking, first from the left and then from the right container. Write the probability of the outcome.

14. 2 green marbles   **15.** 1st green and 2nd white

Solve. *(pages 378–379, 386–387)*

16. Jack's rectangular garden has an area of 60 m². Assume that the lengths of its sides are whole numbers and measure at least 3 m. What are the possible dimensions of the garden?

17. The ratio of maples to oaks in the park is 3:7. There are 27 maples. How many oaks are there?

445

FOR USE AFTER CHECKPOINT 1

Compare the integers. Write < or > to complete.
(pages 396–399)

1. $^-9$ ▢ $^-3$ **2.** $^-6$ ▢ 0 **3.** 5 ▢ $^-6$ **4.** $^-12$ ▢ 6

5. 0 ▢ $^-10$ **6.** 0 ▢ 10 **7.** $^-11$ ▢ 11 **8.** $^-14$ ▢ $^-15$

Add or subtract. *(pages 400–403)*

9. $^-5 + ^-9$ **10.** $^-6 - ^-4$ **11.** $4 + ^-8$ **12.** $5 + ^-5$ **13.** $^-3 + 11$

14. $5 - ^-2$ **15.** $^-2 - 5$ **16.** $8 - 9$ **17.** $^-3 - 0$ **18.** $^-7 - ^-3$

Use the chart. Answer the questions. *(pages 404–405)*

19. The temperature was 0°C. The wind speed rose from 10 km/h to 20 km/h. How did that change the way the temperature felt?

20. The wind remained steady at 20 km/h. The temperature was 8°C. What is the wind chill factor?

WIND CHILL CHART

Temperature (°C)	0	10	20
8	8	5	0
4	4	0	−5
0	0	−4	−10
−4	−4	−8	−15
−8	−8	−13	−21
−12	−12	−17	−26
−16	−16	−22	−31
−20	−20	−26	−36

Wind Speed
(kilometers per hour)

FOR USE AFTER CHECKPOINT 2

Write the ordered pair for the letter.
(pages 406–407)

1. A   **2.** B

3. C   **4.** D

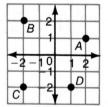

Show the ordered pairs on a grid. Name the figure. *(pages 408–409)*

5. A (3, 2)   B ($^-$3, 2)   C ($^-$3, $^-$2)
D (3, $^-$2)

6. A (0, 3)   B ($^-$3, 0)   C (3, 0)

Solve. *(pages 410–411)*

7. Bowser, Fido, and Rover are a spaniel, a beagle, and a poodle, but not necessarily in that order. Fido is neither the beagle nor the poodle. Rover is not the poodle. Which dog is which?

8. Bill, Phil, and Will's last names are Green, Long, and Good, but not necessarily in that order. Bill's last name is not a color. Will's last name doesn't begin with G. What are their names?

FOR USE AFTER THE CHAPTER TEST

Write < or > to compare the integers. *(pages 398–399)*

1. $^-5$ 5

2. 6   0

3. 0 $^-6$

4. $^-11$ $^-12$

5. $^-200$ 20

6. 5   4

7. $^-54$ 45

8. $^-1$ $^-11$

Write the answer. *(pages 400–403)*

9. $5 + {}^-11$

10. $^-8 + {}^-9$

11. $4 - 12$

12. $3 - {}^-10$

13. $^-7 - {}^-7$

14. $^-4 + 17$

15. $^-2 - 8$

16. $11 + {}^-15$

17. $^-5 + {}^-25$

18. $^-5 - {}^-25$

19. $3 - 13$

20. $^-3 - {}^-13$

Use the chart. Answer the questions. *(pages 404–405)*

21. What is the distance between St. Louis and Tampa?

22. Which is farther, Detroit to St. Louis or Detroit to Tampa?

23. How long a trip would it be from Detroit to Tampa by way of St. Louis?

DISTANCE BETWEEN CITIES (km)

	Detroit	Tampa	St. Louis
Detroit	0	1922	821
Tampa	1922	0	1648
St. Louis	821	1648	0

Locate each point on a grid. *(pages 406–409)*

24. $A(1, {}^-1)$ **25.** $B(^-2, {}^-1)$ **26.** $C(1, 1)$ **27.** $D(^-2, 1)$

Solve. *(pages 410–411)*

28. Al, Hal, and Sal are an author, a hatmaker, and a sailor. None has a job that starts with the same letter as his name. Hal enjoyed the author's last book. Who has which job?

29. Helen, Simon, and Willa are on the soccer, softball, and track teams. Each is on only one team. Helen eats lunch with the soccer and softball players. The soccer player lives next door to Willa. What team is Simon on?

USING ESTIMATION STRATEGIES

Sometimes you may not need an exact answer, and an estimate will do. Each person develops a personal style of estimation to use in practical situations such as shopping, figuring the time needed to complete a job, or walking to a friend's house. In this book strategies for estimation are used that should help you in using math in everyday life. Here are some examples.

Rounding A jar of tomato juice contains 1.89 L. This is about 2 L when rounded to the nearest liter.

The one-way distance from home to the Golden Gate bridge is 87.2 km. When rounded to the greatest place value, the round-trip distance is about 2×90, or 180 km.

Front-end Estimating To estimate the total length, you can use the left digits to add:

$$3 + 4 + 8 + 9 = 24,$$

and compensate by adding on a 1 since the tenths have a sum of about 1. The total length is about 25 m.

3.7 m
4.2 m
8.3 m
9 m

Comparing An estimate for 3.3×6.25 is 3×6, or 18. The exact answer is greater than 18 because 3 and 6 were both rounded down. To find a range of numbers in which $46.2 \div 9$ falls, think: $45 \div 9 = 5$, $54 \div 9 = 6$, so $46.2 \div 9$ is between 5 and 6.

Using Compatible Numbers To estimate $62 \div 8$, you can think of $64 \div 8$, or 8. You found this estimate by identifying a division fact using a number close to 62 as the dividend.

Using Clustering The test scores were 79, 82, 85, 78, and 80. Observe that all the scores cluster around 80, so the sum is about 5×80, or 400.

Using Measurement The staple measures about 1 cm to the nearest cm.

Of the following, 3 lb is the best estimate for the weight of a telephone.

30 lb   3 lb   3 oz

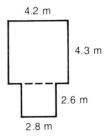

To estimate the area of this room, you can think of it as two rectangles and add their areas.

$$(4 \times 4) + (3 \times 3) = 25$$

The area is about 25 m².

Reading Graphs The height of the bar is about half-way between 100 and 200, so it is about 150.

Sampling and Predicting If about $\frac{1}{10}$ of a good random sample of voters were in favor of a law, then you might predict that about $\frac{1}{10}$ of 10,000 voters, or 1000 voters would vote for the law.

USING MENTAL MATH STRATEGIES

Sometimes you can use mental mathematics to solve problems. You may be doubling a cooking recipe, building a birdhouse, or counting change in a store. You use mental math to find an exact answer without using pencil and paper or a calculator. In this book, strategies for mental math that will help you improve your skills are used. Here are some examples.

Counting On and Back The time elapsed from 11:45 A.M. to 1:42 P.M. can be counted as:

11:45 to 12:00	(15 minutes)
12:00 to 1:42	(1 hour 42 minutes)

The total time is 1 hour 57 minutes.

Using Facts In this division problem, two basic division facts were used to divide mentally.
They were $12 \div 3 = 4$ and $9 \div 3 = 3$.

$$\begin{array}{r} 4.3 \\ 3\overline{)12.9} \end{array}$$

Comparing and Ordering To order the numbers 42.9, 43.6, 42.85, and 43.09 from the greatest to the least, mentally compare the value of the places.

43.6   43.09   42.9   42.85

Using Properties The distributive property lets you work the problem
$(14 \times 3) + (6 \times 3)$ by thinking: $(14 + 6) \times 3$ or $20 \times 3 = 60$.

Using Patterns

$$10 \times 1.3 = 13$$
$$100 \times 1.3 = 130$$
$$1000 \times 1.3 = 1300$$

This pattern helps you determine that $10,000 \times 1.3 = 13,000$.

449

Using Visual Images
You can mentally picture what a figure will look like after a slide, a flip, or a turn.

slide   flip   turn

Changing Numbers and Operations
When working with a percent such as 25%, you may want to change it to $\frac{1}{4}$ or 0.25.

To multiply 0.03×0.46, think:
$3 \times 46 = 3 \times (40 + 6) = 120 + 18 = 138$. Write 0.0138.

To find $\frac{1}{4}$ of \$18, divide \$18 by 4 to get \$4.50.

When adding 198 and 274, you can think of 198 as $200 - 2$. Thus $198 + 274 = 200 + 274 - 2 = 472$.

USING A CALCULATOR

Every calculator is different. You should read the instructions for your calculator to learn how to use it. Most calculators have the keys (buttons) pictured below, but they may be in different places.

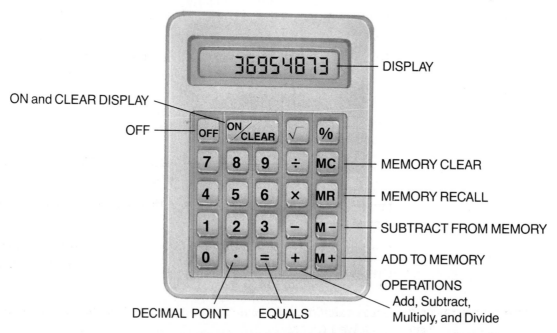

DISPLAY

ON and CLEAR DISPLAY

OFF

MEMORY CLEAR

MEMORY RECALL

SUBTRACT FROM MEMORY

ADD TO MEMORY

OPERATIONS
Add, Subtract, Multiply, and Divide

DECIMAL POINT   EQUALS

The Display
A calculator display usually does not show commas. Usually 8 digits is the most the display will show. A display never shows a dollar sign. You must press the decimal point key to show a decimal number. You press the clear key to remove the display.

The Memory Feature

You can add a given number to several other numbers by using the memory keys.

Add 36 to each of these numbers: 9, 29, 58.

Press   [3] [6] [M+] [9] [+] [MR] [=]
Display   36   36^M   9^M   36^M 45^M

Press   [2] [9] [+] [MR] [=] [5] [8] [+] [MR] [=]
Display   29^M   36^M 65^M   58^M   36^M 94^M

So, 36 + 9 = 45, 36 + 29 = 65, and 36 + 58 = 94.

The Constant Feature

On many calculators the equals key is also a constant key. This feature lets you press the equals key to perform a given operation over and over again with a given number. For example, you can count by twos on the calculator.

Press   [2] [+] [=] [=] [=]   The calculator adds 2 each time
Display   2   2   4   6   8   you press the equals key.

The Percent Key

Many calculators have a percent key. You can use it to solve problems with percents.

Find 50% of 80. On most calculators, enter 80 first.

Press   [8] [0] [×] [5] [0] [%]
Display   80   50   40   50% of 80 is 40.

The π Key

Some calculators have a π key. You can use this key to calculate with a more exact value of π than 3.14.

Find the circumference of a circle with a diameter of 4 cm. Use the formula $C = \pi \times d$.

Press   [π]   [×] [4] [=]   The circumference is
Display   3.1415927   4 12.566371   about 12.57 cm.

The Change-Sign Key

Some calculators have a change-sign key. You can use it to enter a negative number.

Find the sum of ⁻27 and 9.

Press   [2] [7] [+/−] [+] [9] [=]
Display   27   ⁻27   9 ⁻18   ⁻27 + 9 = 18

451

For each problem, choose the method you think is best: calculator, mental math, or estimation. Write C, M, or E. Then solve the problem using that method.

Chapter 1

1. When rounding to the greatest place value, which of these numbers would round to 7000?

   6849   7500   7239   6489   6903   7426

2. Order these numbers from the least to the greatest.

   13,846   14,059   13,946   14,000   13,496

3. The capacity of a container is 2983 mL. About how many liters is this?

4. Tom is 3 ft 10 in. tall. His father is 6 ft 3 in. tall. Is the difference in their heights greater than or less than 3 ft?

Chapter 2

1. What is the difference between 43,789 and the greatest number that can be written with four digits?

2. What is the sum of 68 and 325?

3. There were 23,661 more people at the Sunday baseball game than the Saturday game because of rainy weather on Saturday. There were 36,489 people at the Sunday game. How many people attended the Saturday game?

4. The daily newspaper has a circulation of 139,416, while the Sunday paper has a circulation of 241,385. Would it make sense to say that about 10,000 more newspapers are sold on Sunday than on Saturday?

Chapter 3

1. Is the product of 98 and 26 greater than or less than 2600?

2. What is the product of $862 \times 461 \times 0 \times 312$?

Use this information to solve Exercises 3 and 4.

   Bob had a job that paid $1 the first day, $2 the second day, $4 the third day, and so on. On each day his salary doubled from the previous day.

3. How much money did he earn on the fifteenth day?

4. How much less than the amount that he earned on the fifteenth day did he earn in the first fourteen days combined?

Chapter 4

1. The product of 46 and 8291 is 381,386. What is $381,386 \div 8291$?

2. If $16,501 \div 29 = 569$, is $16,507 \div 29$ between 568 and 569, or between 569 and 570?

3. The altitudes of the California cities of Bakersfield, Fresno, Los Angeles, and Pasadena are 400 ft, 285 ft, 340 ft, and 830 ft. Name two cities, one of which has about twice the altitude of the other.

4. Rich weighs 92 lb. Rich's father weighs 95 lb more than Rich. What is their combined weight?

Chapter 5 **1.** Add and subtract.

2. Is the sum of 3.8, 2.6, and 1.9 greater than or less than 9?

Use the table to solve Exercises 3 and 4.

3. Between which two ages did Andy grow the most?

4. How much more did Andy grow between seven and eight years, than between six and seven years?

ANDY'S HEIGHT

Age	cm
5	104.2
6	113.8
7	118.7
8	125.5

Chapter 6 **1.** Write the next number in the pattern.

40.96   20.48   10.24

2. Which of these numbers have a quotient of about 5 when divided by 2?

9.62   52.2   16.37   11.3   1.2

3. If you and a friend each buy one of each item, how much would you spend together?

Milk: $.89   Dinner Plate: $2.79   Salad: $1.19

4. A can of tomato juice contains 1.36 L. If a juice glass holds 0.15 L, how many glasses of juice does the can hold?

Chapter 7 **1.** What is the perimeter of a square with each side of length 7.2 cm?

2. Which figure has the greater area?

A circle with a diameter of 4 cm
A square with a length of 3.6 cm on each side

3. Is the area of the vegetable garden between 18 m^2 and 28 m^2, or between 28 m^2 and 38 m^2?

3.6 m [   ]
6.9 m

4. Is a 15 ft-strip of lace enough to edge a rectangular tablecloth that is $4\frac{3}{4}$ ft long and $2\frac{1}{8}$ ft wide?

For each problem, choose the method you think is best: calculator, mental math, or estimation. Write C, M, or E. Then solve the problem using that method.

Chapter 8 **1.** Write 6 ft 9 in. in simplest form using only feet, and write $3\frac{1}{2}$ ft using feet and inches.

2. Write each fraction as a decimal that terminates or repeats.
$$\frac{1}{6} \qquad \frac{5}{8} \qquad \frac{4}{9}$$

3. How many multiples of 2 are there between 50 and 70?

4. Order the fractions from greatest to least.
$$\frac{6}{7} \qquad \frac{1}{8} \qquad \frac{4}{9}$$

Chapter 9 **1.** About what is the difference between 20 and the sum of $4\frac{1}{16}$ and $7\frac{14}{17}$?

2. Which is less, $2.625 + 8.49$ or $15 - 1\frac{5}{7}$?

3. Fay took $3\frac{1}{2}$ dollars in dimes and $7\frac{1}{4}$ dollars in quarters to the bank. How much money did she take to the bank?

4. It was necessary to cut off $\frac{1}{4}$ ft from curtains measuring $8\frac{5}{12}$ ft. How long were the curtains after they were cut?

Chapter 10 **1.** About how much money is $10 added to one half of $68.39?

2. Is the product of $2.5 + 1.75$, and 9.126 closer to 10, 50, or 100?

3. In preparing for a party, each of 22 slices of bread was cut into fourths. How many fourths were there?

4. Two fifths of the money collected at the carnival was used to pay workers. If $6859.75 was collected, how much was paid as wages?

Chapter 11 **1.** Are the ratios $\frac{5}{8}$ and $\frac{7}{12}$ equivalent?

2. What is 10% of each number?
$$30 \qquad 65 \qquad \$15 \qquad \$24.50$$

3. Write the numbers from the least to the greatest.
$$16\% \qquad \frac{1}{7} \qquad 0.152 \qquad \frac{2}{15}$$

4. In one year the population of South Dakota was 690,768. If about 5% of the people lived in Brown County, South Dakota, about how many people was this?

Chapter 12

1. Is the area of this figure closer to 10 cm², 12 cm², 14 cm², or 16 cm²?

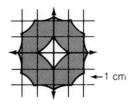

←1 cm

2. How much more will can A hold than can B? Use 3.14 for π.

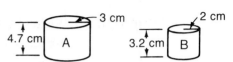

3. If $\frac{1}{2}$ in. on a scale drawing equals one foot, how long will each object be drawn?

    door: 3 ft   wall: 8 ft   wall: 15 ft

4. Which of these boxes holds an amount closest to 100 cm³?

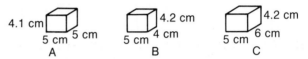

Chapter 13

1. What is the range and mode of this set of data?

    9   4   6   8   9   6   1   6

2. What is the mean of this set of data?

    69   71   74   66   72   75   63

3. The teacher told Alice that her median score on five tests was 89. Alice could only find four of her tests. They had scores of 76, 83, 89, and 92. What can you say about the score of the test that Alice misplaced?

4. The probability of a coin landing heads up after being tossed in the air is $\frac{1}{2}$. If a coin is tossed 4131 times, about how many times would you expect it to land on a head?

Chapter 14

1. Write these integers from the least to the greatest.

    8   ⁻8   0   9   ⁻9   100   ⁻100

2. Add.   642 + ⁻185 + ⁻1263 + 557

3. Let the positive numbers stand for money that Glen has, and the negative numbers stand for money that Glen spends. Is the following sum more than or less than 821?

    821 + ⁻613 + ⁻15 + 183 + ⁻101

4. Imagine that a point located in a coordinate plane has an ordered pair of (5, 9). What point will you get when you move five spaces down?

455

TABLE OF NUMBERS

	A	B	C	D	E	F	G	H
1	71	8	487	678	0.4	1.65	$\frac{1}{4}$	$\frac{3}{4}$
2	5	92	943	899	0.8	3	$\frac{9}{10}$	$\frac{3}{10}$
3	19	9	702	720	0.6	0.3	2	$\frac{2}{5}$
4	35	3	4365	5035	0.1	8.4	$\frac{7}{10}$	$\frac{1}{2}$
5	85	7	2001	1895	0.72	0.23	$\frac{9}{10}$	$\frac{4}{5}$
6	77	47	621	198	0.98	0.85	$2\frac{3}{4}$	$2\frac{1}{4}$
7	22	44	986	1084	1.1	3.5	$5\frac{1}{2}$	$4\frac{1}{4}$
8	48	136	6053	6350	0.2	4.57	$9\frac{1}{2}$	$6\frac{1}{10}$
9	115	19	780	278	8.98	10.7	$1\frac{1}{2}$	5
10	81	79	3200	2300	5.25	6.06	6	$4\frac{3}{4}$
11	42	32	22	12	2.1	2.2	2.3	2.4
12	158	168	178	188	6.8	7.8	8.8	9.8
13	5600	6600	7600	8600	7	7.5	8	8.5
14	1%	10%	25%	50%	75%	20%	40%	80%

Ideas for using this table for mental math, estimation, and calculator activities are found under *Computation Strategies* on the Cumulative Review pages at the end of each chapter of the Teacher's Edition.

GLOSSARY

A

acute angle (p. 182) An angle that measures less than 90°.

acute triangle (p. 189) A triangle with all angles acute.

addend (p. 32) A number being added.

angle (p. 182) Two rays that have a common endpoint.

arc (p. 358) A part of a circle.

area (A) (p. 196) The number of square units that fit inside a figure.

Associative Property of Addition (p. 32) Changing the grouping of the addends does not change the sum.
Example: $(4 + 3) + 7 = 14$
$4 + (3 + 7) = 14$
so $(4 + 3) + 7 = 4 + (3 + 7)$

Associative Property of Multiplication (p. 62) Changing the grouping of the factors does not change the product.
Example: $(2 \times 5) \times 4 = 40$
$2 \times (5 \times 4) = 40$
so $(2 \times 5) \times 4 = 2 \times (5 \times 4)$

average (p. 370) The quotient found by dividing the sum of a group of numbers by the number of addends.

B

bar graph (p. 228) A graph used to compare data.

base (pp. 346, 350) The two congruent parallel faces of a prism or cylinder. The face of a cone or pyramid opposite the vertex.

C

capacity (p. 16) The amount of fluid a container can hold.

Celsius (p. 18) The temperature scale with 0 degrees as the freezing point and 100 degrees as the boiling point.

center (pp. 194, 350) The point that is the same distance from all points on a circle or on a sphere.

centimeter (cm) (pp. 12, 14) A standard metric unit for measuring length.

circle (p. 194) A curved figure in a plane with all points an equal distance from a given point, called the center.

circle graph (p. 376) A circle divided into parts to show data.

circumference (C) (p. 194) The distance around a circle.

common denominator (p. 254) A common multiple of the denominators.

common factor (p. 216) A number that is a factor of two or more numbers. The common factors of 8 and 12 are 1, 2, and 4.

common multiple (p. 214) A number that is a multiple of two or more numbers. Some common multiples of 3 and 4 are 12 and 24.

Commutative Property of Addition (p. 32) Changing the order of the addends does not change the sum.
Example: $7 + 4 = 11$ $\quad$ $4 + 7 = 11$
so $7 + 4 = 4 + 7$

Commutative Property of Multiplication (p. 62) Changing the order of the factors does not change the product.
Example: $5 \times 8 = 40$ $\quad$ $8 \times 5 = 40$
so $5 \times 8 = 8 \times 5$

compatible numbers (p. 108) Numbers that divide easily which are used in estimating quotients.

composite numbers (p. 218) Any whole number greater than 1 that is not a prime.

cone (p. 350) A space figure with one circular base and one vertex.

congruent (p. 338) Having the same shape and size.

cube (p. 348) A space figure with six square faces, twelve edges, and eight vertexes.

cubic centimeter (p. 348) The amount of space contained in a cube with all edges 1 cm long.

cup (c) (p. 22) A United States Customary unit of capacity. 2 c = 1 pt

cylinder (p. 350) A space figure with two parallel, circular, congruent bases.

D

data (p. 368) Numbers that give information.

decimal (p. 118) A number that shows tenths, hundredths, thousandths, and so on. 1.4 and 3.62 are decimals.

decimal point (p. 118) A period used to separate whole numbers from decimals.

decimeter (dm) (p. 164) A metric unit of length. 1 dm = 10 cm

degree (p. 182) A unit for measuring angles.

degrees Celsius (°C) (p. 18) The metric unit for measuring temperature.

degrees Fahrenheit (°F) (p. 399) The U.S. Customary unit for measuring temperature.

denominator (p. 220) The bottom number of a fraction.

diagonal (p. 185) A segment that joins two vertexes of a polygon but is not a side.

diameter (d) (p. 194) The distance across a circle through its center.

difference (p. 32) The answer in subtraction. In the equation 17 − 9 = 8, the difference is 8.

discount (p. 324) A decrease in the price of an item.

Distributive Property (p. 62) The product of a factor and a sum is equal to the sum of the products.
Example: 5 × (3 + 2) = (5 × 3) + (5 × 2)

dividend (p. 90) The number being divided in division. In the equation 36 ÷ 4 = 9, the dividend is 36.

divisible (p. 212) A number can be divided by another number without having a remainder.
Example: 72 is divisible by 3 because 72 ÷ 3 = 24.

divisor (p. 90) The number that divides the dividend in division. In the equation 30 ÷ 5 = 6, the divisor is 5.

double bar graph (p. 372) A graph that uses bars to compare two sets of data simultaneously.

double line graph (p. 374) A graph that uses lines to compare the change over time of two sets of data simultaneously.

E

edge (p. 346) The segment formed when two faces of a space figure meet.

elapsed time (p. 52) The amount of time from one point in time to another.

equation (p. 34) A statement using the equals sign to show that two numbers are equal.
Example: 9 × 6 = 54

equilateral triangle (p. 188) A triangle with three sides of equal length and three angles of equal measure.

equivalent fractions (p. 222) Fractions that name the same number. $\frac{1}{3}$ and $\frac{2}{6}$ are equivalent fractions.

estimate (pp. 7, 38) An answer that is not exact.

even number (p. 218) A number that can be divided by 2 without having a remainder.

expanded form (p. 2) The expanded form of 378 is 300 + 70 + 8.

exponent (p. 76) Names the number of times a factor is used. The exponent in 10^3 is 3.

F

face (p. 346) A side of a space figure.

face

factor (pp. 62, 216) A number being multiplied to obtain a product.

Fahrenheit (p. 399) The temperature scale with 32 degrees as the freezing point and 212 degrees as the boiling point.

flip (p. 336) A figure is reflected about a line.

foot (ft) (p. 20) A United States Customary unit for measuring length. 1 ft = 12 in.

formula (pp. 192, 312) A rule that is written using symbols. Example: $A = l \times w$

fraction (p. 220) A number that compares part of an object or a set with the whole.

front-end estimation (p. 126) Using the digits at the far left in numbers to guess a likely answer.

G

gallon (gal) (p. 22) A United States Customary unit for measuring capacity. 1 gal = 4 qt

gram (g) (p. 16) A standard metric unit for measuring mass. 1000 g = 1 kg

greatest common factor (GCF) (p. 216) The greatest number that is a factor of two or more given numbers. The GCF of 12 and 18 is 6.

H

hexagon (p. 184) A six-sided polygon.

hypotenuse (p. 298) The side opposite the right angle in a right triangle.

I

inch (in.) (p. 20) A United States Customary unit for measuring length. 12 in. = 1 ft.

independent events (p. 382) Events that have no effect on each other.

integers (p. 396) The positive numbers, 1, 2, 3, . . ., the negative numbers, −1, −2, −3, . . . and zero.

intersecting lines (p. 180) Two or more lines that meet or cross at a common point.

isosceles triangle (p. 188) A triangle with two sides of equal length and two angles of equal measure.

K

kilogram (kg) (p. 16) A standard metric unit for measuring mass. 1 kg = 1000 g

kilometer (km) (p. 14) A standard metric unit for measuring length. 1 km = 1000 m

L

least common denominator (LCD) (p. 226) The least common multiple of the denominators of two or more given fractions. The LCD of $\frac{2}{3}$ and $\frac{1}{4}$ is 12.

least common multiple (LCM) (p. 214) The least multiple, excluding 0, of two or more numbers. The LCM of 6 and 10 is 30.

legs (p. 298) The sides of a right triangle that are not the hypotenuse.

line (p. 180) A set of points that extends without end in two opposite directions.

line graph (p. 374) A graph that shows changes in data.

line segment (p. 180) A part of a line that has two end points.

line of symmetry (p. 334) A line that separates a figure into two matching parts.

liter (L) (p. 16) A standard metric unit for measuring capacity. 1 L = 1000 mL

lowest terms (p. 224) When both terms of a fraction have no common factor greater than one. In lowest terms, $\frac{3}{6}$ is $\frac{1}{2}$.

M

mass (p. 16) The amount of matter in an object.

mean (p. 370) The quotient found by dividing the sum of a set of data by the number of items of data.

median (p. 370) The middle number in a set of data after the data is arranged in order from the least to the greatest.

meter (m) (p. 14) A standard metric unit for measuring length. 1 m = 100 cm

mile (mi) (p. 20) A U. S. Customary unit for measuring distance. 1 mi = 5280 ft

milligram (mg) (pp. 104, 166) A metric unit for measuring mass. 1000 mg = 1 g

milliliter (mL) (p. 16) A metric unit for measuring capacity. 1000 mL = 1L

millimeter (mm) (pp. 12, 14) A metric unit for measuring length. 10 mm = 1 cm

mixed number (p. 230) A whole number and a fraction. $2\frac{1}{2}$ is a mixed number.

mode (p. 368) The number that appears most often in a set of data.

multiple (p. 214) The product of a given number and any whole number. A multiple of 3 is 15.

N

negative number (p. 396) A number that is less than zero.

numerator (p. 220) The top number of a fraction.

O

obtuse angle (p. 182) An angle that measures more than 90°.

obtuse triangle (p. 189) A triangle with one obtuse angle.

octagon (p. 184) An eight-sided polygon.

odd number (p. 218) A number that cannot be divided by 2 without a remainder.

opposites (p. 396) Two numbers that are the same distance from zero, but on opposite sides of zero.

Opposites Property of Addition and Subtraction (p. 32) Shows that addition and subtraction are opposite operations.
Example: 9 + 8 = 17 so 17 − 8 = 9.

Opposites Property of Multiplication and Division (p. 88) Dividing by a number is the opposite of multiplying by that number.
Example: 8 × 3 = 24 so 24 ÷ 3 = 8

ordered pair (p. 406) A pair of numbers in which the order shows the location of a point on a grid. (4, 3) is an ordered pair.

ounce (oz) (p. 22) A United States Customary unit for measuring weight. 16 oz = 1 lb

outcome (p. 380) The result of a probability experiment.

P

parallel lines (p. 180) Two or more lines or segments that do not intersect.

parallelogram (p. 186) A quadrilateral with opposite sides parallel.

pentagon (p. 184) A five-sided polygon.

percent (p. 314) Hundredths written with a % sign.
Example: $0.33 = \frac{33}{100} = 33\%$

perimeter (P) (p. 192) The distance around a figure.

perpendicular (p. 180) Two lines that meet or cross to form right angles.

pint (pt) (p. 22) A United States Customary unit of capacity. 1 pt = 2 c

plane (p. 180) A flat surface that goes on and on in all directions.

point (p. 180) An exact location.

polygon (p. 184) A simple closed figure formed by three or more segments.

positive number (p. 396) A number that is greater than zero.

pound (lb) (p. 22) A United States Customary unit of weight. 1 lb = 16 oz

power (p. 76) A product in which all the factors of a number are the same. For example, 2 × 2 × 2 × 2 = 16, so 16 is 2 to the fourth power.

prime factorization (p. 218) The product of prime numbers that names a given number, such as 2 × 2 × 3 × 5 to name 60.

prime number (p. 218) A number with only two factors, itself and 1.

prism (p. 346) A space figure with 5 or more faces. Two of the faces, the bases, are parallel and congruent.

probability (p. 380) The number describing the chance that something will happen.

product (p. 62) The answer in multiplication. In the equation $8 \times 6 = 48$, the product is 48.

Property of One (p. 62) The product of 1 and any number is that number.
Example: $6 \times 1 = 6$

proportion (p. 308) An equation stating that two ratios or rates are equal.

pyramid (p. 346) A space figure with four or more faces. The base can be any polygon. The other faces of the pyramid are triangles.

Q

quadrilateral (p. 184) A four-sided polygon.

quart (qt) (p. 22) A United States Customary unit of capacity. 1 qt = 2 pt

quotient (p. 90) The answer in division. In the equation $56 \div 7 = 8$, the quotient is 8.

R

radius (r) (p. 194) The distance from the center of a circle to any point on the circle.

radius

range (p. 368) The difference between the greatest and the least numbers of given data.

rate (p. 306) A ratio that compares different kinds of quantities.

ratio (p. 304) The quotient of two numbers used to compare one number with the other.
Example: 2 bicycles to 3 cars $= \frac{2}{3}$.

ray (p. 180) A part of a line that has one endpoint and continues in one direction.

reciprocals (p. 286) Two numbers whose product is 1; $2 \times \frac{1}{2} = 1$, 2 and $\frac{1}{2}$ are reciprocals.

rectangle (p. 186) A parallelogram with four right angles.

regular polygon (p. 184) A polygon in which all sides are congruent and all angles are congruent.

remainder (p. 90) In division, the dividend minus the product of the divisor and quotient.

repeating decimal (p. 236) A decimal in which the last digit or block of digits repeats without end.

rhombus (p. 186) A parallelogram that has all sides the same length.

right angle (p. 182) An angle that measures 90°.

right triangle (p. 188) A three-sided polygon that has one right angle and two acute angles.

round (p. 6) To replace a number by the nearest ten, hundred, thousand, and so on. 37 rounded to the nearest ten is 40.

S

sample (p. 386) A part of a large set of data that is used to make predictions.

scale (p. 342) The ratio of the size of a drawing to the actual size.

scale drawing (p. 342) A drawing with the ratio of the measurements equivalent to the measurements of the real object.

scientific notation (p. 174) A way of naming numbers in which a given number is expressed as a product of a number between 1 and 10 and a power of ten.
Example: $43,000 = 4.3 \times 10^4$

sides (p. 184) The segments that make up a polygon.

similar figures (p. 340) Figures that are the same shape but not necessarily the same size.

slide (p. 336) A figure is moved in one direction.

solution (pp. 10, 34) The answer to a problem or equation.

solve (p. 34) Find a number that replaces the variable to form a true equation.

space figure (p. 346) A figure that has three dimensions, length, width, and height.

sphere (p. 350) A shape in space all points of which are the same distance from a point within, the center.

square (p. 186) A rectangle with all sides the same length.

square centimeter (cm²) (p. 196) A metric unit for measuring area.

standard form (p. 2) The usual short form of a number. The standard form of 5 hundreds, 7 tens, and 3 ones is 573.

sum (p. 32) The answer in addition. In the equation 9 + 4 = 13, the sum is 13.

surface area (p. 354) The total area of the faces of a space figure.

symmetrical figure (p. 334) A figure that can be folded so that both halves fit exactly on one another.

T

temperature (pp. 18, 399) Tells how hot or cold something is. Temperature is measured in degrees (°).

terminating decimal (p. 236) A decimal with a limited number of nonzero digits.

terms (p. 222) The numerator and denominator of a fraction.

ton (t) (p. 22) A United States Customary unit of weight. 1 t = 2000 lb.

traversable (p. 206) A network of paths and vertexes that can be traced without lifting your pencil.

trapezoid (p. 186) A quadrilateral with exactly one pair of opposite sides parallel.

tree diagram (p. 384) A picture showing outcomes of an activity.

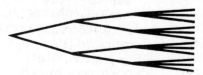

triangle (p. 184) A three-sided polygon.

turn (p. 336) A figure is rotated about a point.

U

unit rate (p. 306) The ratio of a number to 1.

V

variable (p. 34) A letter that takes the place of a number.
Example: 4 + n = 7   n = 3

Venn diagram (p. 190) A diagram to show relationships.

vertex (pp. 182, 184, 346) The common endpoint of two rays of an angle or two segments of a polygon. The intersection of three or more edges of a space figure.

volume (V) (p. 348) The amount of space inside a space figure.

W

word form (p. 2) The word form for the number 4832 is four thousand eight hundred thirty-two.

Y

yard (yd) (p. 20) A United States Customary unit for measuring length. 1 yd = 3 ft

Z

Zero Property of Addition (p. 32) The sum of any number and zero is that number.
Example: 4 + 0 = 4

Zero Property of Multiplication (p. 62) The product of zero and any number is zero.
Example: 7 × 0 = 0

Zero Property of Subtraction (p. 32) The difference between any number and zero is that number. The difference between any number and itself is zero.
Example: 5 − 0 = 5   5 − 5 = 0

INDEX

CREDITS

Cover concept and photography by Lehman Millet Incorporated.
Title page photography by Lehman Millet Incorporated.
Common Art Elements by Linda Phinney.

ILLUSTRATION

Lisa Adams   34
Barbara Adamson   101, 107 (top), 109, 164,
 168, 178, 181 (bottom), 220 (bottom), 221
 (top), 228 (bottom), 229 (top), 240, 246, 254,
 278 (bottom), 286 (bottom), 294 (right), 301,
 311, 313 (bottom), 330, 331, 334, 335, 336,
 337, 338, 339, 341, 344, 345, 348 (top), 350
 (top), 353, 355 (center), 356 (top), 359, 360,
 372, 379, 380 (bottom), 383 (top), 384
 (center), 384 (bottom), 385 (top), 388 (left),
 406, 407, 408, 416, 418
ANCO   181 (center), 182, 186 (bottom), 188,
 189 (left), 192 (bottom), 200 (bottom), 230,
 248, 288 (bottom), 334, 335, 336, 337, 338,
 339, 346, 347, 348 (bottom), 351, 354
 (bottom), 355 (top), 373, 374, 375 (top),
 376, 377, 388 (right)
Barbara Bennett   86, 116, 180, 181 (top), 182
 (top), 184, 185, 186 (top), 190, 191, 193 (top),
 194, 196, 198, 199 (top), 199 (center), 200,
 201 (center), 203, 204, 210, 249, 255 (left),
 358
Paul Breeden   56, 57, 205, 327
Mindy Brooks   174 (line art), 206, 207, 242
 (line art), 243 (line art)
Ruth Brunner-Strosser   241
Bradley Clark   17
Dan Collins   12, 13
Carolyn Croll   10
Robert Crudale   19
Bob Eggleton   4, 5, 175
Gordon Fiedor   50
Simon Galkin   2, 16, 22, 40, 42, 45, 46, 55, 270
Don Gates   212, 217, 282, 292, 294, 348, 401
Bonnie Gee   26, 27, 389, 390, 391, 413
Sylvia Giblin   18, 38, 39
Deirdre Griffin   242
Judith Griffith   138, 139, 269
Sharon Harker   66, 67, 68, 75, 96, 97, 104, 121,
 124, 125, 147, 153 (top), 154, 159, 162, 165,

PHOTOGRAPHY